THE
GOSPELS

THE SERIES

INTERPRETER'S CONCISE COMMENTARY

THE
GOSPELS
A COMMENTARY ON
MATTHEW, MARK, LUKE, JOHN

By
Howard Clark Kee
Lindsey P. Pherigo
William Baird
Massey H. Shepherd, Jr.

Edited by Charles M. Laymon

Abingdon Press
Nashville

Interpreter's Concise Commentary
Volume VI: THE GOSPELS

Copyright © 1971 and 1983 by Abingdon Press

Library of Congress Cataloging in Publication Data

Main entry under title:
The Gospels: a commentary on Matthew, Mark, Luke, John.
  (Interpreter's concise commentary; v. 6)
  "Previously published . . . as part of the Interpreter's
  one-volume commentary on the Bible"—Verso t.p.
  Includes bibliographies.
  1. Bible. N.T. Gospels—Commentaries.   I. Kee, Howard
  Clark.   II. Laymon, Charles M.   III. Series.
  BS491.2.I57   1983 vol. 6   220.7s [226'.07]   83-2508
  [BS2555.3]

ISBN 0-687-19237-4 (pbk.)

(Previously published by Abingdon Press in cloth as part of
The Interpreter's One-Volume Commentary on the Bible, regular ed.
ISBN 0-687-19299-4, thumb-indexed ed. ISBN 0-687-19300-1.)

Scripture quotations unless otherwise noted are from the Revised
Standard Common Bible, copyright © 1973 by the Division of Christian
Education, National Council of Churches, and are used by permission.

MANUFACTURED BY THE PARTHENON PRESS AT
NASHVILLE, TENNESSEE, UNITED STATES OF AMERICA

EDITOR'S PREFACE

to the original edition

A significant commentary on the Bible is both timely and timeless. It is timely in that it takes into consideration newly discovered data from many sources that are pertinent in interpreting the Scriptures, new approaches and perspectives in discerning the meaning of biblical passages, and new insights into the relevancy of the Bible for the times in which we live. It is timeless since it deals with the eternal truths of God's revelation, truths of yesterday, today, and of all the tomorrows that shall be.

This commentary has been written within this perspective. Its authors were selected because of their scholarship, their religious insight, and their ability to communicate with others. Technical discussions do not protrude, yet the most valid and sensitive use of contemporary knowledge underlies the interpretations of the several writings. It has been written for ministers, lay and nonprofessional persons engaged in studying or teaching in the church school, college students and those who are unequipped to follow the more specialized discussions of biblical matters, but who desire a thoroughly valid and perceptive guide in interpreting the Bible.

The authorship of this volume is varied in that scholars were chosen from many groups to contribute to the task. In this sense it is an ecumenical writing. Protestants from numerous denominations, Jews, and also Roman Catholics are represented in the book. Truth cannot be categorized according to its ecclesiastical sources. It is above and beyond such distinctions.

It will be noted that the books of the Apocrypha have been included and interpreted in the same manner as the canonical writings. The value of a knowledge of this body of literature for understanding the historical background and character of the Judaic-Christian tradition has been widely recognized in our time, but commentary treatments of it have not been readily accessible. In addition, the existence of the Revised Standard Version and the New English Bible translations of these documents makes such a commentary upon them as is included here both necessary and significant.

The commentary as a whole avoids taking dogmatic positions or representing any one particular point of view. Its authors were chosen throughout the English-speaking field of informed and recognized biblical scholars. Each author was urged to present freely his own interpretation and, on questions where there was sometimes a diversity of conclusions, each was also asked to define objectively the viewpoints of others while he was offering and defending his own.

Many persons have contributed to the writing and production of this volume. One of the most rewarding of my personal experiences as editor was corresponding with the authors. On every hand there was enthusiasm for the project and warmth of spirit. The authors' commitment to the task and their scholarly sensitivity were evident in all of my relationships with them. The considerate judgments of the manuscript consultants, Morton S. Enslin, Dwight M. Beck, W. F. Stinespring, Virgil M. Rogers, and William L. Reed, were invaluable in the making of the character of the commentary. The copy editors who have worked under the careful and responsible guidance of Mr. Gordon Duncan of Abingdon Press have contributed greatly to the accuracy and readability of the commentary.

—Charles M. Laymon, Editor

PUBLISHER'S PREFACE

The intent of the *Interpreter's Concise Commentary* is to make available to a wider audience the commentary section of *The Interpreter's One-Volume Commentary on the Bible*. In order to do this, the Publisher is presenting the commentary section of the original hardback in this eight-volume paperback set. At the same time, and in conjunction with our wish to make *The Interpreter's One-Volume Commentary* more useful, we have edited the hardback text for the general reader: we have defined most of the technical terms used in the original hardback text; we have tried to divide some of the longer sentences and paragraphs into shorter ones; we have tried to make the sexually stereotyped language used in the original commentary inclusive where it referred to God or to both sexes; and we have explained abbreviations, all in an attempt to make the text more easily read.

The intention behind this paperback arrangement is to provide a handy and compact commentary on those individual sections of the Bible that are of interest to readers. In this paperback format we have not altered the substance of any of the text of the original hardback, which is still available. Rather, our intention is to smooth out some of the scholarly language in order to make the text easier to read. We hope this arrangement will make this widely accepted commentary on the Bible even more profitable for all students of God's Word.

WRITERS

Howard Clark Kee
Rufus Jones Professor of the History of Religion, Bryn Mawr
College, Bryn Mawr, Pennsylvania

Lindsey P. Pherigo
Professor of New Testament and Early Church History, Saint
Paul School of Theology, Kansas City, Missouri

William Baird
Professor of New Testament, Brite Divinity School, Texas
Christian University, Ft. Worth, Texas

Massey H. Shepherd, Jr.
Hodges Professor of Liturgics, The Church Divinity School of
the Pacific, Berkeley, California

CONTENTS

THE GOSPEL
ACCORDING TO MATTHEW

Howard Clark Kee

INTRODUCTION

The first book in the New Testament is one of the three
"Synoptic" gospels. While all four gospels are alike in many ways,
the similarities among Matthew, Mark, and Luke are much
greater than between John and any of the other three. Each of the
three shares most of its material with one or both of the other two.
The word "synoptic" means here "giving a common view" of the
gospel story in which Jesus is the central actor.

Authorship

From the early second century down to the present,
Christians have believed that the first gospel in the New
Testament was also the first to be written and that the author was
Matthew the tax collector, a disciple of Jesus (9:9). The source of
this belief can be traced back as far as about A.D. 130, when
Papias, a bishop in Hierapolis, a city of Asia Minor, wrote a work
titled "Exposition of the Oracles of the Lord." His writing,
which is known only from fragments quoted by later Christian
writers, reports that Matthew, the disciple, compiled the
sayings of the Lord in Hebrew. Those who quoted Papias seem

to have accepted this statement as referring to the Gospel of Matthew.

There are several difficulties with this assumption, however.

(1) The gospel is a rather full account of Jesus' public ministry, not merely a series of sayings.

(2) Detailed analysis of Matthew shows that the author used Mark as one of his sources.

(3) Mark was written in Greek. Therefore Matthew, which used Mark as a source, was written in Greek, not Hebrew.

In view of these difficulties, it is reasonable to assume that Papias is referring, not to Matthew as we know it, but perhaps to a now lost collection of sayings of Jesus.

If we do not accept Papias' statement, then we must admit that we have no evidence for the origin of Matthew and no assurance of its author's name. The gospel itself makes no such claim; indeed all the gospels are anonymous. The names they now bear come from later tradition. We use these names for convenience, but we should recognize that the authority of the writings rested in the power of their message, not in the personal authority of the author.

Date and Place of Composition

In the early second century Christian writings there are a few passages which seem to be quotations from Matthew. The clearest of these comes from Ignatius of Antioch. This suggests that Matthew may have originated in Syria, where Antioch was the chief city. Clues from other early writers suggest that Matthew was written in the area east of Antioch, where there were important colonies of Jews among whom Christianity had quickly spread.

Since Ignatius quoted Matthew around A.D. 115, and since one of its sources, Mark, was likely written around A.D. 70, we may assign a date possibly about A.D. 80-85.

Sources

In addition to Mark, Matthew used a second source—a collection of sayings of Jesus. We have no copy of this document, but it can be reconstructed with reasonable certainty by comparing those passages in Matthew and Luke which have nearly identical material. Often this common material appears in Matthew and Luke in the same order, even though it is not found in Mark, which both Matthew and Luke have also used as a source. It may be that Matthew copied from Luke, or vice versa, but the more likely explanation is that both used a collection of Jesus' sayings which scholars have come to refer to as Q (from the German word *Quelle,* meaning "source"). Since this still does not explain certain features of Matthew and Luke, there may have been slightly different versions of Q in circulation in the pre-Matthean church.

Matthew also has a good deal of material not found in the other gospels. This includes some of the best-known sections of the gospel: much of the Sermon on the Mount, the coming of the Wise Men, the Lord's Prayer (in its more familiar form), the parable of the sheep and the goats, Jesus' calling Peter the rock on which the church will be built. There is no way to tell whether Matthew got this material from a written source or whether it circulated in the church only orally.

In either case, the whole gospel bears the stamp of the author's own special interests and is expressed in his own distinctive words. He is no neutral reporter of traditional information; he has effectively edited his material so that his gospel fulfills his own objectives.

Purpose

Matthew shares with the other gospel writers the aim of presenting Jesus as the Christ. In doing so, they all show how the ministry, death, and resurrection of Jesus are bound up with his role as Messiah. But Matthew is also concerned about the church and its way of life in response to the message of Jesus. Accordingly he has edited the stories and sayings of Jesus in such a way as to point up three claims:

(1) The church is the true Israel, replacing the old Israel in the center of God's purpose.

(2) The church in the present age is a mixed body, including both worthy and unworthy among its members.

(3) The church is called to live a new and higher way of righteousness that exceeds even the strict demands of the Jewish law.

In achieving his aims, Matthew has alternated between narrative and discourse material—accounts of Jesus' acts and reports of his teachings. Thus one receives from this gospel the picture of Jesus as one who not only acts the role of Messiah but also carefully and fully instructs his followers as to the meaning of his ministry. Thus Matthew's aims are served by the very structure he has given to his gospel.

Structure

The main sections of Matthew are as follows:

I. The Coming of Jesus as God's Messiah (chapters 1–2)
II. The Ministry of the Messiah (chapters 3–25)
III. The Humiliation and Exaltation of the Messiah (chapters 26–28)

It is in the long middle section that Matthew's skillful structuring best serves his special aims. Here we see an alternation between narrative and discourse:

Narrative: The Ministry Begun in Galilee (3:1–4:25)
  Discourse: Sermon on the Mount (5:1–7:29)
Narrative: The Authority of Jesus' Ministry (8:1–9:35)
  Discourse: Mission Discourse (9:36–10:42)
Narrative: The Kingdom and Its Coming (11:1–12:50)
  Discourse: Parables of the Kingdom (13:1-52)
Narrative: The Life of the New Community (13:53–17:27)
  Discourse: Greatness and Responsibility (18:1-35)
Narrative: Conflict and Consummation (19:1–24:3)
  Discourse: Revelation of the End (24:4–25:46)

The transitions between these five sections are carefully marked by a repeated phrase, "when Jesus had finished . . ." (7:28; 11:1; 13:53; 19:1; 26:1). It has been suggested that the fivefold structure of this section was meant to imitate the Pentateuch, the five books of the law of Moses.

Whether Matthew consciously copied the structure of the Mosaic law or not, he had a major concern to show that the Old Testament was fulfilled in Jesus Christ. By direct quotation and indirect allusion he keeps pointing his reader to the words of the law and the prophets that have come to fulfillment in the coming of God's Messiah, Jesus. More than 130 different passages from the Old Testament are cited. Some can be readily associated with the events which Matthew claims to be prophetic fulfillment—e.g. the Messiah's birth in Bethlehem (2:5-6; Micah 5:2). Others do not seem to us today to fit—e.g. 2:15, where the return of Jesus from Egypt is seen as the fulfillment of a prophetic reference (Hosea 11:1) to God's call of Israel out of Egypt at the time of the Exodus.

The difficulty with these prophecies is that we think in historical terms and expect an exact association of prediction and fulfillment. The first Christians, like their Jewish contemporaries, considered the Hebrew Scriptures to possess many possibilities of meaning, not all of them by any means self-evident. To discern the many meanings of scripture was first of all a tribute to the divine wisdom that inspired the writings. It was also an evidence of the ingenuity of the interpreter who saw in any given event the fulfillment of a text that others might not have detected. There is a similarity between certain interpretations of the Old Testament found in Matthew and those found in the Dead Sea Scrolls. Those writers likewise believed that the community of God's people to which they belonged was the group for and through whom God would bring his prophetic promises to fulfillment.

Equally important for Matthew is the fulfillment of the *moral* requirements of the law of Moses. The major passage on this theme is 5:17-20, where Jesus tells his disciples that the law is to be fulfilled, that not a letter of it will pass away, that its requirements are not to be in the slightest relaxed, and that their conformity to the law must exceed the strict righteousness observed by the scribes and Pharisees. How radical that demand for righteousness is may be seen in the new formulations of the law set forth in the Sermon on the Mount. But the strictness of moral expectation by the community for which Matthew writes is apparent in his versions of the parables and other sayings of Jesus. Indeed the tone for this emphasis is set in 3:15, where Jesus says: "It is fitting for us to fulfill all righteousness." Even though this is spoken when Jesus accepts baptism at the hand of John, it is a characteristic factor in the gospel as a whole.

I. THE COMING OF GOD'S MESSIAH (1:1–2:23)

1:1-17. *The Genealogy of Jesus.* The Greek word used for **genealogy** (verse 1) is *genesis*, as though the author wanted to stress the continuity between the Old Testament and the new work that God began in Jesus Christ. Mention of **David** and **Abraham** suggests that Jesus is here thought of as in the line of God's people, beginning with Abraham, and in the royal line, for which David is the ideal figure (cf. Psalms 89:3-4; 132:11-12; Acts 2:30).

1:2-17. The descendants are grouped in three sets of fourteen each. Why the number fourteen was chosen is not apparent. Comparison with the Old Testament accounts shows that the lists are not intended to be complete. For example, there are three generations missing after **Uzziah** (verse 9; cf. I Chronicles 3:11-12, where Uzziah = Ahaziah). Furthermore, the genealogy here is not in agreement with that in Luke 3:23-38. Actually the genealogy in Matthew is that of **Joseph**, who is represented as Mary's husband rather than as the actual father of Jesus (verse 16). The purpose of the genealogy is twofold:

(1) to show the continuity of God's purpose among his people, culminating in the call of Abraham (verse 2), the establishment of the kingdom (verses 6-7), the return from exile in Babylon (verse 11), and now the birth of Jesus Christ (verse 16);

(2) to place Jesus in the legal line of the king promised to God's people.

1:18-25. *The Birth of Jesus.* Unlike Luke, who tells of Mary's advance notice of the miraculous birth, Matthew presents only the direct statement that Mary was **with child of the Holy Spirit**. The story shows knowledge of Palestinian customs, such as the binding nature of a betrothal, which was considered as firm an obligation as marriage itself. Joseph decided to deal kindly with Mary, **to divorce her quietly** rather than make a scandal of her seeming breach of the marriage agreement.

1:20-21. Joseph's dream is the first of a series of dreams, revealing each a divine warning or counsel, which occur in Matthew's own material (1:20; 2:12; 2:13; 2:19; 2:22; 27:19). Joseph is addressed as **son of David,** indicating his connection with the kingly line of Israel's history and her hope. The child is to be called *Yeshua* or, in its more familiar Greek form, **Jesus.** The name means literally "he shall save." In the Old Testament the name refers to God's deliverance of his people from their enemies and his vindication of them by the establishment of his kingdom (cf. Psalms 7; 9). By adding the words **save his people from their sins** Matthew pictures Jesus as the one through whom the forgiveness of sins is announced. There had been no tradition in Israel for a messiah who would save from sin.

1:22-25. Here is the first of the explicit claims that prophecy is being fulfilled in Jesus. In Matthew's birth story these prophecies and the incidents which are seen as fulfilling them provide the framework for the entire account: the virgin birth (1:23); the birth in Bethlehem (2:6); the return of the Holy Family from Egypt (2:15); the slaughter of the children by Herod (2:16-17); the move from Bethlehem to Nazareth (2:23). This fulfillment of scripture is evidence that what is occurring in connection with Jesus is the unfolding of God's plan for humanity's redemption.

1:23. The Hebrew original of the verse quoted from Isaiah 7:14 speaks of an *almah*, i.e. a young woman, who **shall conceive and bear a son.** It is the period of conception and birth, not her virginity, that is of importance for Isaiah. The Greek version of

7

the Old Testament in wide use among Jews from the first century B.C. on, the Septuagint, had translated *almah* by the Greek word *parthenos*—**virgin.** Matthew uses this translation, since it suits his purpose of showing that Jesus was divinely conceived in fulfillment of the Hebrew Scriptures.

Although Luke has his own version of the extraordinary birth of Jesus, he does not quote or refer to the virgin birth passage from Isaiah. Neither Mark, nor John, nor Paul has any hint of the virgin birth story. It seems to have become important for the church only in the second century as a way of combatting the charge that Jesus was not truly human. These birth stories insisted that he was truly *born,* although they also served to place Jesus at least on a par with the pagan savior-gods for whom a miraculous birth was claimed. Indeed, the idea of Jesus' virgin birth does not figure at all in the rest of Matthew; it is the conviction that Jesus is **Emmanuel . . . God with us** that is more significant than the circumstances of his birth.

1:14-25. Joseph obeys the instruction of **the angel** in his dream. He takes Mary as his wife and gives Jesus the appointed name.

2:1-12. *The Visit of the Magi.* Matthew makes no attempt to present a full chronological account of the events of Jesus' birth and infancy. We learn that Herod ordered all children up to two years of age be killed. This implies that Jesus was himself already about two when the wise men, or magi, arrived from the East. The magi were astrologers, although they were the closest thing to astronomers that the ancient world knew. They seem to have possessed considerable information about the movement of the stars and planets. But they treated it in magical fashion, tying the heavenly movements in directly with the destiny of humans. It is hard to see why the movements of the stars would have a direct bearing on the coming of a Jewish king. The visit of the magi is symbolic of the divine preparation for the advent of Jesus. Their gifts point to the kingly rights of the child and to the worldwide acknowledgment that he is ultimately to receive.

Herod the king is Herod the Great, who ruled over the Jewish people in Palestine from 37 B.C. to 4 B.C. His father, Antipater, had helped the Romans take control of Palestine following the Roman invasion in 63 B.C. Herod was able to ride out the storms resulting from the power struggle that left Octavian (Augustus) in control of the empire. His marriage to Mariamne, of the authentic Jewish royal line (the Hasmonean family), gave him a touch of respectability. His political and military skill kept him in undisputed control until his death in 4 B.C. In the course of his reign he arranged for the murder of his sons and relatives, as well as of his enemies. The murder of the children is in keeping with his character, although there is no report of this crime from any source other than Matthew.

2:5-6. The birth of the child **in Bethlehem** is seen as the fulfillment of Micah 5:2. This is the only place in the New Testament where Jesus' place of birth is viewed as required by prophecy to be Bethlehem. Although the birth is located here in Luke 2, there is no appeal to this prophecy by Luke. The prophecy is probably referred to in John 7:42, but there it is assumed that Jesus is from Nazareth, not Bethlehem. The Davidic origin of Jesus is attested by Paul (Romans 1:3), but he does not mention Bethlehem and its royal prophecy.

2:9-12. A dream warned the magi not to share in Herod's plot to destroy the one **born king of the Jews,** but they did visit the child, **going into the house** where Mary and Joseph were living. Unlike Luke, Matthew gives no hint that the holy family was merely stopping in Bethlehem for the census, after which they would return to their permanent home in Nazareth. Rather, Matthew implies that Bethlehem was their home. Only in order to escape the vengeance of Herod's son and successor, Archelaus (verse 22), did they change their residence from Bethlehem to Nazareth, **in the district of Galilee.** Herod's son Antipas was ruler of Galilee and of Perea, east of the Jordan River.

2:13-23. *The Flight into Egypt.* The story of the flight into Egypt serves Matthew's purpose by showing that scripture was fulfilled by both the sojourn in Egypt and the return to Nazareth. The great freedom in interpreting scripture that is found among first-century Jews is evident in both aspects of this event. The call of God's son **out of Egypt** (verse 15) is in the Old Testament (Hosea 11:1) a reference to the deliverance of the nation Israel from its period of slavery in Egypt.

2:23. Although we cannot be certain of the scripture referred to here, it is probably an allusion to Isaiah 11:1. There the Messiah is described as a *netzer* (Hebrew for "sprout," or "shoot"), implying that, like a tree cut down, the Davidic dynasty will grow up once more and the kingdom be reestablished. Matthew has taken the consonants of *netzer*—since the vowels were not written in the ancient Hebrew text—and has interpreted them as a prophecy referring to Nazareth: **he shall be called a Nazarene.** This method of scriptural interpretation, far-fetched though it may seem, was in common use among the rabbis of Jesus' time.

The magi's refusal to cooperate after "being warned in a dream," together with the dream of Joseph, caused Herod's plot to fail. His death, which in verse 19 is chronologically linked to the birth of Jesus, gives us our only clue in Matthew as to the date of these events. Since Herod died in 4 B.C., the birth of Jesus would have taken place about two years earlier. The attempt to link these events with the mention in Luke 2:2 of the census "when Quirinius was governor of Syria" only complicates the matter of chronology. Matthew gives us the nearest thing to a fixed date for Jesus' birth.

II. The Ministry of the Messiah (3:1–25:46)

A. The Baptism of Jesus (3:1-17)

3:1-6. *John the Baptist.* Both Christian and Jewish traditions gave John the title **the Baptist,** even though in the earlier account in Mark 1:4 he was known simply as the John who baptizes, or the baptizer. Matthew specifies that he launched his work **in the wilderness of Judea,** the barren territory between the low mountain ridge on which Jerusalem and the cities of Judah lie and the deep cleft where the Jordan River

empties into the Dead Sea. His activity is described as fulfilling
what **was spoken of by the prophet Isaiah: the voice of one
crying in the wilderness.** John's message is identical with that of
Jesus in 4:17: **Repent, for the kingdom of heaven is at hand.** The
term "kingdom of heaven" is used here as by pious Jews to mean
"the kingdom of God," since it was considered irreverent to
pronounce God's name directly.

John's garments are reminiscent of the prophet Elijah, with
whom John is directly identified by Matthew (17:14; cf. Mark 9:13;
see also on Mark 1:6), although John's message more nearly
resembles that of the later prophets, Zechariah or Daniel. His
strange diet of **locusts and wild honey** is an indication of the
ascetic life he lived. The gospels may exaggerate the response to
John—**Jerusalem and all Judea and all the region about the
Jordan**—but the Jewish historian Josephus confirms the wide
appeal that John's ministry had among his contemporaries. They
came, however, not to witness a great sight or to hear a consoling
message, but to confess **their sins.**

3:7-10. *John's Call to Repentance.* Matthew singles out for
attack the Pharisees and the Sadducees (cf. Luke 3:7), who were
the two leading groups within Judaism in the first century. The
Sadducees were from the priestly families. They were
conservative in their view of scripture in that they acknowledged only the first five books of the Old Testament as
authoritative. The **Pharisees** sought to make the ancient faith
and the teachings of scripture relevant to their own day. But
their detailed interpretations often made obedience to the law
burdensome or even avoided the clear intent of the laws
themselves (see below on chapter 23).

They are to accept **baptism** at the hand of John to prepare
themselves for **the wrath to come.** It would appear that John
taught that persons should purify themselves by baptism now so
that they would be ready to pass safely through the fires of
judgment that were to fall. Hence the contrast in verse 11
between baptism with water and baptism with fire. What God
expects of those who call themselves the people of God is **fruit
that befits repentance.** It is not enough to repeat the proud

11

claim that they are **children to Abraham.** God is able to create a new people **from these stones.** The judgment is as sure to come as the tree is sure to fall when **the axe is laid to the root.** The fate of the unrepentant sinner in the judgment will be **the fire, John declares.**

3:11-12. *John's Announcement of the Messiah.* John offers two contrasts between himself and him **who is coming:** (1) The Coming One is **mightier** than John, and (2) he will baptize **with the Holy Spirit and with fire.**

The baptism with fire points to the coming judgment, but there is no clear indication of how the Holy Spirit is related to the fire. It has been suggested that John's original prediction was simply of a baptism with fire and that the early church added the mention of spirit baptism following the Pentecost experience. Whatever the original force of John's words may have been, the early church did not abandon baptism **with water** when it received the Holy Spirit. Rather, water became the symbol of baptism with the Spirit. John expects the Coming One to carry out the judgment he has been predicting. Like grain at threshing time, the worthy will be separated from the useless, here compared with **chaff** fit only for burning **with unquenchable fire.**

3:13-17. *Jesus' Baptism by John.* John's initial refusal to baptize Jesus calls to the reader's attention the fact that it was not appropriate for Jesus, who had no consciousness of sin, to accept a baptism which was a sign of repentance. Further, Matthew's version of this incident suggests that John already recognized who Jesus was and was aware of his own inferiority (but see below on 11:1-9). Jesus' reply sounds a theme which pervades the whole of this gospel: **fulfil all righteousness.** This is developed especially in the Sermon on the Mount. There Jesus exhorts men to be obedient to the law of God in such a radical way as to exceed the zeal of even the Pharisees (5:17-20; see also on Mark 1:9-11).

3:16-17. Unlike Mark, who depicts the coming of the Spirit and the **voice from heaven** as a private experience of Jesus, Matthew implies that the heavenly voice addressed the onlookers, since the words are not addressed to Jesus: **This is my beloved Son, with whom I am well pleased.** This first part of this declaration is reminiscent of Psalm 2:7, where the king of Israel is addressed as the son of God, meaning the one who rules in God's stead. The second half of the statement comes from Isaiah 42:1 and was originally spoken to Israel as the servant people of God. Here, then, are combined two great streams of Jewish hope: the coming of the ideal king and the acceptance of the servant role. Now, however, an individual rather than the nation as a whole becomes the servant.

The descent of the **Spirit** upon Jesus and its appearance **like a dove** are given a somewhat more concrete description in Matthew than in Mark. It is difficult to know what it was about the coming of the Spirit that could be described as "like a dove." The dove in the Old Testament tradition as interpreted in first-century Judaism was the symbol of God's Spirit, hovering over the creation (Genesis 1:2) and caring for his people in the days of their wilderness wanderings (Deuteronomy 32:11).

The whole story of Jesus' baptism has been so overlaid with symbolism that it is no longer possible to separate historical from symbolic elements. The suggestion of some scholars that the entire incident is a legend or a misplaced story of a post-resurrection appearance of Jesus does not help us to understand the incident. Indeed, the fact that Jesus was baptized by John was a source of embarrassment to the early church, since John's followers claimed that Jesus' submission showed John's superiority. Nevertheless, as it stands it symbolizes the entrance of Jesus into his ministry, empowered by God's Spirit and acknowledged by the God-sent forerunner, John the Baptist, as the Coming One.

B. THE TEMPTATION OF JESUS (4:1-11)

4:1. The temptation of Jesus is not an effort on the part of **the devil** to lure Jesus into committing some immoral act. Rather, it is an attempt to force him to set aside his complete obedience to the will of God by adopting an easier way to fulfill his mission. In the gospel tradition the devil (called Satan in Mark, in keeping with the Jewish name for God's archenemy) is waging an unsuccessful effort to wrest final control of the creation from God. The movement of history is the conflict between the kingdom of God and the kingdom of Satan. By offering him enticing possibilities, the devil is here pictured as trying to trick Jesus into submitting to his ways. Although Luke and Matthew present the details of this story in different order from each other, they agree on the main features.

4:2. The **forty days** that the temptation lasted are a round figure for an extended period of time.

4:3-11. The first suggestion of the **tempter** is that Jesus utilize his extraordinary powers to convert **stones** into **bread.** The Roman rulers found very soon that one way to gain the favor of the masses was to distribute free bread. The tempter's proposal follows this line of reasoning. Jesus' response, quoted from Deuteronomy 8:3, affirms that the **word** of God is more vital to man's existence than the food he eats. Jesus' task is to declare God's message, not to fill stomachs.

The second proposal of the tempter is that Jesus demonstrate God's care over him by throwing himself form the **pinnacle of the temple.** But Jesus refuses to put God to the test merely for purposes of public display.

The third offer would have eliminated all the humiliation and suffering that Jesus was to undergo in fulfillment of his mission. All that was required was that Jesus **fall down** in acknowledgment of his subservience to the devil. Jesus will offer **worship** to God alone and will **serve** only the coming of his kingdom. God's continuing favor toward and support of Jesus is portrayed in the attendance of the ministering **angels.**

C. JESUS LAUNCHES HIS MINISTRY (4:12-25)

4:12-17. *Jesus' First Preaching in Galilee.* The indication that Jesus did not begin his public ministry until he **heard that John**

had been arrested has suggested to some interpreters that Jesus and John the Baptist at first carried on their work concurrently (cf. John 4:1), but that Jesus—presumably as a result of disagreement with John—resumed his work only after John was off the scene. This view receives some support from the uncertainty about Jesus' mission implied in the questions John sent to Jesus from prison (see below on 11:1-9). It is possible that Jesus' friendship with religious outcasts was abhorrent to John, with his strict and somber message of doom to sinners.

4:15-16. Matthew sees in the beginning of Jesus' ministry in Galilee the fulfillment of scripture. The fact that it is called **Galilee of the Gentiles** gives the reader the clue that in Matthew's account Jesus' work will culminate with the launching of the mission to the whole world. For the time being, however, his work will be limited to "the lost sheep of the house of Israel" (10:6).

4:17. Jesus' message is presented as identical with that of John: repentance, in light of the inbreaking of the **kingdom of heaven.** The word translated **is at hand** means "has drawn near." Jesus is not declaring, therefore, that the new era of God's sovereign rule has already come, but rather that it has drawn so near that its signs are already evident in the ministry of Jesus. They may be seen in his triumph over the demons (12:28) as well as in the new fellowship he is establishing with the poor and with those considered unworthy by the religious standards of his day (11:19). The whole of Jesus' ministry is in a sense a sign that in his person and work the reign of God has drawn near.

4:18-22. *The Call of the Disciples.* The first four disciples called to follow Jesus are two pairs of brothers; **Simon** (who was given the nickname **Peter,** meaning "rock") and **Andrew** and **James** and **John.** All are **fishermen** by trade; all are called to be **fishers of men.** They are to call all persons from their ordinary way of life in order to prepare for the coming of God's kingdom. Although there is no hint here of prior contact between Jesus and the disciples, there is evidence in John 1:35-42 that Jesus had these men as followers during the period of his association with John the Baptist. But now they followed him **immediately.**

4:23-25. *Scope of the Ministry.* At this point Matthew departs from Mark's order of events and inserts a summary statement which gives a capsule picture of what Jesus did and where he ministered. His work comes under three headings: **teaching . . . preaching . . . healing.**

The teaching was carried on in the Jewish synagogues. This confirms the impression received from the rest of the gospel that Jesus worked almost entirely within the institutions of Judaism, even as he was seeking to transform it in the light of what he knew to be God's redemptive purpose.

The healing activity is as well attested in the gospel tradition as the teaching ministry. Even from polemical Jewish sources we learn that Jesus was believed to possess the power to heal and to expel demons.

The only question in the mind of his detractors was, "Who was the source of his power, God or Satan?" His work attracted the attention of those living outside the bounds of Galilee in such pagan territories as **Syria** and the cities of the **Decapolis.** The latter was a loose confederation of ten Greek cities built by the successors to Alexander the Great and improved by the Romans. They were located in southern Syria and on the east side of the Jordan and were inhabited largely by Gentiles.

The summary passage also serves Matthew as a means of transition from narrative to the first and best known of his great discourses.

D. The Sermon on the Mount (5:1–7:29)

5:1-2. *Introduction.* Jesus went **up on the mountain** to withdraw from the crowds, not to gain a vantage point from which he might be seen and heard. His words are addressed to **his disciples.** No particular mountain seems to be intended; rather Matthew has likely provided the setting, since it contrasts with the "level place" on which Luke locates the comparable "sermon" (Luke 6:17). Matthew does not call this a sermon, and indeed it is not a sermon. It is a bringing together of the teachings of Jesus on the meaning of obedience in such a way as to set forth dramatically his understanding of the radical devotion to God's will that God expects.

In compiling this discourse material Matthew has drawn on the Q source, although he considerably rearranges the material. In addition he has utilized a source uniquely his own among the gospels.

5:3-12. *The Beatitudes*. The Beatitudes have been regarded as timeless rules for the good life. Although one can extract from them certain enduring ethical demands, they are not moral laws, but eschatological promises.

"Eschatology" means literally "the study of the last things," but in relation to the Bible and theology it refers to the events and experiences associated with God's consummation of his purpose in the world—that is, with the coming of his kingdom. Matthew has modified the form of the Beatitudes somewhat. Originally, as evidenced in Luke's version (Luke 6:20-21), they were addressed directly to the hearer ("Blessed are you poor") and made explicit the contrast between man's response to the will of God now and his fate in the kingdom ("Blessed are you that weep *now*, for you shall laugh"). Here they have been changed to sound more like general principles. Matthew may well have expanded the original set, since several of his beatitudes do not appear in Luke.

5:3. The phrase **poor in spirit** does not mean one who is weak in spirit, but one who looks to God alone to preserve him in the midst of his afflictions. He does not live out of his own resources, nor is he relying on his own achievements to overcome the seemingly overwhelming difficulties that he faces—his trust is in God:

> This poor man cried, and the LORD heard him,
> And saved him out of all his troubles (Psalm 34:6).

It is the poor ones who will receive the kingdom, rather than those who are proud and confident in their moral achievements.

5:4. Possibly **those who mourn** refers to persons who are bereaved. If, however, this beatitude is a parallel to the preceding, it may describe those who bewail the present state of affairs in God's world and long for the coming of the new age. God will comfort them by establishing his kingdom.

5:5. This saying, which probably originated with Matthew or his special source, reads like a modification of Psalm 37:11. Moses was called the meekest of men (Numbers 12:3) not on account of his timidity, but because of his awareness of his own limitations and his consequent dependence on God. It is such persons who will **inherit** the kingdom when it is established in **the earth.**

5:6. Matthew has added **and thirst for righteousness** to the simpler form of the saying found in Luke, which pronounces the blessing on those who now "hunger." It is possible that Matthew is using the word "righteousness" in a special eschatological sense to refer to the new situation that will obtain in the earth when God's kingdom is established. His linking of "kingdom" and "righteousness" in 6:33 may confirm this. But in the light of his heavy stress on obedience to the will of God, it seems more likely that he is using righteousness in the sense of holy living. Only those wholly devoted to obedience will be found worthy to see the new age when their aspirations will be **satisfied** by the establishment of God's righteous rule over his obedient people.

5:7-9. Only those who practice **mercy** can expect to receive it from God at the judgment. Only those whose heart is pure can come into God's presence. The **heart** is understood to be far more than the seat of the emotions. It is the center of the inner life, the source of thought and understanding, of will and of decision. A full transformation of the deepest level of life is what is demanded. The direction that this change takes is implied in the call to be **peacemakers,** since this is God's own work in the world. To **be called sons of God** means that one has sought to do what God is doing. In this case it is God's reconciling work in the world in which persons are called to participate.

5:10-12. Those who will one day share in the kingdom are now expected to accept calmly the persecution and reviling which they will receive as a result of their devotion to Jesus and the work of the gospel. They are to understand their harassment as a sign of God's favor rather than as an indication of his displeasure, and therefore to **rejoice**. God has already laid up for them a **reward in heaven**.

5:13-16. *Words on Salt and Light.* These words are addressed to the church, which is called to fulfill its mission as **the salt of the earth** and as **the light of the world.** When salt and light are not fulfilling their proper function, they are utterly useless. But when the church discharges its light-giving role, people glorify, not the church, but God. (See also below on 6:22-23.)

5:17-20. *Words on the Law.* All these words about the law are set in an eschatological setting. They speak of the law's enduring until the end of the age and of the reward that will come in the new age for those who faithfully obey the commandments. Jesus' claim that he has **come** (meaning God has sent him) **to fulfill . . . the law and the prophets** means far more than that he is acting out a role laid down for him in the prediction of the prophets of Israel. It is rather the declaration that both the purpose of God disclosed through the prophets and the demands of God that his people obey him have found their fulfillment in Jesus. There is to be no relaxation of the strictness of the commandments. For Matthew, at least certain aspects of the ceremonial law are as binding as the moral sections (cf. 5:23; 6:17).

5:18. This may have been originally an ironical declaration of Jesus against the Jewish interpreters of the law who, he said, would rather have **heaven and earth pass away** than to have the smallest letter or **dot** of the written law altered (cf. Luke 16:17). But as it stands in Matthew, Jesus is portrayed as laying an extremely heavy burden on his followers, since they are to meet the law's demands in full. They are to surpass the scribes in their zeal, because their **righteousness** is to exceed **that of the scribes and Pharisees,** who make demands that they themselves are not able to carry out. Even these requirements the disciples are to fulfill, Matthew declares (cf. 23:3). What this type of righteousness demands is spelled out in the detailed interpretation of the law that follows.

5:21-26. *Words on Murder and Anger.* The focus shifts from the external meaning of the law against murder (Exodus 20:13; Deuteronomy 5:17) to the inner attitude of the heart. Here there can be no legislation. Hatred and insult are as serious violations of God's will for his people as the overt act of murder. It is God's intention that all persons become reconciled.

To underscore this truth a brief parable is introduced. If an accused person has the prudence to make friends with his accuser while they are on the way to court, how much more should a disciple be reconciled with his brother in this time prior to God's judgment!

5:27-30. *Words on Adultery and Lust.* Merely to stop short of the overt act of adultery is not to obey the intention of God which lies behind the law (Exodus 20:14; Deuteronomy 5:18). To desire another man's wife is as much a violation of God's purpose as is the act of adultery itself. What is demanded is complete self-control of the members of the body, so that obedience may be complete. (See also below on 18:8-9.)

5:31-32. *Words on Divorce.* That this problem was important for the church is evident from the fact that Matthew included both the Q form of the words and that found in Mark. The most radical form appears in Mark 10:11, where Jesus unconditionally denounces divorce and remarriage. Here an exception is made: a man may divorce and marry another if his first wife has been guilty of **unchastity.** But this position is no different from rabbinic interpretation of the law in Jesus' day. Shammai Rabbi insisted on strict, literal observance of Deuteronomy 24:1, where the phrase "because he has found some indecency in her" was understood to mean that he discovered that she had been unfaithful to him.

In Mark 10:2-9 Jesus gives his basis for rejecting divorce. It violates the intention of God in establishing marriage, which is to be an enduring relationship, since it was a part of God's original creative act in fashioning man as male and female. Jesus, therefore, was reminding his hearers of the meaning of marriage. He was not giving a severely strict interpretation of the ancient law on divorce. Matthew, with his interest in legal questions, has introduced the condition in the otherwise unconditional word of Jesus. (See also below on 19:3-9.)

5:33-37. *Words on Swearing and Oaths.* The clue to the interpretation of this passage is given in verse 37: one is always to speak the truth. Persons of truth will not need to add force to their words by an appeal to God or anything that God has created. They will not need to swear by anything, since their word can be relied on as it stands. The phrase which speaks of performing **to the Lord what you have sworn** is probably an addition to the word of Jesus, since it deals with a vow, a promise made to God rather than with an oath, a solemn affirmation made to another person. Jesus declares that when people are truthful, oaths are wholly unnecessary.

5:38-42. *Words on Retaliation.* The ancient Hebrew law of retaliation (Exodus 21:23-25) was an advance over the tribal practices which assumed that a single offense against a member of the tribe called for wholesale destruction of the offending tribe. But Jesus rejects the whole notion of retaliation and demands instead a response to a misdeed that is the reverse of what is expected. He does not recommend such a negative factor as nonresistance. Rather he recommends positive good in the face of evil. Several illustrations are given:

When one is insulted (i.e. struck **on the right cheek**), one is to offer the other cheek as an act of love. This act, because it is not the "normal" human reaction, is intended to challenge the aggressor by grace rather than by retaliation.

When one is sued for the essential clothing, the **coat** (the long garment reaching to the ankles that served as a basic covering for the body), he should offer as well the outer **cloak** (a heavy, more expensive garment which served for protection against sun, cold, or rain, as well as bedding for the night). Again, the act of grace, which contradicts ordinary human reaction to harsh treatment, is intended to overcome the wrongdoer by love instead of by a show of coercive force.

5:41-42. The response of grace is to be seen in reaction not only to private individuals but even to the authorities of the state, when they press one into service. The word translated **forces . . . to go** arose during Persian times. The success of the mail system established by the Persian Empire depended on impressing subjects into service to provide assistance for carrying the mail. Later it came to mean any form of forced assistance to governmental or military authorities.

In a time when Jewish nationalism was urging defiance of Roman rule, it was perilous for a Jew to utter what might sound like a collaborationist appeal. Jesus calls for his followers not only to cooperate with Roman authorities, but also to do twice what is demanded. His aim, of course, is not political collaboration, but shocking one's enemies by an act of grace. The same point is implied by the word to **give** freely to those who beg or borrow. It is the surprising reaction of love that Jesus calls for from his followers.

5:43-48. *Words on Love of Enemies.* The high point of the sermon is reached here. Jesus' moral appeal is grounded in nothing less than the nature of God himself. Those who obey him are to seek to become like him, to become God's **sons.** In Hebrew thinking, to be a son of someone is to resemble him in his manner of life; the sons of darkness, for example, are those whose way of life is that of the Prince of Darkness, Satan. To speak of becoming a son of God does not presuppose some sort of supernatural rebirth; rather it means adopting a new goal and mode of life patterned after the nature of God himself. To adopt this goal, however, is to reverse the ordinary pattern of human behavior, which is to love one's friends and hate one's enemies.

Jewish scholars have pointed out that nowhere in the Old Testament is Israel instructed to "hate your enemies." Although there are in Psalms and some of the prophetic writings appeals to God to bring down judgment on Israel's foes, there is no direct command to hate the enemies. This appeal has, however, been found among the Dead Sea Scrolls, so that it may be this Jewish tradition that Matthew has in mind in verse 43.

That the love which is commanded is more than an emotion is implied both in the parallel command to pray for one's persecutors and in the portrayal of God's love in its active form. God sends **rain** and causes the **sun** to **rise** on all persons, regardless of their moral worth. Even the Gentiles and the tax collectors—both of which groups were despised by pious Jews—observe the rule of treating their own friends kindly. But for the one who would be truly obedient, nothing less than God's own way of working is the ultimate standard.

The call to be **perfect** could be an appeal for maturity and completeness, or it could be based on a Hebrew word which connotes peace, wholeness. In this case, to be perfect would be to share in God's reconciling work (cf. II Corinthians 5:18-19).

6:1-18. *Words on Alms, Prayer, and Fasting.* The three chief pillars of Jewish piety in the first century were alms, fasting, and prayer. Matthew now represents them as established, with significant differences, as a proper part of Christian piety. Here the chief objection to Jewish pious practices is that they were done with hypocrisy and ostentation. Almsgiving accompanied by **trumpet** blasts may be an exaggeration of actual practices, but it points to the fact that perverse human nature may lead to converting an act of charity into a prideful form of public display. Similarly, prayer and fasting are to be purely private acts, involving only God and the penitent one. Fancy **phrases** and drawing attention to one's self-denial make a mockery of the pious acts.

6:9-13. Matthew has inserted at this point what we know as the Lord's Prayer. Comparison with the older form in Luke 11:2-4 shows that in Matthew the prayer has already been somewhat expanded and modified to serve the worship needs of the church. The direct address to God in Luke 11:2, in contrast with the formal address here in verse 9, illustrates the fact that Luke has preserved the older version of the prayer.

6:9-10. To pray **Hallowed be thy name** means more than ascribing honorific titles to God. It means to work as well as pray for the day when God's lordship over the creation will be both universally acknowledged and actualized. "Thy name be hallowed" is but another way of saying **Thy kingdom come,**

which is in turn explained by the words **Thy will be done, on earth as it is in heaven.**

The coming of the kingdom means the fulfillment of God's purpose, the realization of his will in the world that he has made. The Jews believed that God's will already prevailed in heaven; in the last day it would be triumphant on earth as well. The whole of the prayer, like the Beatitudes, is eschatological (see above on 5:3-12); but whereas the Beatitudes are eschatological promises, here we have an eschatological prayer.

6:11-12. The petition for **our daily bread**, literally "our bread for tomorrow," means that we have the right to ask God only for what is essential to our basic day-to-day needs, since our goal is that God will act to fulfill the hope of the kingdom. Meanwhile, we are to pray that God will forgive us for those obligations to him that have gone unfulfilled, our **debts**, while at the same time we are to forgive those who have failed in their responsibilities toward us. Matthew has inserted in verses 14-15 the words of Jesus (cf. Mark 11:25-26) which warn that we cannot expect God's forgiveness if we are unwilling to forgive others.

6:13. The prayer for deliverance from **temptation** and **evil** probably does not refer to temptation to sin, as though God would place us in the position where we would be inclined to immoral actions. Rather it is the notion found in some Jewish writings that just before the end of the age there would occur a time of trial and testing. This period of persecution, with the attempt to turn men aside from the way of faith and obedience, was known as the temptation or the tribulation. It is to be delivered from this situation and from the power of the Evil One (Satan) that Jesus tells the disciples to pray.

6:19-24. *A Collection of Sayings.* The more original form of the word about **treasures** (Luke 13:33-34) is a warning to those preoccupied with the things of this world to divest themselves of such treasures in order to be ready to enter the kingdom. Matthew, in keeping with his stress on righteousness, presents this saying as an appeal to be mindful of the rewards that God is even now laying up for those who are living and serving in a worthy manner. Since God is storing them up, people have no need for worry that they might be lost or harmed, as is the case with the anxiety that always comes from the effort to hold on to earthly possessions.

6:22-23. The strange saying about **light** seems to presuppose that **the eye** is both light and lens by and through which the image of the world enters persons and is comprehended by them. When the eye is functioning properly, we are **full of light;** otherwise we live in darkness. Obviously this is not meant physiologically, but raises the question, How do you view the truth? If you see rightly, then your whole life is illuminated thereby; if not, you remain in the dark.

6:24. The point here is not that possessing wealth and serving God are incompatible, but that *serving* one's possessions (mammon, from an Aramaic word meaning "property" or "riches") cannot coexist with the service of God.

6:25-34. *Words on Freedom from Anxiety.* The familiar King James Version of these sayings carries a mistaken implication in current English when it admonishes to "take no thought" about the necessities of life. The real meaning is **do not be anxious.** The passage seems to embody elements of Hebrew poetry, in which the lines rhyme in their sense rather than in their sounds:

> Look at the birds of the air:
>> They neither sow nor reap,
>> Nor do they gather into barns;
> And yet your heavenly Father feeds them.
> Are you not of more value than they?

> Consider the lilies of the field,
>> How they grow;
>> They neither toil nor spin;
> Yet I tell you, even Solomon in all his glory
>> Was not arrayed like one of these.
> But if God so clothes the grass of the field,
>> Which today is alive
>> And tomorrow is thrown into the oven,
> Will he not much more clothe you, O men of little faith?

Such phrases as **heavenly Father** and **men of little faith** probably originated with Matthew, since they are found only in his gospel. But the passage as a whole breathes the atmosphere of Jewish Palestine and in essence must go back to Jesus.

The message of these words is clear: If God has given man his life, he will surely provide the means of sustaining that life. A human being is here thought of as consisting of a **body**, i.e. a self or form, and **life**, which means the vital force that enables us to live. The form needs to be clothed; the life needs to be sustained. God who gave both will sustain and preserve both. Persons can therefore be free from anxiety when they live in consciousness of dependence upon God. Only those outside the people of God (**Gentiles**) would give way to such foolish anxieties, since God **knows** fully our need. The aim of life is to **seek** for the coming **kingdom.** God will provide for all our needs, just as he will fulfill the promise of the kingdom in his own way and time.

7:1-23. *Another Cluster of Sayings.* In keeping with the Jewish reluctance to pronounce directly the name of God, verses 1-2 mean: Take care how you **judge** others since you will **be judged** by God. He will hold you to account for the way you have dealt with others. The same point is made in Mark 4:24, as well as in Luke 6:37-38, although Luke stresses the generosity of God's grace: "good measure . . . running over."

7:3-5. The word about the **speck** and the **log** in one's eye is a vivid picture of the self-appointed censor of the actions of others who cannot see his own glaring faults. It probably was originally addressed to Jesus' opponents, rather than given as advice to the disciples.

7:6. The saying about giving to **dogs what is holy** and throwing **pearls before swine** is, on the other hand, likely to have been a solemn warning that not all men are ready to receive the mystery of the coming of God's kingdom. Later on the church used this verse to defend its withholding of the sacraments from those it deemed unworthy. Since the saying is found only in Matthew it may have originated among certain exclusivist Jewish Christians.

7:7-11. This is a group of sayings intended to encourage among the disciples the confidence that God is ready and eager to answer prayer. The words are phrased so as to avoid direct mention of God, but the implication is clear: "Ask, and God will give . . .; knock, and God will open to you." An earthly father is given in comparison. If he will grant requests that his son's needs might be met, **how much more will your Father who is in heaven** answer your prayer? The passage is more of a comment on what God is like in his providential care than an absolute guarantee that God will grant any request.

7:12. The so-called Golden Rule is found in one form or another not only in Judaism but also in several other religious traditions. There is in this saying an element of enlightened self-interest which does not reach the height of insight of Jesus' appeal to love one's enemies or to respond to abuse by works of love. It is nevertheless an advance over the form of the saying current in Jewish circles of Jesus' day, which called for men to avoid doing to others what they would not like to have done to themselves.

7:13-14. Similarly, the contrast of the **wide** and the **narrow** gates is paralleled in first-century Judaism, where there was a highly developed tradition of the two ways open to man, one leading to vindication by God and the other to destruction. In one of the rather rare pessimistic notes in the Jesus tradition, it is here declared that those who choose the way that leads to life **are few** in number.

7:15-20. The warning that men display their true worth, not by how they appear, but by what they do, is based on two figures: the wolf disguised as a sheep and the tree that produces worthless fruit. The first image is drawn from Ezekiel 34, which denounces the leaders of Israel for their exploitation of the people. What is in Matthew a general warning against treachery may have been on the lips of Jesus an attack against the ruthless leaders of the nation. Verse 19 is reminiscent of the warning uttered by John the Baptist that those who failed to produce the fruits of right living would be cast into the fires of judgment. People's true nature, therefore, is to be seen in what they do, not in what they merely claim to be.

27

7:21-23. Following through on this theme, Matthew has adapted a saying of Jesus about those who call him **Lord** but do not obey his teachings (Luke 6:46), and has made it into a criterion by which persons will be admitted or refused admission to the **kingdom of heaven.** Here the contrast is between doing the **will of my Father** and merely making a profession of faith in Jesus' name.

7:24-29. *Parable of the Wise and Foolish Builders.* This parable is found in Luke 6:47-49 in an altered form that betrays unfamiliarity with terrain and building methods in Palestine, both of which are accurately reflected in Matthew's version. In Palestine there are many dry stream beds in which a foolish man might more easily build than on the safer slopes. Such a stream bed, called a *"wadi,"* is sandy, so that the foundation could easily be dug and the builder would be saved the effort of carrying stones up the side for the construction of the walls. All would go well until the rainy season came, when the wadi would become a raging torrent. The parable is eschatological (see above on 5:3-12). It raises the question, Are you prepared for the day of judgment? Take care how you are building your life, the parable warns, so that you may be able to stand the testings that will come upon God's people before the kingdom comes in its fullness.

7:28-29. This sentence includes the characteristic words which mark off the divisions of Matthew, **when Jesus finished these sayings.** The remainder is an echo of the recurrent words in Mark (e.g. Mark 1:22), which depict the **authority** that characterized Jesus' ministry and that attracted widespread interest. The **scribes,** the official interpreters of the written and oral law of Judaism, appealed to legal precedent to lend authority to their interpretations. But Jesus did not appeal to authorities; he **had authority.**

E. The Authority of Jesus' Ministry (8:1–9:35)

At this point Matthew resumes the order of events from Mark, which he interrupted after 4:23-25 (cf. Mark 1:39) to insert the Sermon on the Mount. Like his first main division Matthew's second begins with an account of the activity of Jesus drawn mostly from Mark, but with some material from Q as well. All of it has been reworked to suit his own special aims. The miracle stories, for example, are compressed in such a way as to minimize the details of the healing procedures and to emphasize Jesus as the central figure, the Messiah at whose word the healing occurs. Matthew also stresses the power of saving faith on the part of the sick one or of his family.

8:1-4. *The Healing of a Leper.* The Old Testament laws (Leviticus 14) made provision for the ceremonial cleansing of a leper who had been healed. The disease itself is thought to have been anything from a severe skin inflammation to actual leprosy (Hansen's disease), medical terms in antiquity having been so imprecise. How a modern medical observer would describe the disease and its cure in this case there is no way of knowing. But the point of the story is clear. Jesus has the power to heal "every disease" (4:23), and "all who were sick" (8:16). The story also implies that Jesus' ministry fulfills scripture, since he commands compliance with the Mosaic laws.

8:5-13. *The Centurion's Servant.* The authority of Jesus is underlined in this story by having the centurion address him as **Lord**. The Greek word translated "centurion" means literally "leader of one hundred," indicating that the man was a minor officer in the Roman army and hence a Gentile, since Jews were exempted from military service. Matthew does not mention the centurion's assistance to Judaism as does Luke (7:4-5), whose gospel stresses the eagerness of Gentiles to obey the will of God. The weight of Matthew's version falls on the centurion's sense of authority and therefore on his recognition of the authority of Jesus. This awareness of Jesus' power is acclaimed as **faith**—of such kind as Jesus had not seen among Jews.

8:11-13. At this point Matthew has introduced a Q saying (found also in Luke 13:28-29) which anticipates the response of Gentiles to the gospel and their consequent participation in the kingdom of God, replacing the **sons of the kingdom,** who are the unbelieving Jews. Before giving the conclusion of the centurion story from Q, Matthew inserts his favorite phrases about the fate of the wicked in **outer darkness,** where they **will weep and gnash their teeth.** The story ends with the emphasis on the faith of the centurion: **Be it done for you as you have believed.**

8:14-15. *The Healing of Peter's Mother-in-Law.* The brief account of this healing in Mark 1:29-31 is further abbreviated by Matthew. All the references to the other disciples have been omitted. In spite of Matthew's special interest in Peter, no details about Peter's house or family are given.

We can infer only that Peter had a **house** in **Capernaum** (verses 5, 14) and that he was married, although only his mother-in-law is here mentioned. Paul implies that Peter took his wife along with him on his apostolic journeys (I Corinthians 9:5).

8:16-17. *Summary View of Jesus' Healing Ministry.* This brief summary of Jesus' healing work has been taken over from Mark 1:32-34. Matthew had added a quotation from Isaiah 53:4, in keeping with his interest to show that Jesus' work is the fulfillment of the Old Testament. The surprising thing is that it focuses on the healing ministry, rather than on the atoning death, for which the early church found predictions in Isaiah.

8:18-22. *The Cost of Following Jesus.* The first man who volunteers to follow Jesus is warned that to do so will mean giving up the security of his home—Jesus himself has no fixed dwelling place. In his poetic response Jesus refers to himself as **Son of man.** "One like a son of man" is described in Daniel 7:13, probably referring to the human people of God through whom the kingdom is to be established, in contrast to the beast-like appearances of the pagan empires soon to be overthrown. The term appears in the non-canonical book of I Enoch as the title of the redeemer figure sent by God at the end of the age to establish his kingdom. The suffering Son of man is well known from Mark 8:31; 9:31; 10:33. But nowhere in Q, from which Matthew has here drawn, does the Son of man appear as one who suffers. Rather he is pictured either as the coming judge (24:37; Luke 17:26), or simply as a man who came into the world with no special authorization from God (11:19; Luke 7:34).

What may be implied in verse 20 is that, although Jesus possesses the extraordinary powers that the crowds have witnessed in his healings and exorcisms, he comes only as a man. Those attracted to him should be aware that he not only does not have a luxurious way of living to offer but does not even share the certainty of dwelling place that a bird or an animal might have. To follow him is to abandon all earthly security.

8:21-22. Discipleship also may call for neglect of family obligations. Honorable burial of the dead was an important duty for every pious Jew, and especially for a family member. Now Jesus says that one who is thus preoccupied with domestic duties is not ready for the demands of discipleship.

8:23-27. *Stilling the Storm.* Jesus' role as Lord of the Christian congregation is underscored in Matthew's version of this miracle, since his title of "Teacher" in Mark 4:38 has been replaced by **Lord.** Jesus' stilling of the storm is told very briefly. What is stressed is the **little faith** of the disciples and the implication that Jesus is an extraordinary person: **What sort of man is this?**

Rationalistic proposals about the miracle are of little help. For example, a natural subsidence of the storm at the moment that Jesus spoke would make the disciples out as dupes and Jesus as a fraud. The intent of the story is to show that God's authority at work through Jesus is victorious not only over human disease and disorder but also over the destructive powers of nature. Persons are called to a life of faith and trust under such authority.

8:28-34. *Two Demoniacs at Gadara.* Told in greatly abbreviated form (cf. Mark 5:1-20), this tale of the demons being driven out of a man—here two men, in keeping with Matthew's tendency to double the figures—and into a herd of swine lays emphasis on three factors:

(1) the demons' recognition of Jesus' power over them;

(2) the authority of Jesus' word (**Go**);

(3) the rejection by the people, who ask him to leave their vicinity. Mark's vivid detail has been eliminated in order to bring out these points.

9:1-8. *The Healing of the Paralytic.* Here, as in the preceding story, Matthew has eliminated considerable material from the fuller account in Mark. The result is that the authority of Jesus in both healing and forgiving sins is highlighted. This was originally (see on Mark 2:1-12) a story about the healing of a paralytic, but has been combined with a passage claiming the authority of Jesus to forgive sins. Actually Jesus does not forgive sins, but announces that God has forgiven them. To speak in God's name, however, is to invoke his authority, and it is on this ground that he is accused of **blaspheming.** Matthew's use of the phrase **God who had given such authority to men** suggests that the title **Son of man** is meant to imply that Jesus is human. But what a man! To him has been granted this unprecedented power from God. In the stories that follow, Matthew will emphasize the authority that God has given to Jesus, yet without making specific messianic claims in Jesus' behalf.

9:9-13. *The Call of Matthew.* Still following the sequence of events in Mark, Matthew adds one interesting detail at this point. He changes the name of the tax collector from Levi to **Matthew** (Mark 2:14). It has been suggested that the author was intentionally correcting Mark by supplying his own name. But comparison of the lists of the disciples in 10:2-4 with Mark 3:16-19 and Luke 6:14-16 shows that the gospel tradition has not preserved a uniform list of names. The point of this story lies, not in the identity of the man called, but rather in the occupation from which he is called to become a disciple. The men who collected taxes for Rome from their fellow Jews were doubly despised—as traitors to the nation and as often unscrupulous extortioners.

9:10-13. The tradition linked the story of the call of the tax collector with that of the meal which Jesus ate at his home. Such a person was considered ceremonially unclean by Jewish standards. The disregard of dietary and cleansing regulations is further evident in that there were other undesirables present at the same meal.

To eat a meal with someone was considered to be a most intimate kind of personal contact, so that a scrupulous Jew would be extremely careful about the company in which he would share a meal. Jesus, however, has no hesitation about such contacts. Under pressure to account for his lax attitude, he justifies what he is doing on the ground that this is a part of the mission that God has sent him to fulfill: **I came not to call the righteous, but sinners.** The setting of the story, which pictures **Pharisees** as witnessing the meal, is probably artificial, but the message is doubtless historical. Jesus saw his messianic mission as calling into the fellowship of God's people the religious outcasts, rather than as confirming the pridefully righteous in their sense of moral superiority.

9:14-17. *The Question about Fasting.* Several sayings have been brought together in this passage. Only one of these deals directly with fasting, which was likely a serious problem for the early church in its relations of tension with Judaism. The second thrust of the passage is a veiled prediction of Jesus' death, which is here pointed to as the time of sorrow which will come when he has been **taken away from them.** It is in that situation of separation from their Lord that the church will be justified in fasting. The remaining sayings about patches and **wineskins** all point up that when something **new** has come, the **old** is bound to be inadequate. Hence, when the new is added, the old cloth tears and the dry wineskins burst. God is doing a new thing through Jesus, and the older Jewish patterns will be shattered as a result.

9:18-26. *The Ruler's Daughter and the Woman with the Hemorrhage.* This is another in the series of stories that Matthew has reproduced in condensed form (Mark 5:21-43). Much of Mark's vivid detail is accordingly missing, but the now familiar emphasis on the authority of Jesus' word is forcefully presented. Matthew has somewhat blunted the dramatic point of the story, however, by reporting that the little girl was **dead** when the ruler first came to Jesus. Thus the problem created in Mark's version by Jesus' being delayed to heal the woman with the hemorrhage loses its urgency. Matthew has reported that the girl was already dead in order to remove any ambiguity as to whether Jesus merely aroused her from sleep, as verse 24 implies. Jesus, Matthew tells us implicitly, has the power over life and death.

9:27-31. *Two Blind Men at Jericho.* This is a modified and somewhat shorter version of Mark's story of blind Bartimaeus, who was healed near Jericho. Here there are two blind men in an unnamed locale, but otherwise the account differs little from Mark 10:46-52. Matthew has later included Mark's Jericho incident in the same setting and order (20:29-34). But the story is of service to him at this point in his gospel since he is rounding off his account of Jesus' activity before turning to the next great discourse in 9:36–10:42. Once more the point of the story is twofold: the authority of Jesus, who is here greeted as **Son of David** and **Lord,** and the faith of the men who believe that Jesus is able to heal them.

9:32-34. *The Healing of the Dumb Demoniac.* This story sounds like a variant of the more familiar incident in which Jesus' opponents accuse him of being in league with the prince of demons (12:25-29). It serves as a fitting conclusion to Matthew's section on Jesus' healing activity and leads smoothly into the summary statement which follows.

9:35. *Summary of Jesus' Public Ministry.* Each phrase of this brief summary is important. Matthew stresses the comprehensiveness of the ministry—**all the cities and villages**—to show that all Israel had an opportunity to hear and respond to Jesus. The ministry included both **teaching** and **preaching,** as well as **healing** and exorcisms. It is significant that Matthew says the work was carried on **in their synagogues,** suggesting that there is a consciousness within his community of being over against the Jewish community.

F. THE SENDING OF THE TWELVE DISCIPLES (9:36–10:42)

Although less well knit than the Sermon on the Mount, this mission discourse carries throughout the theme that the disciples are sent out in the name of and with the authority of Jesus. Accordingly they can expect persecution for his sake. At the same time they can look forward to the benefits of God's providential care upon their ministry. The material Matthew has here brought together is drawn from both Mark and Q, as well as from his own special source. But the whole bears the unmistakable stamp of his peculiar interests.

9:36-38. *The Needs of the Crowds.* The image of the people of God as a flock **without a shepherd** is a familiar one in the Old Testament and reminds us that Jesus was not concerned merely with the individual. He recognized that men and women of faith can live and flourish only within the people of God, whose shepherd God had appointed him to be. But the work of shepherding the flock of God requires co-workers. Or, to change the figure, as Matthew does, the **harvest,** which will bring to a close this age and establish the kingdom of God, requires **laborers.** It is to share in this work of God that the disciples are called.

10:1-15. *Commissioning the Twelve.* The number twelve may be the historical recollection of the actual number of Jesus' intimate followers, but it has symbolic significance as well. It is not only the number of the tribes of Israel but also the number of eschatological judges that the tradition reports will judge Israel in the Last Day (19:28). The gospel writers seemed to feel that it was important to preserve the "twelve-ness" of the group, as can be inferred from the story of the selection of Judas' replacement in Acts 1.

10:2a. The twelve are here designated **apostles.** This term is transliterated from a Greek word which is itself a translation of a Semitic word meaning originally "one commissioned by the king to fulfill a mission in his name and with his authority." The term "apostle" was probably not used until after the Resurrection, but since the early church is here looking back on the sending of the twelve in the light of its own mission, the use of the term is understandable. It seems to have been used in the New Testament only of those of the first generation of Jesus' followers, those who were specially commissioned by him when he appeared to them risen from the dead.

10:2b-4. The variations in the lists of names of the disciples show that the church preserved a firm tradition only about the inner core of Jesus' followers. The variants of Matthew or Levi have been noted; some ancient manuscripts list Lebbaeus in place of **Thaddaeus.**

The meaning of **Iscariot** in connection with **Judas** is uncertain. Some have tried to associate it with a group of revolutionaries who appeared in Palestine just before the Jewish revolt of A.D. 66-70, and who were known as Sicarii, meaning "dagger-men." But it probaby means only "man of Kerioth," especially since the Sicarii are unknown until more than thirty years after the crucifixion of Jesus.

10:5-6. Although many of the details in the charge to the twelve are found in Mark 6:7-11 or Luke 10:1-16, what is unique here is the limiting of the mission **to the lost sheep of the house of Israel.** Preaching among **Gentiles** and **Samaritans** is specifically forbidden. Some scholars think these words correspond to the historical fact that Jesus restricted his work to his fellow Jews.

But apart from lack of clear evidence that he did so limit his ministry, it must be seen that Matthew understands the work of God to be carried on in two stages, as did Paul: to the Jew first, and then—when the message has been spurned—to the Gentiles. That this is Matthew's view is clear from the universal outreach anticipated in 28:19. "Lost sheep of the house of Israel" could refer to those from among Israel who are lost, or it could mean that all Israel is estranged from God. Probably it is an allusion to the Jews who did not observe the laws of separateness and who were considered by the religious officials as outcasts not worth bothering with.

10:7-15. The nature of the ministry of the twelve directly continues what Jesus has been doing: preaching, healing, raising, cleansing, casting out demons. The saving actions demonstrate the nearness of the kingdom that the preaching proclaims. Matthew goes beyond Mark in further limiting the slim resources that the itinerant messengers of the kingdom are to take with them. Indeed, they appear in Matthew as ascetic

figures, with no **sandals** for their feet and no **staff** to protect
against attackers, human or animal. Unlike Mark, who warns
against moving from house to house in a village until the
preacher finds the most satisfactory accommodations, Matthew
insists that the **house** where the messenger stays must be
worthy. The disciples are to anticipate rejection. But they are to
move on to other places in the expectation that **judgment** such as
fell on the wicked cities of **Sodom and Gomorrah** will fall on
those towns that refuse to receive them and their message.

10:16-25. *The Perils Involved in the Mission.* The sayings
included in this section are drawn in large measure from Mark
13. There they are placed in an apocalyptic discourse, in which
Jesus predicts the tribulations that will overtake God's people
immediately preceding the coming of the **end** of the age. The
situation in which the followers of Jesus experience interroga-
tion and persecution before **councils** and **governors and kings** is
more fitting for later apostolic times than for the period of Jesus'
own ministry, during which his disciples were in direct
association with him. Those who seek faithfully to bear witness
to Christ during this time of persecution will be empowered by
God's **Spirit** so that they will know what they **are to say.**

10:23. One of the most problematical sayings is this explicit
statement that the disciples will not have completed their
mission tour **before the Son of man comes**—that is, before the
age ends and the kingdom of God arrives in its fullness. The
difficulty is that it is nowhere apparent that this event occurred.
There seem to be three major possibilities for explaining this
problem:

(1) Jesus was mistaken;

(2) the prophecy was fulfilled, but in a manner not publicly
observable;

(3) the saying is not authentic, but was created by the early
church for some special purpose.

The first explanation was adopted by Albert Schweitzer, who
declared that Jesus was so disappointed when the kingdom did
not arrive by the time of the disciple's return that he went up to

Jerusalem to force God's hand by acknowledging his messianic role to the authorities.

The second explanation is impossible to sustain, since Matthew ends his gospel with the coming of the kingdom and the end of the age still awaited in the future.

The third explanation is likely to be correct, in that it assumes the saying arose within a group which was concentrating on preaching to Israel, and which expected the end to come before its mission was completed.

10:24-25. Just as Jesus was denounced as being in league with the prince of the demons, **Beelzebul,** so can the disciples expect denunciation as they seek to carry out their mission.

10:26-42. *The Cost and Rewards of Discipleship.* The disciples are promised that God's providential care is over the world, both to judge the wicked who oppose his people and to watch over his own as they go about fulfilling their witness. They are advised that they are to **proclaim** openly the mystery of the kingdom, now only **whispered.** Those who now bear faithful witness will be vindicated before God in the day of judgment; conversely, those who now deny Jesus will be denied **before my Father** in the last day.

10:34-39. So great are the demands of discipleship that obedience leads to conflicts within one's family and opposition by one's own parents. Indeed, devotion to Jesus must take precedence over one's family obligations and affections. For Judaism, where the family with its mutual loyalties is the center of existence, this was an especially radical view. But the paradox of verse 39 is still greater. Full conformity to God's will can be found only by those willing to give up their lives in order that they may find the authentic life God has intended for them to live.

10:40-42. The world's response to the follower of Jesus and its response to Jesus himself cannot be separated, Jesus here declares. Even a simple deed of kindness performed for the benefit of one of his disciples will be noted by God and rewarded.

G. THE KINGDOM AND ITS COMING (11:1–12:50)

This is the activity section of the third main division of Matthew. It is marked off from the preceding section by the stereotyped words of 11:1. The material is drawn about equally from Mark and Q and in general is presented in Mark's sequence.

11:1-9. *John the Baptist and Jesus.* In response to questioners sent by John the Baptist, Jesus interprets his ministry in terms of his redemptive activity rather than by appeal to traditional titles or messianic expectations. In drawing attention to the kinds of healing work he is carrying on, Jesus refers indirectly to such Old Testament passages as Isaiah 29:18-19; 35:5-6; 61:1, though without expressly claiming that in his work these prophecies are fulfilled. Jesus, therefore, does not fit the role of messianic judge that the Baptist has expected. It is not surprising that he has grave doubts as to whether Jesus is in fact **he who is to come.** There is something touching in Jesus' expression of hope that, even though he does not conform to John's expectations, the Baptist will not be offended by him.

11:7-11. At the same time Jesus has a high regard for John. He has only scorn for the crowds who at first flocked out to hear John, but who have ignored his solemn warning of judgment. Jesus is now reported as stating what is a basically Christian understanding of John, although it is possible that the statement includes authentic words of Jesus. John is **more than a prophet;** he is the one who prepares the way for Jesus' coming. Unlike Mark, Matthew explicitly identifies John as **Elijah.** Among all men thus far born there is **no one greater than John.** But those who are even now ready to enter the kingdom of God and are now enjoying its powers in the present are in a relationship to God far superior to that of John.

11:12-19. The period up to John's coming has been filled with violence brought about by the struggle between the power of God and the powers of darkness. Those who triumph in the struggle have already entered the kingdom, at least in an anticipatory way. Instead of thus responding with faith and courage, the present generation, Jesus says, is like some peevish **children** who want neither the solemn asceticism of John (**neither eating nor drinking**) nor the joy of Jesus' fellowship (**a glutton and a drunkard**). Both sets of images are drawn from the Jewish picture of the eschatological age as a time of banqueting and revelry.

The term **Son of man** by which Jesus here refers to himself may imply simply the contrast between John, who came as God's messenger, the prophet, and Jesus, who came as a man among men. God's **wisdom** in working in this paradoxical way will be **justified** by the outcome, which will see the fulfillment of God's redemptive purpose.

11:20-24. *Woes on the Cities of Galilee.* The judgment that will fall on the unrepentant Jewish cities of Galilee is all the more solemn, since even pagan cities such a **Tyre and Sidon . . . would have repented** had they had such an opportunity to see and hear what God is doing to redeem humanity. **It shall be more tolerable** for the heathen cities, since they lacked the opportunity which the cities of Palestine have been given, but to which they have responded not with faith but with hostility.

11:25-30. *Jesus as the Revealer of God.* This section is in three parts, verses 25-26, 27-28, and 29-30. The first subsection is wholly in keeping with Jesus' declaration elsewhere. Persons ready to receive the message of the kingdom are those who by the standards of official religion are ignorant and unable to grasp the learned truths of the scholars of Judaism. Jesus declares, "It is these **babes,** not the self-styled wise, who have laid hold on the truth of what God is doing."

11:27-28. The first and third subsections are thoroughly Jewish. In contrast, this second subsection sounds more like the Gospel of John. For this reason it has been seen by some interpreters as the product of the Greek-speaking church. It could as well, however, be the utterance of a Christian prophet in the Palestinian church, since it was believed that the risen Lord continued to speak to the church through the prophets.

To accept this subsection as authentic, we would have to assume that the earthly Jesus held a view of himself close to that of the creeds formulated in the church in later centuries. On the other hand, since this passage stood in Q, which is thought to have originated in Palestine about A.D. 50, it cannot be a late product. It should be viewed as a formulation of the church on the way to the fully developed Christologies of the second and third centuries.

11:29-30. The third subsection is an invitation to discipleship, to accept the commandments of God as Jesus has set them forth. It is the biblical equivalent of the phrase from the prayer book, "whose service is perfect freedom."

12:1-14. *Controversy Concerning the Sabbath.* Two stories are here reproduced from Mark 2:23–3:6. Both have as their point the question of Jesus' violating or condoning violation of the sabbath law, one of the most sacred of all Jewish institutions. In neither incident is there a problem that the afflicted persons involved will die if their needs are not met instantly. Rather the hungering disciples could surely survive until later in the day and the crippled man could have waited until the next day to be healed. But Jesus faces the issue. The force of the stories in the form in which Matthew has produced them is the lordship of Jesus over the sabbath, as verse 8 declares explicitly.

12:5-6. The point is made even more emphatic by the reference to the superiority of Jesus to the temple. The Jerusalem temple was more than the central shrine for the Jewish people. It was their chief source of pride as one of the great buildings of the world in its time. It was believed to be the place where God was invisibly present in the midst of his people. The nation's continuing acceptability before him depended in large measure on the continuity of the sacrificial system there. It was no small claim, therefore, to assert that Jesus was more important than the temple. Matthew's anti-Jewish viewpoint is once more apparent.

12:8. Matthew has omitted the statement in Mark 2:27 that the sabbath was made for man. Although some scholars think that Jesus' original statement was that man was **lord of the sabbath**, it is clear that for Matthew it is Jesus as **the Son of man**

who exercises rightful authority over even such a venerable institution as the sabbath.

12:14. Jesus' appeal to be more concerned for compassion toward the ill than for observing the law strictly falls on deaf ears. Not only did the onlookers not see in his action the hand of God; they also **took counsel** together, **how to destroy him.** The miracles of Jesus do not convince unbelievers. They merely arouse deepened hostility.

12:15-21. *Response Among the Gentiles.* Building on a tradition preserved in Mark 3:7-12, Matthew has contrasted the opposition of Jewish officials with the receptivity of the Gentiles. Their response is in fulfillment of prophecy (Isaiah 42:1-4)—**and in his name will the Gentiles hope.** In what follows Matthew turns back to the antagonism that Jesus encounters among the Jews, even from within his own family.

12:22-50. *Controversy over the Source of Jesus' Authority.* Matthew has drawn on a Q story of the healing of a man who was **blind and dumb** to serve as his introduction to an incident that was apparently in both Mark and Q: the charge that Jesus was in league with **Beelzebul, the prince of demons.** By this introduction Matthew has obscured what is implied in Mark 3:21, 31-35—that Jesus' family came to the conclusion that he was out of his mind or that he was under the control of demonic forces. Perhaps in his interest to present Mary and Jesus' family in a good light he left this incident out.

12:25-26. Jesus' response to the charge of demonic domination is presented in a form that combines what were probably separate statements on the same general theme of Jesus' conflict with the demonic forces. The first argument is that when a **city** or dynasty (**house**) is **divided against itself,** the consequence is its own destruction. Therefore, it is implied, Jesus' success in destroying the control of the **demons** cannot be attributed to the prince of demons, who would not aid in diminishing his own power.

12:27-28. The second argument is that not everyone who performs exorcisms is in league with Beelzebul, since that would mean that those Pharisees able to cast out demons would be under Beelzebul's control. What is significant in Jesus' exorcisms is not the mere fact that he performs them, but that he discerns in them the power of God at work through the **Spirit.** To the extent that the rule of Satan is being overcome through the exorcisms, to that extent **the kingdom of God has come upon** Jesus' contemporaries.

12:29-30. The coming of God's kingdom is now compared with plundering another man's possessions. Satan is in control in this present age, but Jesus' work is binding **the strong man** (stripping him of his power), and the outcome will be the establishment of God's kingdom.

12:31-37. The question about the sin that **will not be forgiven** is really the question about the source of Jesus' authority. His opponents attribute to Satan the power he wields, whereas it should be attributed to its true source, **the Holy Spirit.** Like a fruit **tree,** the worth of Jesus is to be judged by what he does. There should be no problem in distinguishing God's power at work through Jesus from evil powers at work through evil persons.

12:38-42. Here **the scribes and Pharisees** press their opposition from another angle. They ask him to perform **a sign** from heaven as a way of providing divine authentication for his work. This request he refuses to honor. The only sign to be granted to this **adulterous generation** is **the sign of the prophet Jonah.**

Luke 11:29-32 probably has the more original form of this Q saying, according to which the sign of Jonah was Jonah's message, which carried its own authority without any miracles or divine attestations. Matthew has added an interpretation which sees in the sign of Jonah a prediction of Jesus' resurrection. If this had been the original intention of the saying, it is difficult to imagine why Luke would have omitted it from his version. The period of **three days and three nights** does not fit the gospel tradition's chronology of the Resurrection—that the interval in the tomb lasted part of three days, but not three nights as well. The interpretation seems to have arisen from Matthew's interest in the specific, detailed fulfillment of prophecy.

The rest of the passage shows that what was significant about Jonah was not his experience inside the whale but his **preaching**, in response to which the people of Nineveh repented. Similarly it was the **wisdom of Solomon** that led the queen of Sheba to journey **from the ends of the earth** in order that she might hear it. One greater in wisdom and with a greater message is here. Israel must not seek for signs, but heed the message.

12:43-45. The implied judgment on the unrepentant nation is carried further by the story of the man who, once cleansed of a demon, in the end is worse off than ever, possessed **by seven other spirits more evil than** the first. The point is obvious: Israel had her chance to be God's holy people; if now she turns from him she will be many times worse off than before. Probably the original force of the saying, if it is authentic, was simply that it was not enough for a person to be liberated from demonic control. Unless one submitted oneself to the power of God, one would be in a worse condition than before the exorcism was performed.

12:46-50. The concluding challenge to Jesus' authority comes from his own family. Although the direct charge that "he is beside himself" (Mark 3:21) has been omitted by Matthew, the sense of hostility is evident in Jesus' response, wherein he redefines what the family relationship is. The bonds that link together those who are seeking to do **the will** of God are not only more enduring but more important than the ties of the family.

H. THE PARABLES OF THE KINGDOM (13:1-52)

13:1-9. *The Parable of the Sower.* Following a somewhat stylized introduction in which Jesus is pictured sitting in **a boat** with **great crowds** gathered along **the beach,** Matthew describes Jesus' teaching **in parables,** launching without explanation into the parable of the sower. Unlike most of the parables subsequently reported by Matthew this one is not introduced by "The kingdom of God is like . . .," but it is related to the coming of the kingdom nonetheless. The question is how and with what intention.

13:3*b*-8. Let us set aside for the moment the allegorical interpretation given in verses 18-23. If we take the parable as it now stands, its point lies in the contrast between the mixed results that the beginning of the work brings forth and the astonishingly fruitful outcome in the harvest. The parable, then, is an encouragement by Jesus to his followers, warning them that much of their work in proclaiming the coming kingdom will be wasted effort, but promising them that God will bring forth results far exceeding their expectations. The parable is told against the background of what are to us strange farming methods, such as sowing before plowing or before the ground has been cleared.

13:9. The closing sentence, **He who has ears, let him hear,** was probably a free-floating saying of Jesus which was attached by the tradition or by Mark to this parable, even though it is not directly relevant to its point.

13:10-17. *The Purpose of Speaking in Parables.* A parable may be defined as an extended metaphor in which the comparison is based on a brief narrative rather than on a simple likeness to another object. Parables were in wide use among the rabbis of Jesus' day, although they were not common in the Gentile world. What was widely used there in teaching and literary endeavors was allegory, in which each element of a narrative represents symbolically a reality in another sphere. For example, the Greeks allegorized the Homeric myths, so that the tales of the conflicts and schemes of the Olympian deities became symbolic portrayals of the conflicts of natural forces.

The Semitic word which lies behind the Greek word "parable" can mean not only the literary form we know as parable, but also an enigma, puzzle, or riddle. When Mark links up these possibilities with the "secret" or "mystery of the kingdom," the result is to suggest that Jesus taught in parables so that those outside the circle of his followers might not be able to discern his meaning. Matthew has somewhat modified the force of this statement in three directions:

(1) He has changed the secret to **secrets,** thus implying that what is involved is not merely the clue to the coming of the kingdom, but private information about its nature.

(2) By introducing verse 12 (cf. Mark 4:25) at this point, and by quoting (from the Septuagint, not the Hebrew) the full passage from Isaiah 6:9-10, he has stressed that Israel's inability to comprehend what God is doing in Jesus is a fulfillment of prophecy.

(3) By changing "so that" (Mark 4:12) to **because,** Matthew quotes Jesus as saying that the *result* of Israel's willful blindness is that they do not discern the mysteries of the kingdom. This is in contrast to Mark's flat statement that Jesus' teaching in parables is *intended* to prevent Israel from discerning the secret of the kingdom.

13:16-17. It is fitting, therefore, for Matthew to introduce at this point from Q (cf. Luke 10:23-24) Jesus' pronouncement of the blessedness of the disciples to whom the secrets have been given. They now understand what the **prophets and righteous men** could discern only dimly, if at all.

13:18-23. *The Interpretation of the Parable of the Sower.* The process of allegorization by which the church has tried to understand the parables of Jesus, and has accordingly distorted them, is apparent in the explanation of the parable of the sower that Matthew has reproduced from Mark 4:13-20. Each point of the parable takes on special significance; but, as so often happens in allegory, the explanation cannot be carried through with consistency. At first the soil is the one who **hears,** the seed is **the word,** and the enemy is **the evil one.** But suddenly the hearers are compared with the seed **sown on rocky ground.** The inconsistency continues, with the hearers compared with the soil and then with the seed or the plant. Instead of a message of encouragement addressed to the messengers, the parable has become a word of warning addressed to the church. It no longer says, "Sow with assurance," but, "Receive the word with fruitfulness or fear the outcome."

13:24-30. *The Parable of the Weeds.* The original force of this parable is probably similar in part to that of the parable of the sower: carry on your work faithfully in spite of mixed results. It is a word of encouragement. Only in this case it is based, not on the astonishing results, but on the promise that God will evaluate the results in the judgment. In verses 36-43, however, Matthew has furnished an allegorical interpretation which radically alters its meaning and enables him to introduce some of the distinctive features of his own theology.

13:31-32. *The Parable of the Mustard Seed.* In abbreviating somewhat from Mark 4:30-32, Matthew has shifted the point of this parable so that the contrast is no longer between the tiny seed and the large shrub, but between the seed and its supernatural transformation into **a tree.** In this and the preceding parable the characteristic introductory phrase appears, **The kingdom of heaven is like . . . .** But the comparison is not between the kingdom and the seed or those who sow the seed, but between some aspect of the kingdom and the whole incident. It might be clearer to translate or paraphrase this introductory formula as: "It is with the kingdom of God as it is with the following incident." The story would then point to the almost unnoticed beginnings of the work of the kingdom in the ministry of Jesus as contrasted with the surprisingly great results that are promised in the eschatological fulfillment.

13:33. *The Parable of the Leaven.* As it stands, this parable also makes the point of contrasting the small beginnings with the extensive results of the power of the kingdom now at work. The saying comes from the Q source, as would appear from the parallel in Luke 13:20-21 and from its nonappearance in Mark, which Matthew is otherwise following at this point. It is likely, however, that this saying originally did not refer to the hidden working of the powers of the kingdom, but to the stealthy operation of the powers of evil. The figure of leaven is used elsewhere in the Synoptic gospels to refer to evil (16:6; Mark

8:15; Luke 12:1). Similarly, Paul uses leaven as a symbol of evil that is seeking to pervade the Christian community (I Corinthians 5:6). The Corinthian Christians are called to purge out this corrupting influence in order that they might be the pure loaf. Matthew, however, has clearly understood it as the silent action of the coming kingdom of God.

13:34-35. *Why Jesus Uses Parables.* Matthew has modified Mark's form of these words (Mark 4:33-34), where the meaning is that the parables were Jesus' way of keeping the secret of the kingdom within the inner circle of the disciples. The quotation is not from a **prophet** (some ancient manuscripts read "the prophet Isaiah"), but from Psalm 78:2. What is important for Matthew is that even the form of Jesus' teachings—in this case, **in parables**—is a part of the divine plan laid down in advance in the scriptures.

13:36-43. *The Interpretation of the Parable of the Weeds.* Once more we have an allegorical interpretation of a parable, but this time it is from Matthew rather than from the tradition on which he draws. Verse 41 gives us a clue to one of the main themes of Matthew's understanding of the church and its destiny. The kingdom of the **Son of man** is the church (cf. **his kingdom,** verse 41) in contrast with the **kingdom of their Father** (verse 43), which is the new age, from which all evil persons have been removed. The church, therefore, is a mixed body, containing both good and bad.

The point of the interpretation is that the task of differentiating worthy from unworthy members is not up to the church, but will be accomplished by the Son of man as judge at **the close of the age.** The **evildoers** will be punished and will **weep and gnash their teeth** in anguish, as Matthew delights to say. His designation for the good is **the righteous,** which, as has been noted, is a pervasive theme in this gospel.

13:44-46. *Parables of the Treasure and the Pearl.* Both these parables point to the supreme importance of sharing in the kingdom of God, in comparison with which every other value should be sacrificed. The covering up and the secrecy about the treasure are not the significant points. Rather it is that the man sells all that he has in order to gain one thing—the kingdom.

13:47-50. *The Parable of the Net.* The specific details of this parable are reminiscent of the parable of the weeds as interpreted by Matthew in verses 40 and 42, including the burning of the bad and their anguished weeping and gnashing of teeth. The parable is here used to warn that the good and bad will be separated from within the church at the last judgment, and the unrighteous will be punished. The explanation given in verses 49 and 50 is almost certainly not authentic, but it is an extension of Matthew's own views. The fact that the way of handling inedible fish would not be to burn them demonstrates the artificiality of the parable as it stands.

13:51-52. *The Parable of the Householder.* Here we have the clearest hint as to the way Matthew viewed himself. He is a **scribe,** and therefore one who through reinterpreting the will of God as embodied in the scriptures, adopted the role of the leaders of Pharisaic Judaism, whose task was to study and transmit the ongoing interpretations of the law. The special training of the Christian scribe, however, enabled him to do more than merely preserve the tradition; he brought out new realities as well from the treasure of scripture and the gospel tradition. This is, of course, precisely what Matthew is engaged in: showing from the law and the prophets how Jesus is the fulfillment of the hopes of Israel and the one through whom God is establishing the true Israel. The passage tells nothing about Jesus' understanding of his mission; it tells a great deal about Matthew's understanding of his own.

I. THE LIFE OF THE NEW COMMUNITY (13:53–18:35)

Appropriately Matthew begins the action section of the fourth main division of his gospel with the account of Jesus' rejection by official Judaism represented by the synagogue leaders in Nazareth. At this point he resumes following Mark's sequence of events. Verse 53 marks off the main division with the words **when Jesus had finished . . . .**

13:53-58. *The Rejection at Nazareth.* Once again we see that the opportunity to observe the **mighty works** Jesus performed did not convince his opponents that God was at work through him. Instead **they took offense at him.** Since he had come from their own town and his family was known to them, they implied that a man of such humble origins could not possibly be God's agent. It is noteworthy that they regard him as **the carpenter's son,** meaning, of course, Joseph's. There is no hint here of supernatural origin. At this point Matthew has diverged from Mark, who (in the most reliable manuscripts) quotes the townspeople as referring to Jesus as simply "the carpenter" (Mark 6:3). It may be that Matthew considered it undignified to speak of Jesus as a carpenter, but his version of the saying raises more serious questions by suggesting that Joseph was Jesus' father. It should be kept in mind that John likewise speaks of Joseph as the father of Jesus and contains no hint of the supernatural birth (cf. John 1:45). John further assumes that Jesus was born in Galilee rather than Bethlehem (John 7:41).

14:1-12. *Herod and John the Baptist.* In Mark 6:14-29 the story of the death of John the Baptist is told as though the evangelist wants to take up the time while the disciples are out on their mission journey. In Matthew the incident serves as a warning to Jesus of the rejection that he can expect from the governmental officials as well as from the religious leaders. News of John's death leads Jesus to withdraw, at least for the moment, from public activity. The gruesome story of the mode and motive of John's murder is presented in shortened form by Matthew. The **Herod** spoken of here is not Herod the Great of the infancy stories, but his son, Herod Antipas, who was ruler of Galilee and Perea. Judea, in which Jerusalem was situated, was under the direct control of the Roman governors; but when Jesus was in Galilee, the person who had life-and-death control over him was Herod Antipas.

14:13-21. *The Feeding of the Five Thousand.* This story, which is one of the few incidents to be reported by all four of the gospel writers, is filled with symbolic elements arising from the eucharistic practices of the early church. The words of blessing and distribution follow quite precisely the traditional words of ritual of the Lord's Supper. This is not to suggest that there is nothing historical about the event. It is rather to suggest that what is historical is so overlaid with what is symbolic that the two can no longer be differentiated sharply.

Many rationalistic explanations have been offered for the miracle of the loaves and the fishes, but none of them is really helpful in understanding the story. Albert Schweitzer suggested that, although in actuality each person received only a tiny fragment of food, the joyous realization that the kingdom of God was breaking in through the ministry of Jesus was so powerful that each felt satisfied. A century ago it was common to propose that the crowd had brought food but kept it concealed until the small boy (mentioned only in John 6:9) offered to share his lunch and shamed the others thereby into offering theirs. But such explanations have missed the point of the story, that Jesus is able to supply all needs in abundance. John has seen this most clearly in linking the feeding story directly with the discourse on the bread from heaven.

14:17-19. The **loaves** are obviously significant in the early church in connection with the Eucharist, or the Lord's Supper. But the **fish** were also important as a Christian symbol. The fact that the letters of the Greek word for "fish," *ichthus*, were the initials of the full title of Jesus as worshiped in the church—*Iesous Christos Theou Uios Soter* (Jesus Christ God's Son, Savior)—made this symbol especially appealing.

14:20-21. The tradition emphasizes that the miracle really did occur by the many fragments remaining and by mentioning the note (not mentioned in Mark 6:44) that the number five thousand did not include the women and children. This comment is in keeping with Matthew's tendency to heighten the miraculous element.

14:22-33. *Walking on the Water.* Jesus' power over nature in creating bread to feed the multitudes is seen here once more in his walking on the water. The account has many of the characteristics of stories told about other great figures in various religions and cultures. It is presented here to show that the authority of Jesus extends not only to sin and sickness but to the forces of nature as well. God's kingdom must be sovereign over the whole of the creation, not merely the world of humans. The account is full of vivid detail about **the boat . . . beaten by the waves** and **the disciples,** who **were terrified.** To the community of faith, as to the distraught disciples, comes Jesus' word: **Take heart, it is I; have no fear.** The intention of the story is made clear in verse 33, where Jesus is acclaimed as **the Son of God.**

14:28-33. To Mark's account of this incident Matthew has appended a brief account concerning Peter, which presents vividly and succinctly Peter's brashness (**bid me come to you**), his lack of courage (**he was afraid**), but also his ultimate faith in Jesus (**Lord, save me**). The presence of Matthew's favorite phrase **little faith** suggests either that he has created this story or that he has reworked it to suit his purpose.

14:34-36. *Healings at Gennesaret.* This brief narrative is in the nature of a summary of Jesus' ministry of healing. The exact location of Gennesaret is not known, although it was probably an area on the northwest shore of the Sea of Galilee.

15:1-20. *How Does a Person Become Defiled?* For first-century Christianity, especially where there was close contact with Jews, there was a perennial problem as to the extent to which Jewish laws were binding on Christians. In addition to written laws from scripture there were the detailed oral laws accumulated over the centuries. There are two main issues discussed here: honoring one's parents in keeping with the fifth commandment, and preserving ones ceremonial purity in keeping with the dietary laws and traditions.

15:3-9. Jesus' criticism in relation to the law commanding **honor** to parents is that the oral tradition has replaced the written law. According to the oral tradition, a man could announce that his possessions had all been **given to God,** which was understood as freeing him from any obligation to support his parents. The hypocrisy of this action was compounded by the fact that, in the name of piety toward God, a person evaded direct responsibility to obey the express command of God. By placing the quotation from Isaiah after the passage exposing the hypocrisy of the oral tradition, Matthew has rendered the point about **the precepts of men** even more than does Mark.

15:10-20. The critique of the regulations about ritual cleanliness is even more radical. Verse 11, with its claim that one is defiled not by what enters the mouth but by what comes out of the heart, implies the setting aside of the entire dietary and ritual cleansing code, oral and written. The direction of the oral law had been to expand the dietary and cleansing regulations. Jesus now renders them all irrelevant to the question of genuine purity. It is the **heart** (the will) that needs to be cleansed, not the **hands.** The question about the parable in Mark 7:17 refers to Jesus' statement about what constitutes defilement. Matthew links it with a veiled denunciation of the leaders of Israel as constituting a group which has no rightful claim to call itself the people of God: they are a **plant which my heavenly Father has not planted . . .; they are blind guides.** Thus Matthew has transformed a critique of Jewish institutions into a repudiation of Judaism itself. Clearly he is writing from within a situation in which the church is set over against Judaism.

15:21-31. *Mercy for the Outcasts.* The first incident in this section takes place in Gentile territory visited by Jesus following his rejection in Galilee. **Tyre and Sidon** lie just to the north of Palestine along the Mediterranean coast in what is now Lebanon. The inhabitants of this area were racially and linguistically connected with the ancient Canaanites, who lived in Palestine at the time of the coming of the Israelites. Matthew prefers **Canaanite** to the term common in his time, "Syrophoenician" (Mark 7:26). It has been conjectured that Matthew's use of the old name, which was still preferred in the first century by the inhabitants themselves, indicates that the church for which he wrote was located in this area. Yet it is in his gospel that the woman addresses Jesus as **Son of David,** a title which gives expression to the hopes of Israel for the reestablishment of the Davidic kingship, and which is scarcely appropriate for a Canaanite woman.

15:24-28. The comparison Jesus draws between allowing

Gentiles to share in the benefits of the kingdom and throwing **the children's bread . . . to the dogs** does not sound like a charitable response to a gravely concerned mother. Attempts to account for this as spoken in jest do not ease the difficulty at all. We should probably see here either the inner struggle of Jesus when confronted with the request to extend his mission beyond the Jewish limits in which he had begun it, or the struggle within the early church as to whether the message and powers of the kingdom of God were open to Gentiles as well as Jews. The reappearance of the phrase **the lost sheep of the house of Israel** (cf. 10:6) strengthens the impression that this story is preserved because of its bearing on the question of the limits of the church's mission. The obvious answer is that the mission is to be extended to wherever it encounters **faith.**

15:29-31. Matthew has omitted Mark's account of the healing of the deaf mute (Mark 7:32-36), limiting himself instead to a general statement of the types of sufferers that Jesus healed: **the lame, the maimed, the blind, the dumb.** The important thing is that he healed them, and in so doing raised the question among the onlookers as to the source of his powers.

These incidents would remind the gospel's readers of the prophecies of Isaiah 29:18 and 35:5-6. It is not only as redemptive events in themselves that these healings are important; they are manifestations of God's fulfillment of his purpose of redemption of the world through Jesus.

15:32-39. *The Feeding of the Four Thousand.* The oral stage of transmission of the Synoptic gospel stories and sayings seems to have preserved two different versions of the feeding incident. Mark recorded them both and Matthew has followed his example (cf. 14:31-21). Presumably this feeding took place on Gentile soil, since the last place-names mentioned (in Mark 7:31) were the cities of the Decapolis (see above on 4:25).

It is likely that the number of baskets filled with fragments, **seven,** is symbolic of the mission to the Gentiles, just as the twelve baskets in the earlier account symbolize the mission to the Jews. This division of labor and these numbers appear in Acts 6:2-3, where the church assigns different responsibilities to two groups: the twelve from among the Hebrews and the seven from among the Greeks (Gentiles).

16:1-12. *Unbelief of the Pharisees.* Following Mark, Matthew presents here the brief account of Jesus' refusal to give **a sign** in response to the demand from his opponents. But Matthew has introduced two elements not found in Mark 8:12, where there is simply a categorical refusal.

First there is a saying from Q (cf. Luke 12:54-56) in which Jesus scoffs at his detractors, since they can predict the next day's weather by reading certain signs in the sky but cannot discern the signs that **the times** are about to change and that God is already performing signs of the inbreaking of the new age.

The second innovation is the combining of Mark's form with the Q form to create a new composite saying, which declares that no sign will be given **except the sign of Jonah.** Here no specification of this sign of Jonah is given, although in 12:38-40 Matthew has linked it with the burial and resurrection of Jesus. Jesus' point is that the signs of the kingdom are to be discerned in the works which he is performing, but they will not be performed merely to satisfy the curiosity of his critics.

16:5-12. The story of the feeding of the multitudes is once more recalled. The disciples have forgotten to bring along **bread,** and their negligence becomes the occasion for a curious explanation which is as difficult and enigmatic as the events which it purports to explain. **The leaven of the Pharisees and Sadducees** is interpreted as referring to their **teaching,** which is not according to the truth and therefore works its harmful influence. Jesus warns his followers to **beware of** this teaching.

But the reference to the two feedings, of five and four thousand respectively, is presented as though it were self-explanatory, which it is not. Matthew's implication is that the feeding stories contain some teaching of the truth, which his followers are supposed to grasp.

No specific accusation is brought against the teaching of the Pharisees or the Sadducees, except the warning of the error which it contains. Elsewhere in Matthew the Sadducees come under indirect attack for their rejection of the belief in the resurrection (22:23-33), while the Pharisees are repeatedly denounced as hypocrites, whose traditions and burdensome regulations stand in the way of men's obedience to the will of God.

16:13-23. *Confession of Jesus' Messiahship.* In all three Synoptic gospels the incident at Caesarea Philippi marks a turning point in the story of Jesus. From this point on Jesus begins to speak of his destiny in terms of his suffering and death, rather than speaking only of the coming of the kingdom of God. By far the fullest account of this incident is in Matthew.

16:13a. The city of **Caesarea Philippi** was located at the sources of the Jordan. It was enlarged and renamed by Herod's son, Philip, in honor of Caesar Augustus (or possibly Tiberius) and of himself. The site of a pagan shrine to Pan, it was a Gentile region outside the bounds of Jewish Palestine. Since the city had no known significance for the early church apart from this event, it can scarcely have been the imagination of the church that located the event here. In short, this appears to be one of the firm topographical references in the gospels.

16:13b. Unlike Mark 8:27, where Jesus simply asks who men say he is, Matthew reports Jesus as designating himself as the **Son of man.** The term "son of man" is used in Daniel 7:13, not as a title, but as a way of contrasting the kingdom of God, which is compared to a human being (literally a son of man) with the kingdoms of the idolatrous world powers, which are depicted as horrendous beasts. In the book of I Enoch the Son of man is a title for a heavenly personage who comes to earth to judge the enemies of God and establish his rule in the earth. This document apparently incorporates ideas of God's redemptive agent that were abroad in Judaism before the birth of Jesus. It appears, therefore, that Matthew is placing a Christian witness to Jesus as the Son of man on the lips of Jesus himself. The actual question was perhaps more tentative with regard to Jesus' messianic mission.

16:14ab. The answers to his question are varied. Those who say **John the Baptist** apparently shared with Herod Antipas the belief that Jesus was John raised from the dead. Indeed, the fact that both men announced the end of the age, the coming judgment, and the establishment of God's kingdom would make the confusion easy to understand. The association of Jesus with **Elijah** was a natural development, since Jewish tradition expected that Elijah would reappear on the earth in the last days to prepare for the coming of the Lord God (Malachi 4:5). It is possible that there were some Christians who identified Jesus with Elijah, but Matthew is quite explicit that John the Baptist is Elijah (17:13), even though in John 1:21 the Baptist flatly rejects this role.

16:14*cd*. Linking Jesus with **Jeremiah** was understandable, since it was he who had predicted the establishment of the new covenant (Jeremiah 31:31-40), and the words of Jesus mirrored the language of the new covenant (26:28). Otherwise there is no tradition of Jeremiah's returning at the end time, such as there is concerning Elijah and Enoch.

The answer **one of the prophets** is obviously rather vague. But it may have been originally "the prophet." In that case it would have had great significance, since Deuteronomy 18:15-22 promised that in the days of the restoration of the nation God would send them a greater prophet like Moses, to whom the nation would finally give obedience.

16:15-16. When Jesus' question is turned directly to the disciples themselves, it is Peter as usual who is the spokesman for the group. Matthew gives his answer in fuller form than in Mark 8:29: **You are the Christ, the Son of the living God.** It is remarkable that the tradition speaks here of *the* Christ, that is, Messiah, meaning "anointed" by God to perform a prescribed task. The term is used in the Old Testament of a pagan ruler who does God's bidding (Isaiah 45:1) as well as of Israel's king (Psalm 45:6-7). Actually there was not a single image of such a redemptive figure that could be designated as "the Christ." Perhaps the closest one could come to this would be the nationalistic hope of the reinstatement of the monarchy, with God's anointed one (Christ) ruling as his vicegerent over his people. Since the king would be spoken of as God's son (Psalm

2:6-7), this may be the implication of the title that Peter ascribes to Jesus.

16:17. The words which follow are found only in Matthew and are among the most controversial in the whole of the New Testament. There is evidence of Semitic forms of speech behind the Greek text of Matthew here, but that does not prove that these words are authentic. It shows only that they likely originated in a Semitic-speaking community.

Peter is addressed by his Semitic name, **Simon Bar-Jona,** which means simply "Simon son of Jonah." He is here given the nickname *Kepha* (Cephas; cf. John 1:42), an Aramaic word meaning "rock," which is translated into Greek as *Petros.* What Peter has affirmed has not been disclosed to him by any human agency (by **flesh and blood**), but directly by God himself. Matthew's use of the phrase **my Father who is in heaven** shows that he has reworked the tradition, adding his own favorite phrases.

16:18-19. Peter's nickname now becomes the basis for a play on words. Peter *(Kepha)* is to be the rock *(kepha)* on which the church will be built. Only in Matthew (here and at 18:17) among all four gospels is the church mentioned directly. This suggests that the passage in its present form is the product of the church rather than an authentic word of Jesus. Attempts have been made to demonstrate the authenticity of the words, but only by assuming that they were spoken by Jesus after the Resurrection. The designation of Peter as "the rock" does not view him as the first bishop of Rome and the founder of the Roman Catholic hierarchy, but as the first witness of the Resurrection and therefore as the prime apostolic witness that God raised Jesus from the dead (I Corinthians 15:5).

The word translated **church** (Greek *ekklesia*) refers to the community of faith, not to an ecclesiastical organization as the church later came to be. The authority to **bind** and **loose** has to do with the regulation of the inner life of the community. It has its parallel in the work of the rabbis as interpreters of the law, deciding what is permissible for the faithful and what is not. The promise here given is that they are not exercising this authority in independence. Rather God's plan is being worked out through what they do. The binding and loosing **on earth** has its counterpart **in heaven.**

16:20. The charge to **tell no one,** if authentic, may have been originally a blanket rejection by Jesus of the title of Messiah. Nowhere is there a record of his assigning this title to himself. Instead, he repeatedly calls attention to the implications of his work for the coming of the kingdom. He regards his mission as messianic without identifying himself as the Messiah. Here, in any case, he orders his followers to be silent concerning his role as the Messiah.

16:21-23. When, however, Jesus starts to explain to his followers that his mission involves his own suffering and death, Peter rejects this notion vehemently. He in turn is denounced as the spokesman for **Satan,** the enemy of God's purpose through Jesus.

It is likely that the specific details of Jesus' prediction of the Passion have been introduced into the tradition after the events occurred. But there is no reason to doubt that Jesus foresaw his death, that he viewed it as a part of the divine purpose, and that he forewarned his disciples concerning it. It is equally likely that they failed to understand the seriousness of his warning or to discern any connection between his death and the coming of the kingdom of God. Only in the light of the Resurrection did this connection begin to become clear.

The prediction is repeated twice (17:22-23; 20:17-19). In all three cases Matthew corrects Mark's dating of the Resurrection from "after three days" (Mark 8:31; 9:31; 10:34) to **on the third day.** What is perhaps more significant is that in all three (though not in 27:63-64 and 28:6-7) Matthew alters Mark's active voice, "he will rise," to the passive, **he will be raised.** The oldest witnesses to the Resurrection—Paul's letters and the traditions of early preaching in the first half of Acts—say that God raised Jesus rather than that Jesus rose.

16:24-28. *Conditions of Discipleship.* Just as Jesus called his followers to share in the works of the kingdom, so he began to announce that they must be prepared to share in his sufferings.

It has been suggested that **take up his cross** originally referred, not to the instrument of Jesus' death, but to acceptance of the stigma attached to him and his work. But clearly the tradition and the gospel writers understand these sayings to speak of sharing in the sufferings of Christ in the light of the cross. For one to accept this way of life means to **deny himself**, even to **lose . . . his life** in order that he may find the true way to life that God alone can provide. There is no way to recover the loss resulting from a wasted life—nothing can one **give in return for** it.

16:27. The seriousness of the situation is heightened by the warning that **the Son of man is to come** as judge. He will mete out rewards and punishment approprite to the stewardship that men have performed with their own lives. It is remarkable that here, as is nearly always the case where the coming Son of man is mentioned in the Synoptic tradition, Jesus speaks of him in the third peron, as if it is someone other than himself. The contrast between himself and the Son of man is more evident in Mark 8:38, but it is implied here and also in verse 28.

16:28. This saying raises another kind of difficulty, since it declares that the coming of the Son of man, whose advent will mark the end of the present age, will take place during the lifetime of some of Jesus' disciples. On this basis, therefore, the end should have occurred sometime between A.D. 70 and 100, depending on how long the last of Jesus' followers lived.

Some interpreters try to get around the difficulty by suggesting that the kingdom's coming is to be seen in the transfiguration story which follows immediately. Others think the **coming in his kingdom** refers to the resurrection of Jesus. But if we take the humanity of Jesus with full seriousness, we should perhaps acknowledge that he, in the sense of urgency and power that attended his ministry, actually expected the end to come within that generation.

Although his expectation was not fulfilled in that form, the experience of his resurrection and the consequent powerful coming of the Spirit upon the church produced transforming effects in the lives of men of faith. This led the church to conclude that the signs of the kingdom were in fact present in

the ministry of Jesus, even though the consummation did not
occur at the point in time that Jesus seems to have expected it.

17:1-8. *The Transfiguration.* Many interpreters have found
in this story a kind of advance viewing of the glory of the risen
Christ. It is surely so understood by the author of II Peter
1:17-18, who speaks as though he had been present when the
revelation of Christ's glory took place. More likely, however,
the story is the product of the early church, which rightly saw in
the redemptive significance of Jesus many parallels with the
great redemptive act of God in behalf of old Israel—the Exodus
and the giving of the law at Sinai.

It is with the latter that the analogies are most clearly to be
seen: withdrawn on a mountain, God's servant hears the voice of
God speaking out of a cloud, as a consequence of which his very
appearance is changed. We see these features in the story: a
**high mountain; apart; his face shone; a bright cloud
overshadowed them; a voice from the cloud said, "This is my
beloved Son."** Significantly, the voice from the cloud uses the
same words and confirms the message which came from heaven
at the baptism of Jesus (3:17).

It is difficult to understand how the disciples could have
missed Jesus' intention so completely—as they in fact did—if
they had had such divine communications as these. Even if we
assume that there was some historical experience behind this
account—such as a corporate vision by the inner group of
disciples—we would still have to acknowledge that the account
has now been overlaid with Old Testament imagery.

The point of the story in the purpose of the gospel writers is
clear and important: God's redemptive purpose through Jesus
did not start with the Cross and the Resurrection, but was
operative throughout the whole of his earthly life and ministry.
Furthermore, those whose eyes were opened in the light of the
Resurrection to discern the glory that was present in the earthly
life were the disciples, among whom the prime witnesses were
Peter and James and John. In spite of the idle proposal to build
three booths, as though this would in some way preserve this
moment of glory (Mark 9:6 tells us Peter suggested this for want

of anything better to say), the scene quickly fades, **Moses** and
Elijah vanish, and **Jesus only** remains.

17:9-13. *The Coming of Elijah.* Frequently in Mark, Jesus
commands the disciples to be silent about what they know of
him. Matthew has here taken over Jesus' instruction (cf. Mark
9:9), although he has omitted the suggestion that the disciples
did not understand what being **raised from the dead** meant. The
movement of thought is somewhat awkward in Mark, but
Matthew has sought to give a unity to the whole by referring in
verse 12 once more to the Son of man and his suffering. It is not
known which scribes expected Elijah to come **first** in order to
restore all things, nor is it known what "first" implies, whether
before the Messiah (Matthew presumably understands it in this
way) or before the end. The argument now runs, Elijah has
come and has suffered—that is, **John the Baptist,** as verse 13
makes explicit. Suffering will also befall the one whose
forerunner Elijah was—that is, the Son of man.

17:14-21. *Healing the Epileptic Boy.* Matthew's version of this
story is considerably abbreviated, but it is told in such a way as to
minimize the miracle itself and to emphasize the inability of the
disciples to perform the healing. Stress is laid on the faults of this
generation (it is **faithless and perverse**) and on the failings of the
disciples (they have **little faith**). To this rebuke Matthew adds
the word about **faith as a grain of mustard seed,** by which men
and women of faith are able to accomplish the seemingly
impossible.

17:22-23. *The Passion Predicted Again.* The second direct
prediction of the Passion is not so detailed as the first (16:21).
This time Mark comments that the disciples "did not
understand" and were "afraid to ask" for an explanation (Mark
9:32), but Matthew says merely that they were **greatly
distressed.**

17:24-27. *The Coin in the Fish's Mouth.* It is an understate-
ment to say that this story, perhaps more than any other of the
Synoptic miracles, stretches modern credulity. Attempts have
been made at rationalistic explanations and at allegorical
interpretation, but neither approach is really fruitful. It seems

rather to be a story that arose, or at least that assumed its present form, in the days when serious questions were beginning to arise as to the relation of the young church to the Roman state. Following the destruction of the temple in Jerusalem in A.D. 70, the Romans continued to collect the half-shekel tax originally designated for support of the temple, but channeled the funds into support for the pagan temple of Jupiter. The purpose behind the story is to tell inquiring or reluctant Christians that, although their freedom as children of God releases them from a moral obligation to pay such a tax, it is better to avoid **offense** by paying it. The story thus serves to provide the sanction of Jesus' reaction to the problem for Christians who face the difficulty of whether or not to obey the pagan state.

18:1-5. *True Greatness.* Matthew has changed the discussion among the disciples as to which of them was the greatest (Mark 9:33-34) into a question, **Who is the greatest in the kingdom of heaven?** The older form of Jesus' answer (Mark 10:15) does not specify what it is about a child that prepares one for admission to the kingdom. But for Matthew, to become like a child one **humbles himself.** Humility, then, is the guarantee to greatness in the kingdom.

18:5. Mention of the child calls to mind another saying about children, according to which receiving **one such child** is the same as receiving Jesus. This is a recurrent theme in the tradition. The treatment accorded the followers of Jesus or those who come in his name is actually treatment offered to Jesus himself. Matthew has the fullest statement on this theme in the parable of the last judgment (25:31-46), which is found in his gospel alone.

18:6-35. *Mutual Responsibilities.* We now have a series of loosely connected sayings dealing with the general theme of the solemn obligations that fall upon those who share in the life of the Christian community. The sayings were probably addressed originally to Jesus' disciples, but they have been placed here in a setting which makes them a set of regulations for guiding the inner life of the church. The train of thought moves easily from the children spoken of in the previous section to the **little ones.**

These are not children in the literal sense, but those who have newly come into the fellowship of the community. To cause them to stumble (see below on 18:7) as they begin the life of faith is a grievous sin. The consequences of such action are so grave that Jesus here advises the guilty person—using typical Semitic overstatement—to try to flee from the wrath of God's judgment by drowning himself in the **depth of the sea.**

18:7. This saying reiterates the theme of the preceding. The Revised Standard Version confuses the meaning by translating the word for "stumbling blocks" as **temptations to sin.** There is no suggestion here of a conscious luring of the little one to sin or even of some testing experience that must be undergone to fulfill one's witness. Rather it is acknowledged that factors will arise in the world which will cause those of weak faith to stumble. Those through whom these occasions for stumbling occur will be held accountable to God.

18:8-9. Persons of faith are to exercise control over their own faculties, so that what is handled, what is entered into, and what is seen is not outside the range of their responsibility and therefore not beyond those factors for which God will hold them accountable. In vivid imagery, repeated from 5:29-30, Jesus tells his followers they must be ready to **cut . . . off** the offending **hand** or **foot** or to **pluck . . . out** the offending **eye.** Nothing less than complete self-control is expected of those who would enter the life of the age to come. The alternative is to yield to unworthy motives and urges, and the consequence will be exclusion from the presence of God. The **hell of fire** is an image taken over from ancient Israel, when the Valley of Hinnom (Gehenna) was the place of refuse for the city of Jerusalem. Its smoldering fires made it an obvious symbol for the fate of the worthless and the useless.

18:10-14. Concern for **these little ones** continues. Matthew has placed here the parable of the lost sheep, which he drew from his Q source (cf. Luke 15:3-7). By referring to the little ones at the beginning and ending of the parable Matthew has given it a new direction. In the original form it speaks of the joy of God at the recovery of one of his own children who repents. Here it is the welfare of the little ones that is stressed.

The parable was probably addressed originally to Jesus' critics, who objected to his interest in the outcasts and the sinners. In Matthew's setting it is addressed to the church leadership, which is being called to account for the welfare of the weak in faith, the new converts. God's concern for these is to be reflected in the leaders' active concern for the immature believers within the community. The notion that **their angels always behold the face of my Father** is seen in the rabbinic teachings of the time, according to which angels watch over men and have direct access to God. The little ones are therefore always under the eyes of Providence.

18:15-35. The remainder of this section deals in a variety of ways with the question of resolving disputes within the community. Matthew is concerned with lining out procedures for dealing with disputes. Verse 15 presents the first stage: the one offended is to take the initiative in settling matters privately with the **brother** who has caused the offense. If this does not work, stage two is to be put into effect: **one or two others** are to listen to the dispute as **witnesses,** in accord with the Old Testament method of gathering evidence (Deuteronomy 19:15). If this also proves to be ineffective, the third stage comes into operation: there is a hearing on the issue before **the church,** i.e. the entire congregation. If no settlement can be reached on this basis, the offending member is to be put out of the community, as Israel would treat a **Gentile and a tax collector.**

Here is the beginning of judicial procedure within the church and the first suggestion of a process of excommunication. It seems certain that such advanced regulations did not come from Jesus, but from the early church itself, operating in keeping with what it understood to be his intention.

18:18-20. The authority exercised in the church is understood to have heavenly sanction, since it is believed that there is an exact correspondence between the will of God in heaven and the functioning of the authorities within the church on earth. The moral decisions of the community are to be equated with the moral judgments of God. This same element of correspondence is to be seen between the petitions of the church on earth and the will of God in heaven. Prayer is not a purely private matter, but an expression of the will of **two** or more. **Anything they ask,** God will do. The safeguard in what may appear to be a blanket promise is the presence of the living Christ in the midst of the community: **There am I in the midst** of the church. This theme will reappear in the closing words of the gospel, 28:20.

18:21-22. Again as spokesman for the group of disciples, **Peter** asks for a ruling as to the number of times one must forgive the person who has committed a wrong. He thinks that he is being most charitable in suggesting that he will forgive someone **seven times.** Note the parallel between this passage and the cry of vengeance in Genesis 4:24:

> If Cain is avenged sevenfold,
> truly Lamech seventy-sevenfold.

In the pre-Israelite period vengeance toward one who had done wrong knew no limits. Jesus is here saying that, among those who await the coming of God's kingdom, mercy can have no limits. **Seventy times seven** is not to be taken literally. It points rather to the limitless grace which is to be displayed by the child of God.

18:23-33. The **therefore** shows that Matthew intends the parable to be a comment on the same theme. **The kingdom of heaven** is being compared, not with the **king** only, but with the whole story that follows.

Strictly speaking, the parable tells more about the nature of God than about the nature of the kingdom. The story is vivid, even though the details seem overdrawn. The debtor owes the king the equivalent of $10 million. The aim is to depict the debt as the greatest imaginable to a first-century mind. Hence we have the highest number in normal usage (**ten thousand**) and the largest monetary unit (**talent**). But **the servant** who owes this enormous debt is himself owed about $20. The king is willing to forgive the huge sum, but the wretched servant will not forgive his debtor, insisting rather that the man be put in debtors' **prison.** When word of this reaches the king, he reminds the servant of the great debt that has been forgiven and asks why he could not likewise have shown **mercy.**

18:34-35. It is likely that the original parable ended with the question in verse 33. Matthew's concern for the punishment of the wicked shows up in the lines which have been added, according to which the king delivers up the servant to the torturers (the Revised Standard Version has toned this down to read **jailers).** Apparently it is to be assumed that the servant's family would put up the money for his release and bring his torment to an end. But this detail blunts the point, which must have been: If God has forgiven us all, how much more should we be ready to forgive those who have done wrong to us! Matthew states it in the negative: God will punish you **if you do not forgive your brother from your heart.**

J. CONFLICT AND CONSUMMATION (19:1–25:46)

This is the last main division of Matthew's fivefold structure. It begins with a series of controversy stories. Throughout there is a sense of mounting hostility between Jesus and the leaders of Judaism. The ground of that hostility and Matthew's own vengeful attitude toward the Jews is made clear in these chapters.

19:1-12. *Marriage, Divorce, and Celibacy.* This section opens with Matthew's typical transitional phrase, **now when Jesus had finished . . . ,** which is followed by a strange reference to **the region of Judea beyond the Jordan.** Both Mark and John depict Jesus as carrying on a ministry east of the Jordan. One interesting theory is that this ministry was carried on in an interim after Jesus' confrontation with the Jewish authorities at his cleansing of the temple and before the final events in Jerusalem, all of which (the theory runs) have been telescoped into a single week by Mark. Actually the nature of Jesus' activity is such that the location is of little consequence in any case.

19:3-8. The first issue between Jesus and the Jewish leaders is divorce. This theme has already been touched on in the Sermon on the Mount. Verse 3 sets the issue in the framework of the controversies that were going on within Judaism: What are the conditions, if any, under which it is **lawful to divorce one's wife?** As already noted (see above on 5:31-32), Jesus refused to take sides on this legal dispute. Instead he rejected the practice of divorce and remarriage as contrary to the will of God. The basis for interpreting the will of God is given in greater detail here.

Matthew has rearranged two strands of tradition from Mark 10:2-9—the denunciation of the practice of divorce and the appeal to Genesis 1:27; 2:24 for the stability of the marriage relationship. He has thus made the argument more compelling than it is in Mark. God has indicated by creating persons as sexual beings that he intended for man and woman to be joined and remain joined together. There is no place in his purpose for divorce. Matthew repeats (verses 4, 8) that God had in mind this intention of indissoluble unity **from the beginning.**

19:9. Repeated from 5:32 is the one condition under which divorce is to be permitted—**unchastity.** This has the effect of setting aside the unconditional rejection of divorce and remarriage in Mark 10:11, which was surely the teaching of Jesus himself. Matthew shows that the early church was not able to live by the radical demands of Jesus, but had instead to modify them in order to make them—as it thought—practicable.

19:10-12. This paragraph includes material found only in Matthew. The disciples' comment in verse 10 uses terms which sound like Paul when he is speaking about the advantages of being single (I Corinthians 7:25-40). The reply, however, goes beyond anything found in Paul. Three categories of eunuchs are indicated here: (1) those who are congenitally impotent; (2) those who have been castrated; (3) those who voluntarily abstain from sexual relationships. Occasionally the words—**eunuchs who have made themselves eunuchs for the sake of the kingdom of heaven**—have been taken literally. This was true in the case of Origen, the learned biblical scholar of the church in Alexandria in the early third century. But the saying likely reflects the growing tendency of the church, even by the end of the first century, to regard abstinence from the marriage relationship as a sign of holiness. The passage tells us about the early church; it reveals nothing about the attitude of Jesus toward marriage.

19:13-15. *Children and the Kingdom of God.* These sayings are of a piece with those found in 18:1-4, where becoming like a child is considered a prerequisite for entering the kingdom.

19:16-30. *How to Inherit Eternal Life.* Jesus' refusal to be called "good" in Mark 10:18 is modified in Matthew to read: **Why do you ask me about what is good?** It appears that Matthew has sought to avoid the implication in Mark that there is a contrast between the goodness of God and that of Jesus. But the original force of the saying of Jesus shows through in the statement, **One there is who is good,** meaning God is the only one who is good in the full sense.

19:17c-22. The thought then turns to the man's question as to **what good deed** he must do **to have eternal life.** The answer of Jesus is simply to recite the commandments, although the commandment about loving God with all one's heart is omitted, as it is in the accounts of the other evangelists. The young man replies with supreme moral confidence: **all these I have observed.** But Jesus' proposal that he sell his possessions and give the money to the poor is utterly discouraging to him, and he leaves sorrowful.

The highest good in this man's life is not his exemplary conformity to the moral requirements of his religion, but the possession of wealth. He cannot bring himself to part with the **great possessions** which he holds so dear and fling himself upon God's providential care. He lives, not by faith, but by holding on to what he has. Accordingly he is not ready to **enter the kingdom of heaven.** It should be noted that Matthew treats **eternal life** (verse 16) and entering the kingdom as virtually synonymous. Eternal life probably means here, not everlasting life, but the life of the age to come, since the Greek word *aionios,* translated "eternal," is related to the word *aion,* meaning "age."

19:23-24. The comment made to the disciples is appropriate, even though it may have been spoken originally in a different circumstance. It is in keeping with the promise that the poor are those who will possess the kingdom. Verse 24 presents a vivid image of the difficulty that the **rich man** faces in the familiar comparison with the **camel** going **through the eye of a needle.**

The attempts to make this figure less grotesque have been ingenious. It has been suggested that it can be translated as "it is easier for a rope to pass through a needle's eye." A more romantic proposal speaks of a gate left open after the large city gates are closed, so small that the camel must have its burden stripped off before it can pass through. But anyone who has witnessed a camel arising or settling down and has heard its raucous cries of complaint at changing its position will appreciate the superb irony in the notion that a camel could ever make it through the eye of a needle.

19:25-30. The disciples' response is understandable; salvation on these terms is humanly impossible. And Jesus agrees that it is. But it is possible **with God,** whose kingdom it is, and who gives us the possibility of entering it by his grace, not by our merits. Human greed once more asserts itself when **Peter** asks what Jesus' disciples will gain in exchange for what they have given up to follow him.

In giving Jesus' reply Matthew has omitted much of the strange detail about the two stages in the disciples' reward described in Mark (10:29-30), but has added a Q saying (cf. Luke 22:28-30) about the role of the disciples as judges, seated with the Son of man in the age to come. But further, Matthew continues, there will be a **hundredfold** reward for accepting the deprivations that go with discipleship, and beyond the reward is the possibility of entering the **life** of the age to come. The concluding comment is found in many contexts in the Synoptic tradition and adds nothing to the meaning of the section here.

20:1-16. *The Laborers in the Vineyard.* Only Matthew has preserved this, one of the more problematical parables. The whole story runs counter to a sense of fairness. It would be preposterous to look to this parable in defense of uncondition- ally free enterprise or as a basis for labor-management relationships. The parable presupposes the situation in first-century Palestine.

The **householder** does not have a crew of regular workers, but is dependent instead on the occasional help of men from the village. The first group of workers went out to the fields at sunrise (**early in the morning**), the next at nine o'clock, and next at noon the next at three in the afternoon, and the last group at five. At sundown (the twelfth hour) all were called together to be paid. When those who had worked only one hour received an amount (**a denarius,** equal to about 20 cents) that was considered generous for a full day's work, the others must have quickly calculated how much more they would receive. To their astonishment and chagrin, all received the same.

That **they grumbled** is understandable, especially to anyone who has worked under the hot Palestinian sun. The householder will not yield to their complaints, however, since he insists that he is free to be equally generous with all. He is sovereign over his own lands and household; if he chooses to, he can give freely to all. There is no ground for complaint, he insists, against such action.

20:15. The two main points of the story appear in the double question which probably brought the original parable to a close: **Am I not allowed to do what I choose with what belongs to me? Or do you begrudge my generosity?** The householder operates by the standard of grace, not of merit. The laborers are so bound to legalistic thinking that they cannot conceive of anyone motivated by grace alone. The central actor is the generous householder, not the disgruntled employees. The parable is a defense of Jesus' message of God's grace to all against the attacks of the defenders of a religion of meritorious works.

20:16. The concluding comment, which is nearly identical with 19:30, blunts the point of the parable by drawing attention to the irrelevant fact that those workers who came last are paid first. The saying floated freely in the tradition and has been attached to the parable because of the purely verbal connection with the order in which the workers are paid. This conclusion, however, has led some to interpret the parable as though it were a contrast between the Jews, who came to God's vineyard first, and the Gentiles, who came last.

20:17-19. *Prediction of the Passion.* This is the third and most detailed of the predictions of the Passion, which began following Peter's confession at Caesarea Philippi (see above on 16:21-23). It is spoken here in connection with the movement of Jesus from the area east of the Jordan, through Jericho, and so up to Jerusalem. The consensus of the gospel tradition on Jesus' decision to leave Galilee and go to Jerusalem, there to confront the religious leaders of the nation, probably rests on historical fact. Identifying himself as the **Son of man,** Jesus reportedly predicts the main outlines of the passion events: seizure by the priests, condemnation, deliverance into Gentile hands, mocking, scourging, and crucifixion, followed by resurrection on the third day. The reader is now fully alerted as to what is in store for Jesus in Jerusalem.

20:20-28. *On Becoming a Servant.* The occasion for this statement about becoming a servant is the request for a place of special favor for the **sons of Zebedee,** James and John. Whereas in Mark 10:35 these disciples themselves make the request, according to Matthew the petition is voiced by their **mother.** The change has the effect of softening the seeming audacity of the sons of Zebedee. Jesus' reply, however, is addressed to the two disciples: **Are you able to drink the cup that I am to drink?**

The fact that Jesus does not here speak of his passion in the specific terms of the previous section, added to the report preserved by the early church that John lived to an advanced age rather than dying as a martyr, has led many scholars to the conclusion that here we have an authentic word of Jesus in which he anticipates his own death and that of his followers. The cup is clearly the cup of suffering—and in this case suffering which leads to death. The response of the disciples is glibly uttered with no awareness of the real consequences: **We are able.**

20:23. The first clause of Jesus' reply is a warning to the sons of Zebedee that they *will* experience martyrdom. But the rest of the verse returns to the theme of their original request, to which

Jesus replies that the awarding of places in the age to come is the work of **my Father** and **not mine to grant.** Some interpreters have found in these two parts of Jesus' response a contradiction. On the one hand he suggests that one should not aspire to a place of honor in the age to come since it always involves suffering. On the other hand he declares that it is not his prerogative to award honors. One thing is sure, Jesus would scarcely have taught his followers to accept suffering with the motive of gaining places of honor in the new age. Possibly the original form of this incident dealt only with preference in the new age, and the tradition added the words about suffering. But we cannot determine by current standards of logic what would be the line of reasoning for first-century Jews, steeped in apocalyptic ways of thinking.

20:24-28. The climax of the section comes in the contrast between the ordinary way people exercise authority over others when they **lord it over them** and the way God's power is evident through one who accepts the **servant** role. Verse 28 is perhaps a comment of the early church on the significance of Jesus as servant. The Son of man announces that he will **give his life a ransom for many** (the latter phrase reflecting the language of Isaiah 53:11). The Son of man was for Judaism a figure of triumph; the servant was a figure of humiliation. Jesus is here seen as one who moves through humiliation to triumph. (See also on Mark 10:42-45.)

20:29-34. *The Blind Men at Jericho.* Instead of a single blind man, as in the Bartimaeus story (Mark 10:46-52), Matthew reports Jesus as healing **two blind men** on the way out of Jericho. Twice they cry out to Jesus, whom they address as **Son of David,** thereby calling to mind the traditional messianic hope of Israel for the restoration of the Davidic kingship. But the second time they also call Jesus **Lord,** which is clearly a title attributed to Jesus in the earliest Christian communities, following his resurrection. Again they call him **Lord** when they beseech him to heal their blindness. Emphasizing Jesus' compassion on their condition, Matthew tells us that they were healed **and followed him.**

There is a deep symbolic touch in this story, which informs us that on the way to Jerusalem, where he is to present his claims before the official spokesmen for the Jewish people, only the blind can see who Jesus really is.

21:1-9. *The Entry into Jerusalem.* The most direct route from Jericho to Jerusalem leads through the wilderness of Judea, over the top of the **Mount of Olives,** and down the slopes into the city of Jerusalem. The Mount of Olives is a part of the ridge that runs north and south throughout central Palestine, sloping off gradually toward the Mediterranean on the west, and on the east dropping abruptly into the Jordan Valley, which at its lower end is more then 1,200 feet below the level of the Mediterranean. The climb from Jericho to the summit of the Mount of Olives is about 3,600 feet. From the crest of the ridge at the Mount of Olives one can see the whole of Jerusalem spread out on the lower hills below. **Bethphage** was a village on the eastern slope of the Mount of Olives—the last settlement through which one would pass before reaching Jerusalem. **The village opposite,** where the disciples were to find the ass and the colt, may have been Bethany, just to the southeast of Bethphage.

21:2-5. There is an element of mystery about the prearrangement with the owner for making the animals available. The only point in obtaining two animals—one would have been quite sufficient for transporting Jesus, as Mark 11:2 makes clear—is that a literal reading of the poetic words of Zechariah 9:9 implies that there were both an **ass** and a **colt** on which the eschatological king would ride into the city. Matthew, misunderstanding Hebrew poetic parallelism, by which the lines were matched by sense rather than by sound, considered it essential to add the second animal.

If Jesus arranged this in advance, he was obviously intent on enacting this prophetic promise. It is possible, however, that he simply rode into the city, and his followers, recalling the prophecy, interpreted his action in this way.

21:9. The greetings of the crowd, **Hosanna,** and **Blessed is he who comes in the name of the Lord,** are quoted from Psalm 118:25-26. This psalm was originally used as a greeting to the pilgrims who came up to the Jerusalem temple to worship. The phrase "in the name of the Lord" was intended to be linked with "blessed," and "he who enters [comes]" meant "he who comes to worship." Its meaning has been altered, so that now it is an acclamation of the one who comes as the Messiah. Similarly, **Hosanna** (meaning "Save us") **in the highest** meant that the prayer for salvation was addressed to the Highest One, i.e. to God. Here, however, it implies that the prayer is uttered at the highest level or with the utmost earnestness of devotion.

21:10-7. *Jesus in the Temple.* Matthew alone suggests that **all the city** took notice of Jesus' entry into Jerusalem. The way Jesus was identified by the crowds is noteworthy, since it is in many respects an accurate description of what he must have seemed to even sympathetic observers: **the prophet Jesus from Nazareth of Galilee.** He comes without official standing, authorization, or credentials. His message and actions carry their own authorization. Nowhere is this authority more forcefully seen than in the cleansing of the temple.

21:12-13. By driving out the money-changers and the sellers of small animals for sacrifice Jesus threatened the economic functioning of the temple, which must surely have been one of the largest commercial enterprises in Palestine. All contributions to the temple had to be made in Jewish money, so that Jews from the lands of the Roman Empire and beyond who came to Jerusalem had to exchange their local money for Jerusalem coinage—to the benefit of the money-changers, of course.

It is the commercialism of the temple area that Jesus denounces by quoting from Isaiah 56:7 and Jeremiah 7:11. The former reads: "My house shall be called a house of prayer for all peoples." Mark 11:17 quotes it in its entirety, but Matthew strangely omits the last phrase. This heightens the denunciation, but misses the point that the Court of the Gentiles, where the commercialism was located, was intended to be a place where all people of whatever nation could approach God.

21:14-16. The reaction of the priests is understandably hostile and regrettably vindictive. They are not impressed favorably by **the wonderful things that he did.** Those disposed to think ill of

Jesus are never persuaded by his extraordinary powers, as is seen from the gospel tradition throughout. Matthew, with his feel for paradox, represents the children echoing the cry of the crowds, **Hosanna to the Son of David.** Once more the simpleminded can perceive what is hidden from the eyes of the learned—that Jesus is the Messiah. This incident also provides Matthew the occasion to see the fulfillment of scripture (Psalm 8:2) in that the **babes** are those who utter **praise** to God's Chosen One.

21:17. Following this display of authority and the resulting determination on the part of the leaders to destroy him, Jesus withdraws from the city to the nearby village of **Bethany.** Jewish custom required all pilgrims to be within the city during the celebration of the Passover, the feast in which Israel celebrated its deliverance from bondage in Egypt. But since the city could not hold the crowds that flocked to it on festival occasions, the city limits were technically expanded to include surrounding towns, such as Bethany.

21:18-22. *Cursing the Fig Tree.* As a straightforward story this account of the cursing of the fig tree is difficult to comprehend. It seems like an act of petuance on the part of Jesus to curse a tree because it cannot provide fruit at the moment that he is hungry. The curse was evidently effective, since **the fig tree withered at once.**

It would appear, however, that the story is largely symbolic, at least in its present form. It points to the nation Israel, which has not brought forth the fruits of repentance (in the phrase of John the Baptist) and is therefore depicted by the Synoptic tradition as under God's curse. Whatever historical elements there may have been behind this account have been obscured by the tradition in its eagerness to point out that God's favor no longer rests on the nation that rejected his Messiah.

21:20-22. The explanation of the cursed fig tree requested by the disciples does not really speak to the problem, but becomes instead an appeal for confidence in prayer. Matthew's appeal for persons to have great faith is introduced here once more.

21:23-27. *The Source of Jesus' Authority.* In a section in which Matthew follows Mark 11:27-33 very closely Jesus is questioned by the Jewish leaders as to the source of the authority by which he acts and teaches. His response is in turn a question which requires them to take a stand on the role of John the Baptist, whether he was from God or not. The enormous popular following of John is attested by Josephus, the Jewish historian of the period. The leaders would incriminate themselves if they acknowledged the divine origin of John's ministry, snce they had not heeded John. On the other hand they would risk the resentment of the people if they denied that God had commissioned John. Jesus leaves them with precisely the same dilemma regarding the source of his authority. Jesus seems to see in the work of John more than an analogy to his own work. Rather he sees a continuity between John's ministry and his own—not merely historical, in that they were earlier associated, but also theological, in that God, who began a new thing with the coming of John, is bringing it to completion through Jesus.

21:28-32. *The Two Sons.* Here begins a series of three parables, only the second of which is found at this point in Mark's account. The first, which appears only in Matthew, culminates in a question, as indeed many of the parables probably did in their original form. The son who refused to work but changed his mind and did is contrasted with the son who agreed to work but did not actually go. Jesus turns this question to those who are presumably his critics: **Which of the two did the will of his father?** The critics, perhaps unwittingly, condemn themselves in their answer: **the first.** Jesus' response goes to the heart of his message. What God calls for is repentance on the part of those who are in need of his grace and are willing to acknowledge their need. The proud, self-righteous, "religious" people do not know of their own need and refuse the message. The religious leaders have refused to repent, and therefore the outcasts—**the tax collectors and the harlots**—who have repented will enter the kingdom of God first. The cloak of religious respectability means nothing in God's sight, unless the person is genuinely repentant, as these poor sinners are.

21:33-46. *The Wicked Vineyard Workers.* Once more Matthew has provided us with both a parable (from Mark 12:1-12) and his understanding of its meaning. The picture in the parable is of a vineyard, whose absentee owner is naturally interested in receiving the earnings from the tenants who are working it in his absence. The brief description of the vineyard fits the conditions in first-century Palestine—a crude **tower** for watchmen, a protective **hedge**, or fence, to discourage marauders, human or otherwise, and a **wine press** dug out of the soft limestone of the Palestinian hills. The **fruit** that is sought is not the grapes, but the money earned by the sale of the wine.

The **servants** who come to collect from the tenants are beaten, stoned, and killed. Finally the **son** of the owner is put to death, on the assumption that with the heir of the owner gone, the tenants can claim the property by reason of their occupying it. The owner then comes to destroy the tenants and to turn over the stewardship of his property to others, who will produce for him the results appropriate to their labor in his vineyard.

The background of this image is the allegory of the vine in Isaiah 5, where it is explicitly stated that the vineyard is the house of Israel and that the owner is the Lord of Hosts. The implication of Jesus' parable is obvious. Israel's role as the people of God has not been faithfully discharged; indeed, God's servants have been rejected by Israel, which is soon to reject his Son. A slight shift in detail from Mark 12:8, "killed him and cast him out of the vineyard," to Matthew's **cast him out of the vineyard, and killed him,** shows how the course of events in the Passion influenced this parable, since Jesus was actually taken out of the city first and then killed.

21:41-46. Matthew's vindictiveness against the Jewish leaders is evident in the details which he adds to the words of judgment. The tenants are for him **wretches**, whose fate is a **miserable death.** The new tenants can be counted on to produce according to expectations. After quoting one of the favorite texts of the early church (Psalm 118:22-23), which speaks of the Messiah as the rejected **stone** now become the cornerstone of God's new building, Matthew returns to an agricultural image and points to

the church as the **nation** which will replace Israel in the purpose
of God. The point is not lost on the Jewish leaders, who
recognize that Jesus **was speaking about them.**

The parable verges on allegory, so that it is difficult to
determine how much of it in its present form may be traced back
to Jesus and how much has originated in the situation of conflict
between the church and Judaism in the later first century. Its
main outlines are present in Mark's version, but it may have
assumed that form in the years just before the final break
between the church and Judaism, which occurred in the period
A.D. 66-70.

22:1-14. *The King's Marriage Feast.* There are many
significant differences between Matthew's version of this
parable and that found in Luke 14:16-24. Luke depicts a man
giving a banquet; Matthew presents a king giving a wedding
feast for his son. Matthew's allegorical interest is obvious. This
passage now has become an allegory of God's preparation for the
eschatological time of joy, described under the favorite Semitic
image of a wedding. The allegorical factor of the church as the
bride of the king's son is surprisingly absent, however.

22:3-6. The invitation was issued, in Palestinian fashion, in
two stages: a preliminary announcement that the feast was being
planned and a final notice that preparations were now
completed. Those invited did not take the invitation seriously,
but went about the routine business of life, **one to his farm,
another to his business.** Others abused the servants sent with
the invitation.

22:7. The reaction attributed to the king shows once more the
allegorical reworking of the parable in the light of historical
developments. The king **sent his troops** and **burned their city,**
an unmistakable allusion to the coming of the Roman
troops—viewed as the instruments of God's judgment on the
nation Israel—and the destruction of the city of Jerusalem in
A.D. 70.

22:8-10. The parable now shifts to a second phase. Those
originally invited have proved to be **not worthy** (a favorite term
of Matthew). Accordingly the invitation is to be sent

everywhere, into the wide **thoroughfares** and the narrow **streets,** that is, to all people. The result is a wide response. That the persons who come are both good and bad is characteristic of Matthew's view of the church (see above on 13:36-43).

22:11-14. Those who have failed to provide themselves with the **wedding garment** of righteousness (another favorite teaching of Matthew) will be **cast . . . into the outer darkness** (Matthew's typical phrase for the fate of the unrighteous). The concluding saying, which probably was preserved in the oral tradition without a specific context, serves Matthew's purpose here, since it contrasts the wide sweep of the invitation to accept the gospel and the small number of those actually found worthy.

22:15-22. *Tribute to Caesar.* This is the first of four controversy stories which serve to bring out some of the issues not only between Jesus and his critics but between the church and Judaism. The first has to do with the payment of a head tax of one denarius (about 20 cents) required by Rome from all subject people. The question is raised by representatives of two groups: the Pharisees, who objected strenuously to having to pay the tax, and the Herodians, who presumably favored the tax, since they were sympathetic with the family of the Herods, who ruled as Rome's puppets.

For Jesus to have sided with the Herodians would have alienated all who longed for Israel's freedom. To have sided with the opponents of the tax would have laid Jesus open to charges of subversion. His answer has the effect of thrusting the decision back on his interrogators, since one must still determine what is rightfully **Caesar's** and what can be claimed by **God** alone.

22:23-33. *The Question Concerning the Resurrection.* The issue here is not the resurrection of Jesus, but whether there is a resurrection of the faithful at all. The **Sadducees** rejected such a teaching, since it could not be documented in the first five books of the Old Testament, which they alone recognized as scripture. The question presupposes the Jewish custom of levirate marriage, which required the surviving brother of a deceased husband to marry his brother's widow. In this story, which must have been a stock question raised by those skeptical about the possibility of a resurrection, the woman becomes the wife of seven brothers successively as each dies and the next brother takes her as his wife.

Jesus does not deal with the problem on the ridiculous terms in which it was raised. Instead he points to the transformation of human existence which is involved in the resurrection life. He describes it only indirectly when he says that marriage has no place in it. His statement that it is like that of the **angels in heaven** is not much help, since we know nothing of the character of angelic or heavenly existence.

22:31-33. The conclusion of the discussion, in which appeal is made to scripture (Exodus 3:6), does not fit neatly with what has gone before, since the quotation says nothing directly about resurrection. The weight of the argument falls on the tense of **I am the God**—that is, God's relationship to Abraham, Isaac, and Jacob is a continuing one, even though these patriarchs were from successive generations and all have long since died. He was and still is their God; therefore he is the God **of the living.** What is implied in this argument is not resurrection of the dead, but the personal survival of God's people.

22:34-40. *The Great Commandment.* The questioning of Jesus now passes from the Sadducees to the Pharisees. Their question, which seems to have been raised often by the rabbis, is: **Which is the great commandment in the law?** In reply Jesus links together the commandments to love God (Deuteronomy 6:5) and to love one's neighbor (Leviticus 19:18). The rabbinic interpreters of the law seem to have done this. What was new was not the content of Jesus' teaching on this subject but his redefinition of what the love of God was—how it manifested itself, and who one's neighbor is. In this expansion of the horizons of obligation, as well as in the way of life that accompanied and exemplified his teachings, lay the revolutionary, new element of Jesus' ministry.

22:41-46. *David's Son.* The last of the four controversies involves a question raised by Jesus rather than by his opponents. It was widely understood that the eschatological king of Israel—the Messiah, **the Christ**—would be a descendant of the royal line, a **son of David.** When the Pharisees answer, Jesus cites the opening lines of Psalm 110, one of the most notable of the messianic psalms, even though the word "messiah" is not used in it. One would suppose that the son would be subordinate to the father, and yet here David (for Jesus shares with his hearers the assumption of this authorship) speaks of the subject of his psalm as **my Lord.**

Jesus offers no solution to this dilemma. At first glance the implication might seem to be that he is denying his Davidic descent. But Matthew, in taking this story from Mark 12:35-37, surely did not so understand it. Rather Matthew's interpretation must be that Jesus is not merely Son of David but more; he is Lord.

Although some interpreters have assumed that Jesus was here wrestling with questions concerning his own messianic consciousness, it is more likely that a controversy which arose in the early church is here attributed to Jesus. It was the church which acclaimed him as Lord. Very early in the church he was also asserted to have been born of David's lineage (Romans 1:3). It was the attempt to bring these two affirmations together, in a situation of controversy with the Jews over the interpretation of scripture, that seems to lie behind this discussion.

23:1-36. *Woes Against the Pharisees.* This long discourse, in which the Pharisees are denounced for their hypocrisy rather than for the content of their teaching, appears only in Matthew, although parts of the material are found scattered through the other two Synoptic gospels. It seems to be Matthew's creation, even though there is no reason to doubt that it includes authentic words of Jesus. The vindictive attitude toward the Pharisees should probably be credited to Matthew or to the church for which he is the spokesman.

23:3-12. Jesus' first criticism is against the hypocrisy and ostentation with which the Pharisees go about their religious living. There is no complaint against their teaching—**practice and observe whatever they tell you.** What is objectionable is the way they live. They think up burdensome moral obligations for others which they are unwilling themselves to assume, and they

strut their piety in public, taking delight in fancy robes and
honorific titles. By contrast the disciples are to be humble. At
this point the terminology of the early church—**one Father . . .
in heaven; . . . one master, the Christ**—betrays that we are
here dealing with church teaching rather than words of Jesus.

23:13-32. The Pharisees' favorite acts of piety are now
enumerated and denounced: making converts to Judaism who
are more flagrant violators of the intention of the law than the
Pharisees themselves; trying to guarantee their word by means
of oaths, while in actuality making pious excuses for telling lies;
worrying about petty matters of legal observance while ignoring
serious trespasses of God's will; paying attention to externals
while the inner life is corrupt; piously honoring the tombs of the
prophets while opposing the messengers of God and seeking to
have them killed.

23:33-36. This last issue, which brings the section to a climax,
moves beyond the time of Jesus to the period of violent hostility
between Judaism and the church. It is here claimed that the
whole history of the people of Israel as recorded in scripture is
one of rejection and murder of those who have spoken for God.
The first book of the Hebrew Bible reports near its beginning
the murder of a faithful worshiper of God, **Abel.** The last book
records that a faithful priest, **Zechariah,** was murdered within
the court of the temple when he tried to call the people to obey
the commandments of God (II Chronicles 24:20-21; **the son of
Barachiah,** not found in Luke 11:51, is apparently an error
based on Zechariah 1:1). The clear implication is that this
pattern of murderous rejection of God's messengers has
continued in the response of the Jewish leaders to Jesus and to
his messengers now at work among them.

It is interesting to see how these messengers are described:
prophets and wise men and scribes. None of these offices except
that of prophet is familiar to us from other parts of the New
Testament. This suggests that in the section of the church for
which Matthew was writing there were functions which closely
resembled the Jewish institutions. It is ironic, and yet
psychologically quite understandable, that the segment of the

church that was in many ways most Jewish should at the same time be most bitterly denunciatory of Judaism and its official leadership.

23:37–24:3. This section consists of two parts:

(1) Jesus' lament over the impending destruction of the city, in the light of his ceaseless yearning for the city (here symbolizing the nation) to repent. The warning is given that the next opportunity to see Jesus will come when he is disclosed in his eschatological glory. The passage has apparently been reworked by the early church and cannot all be traced back to Jesus.

(2) The announcement that the temple will be destroyed. The source for great pride among the Jews of the world in the first century, the temple must have appeared as though it would stand forever. It seems to be historically certain that Jesus did predict the temple's destruction, since this is the issue that is raised repeatedly and in various forms in connection with his trial. The question raised by the disciples as to the time when this catastrophe will occur becomes the occasion for the apocalyptic discourse which follows in all three of the Synoptic gospels.

24:4–25:46. *The Apocalypse.* Matthew is here writing in language and employing imagery that is characteristic of the apocalyptic writings of Judaism in the period about the time of Jesus' birth. The word "apocalypse" means simply "revelation," and apocalyptic writings claim to be revelations of future events which God made known to eminent persons—Moses, Daniel, John, for example. Matthew adopts and expands Mark 13:3-37 in order to describe the conditions that will obtain on earth in the time immediately preceding the coming of the Son of man, which will mark the end of the age. To Mark's material Matthew has added some extended parables and a group of sayings about the need to be watchful, since no one can predict when the end will come.

24:4–36. *Signs of the End.* The signs which will give warning of the approaching end are rather general in nature: claims of false Christs, international strife, and natural disturbances. But these are but **the beginning of the birth-pangs.** The word used here is almost a technical term for the difficulties that the people of God must pass through before their deliverance comes.

24:9-14. The theme now turns to the way that the time of tribulation will affect the people of God directly. They may expect to be brought to trial before civil authorities, to be universally **hated,** to be victimized by **false prophets.** But if they are able to maintain their witness faithful **to the end,** they can be confident that God will preserve them—they **will be saved.** But before the end can possibly arrive, the world mission of the church must be carried out **to all nations.** This represents a shift from the strategy that Matthew portrays during the opening of Jesus' ministry, when the mission was to be limited strictly to Israel (10:6).

24:15-22. There is one clear sign by which the community can recognize the approach of the end—**the desolating sacrilege . . . in the holy place.** Daniel 9:27; 11:31, and 12:11 were written about the erection in the temple of an image of a pagan god in the time of the Maccabees. The passages are here interpreted as predicting desecration of the temple by the Romans. The fact that in this apocalypse Mark, followed by Matthew and Luke, is reproducing a document is disclosed by the phrase **let the reader understand,** which could not conceivably have been a part of an oral statement by Jesus himself. Some scholars think this is part of a warning sheet distributed among the Christians in Jerusalem just prior to the fall of the city in A.D. 70, on the basis of which advice the Jerusalem Christians fled to the city of Pella east of the Jordan. The need for sudden flight could explain the details about not entering the **house,** not stopping to take up one's **mantle,** and the difficulty of flight **in winter,** when the Jordan would be at flood stage.

24:23-31. The warning ends with the announcement of the unprecedented difficultes that will come on the earth before the consummation occurs. The themes of false messianic claimants, the impossibility of accurately predicting the sudden end, the natural disturbances that will accompany the coming of the **Son of man** are repeated once more.

24:32-36. The section ends with the analogy of a fig tree: when the first signs are evident, the time of fruition is not far off. But even so, no one, not even **the Son,** can predict the exact time of the end, since this is known to God alone. The apocalypse in its present form draws on traditional apocalyptic material and on various strands of the gospel tradition. It reveals more of the situation of the church in the midst of conflict and persecution than it does of the time of Jesus.

24:37-51. *The Need for Watchfulness.* Using material from Q, which is scattered in Luke's version, Matthew heightens the sense of the need for watchfulness by appeal to three analogies:

(1) In **the days of Noah** people were preoccupied with the affairs of life and therefore totally unprepared for the judgment of God that fell on the whole world. Thus in the last days persons will be taken away in judgment without warning as the indifferent contemporaries of Noah were.

(2) A parabolic word concerning a **householder** who is not prepared for the coming of a **thief** points to the need for preparedness in light of the unpredictability of the end.

(3) Just as the owner of a **household,** when making arrangements for the handling of affairs in his absence, commissions a trusted **servant** to perform his duties and expects him to fulfill these obligations faithfully, so the disciples are charged to be diligent in their work since it is impossible to determine when the absent Lord will return.

My master is delayed may well have originated in the early church at a time when the keenness of expectation of the coming of Christ had begun to wane. Men were growing lax or exploiting for their own ends the authority entrusted to them within the church. This parable serves to warn against such behavior by reminding them that they must be ever ready for the coming of the end.

25:1-30. *The Parables of Watchfulness.* Here are two familiar parables. The point of each is the need to be ready for the unpredictable coming of the Lord. The first, found only in

Matthew, involves **ten maidens** following the marriage customs of first-century Palestine. That no mention is made of the bride (that is, the church) shows that this has not become a full-fledged allegory. The **wise** maidens are prepared, no matter how long the wait may be; the **foolish** are not ready and find themselves excluded. Lest the reader miss the point, Matthew adds: **Watch, therefore, for you know neither the day nor the hour.**

25:14-30. The parable of the **talents,** adapted from Q (cf. Luke 19:12-27), is also intended as a message on the need for faithful stewardship during the interim before the end—an interim for which no one can predict the terminus. The responsibilities assigned differ widely: **one . . . two . . . five talents** (worth about $1,000 each). The issue is stewardship in light of the unexpected return of the owner. Matthew depicts the fate of the irresponsible servant in his favorite terms: **men will weep and gnash their teeth.**

25:31-46. *The Last Judgment.* This final parable does not appear elsewhere in the New Testament. It gives evidence of Matthew's own special language and theological interests (e.g. the kingdom of the Father contrasted with the Kingdom of the Son of man). Yet it preserves a theme that is found throughout the gospel tradition: that the decisions made by men now in relation to Jesus determine their destiny in the age to come.

The **Son of man** appears here as the judge, which is his traditional role in the apocalyptic view. All the nations are judged, not merely Israel. They are separated into the **sheep** and the **goats**—those who are or are not worthy to enter the Father's kingdom. The criterion for their separation is whether they have performed acts of mercy toward the **least of these my brethren.** Some interpreters think this phrase meant originally the disciples, who were to be received in Christ's name, but it is more likely that the parable now is extended to include all humanity. **My brethren** refers to any human beings who are in need. To receive such a one is to receive Christ; to refuse to aid such a one is to refuse Christ. The surprising element in this parable-like description of the judgment is that those who are welcomed into the kingdom have had no consciousness that the acts of mercy they performed had any relationship to Christ, much less to their eternal destiny. They acted because their brethren were in need, not in order to earn a reward or to merit admission to the kingdom.

III. The Humiliation and Exaltation of the Son of Man (26:1–28:20)

26:1-16. *The Death of Jesus Plotted and Foretold.* The familiar words **when Jesus had finished . . .** open this final division of the gospel. Matthew follows Mark's telescoped chronology of Holy Week, so that only **two days** elapse between the launching of the plot by the **chief priests and the elders** to destroy Jesus and the carrying out of their plans on the night of **the Passover.**

Commentators have drawn attention to the stated wish of the plotters to take Jesus secretly and **not during the feast** in order to avoid a popular uprising in his support. This would imply that the trial took place at some time other than on the Passover day. But the imagery of the Passover so influenced the Christian understanding of the Last Supper and of the death of Jesus that Passover and Last Supper are interwoven in the present form of the tradition.

26:6-13. The anointing of Jesus by **a woman . . . at Bethany** is an enacted prediction of his death. The incident provides the opportunity to demonstrate the lack of understanding by the disciples, who complain about the waste of such **a large sum.** But it is also the occasion to praise the woman, who shows greater insight and devotion at this moment than any other follower of Jesus. In its present form the story reflects the opinion of the early church, even though it may also reproduce the outlines of an actual historical occurrence.

26:14-16. The final stage in the plot to destroy Jesus takes place when Judas Iscariot agrees to **deliver** Jesus over **to the chief priests** in exchange for a sum of money. The specific amount may have been fixed by the tradition when it saw a connection between Zechariah 11:12 and the traitorous act. Why Judas betrayed Jesus cannot be determined. The notion that he was disappointed because Jesus did not lead an uprising against Rome is no more than a romantic guess. What Judas betrayed is not clear, either, though it may be simply that Judas agreed to lead the guards to the place where Jesus spent the night outside the city walls, so that he could be taken by stealth.

26:17-29. *The Last Supper.* In Jewish practice **the first day of Unleavened Bread** was the occasion for the celebration of the Passover meal, which was eaten during the night by the family. The account in Matthew states that this was the day when preparations were made for the feast. John probably has the historically correct chronology in considering the Friday afternoon on which Jesus was put to death to be the day of Preparation, which according to Jewish thinking began at sundown on Thursday night—hence the reluctance of the Jews to defile themselves by entering Pilate's hall.

It is doubtful that the last meal of Jesus was a Passover meal, especially since most of the characteristic elements of that meal (lamb, bitter herbs, etc.) are missing in the gospel accounts. Probably the Christian understanding of the death of Jesus in the light of the Passover tradition—that is, as God's new act of delivering his people—has influenced the reporting of the Last Supper.

26:18-23. The circumstances surrounding the preparation have an almost miraculous quality about them, although Matthew has omitted some of the detail from his version (cf. Mark 14:12-16). The whole account of the supper is closely linked with Old Testament passages considered to have been fulfilled by Jesus in the passion events. Therefore it is difficult to tell where historical recollection leaves off and the influence of scripture begins. One such detail is the saying about the betrayer eating from the common **dish** with Jesus, which recalls Psalm 41:9.

26:24. This verse is of special interest, since it brings together the elements of human freedom (Judas' intention to betray Jesus) and divine determination (the prediction of the death of the Son of man). In actuality, there is no passage in scripture or known extra-biblical writings where **it is written** that **the Son of man** will go the way of suffering and death. Evidently this saying is based on equating the Son of man with the suffering servant of Isaiah 42–53 (see above on 8:18-22; 16:13*b*).

26:25. Judas identifies himself by his very question as the one who will betray Jesus to his enemies. The seemingly noncommittal answer of Jesus, **You have said so,** implies that Judas has spoken the truth. This revelation of the traitor to the other disciples is not found in Matthew's source, which is Mark 14:17-21, or in Luke 22:21-23 (cf. John 19:21-30).

26:26-28. The taking of bread and the drinking of the cup are described as occurring during the course of the meal, rather than as a separate ceremony. In all likelihood this was the way the earliest church celebrated the Supper until excesses at the common meal required that the meal and the Eucharist (meaning service of thanksgiving) be separated. The words **took . . . blessed . . . broke . . . gave** all became the technical terms for the celebration of the Lord's Supper in the church. It was God who was blessed, not the bread that was in some way sanctified. The **bread** symbolizes Jesus' total self, which is given for all persons. The **cup** symbolizes the life of Jesus, which is offered up to seal the new **covenant** by which God is calling into being his new people, the church. Matthew's special interest in sin and forgiveness is evident in the addition of the phrase **for the forgiveness of sins.**

26:29. The element in the Eucharist which was probably of the greatest importance for Jesus and for the earliest Christian community was the conviction that the meal which Jesus was celebrating with his followers was a foretaste of the full fellowship to be experienced when the kingdom of God has come and all God's people are gathered into one. Then the **fruit of the vine** will be drunk once more in **my Father's kingdom.**

26:30-35. *Jesus in Gethsemane.* Leaving Jerusalem after the meal, Jesus and the disciples go out east of the city across the Kidron Valley, which separates the city from the **Mount of Olives.** Jesus predicts that the disciples will desert him, in fulfillment of scripture (Zechariah 13:7). But they will be restored following his being **raised,** when he will **go before,** or precede, them **to Galilee.** Peter makes the idle boast that he will stand true to Jesus, but his claim is immediately discredited by Jesus' prediction of Peter's threefold denial.

The promise of the appearance of the risen Lord in Galilee is one of two strands in the gospel tradition, the other of which reports the appearances as occurring in the vicinity of Jerusalem (Luke 24; John 20).

26:36-46. The meaning of the name **Gethsemane,** "olive press," suggests that it may have been a grove of olive trees of the sort still to be seen on the western slope of the Mount of Olives. The vivid account of Jesus' struggle points up the inability of the disciples to grasp the seriousness of the occasion, since they soon are **sleeping.** The possibility of our having here an eyewitness account of the struggle of Jesus is slim, since by definition no one was there to observe except the disciples, who were asleep. It is probably an imaginative account, but it does reflect accurately the issue that would have confronted Jesus under the circumstances: the temptation to flee, and thus avoid the inevitable trial and death that he must have known awaited him. With the arrival of Judas the movement of events is inexorable.

26:47-75. *The Seizure and Hearing by the Jewish Authorities.* The group that arrests Jesus is a **crowd** sent by **the chief priests and the elders,** who together made up the sanhedrin, a kind of senate that was permitted by the Romans to exercise considerable authority. A false show of affection by Judas and a mistaken effort at protection by one of the disciples lead Jesus to declare, according to Matthew's addition, that he will not invoke the support of **angels** in order to save himself, since his death is so that **the scriptures** may **be fulfilled.** The entire group of disciples abandon him to his fate.

26:57-68. The sanhedrin is convened in the house of the high priest, **Caiaphas.** The only charge that can be lodged against Jesus is that he is going **to destroy the temple of God, and to build it in three days.** To this Jesus offers no reply or defense.

He answers the high priest's question as to whether he is **the Christ** with the same equivocal words he had spoken to Judas: **You have said so** (cf. the unequivocal "I am" in Mark 14:62).

Then he turns to the prediction of the coming of **the Son of Man** (cf. 24:30; Psalm 110:1; Daniel 7:13), which is interpreted as a claim that he is the Son of man. The charge of **blasphemy** is brought against him, which was punishable by death at the hands of the Jews, by Roman agreement with the Jewish authorities of the time.

26:69-75. At this time **Peter,** under pressure from various members of the crowd, denies that he has had any acquaintance with Jesus. In adapting Mark 14:66-72 Matthew alters several details of the story—for example, Peter is recognized by his northern **accent.** Matthew emphasizes the bitterness of Peter's remorse in verse 75.

27:1-26. *The Hearing Before Pilate and the Condemnation.* On the morning following the hearing before the sanhedrin, which would be still the day of Preparation for the Passover by Jewish reckoning, Jesus is turned over to **Pilate,** the provincial governor. Since A.D. 6 Rome had ruled Judea directly by governors, after Archelaus, son of Herod, had proved a hopelessly inefficient administrator.

27:11-18. Pilate's questions concern Jesus' political ambitions: **Are you the King of the Jews?** By this time Pilate had been forced on several occasions to put down incipient messianic revolutionary movements. Although there is no record of such a practice from Jewish or Roman sources, the gospels report that Pilate had a custom of granting amnesty to a prisoner on the occasion of the Passover. The tradition hints that Barabbas was himself an insurrectionist (see on Mark 15:7), but Matthew describes him only as a **notorious prisoner.**

27:19. Only in Matthew is there the report of the dream of Pilate's **wife,** which is presented as a divine warning that Jesus is innocent.

27:20-23. The crowd's choice is for the release of Barabbas, and they cry out for the crucifixion of Jesus. This was a mode of execution used by the Romans alone and would be appropriate for one charged with revolutionary aims.

27:24-26. Pilate accedes to their demand, even though no evidence is adduced to support the charge. He publicly discharges himself from responsibility for Jesus' death by washing his hands before the crowd. Matthew emphasizes that the Jews accept the responsibility, even though both the charge and the mode of execution are related to Roman rather than Jewish law. The bitter words he attributes to the Jews have caused endless harm in arousing anti-Jewish emotions: **His blood be on us and on our children.**

27:27-66. *The Crucifixion and Burial.* The **plaiting** and placing of the **crown of thorns,** as well as **the scarlet robe** and the **reed** as a mock scepter, point to the scorn of Jesus by the Roman soldiers as a kingly pretender. This confirms the impression that the historical basis for the death of Jesus was not ultimately the rejection of him and his message by Israel, but the Roman determination to execute all possible leaders of freedom movements among the Jewish nationalists.

27:32. Concerning the man who was **compelled to carry** Jesus' **cross** see on Mark 15:21.

27:33. The fact that the name **Golgotha** must be interpreted as **the place of a skull** shows that Matthew is writing for non-Semitic-speaking people. The name of the place might imply nothing more than an association of the spot with the dead, but it has been thought to be due to a domelike limestone outcropping that may have resembled a skull. The traditional site of the crucifixion and burial, now enclosed by the Church of the Holy Sepulcher, lay outside the walls of the city in Jesus' time.

27:34-44. The soldiers offer Jesus a sedative in the form of **wine . . . mingled with gall.** Matthew uses "gall" in place of "myrrh" (Mark 15:23), probably under the influence of Psalm 69:21: "They gave me poison (gall) for food, and . . . vinegar (sour wine) to drink." The casting of lots for Jesus' garments corresponds to Psalm 22:18, and the derision of the passersby to

Psalm 22:7. A taunt added by Matthew in verse 43 accords with Psalm 22:8.

The **two robbers . . . crucified with him** are actually insurrectionists, so that the ironic title **This is Jesus the King of the Jews** completes the picture of the Roman vengeance on those accused of fomenting political revolution. The taunts of the other condemned men follow the lines of Jewish objection to Jesus, however—his claims about destroying and rebuilding the temple and about being the Messiah. **The chief priests, with the scribes and elders,** in their mockery unwittingly bear witness to who Jesus really is—**the King of Israel, . . . the Son of God.**

27:45-50. There is **darkness over all the land** (or the whole earth) from noon until 3 P.M. Jesus' cry to God. Matthew gives this in a form somewhat imperfectly transliterated from Hebrew (**Eli, Eli, lama sabachthani**) instead of the Aramaic of Mark 15:34. It is a quotation from Psalm 22:1.

Even in the depths of a sense of abandonment Jesus nevertheless cries out to God. The crowd, misunderstanding, thinks he is calling for **Elijah** to come and deliver him from his agony. The **vinegar** is probably the sedative of verse 34, though a different Greek word is used. Jesus uttered a loud cry and, Matthew implies, **yielded up his spirit by an act of will, rather than merely dying of exhaustion, as was the usual case with those who were crucified.**

27:51-54. At the moment of Jesus' death, Matthew reports, not only was the temple **curtain . . . torn in two,** but an earthquake shook the city and opened **tombs,** from which came forth the departed **saints.** This group of incidents is full of symbolic meaning. The torn temple curtain suggests that Jesus' death opened up the way into the presence of God, who, according to Jewish beliefs, was invisibly present behind the curtain of the temple and accessible directly only to the high priest. The appearance of the saints is a foretaste of the resurrection, although it is odd to have it occur even before the resurrection of Jesus. The pagan centurion acknowledges what the religious leaders cannot see: **Truly this was the Son of God!**

27:55-61. The only witnesses of the crucifixion from among

Jesus' followers are the group of **women . . . from Galilee,** who watch **from afar.** But just before sunset, when the feast day would begin, **Joseph,** from the village of **Arimathea** in the hill country northwest of Jerusalem, received permission from Pilate to remove the body. This was an act of piety, since the Jews believed that a dead body exposed polluted the sabbath. Hastily, and without adequate preparation of the body, Jesus was placed in a tomb that Joseph owned, recently hewn from the soft limestone of the hills on which Jerusalem stands. The women saw the place and presumably made plans to return at the earliest possible moment to complete the preparation of the body, which could not be carried out on the sabbath just then beginning.

27:62-66. The chronological reference here is problematical, since it would suggest that the Jewish leaders approached Pilate on the sabbath itself with their request for a guard at the tomb. The story, which is found only in Matthew, is probably not historical, but arose at a time when Jews were charging that the resurrection claims of the Christians were a hoax and that the disciples had actually stolen the body of Jesus. It was introduced to show that even official action by Pilate could not have prevented the Resurrection from occurring.

28:1-15. *The Women at the Tomb.* In spite of all precautions, when the women arrived on Sunday morning to complete the preparation of the body, Jesus had already been raised. Verses 2-4, found only in Matthew, describe the miraculous events that followed the Resurrection. Instead of a young man in white at the tomb (Mark 16:5), Matthew reports **an angel** descending **from heaven,** an **earthquake,** the stone **rolled back,** the swooning of **the guards,** and the understandable astonishment of the women. The stone was shaped like a millstone and placed in a groove in such a way that gravity would cause it to roll down and block the doorlike opening to the tomb. The purpose in rolling back the stone is to allow the women to **see** that Jesus **has risen,** rather than to allow Jesus to come out.

28:7-10. There follows the instruction, recalling 26:32, to return to **Galilee,** to which Jesus is even now **going.** There the appearances of the risen Christ will occur. There is, however, a brief encounter between the risen Christ and the women, but its net effect is to underscore the importance of the disciples' return to Galilee.

28:11-15. The attempt by the Jewish leaders to discredit the story of the Resurrection builds on the earlier report about a guard at the tomb. Since the soldiers were by this testimony asleep when the body was removed, their word could not be credited in any case. Like the earlier part of the guard incident, it arises in a situation of mutual hostility between Jew and Christian.

28:16-20a. *The Commissioning of the Disciples.* Here, more than anywhere else in his gospel, Matthew discloses the main themes of his interest. The disciples have returned to Galilee. Even when they encounter Jesus risen from the dead, some are still unbelieving. This accords with Matthew's picture of the church as a mixture of faith and unfaith (see also on Mark 16:8). Jesus now appears as a figure of complete **authority in heaven and on earth.** It is he as the authoritative one who sends forth the disciples.

Their task is threefold:

(1) Going among **all nations,** seeking to **make disciples,** i.e. to summon those who will follow Jesus and be the bearers of his word and his authority.

(2) **Baptizing** the new disciples in the full trinitarian **name** of God: **Father . . . Son . . . Holy Spirit.** This is one of the few places in the New Testament where the names of the Trinity are explicitly used.

(3) **Teaching** obedience to Jesus' commandments in their entirety.

28:20b. The commission ends with a promise of the invisible presence of the authoritative Lord with his disciples **to the close of the age.** Then, as Matthew has already informed his readers elsewhere, the Son of man will be visibly present to his people in the kingdom of God. Meanwhile, both their responsibilities and their resources have been made available by the risen Lord for the fulfillment of their appointed task.

THE GOSPEL ACCORDING TO MARK

Lindsey P. Pherigo

INTRODUCTION

Modern scholarship is in broad agreement with the second-century traditions about this gospel:

(1) It was written by a man named Mark, a missionary companion of both Peter and Paul;

(2) It was written in Rome, far away from local traditions about Jesus;

(3) It dates from after the death of Peter (A.D. 64), at least thirty-five years after the events described.

This gospel represents, therefore, a collection of traditions gathered, arranged, and edited by one who did not participate in the events personally. It is one of the three "Synoptic" gospels.

Relation to Matthew and Luke

Literary analysis of the agreements and differences among the first three gospels has established that Mark was the earliest of the three and was used independently by both Matthew and Luke as their major source of information about the life of Jesus. This twofold reliance on Mark verifies its general historical reliability. The fact that the two later gospels have incorporated practically all of it in their accounts indicates that they intended to replace Mark rather than simply to supplement it.

The changes introduced by Matthew and Luke are noted in the following commentary. They show how this earliest gospel was understood in its own day and help us to grasp its original purpose.

Date and Occasion

The tradition that Mark put together his gospel after the death of Peter and the manner of its use by Matthew and Luke limit the date of writing to the period from A.D. 64 to around 75.

Many have assumed a date during Nero's persecution of the Roman Christians (A.D. 64-68). Accordingly they have deduced that Mark's chief motive in writing was to encourage his fellow church members facing this crisis. His reporting of Jesus' teaching about the costs of discipleship and the large space he devotes to Jesus' own example of martyrdom are cited as confirmation. This emphasis no doubt reflects persecution, in recent memory if not as a present peril, but it is not pervasive enough to explain the whole gospel.

Many also have sought for evidence that Mark knew of the Romans' capture of Jerusalem and destruction of the temple in A.D. 70. Finding no unmistakable allusions to this, they have assumed that he must have written before this date. It is not certain, however, that Mark would necessarily allude to this event if he knew of it; and in fact there may be allusions to it in 12:9 and 13:2, 14 (cf. 9:1; 13:30). Thus the fact that Mark's work had circulated long enough to survive the attempts of Matthew and Luke to replace it provides the only sure limit to its date.

During the whole period in which this gospel could have been written, Christianity was in transition from its original home in Palestinian Judaism to the Gentile culture of the Roman Empire. The older Christianity held tenaciously to the traditional Jewish customs, such as circumcision and the food laws, but the newer Gentile version abandoned these entirely. More significantly, the older Christianity understood Jesus mainly under the Jewish concept of the Messiah, whereas the newer found more meaning in him as a divine being, the Son of God, Lord, and Savior. The older view clung to the Jewish concept of religion as obedience to God's will, whereas the newer openly abandoned this as hopeless by one's own effort. The newer Christians espoused a religion which redeemed one from slavery to sin by an act of God's grace, the Christ event.

Against this transition background Mark presents Jesus from the newer Gentile Christian viewpoint. Although not strictly Pauline in his terminology, Mark reflects an understanding of the problem of human nature, the person of Christ, and the nature of salvation quite closely related to that found in the letters of Paul. These letters, therefore, as parallel expressions of early Gentile Christianity, help us more than any other part of the New Testament to understand the religious message of Mark. Matthew and Luke repeat the story of Jesus from a more conservative position.

All cultural transitions are marked by tension between the conservatives who defend the older and the liberals who introduce the newer. Since the twelve disciples of Jesus became the leaders of the conservatives, Mark shared Paul's coolness and reserve toward their authority (cf. I Corinthians 9:1-18; Galatians 2:1-10). He makes it plain to the reader that the twelve never understood Jesus properly and therefore are not the best guides.

This is not a frank and naïve report of their weaknesses in a period before apostolic veneration began. Mark is helping the reader to understand why the view of Jesus among the conservative Jewish Christians is so unsatisfactory to the Gentile Christian church. Matthew and Luke systematically alter this portrayal of the twelve to give readers confidence in their leadership.

Authorship

Tradition has given the author of this gospel the name Mark. From early times he has been identified with John Mark, kinsman of Barnabas. Many scholars today accept this identification, largely on the basis that a gospel would not be attributed to so remote a witness unless he was actually the author. However, if a gospel author named Mark was otherwise unknown, there would be a strong tendency to identify him with any known early Christian of that name, even one with so little authority as John Mark.

Careful study of the book itself makes it difficult to believe that the author was John Mark of Jerusalem, because he seems to treat both Palestine and Palestinian Judaism as an outsider. His attitude toward the disciples and his reflection of the Pauline viewpoint, as noted above, make it probable that he was a prominent member of the Gentile Christian community. His background must have been the liberal Hellenistic Judaism of the Roman Empire rather than the traditional Judaism of Jerusalem. The strong Semitic coloring of some of his writing can be attributed to the sources he used rather than to his own experience.

There is no reason to doubt a tradition that the author derived much of his information about Jesus from the sermon of Peter. But it must be remembered that he presents this information from a Gentile Christian point of view, and that he also includes much that did not come from apostolic memory at all. In Gentile Christianity a great deal of reliance was placed on learning of Jesus from Old Testament statements believed to be about him.

I. The Beginnings

A. Introduction to the Book (1:1)

Mark begins his book very abruptly with a terse phrase like a title. It is not a complete sentence. It can be taken as the introduction to the whole book, but more likely it was intended simply to introduce the first part of the story, the work of John the Baptist. Some ancient manuscripts have the descriptive phrase **the Son of God** at the end, and others do not have it; but whatever its origin it expresses well the main viewpoint of Mark about Jesus. In this book Jesus of Nazareth is not merely the Jewish Messiah (translated into Greek as the **Christ**). He is the strong Son of God, able to deliver us from the powers of evil around us that hold us in bondage. On **the gospel** see below on verses 14 and 15.

B. JOHN THE BAPTIST (1:2-11)

1:2-3. *The Introduction to John.* The story of John is introduced by quoting Old Testament prophecy. The quotation shows that Mark was apparently not a careful scholar of the Hebrew Bible. He was probably drawing on popular quotations already in circulation in Christian communities and did not check his references very carefully. His main point is quite sound, but he has made two interesting mistakes in presenting it.

In the first place Mark has put together two separate quotations and attributed both to Isaiah. Actually the first quotation seems to be a free version of Malachi 3:1, although the first part of it is exactly like the Septuagint version of Exodus 23:20. The second one is from Isaiah 40:3. In Matthew and Luke this error is corrected (Matthew 3:3, Luke 3:4).

In the second place the use to which the second quotation is put reflects unfavorably on Mark's understanding of Hebrew poetry. The main trait of this poetry is not sound rhyme, like our poetry, but idea rhyme. Everything is usually said twice; the second line repeats, in different words, the idea of the first line. Thus the Old Testament form of this verse in Isaiah 40:3, as set up in poetical form, reads:

A voice cries:
"¹In the wilderness ²prepare ³the way ⁴of the Lord,
¹In the desert ²make straight ³a highway ⁴for our God."

As Mark uses it, however, the phrase **in the wilderness** is taken out of the poem itself and made into a phrase describing **the**

voice of one crying. The change makes the prophecy fit John more closely.

This became a standardized treatment of this quotation in the early church, and may already have become part of the tradition before Mark wrote his gospel. The idea behind the original poem is the custom of an oriental monarch traveling over territory where there was no road. Before him went a crew of workers, making the rough places smooth enough for the king's chariot. Everybody should be preparing the way for the coming of the Lord. This is what John did for Jesus and why the early church felt that this scripture fitted John so well. It seemed perfectly justifiable to make it fit a bit better.

1:4-8. *The Ministry of John.* This is the earliest account of John and his work. Josephus, a Jewish historian of the last part of the first century, wrote of John that he "was a good man, and commanded the Jews to exercise virtue, both as to righteousness towards one another, and piety towards God, and so to come to baptism" (Antiquities of the Jews XVIII. 5.2). John's baptism was **a baptism of repentance for the forgiveness of sins.** As such it was very much like the old prophetic message. The exact manner of baptism that John used is nowhere described. Neither is it known how it arose. It seems probable that it was not introduced by John but was already a familiar custom. It probably signified a cleansing or purification, and it was most likely a regular immersion, rather than a pouring or a sprinkling.

1:6. The description of John is that of a simple ascetic. **Camel's hair** may mean either a skin from a camel or a fabric woven from camel's hair. The latter was common and cheap, and so is more probable. The **leather girdle around his waist** reflects the description of Elijah in the Septuagint translation II Kings 1:8, where exactly the same phrase is used of Elijah. In fact this description of Elijah's characteristic appearance so closely parallels Mark's description of John that it must be assumed that Elijah established (or illustrates) a prophetic costume which John accepted as his own. The Christian view of John as the forerunner of Jesus naturally assumed that he dressed in accord with his role. The link with Elijah is more basic than one of costume, however (see below on 9:13). Eating **locusts and wild honey** is common among the poor bedouin of Palestine and Arabia.

1:7. The teaching of John is given only in the barest outline. All the other gospels give more attention to this. The description could easily be predicted in the light of John's role as the messianic forerunner. **After me comes he who is mightier than I** is simply putting his basic role into proclamation form. The word translated "mightier" is one often associated with great supernatural beings.

1:8. The words **I have baptized you** certainly make it probable that baptism was something that John did for (or to) the one being baptized, rather than something which they did for themselves. **With water** is more explicit than the underlying Greek text; "in water" would be equally correct and fits baptism by immersion better.

The contrast between the baptism in water of John and the baptism in the Holy Spirit of Jesus has some puzzling aspects. Does Mark suggest that Spirit baptism will replace water baptism? Does he mean that Jesus will add the Spirit to the water-baptism ritual? There is some confusion here in the earliest record, and it is not clear whether Jesus himself practiced water baptism (as affirmed in John 3:22; 4:1, but denied in John 4:2), or whether the practice began after the Resurrection with the coming of the Holy Spirit. The origins of Christian baptism, unfortunately, are obscure.

1:9-11. *The Baptism of Jesus.* Jesus' baptism by John marks the real beginning of the gospel story. What Jesus did before that event is of no interest to Mark. The baptism itself is one of those parts of the gospel story that seems most historically sound. It was a source of embarrassment to the early Christians on two counts and therefore is not likely to be the result of a development within Christian piety.

One embarrassing aspect stems from the nature of John's baptism. All accounts agree that it was a baptism "of repentance for the forgiveness of sins" (1:4; cf. Matthew 3:6; Luke 3:3). If Jesus was baptized by John, then the inference is that he too had repented and was seeking forgiveness of his sins. Since Christians began very early to believe that Jesus had been sinless (cf. Hebrews 4:15; I Peter 2:22), his coming to John for baptism began to need explanation. Matthew is the only gospel in the New Testament that attempts to deal directly with this problem (see on Matthew 3:14-15), and it is not very successful.

The other embarrassing aspect of the baptism is that it puts Jesus in an inferior position to John. John's religious movement and Jesus' continued to exist as separate and even rival groups (see below on 2:18-22). In this situation the disciples of John had the advantage of claiming that their master was the superior one because he had baptized Jesus. John's gospel is especially sensitive to this situation. Not only does it represent John as expressly denying all claims to superiority (1:20; 3:28) and acknowledging his inferiority (3:29), but it even omits any account of the baptism.

1:10. The word translated **immediately** is a common connective in Mark, being used forty-one times. It is not to be taken as necessarily suggesting speedy action, or a rapid succession of events. Rather it is primarily a literary device and usually expresses mere sequence. The fact that **he came up out of the water** makes it probable that the baptism took place in the Jordan River itself, rather than on its banks.

He saw (i.e. Jesus saw) by the most natural reading means that in Mark's view no one else shared this experience of Jesus. The voice in verse 11 is also apparently addressed to him alone. That it was a personal religious experience of Jesus seems to be required by the historical evidence that John was not aware of Jesus' messiahship, according to the views of all the first three gospels (cf. Matthew 11:2-6; Luke 7:18-23).

The heavens opened is a fairly mild translation of a rather violent Greek word meaning "split apart." It was commonly believed among Jews of this period that direct communication from heaven was quite rare and involved a rending of the barrier between heaven and earth. **The Spirit descending upon him like a dove,** the second thing he saw, also reads like a personal experience. The symbolism of the dove as representing the

Holy Spirit is obscure. It is interesting to note that both Matthew (3:16) and Luke (3:22), in retelling the story of Jesus' baptismal experience, describe it as an objective event.

1:11. The **voice** that **came from heaven** is a special, but familiar, feature of Jewish piety. Note that the voice is addressed to Jesus himself, not to the bystanders, as in Matthew 3:17. This type of voice is a familiar part of a visionary experience and occurs again on the Mount of Transfiguration (see below on 9:2-8). A striking example of this type of thing is the experience of Paul on the road to Damascus (Acts 9:1-9). It includes both "seeing" and "hearing" and is later described as a "heavenly vision" (Acts 26:19). What the voice said to Jesus recalls Psalm 2:7, which is one of the "enthronement" psalms used during the coronation of a king of Israel. It also recalls Isaiah 42:1, the consecration of God's servant. It is not, however, an exact quotation of anything in the Old Testament.

C. THE TEMPTATION OF JESUS (1:12-13)

The temptation of Jesus is only briefly told in Mark. It is greatly elaborated in both Matthew and Luke, but eliminated entirely in John. It finds a parallel in the life of many a saint. That the newly baptized convert entered immediately into temptation was certainly true in Mark's time.

1:12. The **wilderness** is not identified and may be a symbolic name for the home of evil spirits.

1:13. The number **forty** is an expression commonly used in the Old Testament to indicate a fairly long period of time. **Tempted by Satan** is the customary late Jewish understanding of temptation. Satan was God's enemy, and God and Satan were engaged in an all-out war, in which Satan tried mightily to increase his forces of rebellion. This ancient view of the temptation process would be explained by most people today in other terms, but the underlying reality is just as much a problem now as it was then. The **wild beasts** and the **angels** are symbolic of the personnel of the opposing armies of Satan and God.

II. THE MINISTRY IN GALILEE (1:14–8:26)

A. INTRODUCTION TO THE MINISTRY OF JESUS (1:14-15)

1:14. The first three gospels make it plain that the ministries of John and Jesus were successive, that Jesus did not begin his preaching and religious work until **after John was arrested.** This is easier to fit in with the Christian interpretation of the work of John as a forerunner of Jesus. The report of John (3:22-24; 4:1) that their ministries overlapped is more difficult, but it is likely to be more historical in the light of subsequent events. **Galilee** was the scene of most of Jesus' ministry.

Preaching the gospel is a favorite Markan expression and typical of the viewpoint of early Gentile Christianity. The "gospel" is not a collection of teachings by Jesus but the proclamation that God has acted in Christ to save the world. It is a message about Jesus rather than a message by him. Only in the gospel of John are these two united so that Jesus is represented as preaching a message about himself.

1:15. The proclamation that **the time is fulfilled** refers to the common understanding of the time that God planned to end the present age and begin a new one. The old age of strife and evil and opposition to God would be replaced by **the kingdom of God.** This great event is the theme of all apocalyptic books, such as the book of Revelation. Jesus not only shared this eschatological hope (i.e. a hope that the end of this evil age would surely come) but believed that according to God's schedule the time for accomplishing it was in his own day (see below on 9:1). **The time** of waiting **is fulfilled, and the kingdom of God is at hand.**

Repent is not a characteristic theme in Mark (or in Paul, or in Gentile Christianity in general). Repentance implies real personal freedom, whereas early Gentile Christianity proclaimed Christ as God's rescue act, redeeming lost and helpless humanity from its slavery to sin. Repentance is a major theme in Luke's presentation of Jesus' teachings, but the message of salvation there is more closely related to a Jewish obedience-centered religion. In contrast, Mark proclaims a strong Son of God who overpowers our enemy for us. **Believe in the gospel** lies close to the heart of Mark's message to the reader. The story of Jesus is the gospel. To be a Christian and to know redemption is to believe in this story about God's gracious rescue act.

B. THE CALL OF THE FIRST DISCIPLES (1:16-20)

Mark's version of the call of the first disciples is the most popular one. It is repeated without significant change in Matthew. Its popularity is due not simply to its use in Matthew but to the fact that from the beginning it has been useful to preachers. It is not only an account of the first disciples but also a picture of the ideal response of every person. When the voice of Jesus calls, we should drop everything and respond. Note the double emphasis: verses 16-18 make the point first, then verses 19-20 repeat it.

Luke's version (5:1-11) expands the story with other material that appears elsewhere in the other gospels, and John (1:35-51) has an account which is distinctly different from both Mark's and Luke's. The example of instantaneous response is apparently what Mark is emphasizing.

1:16. The generalized reference to **by the Sea of Galilee** is characteristic of Mark's geographical notices. **Simon** is later called Peter (see below on 3:16).

1:17. The **fishers of men** saying is the key to the whole account and was probably better known in the early church than the exact details of the call of the first disciples.

C. FIRST ACTIVITIES (1:21–2:12)

1:21-28. *The Beginnings in Capernaum.* The very first event of Jesus' ministry, as Mark presents it, is one that expresses his authority. In the introduction to the story Jesus appears as **one**

who had authority, in contrast to **the scribes.** Jesus did not depend on the authority of some previous expert but was the expert himself. He did not quote the "authorities" but acted like one himself. By this opening event Mark wishes to inform the reader that Jesus was not an ordinary human but a superhuman being. It was indeed the Son of God, come to rescue people from the demonic forces which enslave them.

1:21. The city of **Capernaum,** on the northwest shore of the Sea of Galilee was apparently the chosen headquarters of Jesus' mission. The gospels all witness to Jesus' loyalty to the **synagogue** of his time. He apparently made no effort to establish a new type of worship but worked only to purify the old.

1:22. The **scribes** were the experts in the laws of the first five books of the Bible. As such they were often consulted by the people when the authority of Moses was desired on a question.

1:23. The term **unclean spirit** is common in the New Testament for a demon. Demon possession was widely held responsible for many human ills in Jesus' time. Humans were at the mercy of these demons, unless under the protection of some stronger spiritual power. Jesus' own belief cannot now be recovered. In any case his effectiveness in healing people who believed in demon possession would require that he seem to believe it also, whether or not he actually did.

1:24. The designation **Jesus of Nazareth** would certainly imply to the ancient reader that Jesus was born in Nazareth. In identifying a man by a place name, like "Saul of Tarsus" or "Joseph of Arimathea," the custom of the times was to use his birthplace, not his present residence. Mark and John knew nothing of the Bethlehem tradition found in Matthew and Luke. There is a possibility, however, that "of Nazareth" (literally "the Nazarene") is not a place name reference at all, but a party name, like "Simon the Zealot."

Have you come to destroy us? is the basic question. Mark's answer is clear: yes, he has. In fact, it probably should be read, not as a question at all, but as an exclamatory declaration, a defiant cry.

The Holy One of God is an excellent and appropriate title for

Jesus. It shows again that Jesus is a superhuman person. Mark intended to reveal clearly to the reader what the contemporaries of the event did not recognize at all. All the way through this gospel only the demons recognize Jesus as he really is. By means of the dialogue with demons the reader is kept fully informed.

1:25. The rebuke of Jesus is not intended to be a denial of his title "the Holy One of God," but rather a suppression of it. **Be silent** is Jesus' constant command to the demons who recognize him. This is Mark's answer to the pressing question of his own day: "Why wasn't Jesus recognized as the Son of God during his earthly lifetime?" He was recognized, Mark says, but only by the demons, and he silenced them.

1:28. The vagueness of **the surrounding region of Galilee** is characteristic of Mark's geographical notices.

1:29-31. *Healing Simon Peter's Mother-in-Law.* This healing of Simon's mother-in-law is a second example of Jesus' power. He does not rely on magical formulas that bring some outside supernatural force into the situation, but he himself is the power to heal.

1:29. The natural assumption is that **Simon and Andrew** had their home in Capernaum. The fact that his early disciples lived there may have been a factor in Jesus' apparent decision to make Capernaum his headquarters (see below on 2:1).

1:30. That Simon's mother-in-law lived with him makes it highly probable that his wife did also. Becoming a disciple of Jesus, therefore, did not necessarily mean the repudiation of normal human relationships. Simon Peter's wife seems to have accompanied him on his later apostolic journeys, as did the wives of the other apostles.

1:32-34. *Other Healings.* These two specific healing incidents are followed by a statement of healings in general. Some of these are exorcisms, others are not. In the exorcisms Jesus characteristically **would not permit the demons to speak, because they knew him.**

1:35-39. *Departure from Capernaum.* In general this is an account of the extension of Jesus' ministry into all of Galilee. He was not merely a local healer and teacher in Capernaum.

1:35. The **lonely place** to which Jesus retired was not the wilderness, for the country around ancient Capernaum was probably cultivated.

1:38. The natural effect of this verse, taken alone, would be to suggest that Jesus felt that his ministry to health problems was crowding out his preaching, but the next verse makes this unlikely. What does Jesus mean when he says, **That is why I came out?** Does he mean to explain why he left (came out of) Capernaum and went to the other towns of Galilee? Luke understands it differently and makes it refer to the basic purpose of Jesus' ministry (Luke 4:43). The former meaning is most harmonious with Mark's overall viewpoint, the latter with Luke's.

1:40-45. *Healing a Leper.* It is noteworthy that Mark's first emphasis is on Jesus' power to heal. Who Jesus was, rather than what he taught, is the main interest of Mark.

1:41. The phrase **moved with pity** is not nearly so simple as it seems. It is probably a substitution for an original "being angry," which is preserved in some of the ancient mauscripts. The phrase is omitted in both the later accounts (Matthew 8:3; Luke 5:13) as is any sign of emotion on the part of Jesus. If it did originally read "being angry," the meaning is obscure. That it was omitted by Matthew and Luke and changed to "moved with pity" in later copies of Mark suggests that it was as difficult for ancient interpreters as for us (see below on 3:5).

1:42. The disease **leprosy** was not diagnosed precisely in ancient times; the term covered a variety of skin diseases and blemishes. It is hopeless to attempt a diagnosis of this man's ailment now.

1:44. The admonition to **say nothing to any one** does not reflect Jesus' concern in Mark to keep secret his true identity, but is intended to put limits on his popularity as a healer. Spiritual healers were relatively common in those days, and the curing of leprosy would not automatically cause the healer to be regarded as a supernatural being.

1:45. Jesus' popularity as a healer becomes so great that he cannot **openly enter a town.**

2:1-12. *Healing a Paralytic.* This is a complex healing story. As literature it seems to be a combination of two stories. The first story, a healing miracle, is more complete (verses 1–5*a*, 11-12). The second (incomplete; verses 5*b*-10) is inserted into the first.

The second story here is controlled by a theological interest—the power of Jesus to forgive sins. It is primarily a dialogue between Jesus and his enemies, the scribes. The first story is set in his Capernaum home, where he is surrounded by his followers and disciples. The original setting of the second story is now lost, but it was probably a public healing of another paralytic, hence the later confusion of the two accounts. The combination is repeated in both Matthew (9:1-8) and Luke (5:17-26).

2:1. The idiom **at home** (literally "in a house") seems to mean that Jesus was in the house where he lived. Scholars are divided in interpreting this as Simon's house (based on 1:29-31) or Jesus' own house (the more natural meaning of the Greek; see below on 2:15 and 2:17).

2:4. The exact meaning of **they removed the roof** is obscure; ancient interpreters were as puzzled as modern scholars. Luke's view of it is given in Luke 5:19. Matthew omitted it.

2:5a. The **faith** of the men who brought the paralytic is emphasized, rather than the paralytic's faith. This first story continues at verse 11.

2:5b. This is the only use in Mark of **my son** (literally "child") as a term of address. Although the term is used elsewhere in Luke, it is somewhat strange that Luke's parallel (5:20) here changes "child" to the more impersonal "man." This suggests fear that the use of "my son" might be cited to justify the charge of blasphemy which follows, inferring that Jesus was now claiming the role of the heavenly Father.

To say **your sins are forgiven** as a healing formula implies an association between sin and sickness. This was certainly traditional in Judaism, but it is not Mark's intention to raise this problem. Here it is simply a question of Jesus' authority and his power. Luke reports teachings of Jesus that deny a causal

111

relationship between sin and calamity (Luke 13:1-5). Perhaps in this story the paralytic is under the old view.

2:7. In Mark's theology Jesus is the incarnation of God's Spirit, as described in 1:9-11, and therefore **can forgive sins.** In Jewish eyes this would be regarded as **blasphemy.** As the son of man coming to judge the world (implied in passages like 8:38; 9:1; 13:26, but plainly stated in Matthew 19:28), he clearly has the authority to forgive sins now.

2:10. The phrase **Son of man** is an old Jewish idiom meaning simply "man," as illustrated best in the poetry of Psalm 8:4 or in Ezekiel 11:2. In later Judaism, however, it came to be a special term for a superhuman being coming on the clouds of heaven to deliver the righteous from the hands of their enemies. It seems to be used in this latter sense here.

D. First Conflicts (2:13–3:6)

2:13-14. *The Call of Levi.* The call of Levi follows the pattern of 1:16-20; Jesus calls and there is immediate and unquestioning response. The identification of this disciple is difficult. He does not appear in any of the official lists of the twelve (see below on 3:13-19). Identified here as **the son of Alphaeus** (lit. "the one belonging to Alphaeus"), he may be related to, or the same as, "James the son of Alphaeus" of 3:18. Luke retains the name "Levi" but not "the son of Alphaeus" (Luke 5:27). Matthew replaces "Levi" by "Matthew" (9:9) and does not mention Alphaeus. Were Levi and James brothers? Are they supposed to be the same? Are Matthew and Levi the same? Are all three the same? There is also a possible connection between Levi and Thaddaeus (3:18). That there is considerable confusion in the manuscripts where these names occur shows that it has been a problem from the earliest times.

2:15-17. *Association with Sinners.* The calling of a tax collector into the disciple group is here naturally coupled with a popular story about Jesus' reply to those who criticized his association with **tax collectors and sinners.** The story seems to belong later in his ministry than Mark has placed it, because it refers to his **disciples** as **many** (only five have been mentioned to this point).

2:15. The Greek for **sat** is "reclined," in the Gentile eating style familiar to Mark. **In his house** may mean Jesus' house (see above on 2:1) or Levi's house; the Greek is as ambiguous as the English. Luke 5:29 interprets Mark to mean Levi's house, but the presence of scribes there is not likely. **Sinners** here are Jews who are not scrupulous in observance of the details of the ritual law, rather than criminals or moral degenerates. The punctuation used by the Revised Standard Version is possible, but more natural is the reading "and his disciples, for they were many, and they followed him." The awkwardness here is a trait of Mark's style.

2:16. The phrase **the scribes of the Pharisees** is used only here; "scribes of the Pharisees' party" (Acts 23:9) expresses the idea more accurately. They would not necessairly have to be present at the dinner and probably should be thought of as criticizing him among themselves. The whole matter of table fellowship was a problem in the early church, and the Gentile Christians were most sensitive here.

2:17. This saying of Jesus was probably proverbial and is merely applied here to this situation. It fits the call of a sinner into the disciple group (verses 13-14) but not the question of eating with sinners. **To call** probably does not refer to table fellowship at all; Luke interprets it as a call "to repentance" (5:32). If "call" does mean "invite to dinner," then Jesus would have to be acting as host, presumably in his own house.

2:18-22. *Jesus and Fasting.* To a short incident about fasting Mark adds two sayings that symbolize the relationship between Christianity and Judaism. The fasting question reveals that John's disciples and Jesus' are independent groups, following different customs (cf. Matthew 9:14; John 4:1; Acts 19:1-5). It also reflects a tradition that Jesus and his disciples were not ascetic (cf. Matthew 11:18-19; Luke 7:33-34).

2:18. The words **and people came** (literally "and they came") are typically ambiguous. Matthew (9:14) interprets the questioners to be John's disciples and rewords accordingly. Luke associates them with "the Pharisees and their scribes" (5:30, 33) of the previous incident, thus welding the two units into one.

Fasting may refer to a general practice, but more likely it refers to one of the special periods of fasting in the Jewish calendar, abandoned by Gentile Christianity.

2:19-20. This answer is expressed in the language of the early Christian community and from the viewpoint of this community, which now has some established fast days of its own. The problem being faced is: Why does the church have fast days if Jesus and his disciples did not observe them? The answer is that Christian fasting is a memorial of his death and therefore was inappropriate in the days before his death.

2:21-22. In these two parallel analogies there is a recognition that Christianity and Judaism are incompatible. This is the typical Gentile Christian view. It is too radical for Matthew and Luke; see their independent additions (Matthew 9:17; Luke 5:39). Mark's use of these sayings, however, is probably not the way Jesus used them, for Jesus was not this radical either. The original purpose is now lost.

2:23-28. *Sabbath Violation.* This story intends to show in another way the difference between the religion of Jesus and Jewish legalism. It is officially a sabbath violation story, although the unlawfulness of the action described is not clear. The historical inaccuracies (see below on verse 26) show further the Gentile Christian background of Mark. The story seems to culminate in the strongest anti-sabbath statement in the gospels, omitted in both the parallel versions.

2:23. In the Greek manuscripts this action is not clear. Matthew (12:1) makes the offense plucking and eating; Luke (6:1) makes it a kind of crude threshing ("rubbing them in their hands"). The Pharisees permitted "plucking and eating" in case of need, but not harvesting or threshing. Perhaps Mark is caricaturing Pharisaic legalism.

2:26. The reference **when Abiathar was high priest** has two inaccuracies:

(1) There was no high priest in David's time; this office developed much later.

(2) The Old Testament account (I Samuel 21:1-6) gives the name of the priest as Ahimelech. Matthew 12:4 and Luke 6:4 correct these errors. Mark characteristically reflects less accurate knowledge of Palestine, the Old Testament and Jewish affairs in general than Matthew and Luke.

2:27. This is a most remarkable statement, that was certainly understood in early Gentile Christianity as laying the foundation for abandoning the sabbath entirely. Both Matthew and Luke omit it. The changeover from sabbath (Saturday in the Gentile calendar) to Sunday as the day of worship was accomplished by the early second century.

2:28. This seems to justify Jesus' action on the ground that he was privileged to do things on the sabbath that ordinary people should not.

3:1-6. *Healing the Withered Hand.* This is another sabbath violation story. It is simply a deliberate healing to prove a point. The Pharisees permitted medical attention on the sabbath only when life was in danger.

3:4. The question of Jesus (preserved in Luke 6:9) becomes actual legislation in Matthew 12:12.

3:5. The phrase **with anger** is a sign of the emotional involvement of Jesus in this cause, and is omitted in Matthew 12:12 and Luke 6:10 (see above on 1:41).

3:6. The name **Herodians** implies that they were partisans of Herod Antipas and friends of the Herodian dynasty.

E. Editorial Summary (3:7-12)

This paragraph is a general statement of the popularity of Jesus at the height of his Galilean ministry.

3:7-8. These verses list in succession the peoples attracted to Jesus. Not only Galileans but many from faraway places come to him. This is the first mention of Judeans as followers of Jesus.

3:9. This verse prepares the reader for the incident to be described in 4:1. The word translated as **crush** is one that means "squeeze," or "compress."

3:10. In both Matthew's version (12:15) and Luke's (6:17-19) Jesus "healed them all," rather than **healed many.** The word **diseases** is not a medical but a disciplinary term. It means literally a whipping or a scourging and is translated that way in Acts 22:24 and Hebrews 11:36. The idea is that some illnesses or diseases are sent by God as punishment.

3:11. The testimony of **the unclean spirits** is a clear revelation of Mark's theology. How would the author have learned of this if no one except Jesus was aware of it? This is communication between the author and the reader to remind the readers of the true understanding of Jesus. **The Son of God** is not a messianic title; it is the title of a supernatural being, a divine being. It expresses Mark's convictions about Jesus as a guide to the readers.

3:12. As earlier (1:24-25), and consistently throughout the gospel, Jesus' true identity as a divine being (Son of God rather than Jewish Messiah) is not revealed to his associates. The demons know it, but are forbidden to reveal it.

F. The Twelve Disciples (3:13-19*a*)

The appointment of the twelve looks far more simple than it actually is. The unsystematic use of different kinds of names, the omission of Levi, whose call has already been described, and the use of strange terms like **Iscariot** make it highly likely that Mark is here simply handing on a traditional list. Since the setting of the appointment is very vague and general, it should be assumed that the evangelist has provided this setting himself, as a good author would.

The idea of **twelve** chief disciples is deeply rooted in early Christian tradition. The earliest reference is in I Corinthians 15:5. It occurs in all the gospels, but with interesting differences in details. It is possible that the idea of the twelve is a later

development which was mistakenly believed to have been
established by Jesus.

There were twelve tribes of Israel, so twelve missionary aides
is a convenient number. However, most of the names in the list
do not emerge in early Christian tradition as real actors on the
stage of history. We may therefore suspect that to a small
handful of actual leaders were added others not so important to
bring the number up to the desired twelve. Discrepancies in the
two extant lists (Mark's and Luke's) seem to support this.

But the problem cannot be solved on the basis of surviving
evidence. It may be sufficient to note that Mark's list is followed
by Matthew (10:1-4) and that Luke's changes (6:12-16) are
repeated in Acts 1:13. John mentions the twelve (6:70; 20:24)
but nowhere gives a list. He does not even mention by name
James and John and includes disciples, like Nathanael,
Nicodemus, and Lazarus, who do not appear in either of the lists
of the twelve.

3:13. It is implied that there was a larger group with Jesus and
that out of these he chose twelve. Luke 6:13 makes this explicit.

3:14-15. The expressed purpose of the twelve is **to preach and
have authority to cast out demons.** There seems to be no
indication here of their future role as general overseers of the
church, as described in Acts. Mark, as a spokesman for Gentile
Christianity in general, may be reflecting the resistance of
Gentile Christianty to the administrative leadership of the
twelve. It is probably significant that Luke leaves this statement
of purpose out entirely.

3:16. It is strange that Simon Peter is separated from his
brother Andrew in this list. Both Matthew and Luke rearrange
the order to bring the brothers together. Mark may have chosen
his arrangement to give precedence to the ones who seem to
have been the actual leaders—Peter, James, and John. This trio
is customary in Mark. Andrew simply was not as important, so
Mark puts him in the group of those who are only names to us.
The list in Acts 1:13 follows Mark in this, as over against
Matthew and Luke.

The surnaming of Simon with the name "rock" (**Peter** in

Greek; "Cephas" in Aramaic) is not reported as a special event in Mark, as it is in Matthew 16:17-18 and John 1:42. This, however, is a transitional verse in Mark. Before this the disciple is called Simon; after this (except in 14:37) he is called Peter.

3:17. The surname **Boanerges** seems to be a corrupt transliteration of an original Hebrew or Aramaic title that is difficult to recover. Even the early explanation, **sons of thunder**, has an uncertain meaning—possibly related to Luke 9:54. "Boanerges" might mean that they were twins. It probably refers to a personality trait in the two brothers.

3:18. Though mentioned several times in John, **Philip** does not appear in the first three gospels, or in Acts, except in the lists of the twelve. The deacon Philip of Acts is a different person.

Bartholomew appears not to be a personal name, but an identification based on family. Translated back into Aramaic it would be "son of Talmai." It is possible that the names Nathanael and Bartholomew refer to the same man, Nathanael son of Talmai.

Matthew has somehow replaced Levi, who was called earlier (2:14) but is not included in the list. Matthew identifies this man as "the tax collector" and substitutes this name for Levi in the story of his call (see above on 2:13-17).

Thomas is identified by John (11:16; 20:24; 21:2) as the one "called the Twin" (transliterated as "Didymus" in the King James Version), but any more exact meaning is unknown.

James the son of Alphaeus is identified this way to distinguish him from James the son of Zebedee. Since Levi was earlier identified as "the son of Alphaeus" (2:14), some have guessed either that James and Levi are the same or that they were brothers. Is he the same person as "James the younger" of 15:40?

Thaddaeus is the most obscure of all. The manuscripts have different readings, some having "Lebbaeus." The lists of the twelve in Luke and Acts substitute "Judas the son of James" for Thaddaeus. All are otherwise unknown.

Simon the Cananaean was a political zealot. "Cananaean" and "zealot" were apparently older and newer terms for members of the extreme nationalist movement in Palestine. Luke's reading, "Simon who was called the Zealot" (6:15), is probably justified.

3:19a. The surname **Iscariot** is obscure in meaning. It has been guessed that it means "man of Kerioth" (either a village twelve miles south of Hebron or one in Moab). Another guess is "assassin." Since Mark offers no explanation, it may have been obscure to him also.

G. THE DEMON-POSSESSION CHARGE (3:19b-35)

This section is a remarkable revelation of the relationship between Jesus and his family. They were blind to his true significance as the Son of God and came to rescue him from the consequences of his "condition," **for people were saying, "He is beside himself"** (that is, demon-possessed). Verse 21 should be followed immediately by verse 31 to get the force of this section. Verses 22-30 interrupt the natural flow of the family incident and were probably added here because they denounce the demon-possession accusation. For study purposes read verses 19b-21 with verses 31-35, and verses 22-30 separately.

3:19b-21. Note that both Matthew and Luke omit these verses. Since, however, the verses provide the reason for Jesus' refusal to go with his family, they are necessary for the best understanding of verses 31-35. Matthew and Luke, in harmony with their infancy narratives, carefully eliminate any suggestion that Jesus was not accepted by his own family. Note also the omission of Mark's phrase "among his own kin" (6:4) in the parallels of Matthew 13:57 and Luke 4:24. On **home** see above on 2:1.

3:21. To seize him implies concern for his safety and welfare. **Beside himself** means that his spirit was outside his body, which was being directed by a foreign spirit (a demon).

3:22-30. The purpose of this interruption of the family incident is to make plain that Jesus was not demon-possessed. It was the Holy Spirit of God, not a demon, that possessed him. Two originally independent traditions seem to be combined here to make the point: verses 22-26, the reply to the scribes, and verses 27-30, which are two sayings of Jesus.

3:22-26. Though other sources have been suggested, the name **Beelzebul** probably comes from an ancient title of the god Baal. Most interpreters, including Matthew and Luke, have understood Beelzebul and Satan to be alternate names for **the prince of demons.** Mark's two clauses quoted from the scribes can be read, however, as two entirely separate accusations. Since Jesus' reply answers only the second, it is possible that Mark has used an isolated bit from another tradition. **He is possessed by Beelzebul,** thus forms a bridge from the family theory of demon possession to the interpolated story of Jesus' decisive refutation of the charge that his power came from **Satan.**

3:27. Here the argument shifts. Jesus' exorcisms prove that **the strong man** (Satan) is bound. The ultimate defeat of Satan and his kingdom is clearly forecast; even now his **house** is being plundered. Some have seen a word play in the fact that the apparent meaning of Beelzebul is "master of the house."

3:28-30. This "unforgivable sin" saying has been a problem to Bible interpreters in every age. In this context it refers to failure to recognize the Holy Spirit—calling it a demon. But verse 30 is found in Mark only. The heart of the saying is stated in Matthew 12:31 without an explanation and in Luke 12:10 also in an entirely different setting. Mark's interpretation (in verse 30) remains the most satisfactory.

3:31-35. Jesus' family appears only twice in Mark, here and in 6:1-6. Both times the family members appear as outsiders rather than sympathetic members of his group. True brotherhood and true kinship is spiritual, not physical.

3:31. Jesus' **mother** is mentioned only twice in Mark, here and in 6:3. His father, or the father in his family, is never mentioned. **His brothers** appear once more in 6:3, where they are named. From the references here and elsewhere in the New Testament there is no reason to think of them except in the ordinary sense as blood brothers. Roman Catholic teaching, believing in the doctrine of the perpetual virginity of Mary, has traditionally explained the brothers as cousins (children of Mary's sister) or legal stepbrothers (children of Mary's husband by a supposed earlier marriage).

H.Teaching by Parables (4:1-34)

4:1-9. *The Sower.* The parable of the sower introduces a section dealing with parables and their purpose and use. In general a parable as a teaching device is best understood as a story to illustrate a teaching.

4:1. The setting, teaching from a **boat** to a **crowd . . . on the land,** is retained in Matthew's parallel account (13:1-2), but Luke moves this setting to a different point (5:3) and has this parable taught in an ordinary setting (8:4).

4:2. The use of **parables** was characteristic of the teaching of Jesus.

4:3-8. This parable itself might more accurately be described as the parable of four kinds of soil. Like the other parables in this section, it does not so much contain a positive teaching of Jesus as explain why his teaching was not always immediately successful.

4:9. This formula appears at the end of the parable in all of the first three gospels, and appears again in 4:23. It indicates the need to be careful in interpreting the meaning because it is either difficult or commonly misunderstood. Whether this is intended to be a saying of Jesus or of Mark is not clear, but probably it is Mark's. It prepares the reader, at least, for the explanation to follow.

4:10-12. *The Purpose of the Parables.* This explanation that the purpose of parables was to conceal truth from outsiders is rooted in doctrine rather than history. Such a purpose would be naturally assumed in the environment of early Gentile Christianity, but in the practice of Jesus parables were obviously to make truth plain to all hearers (see verses 21-25).

The difficulty here arises from the fact that Mark added an originally independent saying (verses 11-12) to this context (note that verse 10 leads directly into verse 13). He seems to have felt that this was a proper place for a saying about parables, but he may have misunderstood the meaning of **in parables** in verse 11. Rather than referring to the story parables of Jesus, it probably here means "in riddles" (the same word in Aramaic or Hebrew), making the sense of the saying: "For those outside everything becomes a riddle." The gospel as preached in early Gentile Christianity begins with a faith relationship, and without that the whole message is foolishness.

4:13-20. *The Sower Parable Explained.* Since the explanation of the parable offered here is an allegorical one (see on Matthew 13:10-17), most scholars regard it as a later development in the transmission of early traditions about the teachings of Jesus. Mark has in effect brought the parable up to date and made it refer to the apostolic preaching of his own time.

4:13. Jesus' comment about the failure of the twelve to understand his parable is omitted in the parallel versions of Matthew 13:18 and Luke 8:11, in harmony with their respect for the authority of the twelve.

4:14. In Mark's time **the sower** is the apostolic preacher. **The word** is the gospel proclamation, the good news about Christ.

4:21-25. *Sayings About Parables.* Mark understands these verses to shed light on Jesus' use of parables. They are to enlighten, rather than confuse, their hearers. The arrangement is editorial here, as the parallels in Matthew and Luke show. A table of these parallels will show the situation clearly.

MATT.		MARK 4		LUKE
5:15	=	21	=	8:16; 11:33
10:26	=	22	=	8:17; 12:2
13:9, etc.	=	23	=	8:8b, etc.
		24a	=	8:18a
7:2	=	24b	=	6:38
13:12; 25:29	=	25	=	8:18b; 19:26

It is safe to conclude that the sayings contained in these verses are remnants of much longer original teachings, the context of which is now lost. They are pithy and terse, and should be interpreted simply in terms of their content, without regard to their present context.

4:22-23. Eventually all mysteries will be cleared up. On verse 23 see above on verse 9.

4:24-25. The first part of verse 24 is connected directly to verse 25 in one of Luke's parallels (8:18), with a resulting difference in meaning. Mark's coupling of two sayings in verse 24 forms an exhortation to be careful to hear correctly and seems to make understanding conditional on sharing.

Verse 25 has long been a troublesome saying. On the surface it seems unfair, but on deeper thought it is an accurate reflection of the way things actually are. The parable of the talents (or pounds) makes this point in more detail (Matthew 25:14-30; Luke 19:12-27).

4:26-29. *The Seed Growing Secretly.* This parable, omitted from both Matthew and Luke, is rather difficult. It points to the kingdom as a divine act rather than a human accomplishment. It calls on people to be patient with the delay of the kingdom in coming.

4:30-32. *The Mustard Seed.* This parable might illustrate the ways the kingdom **grows,** gradually and naturally instead of suddenly and dramatically. But it is more harmonious with the other teachings to see it as a contrast between the small, insignificant beginnings of the Christian movement and the final tremendous kingdom that is its destiny. Mark has grouped these three "seed parables" together out of some conviction that they teach related truths about the kingdom of God.

I. SPECIAL MIRACLES (4:35-5:43)

4:35-41. *The Storm at Sea.* The stilling of the storm is clearly a demonstration of Jesus' power over nature. It is possible, but beside the point, to try to give it a natural explanation.

4:38. The reaction of the disciples is presented quite unfavorably. They rebuke Jesus for his lack of concern. Matthew

8:25 and Luke 8:24 change this rebuke into an appeal for help.

4:39. It is a pathetic kind of rationalization to explain Jesus' command **Peace! Be still!** as originally directed to the disciples rather than the wind. The intention here is clearly to portray Jesus as Lord of nature.

4:41. The disciples, however, do not grasp the significance of Jesus' action. They are amazed, but left bewildered, as usual in Mark.

5:1-20. *The Demonic Legion.* The story of the Gerasene demoniac teaches the same basic truth about Jesus as the account of the stilling of the storm. Both the howling wind and the howling demon are subject to the Son of God. At his command both the sea and the man find their peace. The history of this story is complex. The setting is clear in general, but not in detail.

Luke (8:26-39) uses the full story almost as it appears in Mark. Matthew (8:28-34) drastically abbreviates it and yet makes it the story of two demon-possessed men instead of one. The background of the story is more Gentile than Jewish (Jews did not keep swine, and Palestine is a difficult setting for Gentiles to have such a large herd). To complicate matters further, there are some other versions of this story, with other exorcists as heroes. The probabilities are that this was a popular story that got attached to Jesus in the tradition of early Gentile Christianity.

5:1. The general location is reported to be the eastern shore of the Sea of Galilee but the exact location is reported in different ways. The oldest and best manuscripts have Gerasa, but this is too far from the Sea of Galilee to fit well. Matthew changes this to Gadara ("the country of the Gadarenes," 8:28), but this, though nearer, is still too far from the water. Later copyists changed both to "Gergesa," which may correspond to some ruins on the east side of the sea. It remains a problem.

5:2. Palestinian burials were often in caves set aside as **tombs.** It was commonly believed that demons lived in them.

5:6. As is usual in Mark, **he ran and worshiped him** means that the demons, not the man, recognized Jesus.

5:7-8. The story is awkwardly told at this point, with the demonic response coming before the command of Jesus.

5:9. The name **Legion** suggests that many demons, rather than one demon, were possessing the man, and this meaning is confirmed by the following phrase, **for we are many.** A Roman legion at full strength numbered 6,000 men.

5:10. The term **out of the country** probably means out of the inhabited area and into the desert, a traditional haunt of evil spirits.

5:11-13. The plight of the poor pigs would scarcely have been of concern to the early Christian. The naturalistic theory that the pigs were stampeded by the antics of an insane man undercuts the main point of the story, which is Jesus' control over the demons.

5:20. The Decapolis was a group of ten Gentile cities in the area between Judea and Galilee on both sides of the Jordan.

5:21-43. *Jairus' Daughter.* This account is an unusual combination of two miracle stories, one contained within the other. Matthew 9:18-26 retells Mark's version more briefly and places it earlier. Luke 8:40-56 parallels Mark.

5:21. The seaside setting of Mark is abandoned by both Matthew and Luke.

5:22. The ancient Palestinian synagogue usually had only one **ruler,** but the author may mean one of the class of synagogue rulers.

5:23. It is difficult to know whether the author intended this account to be a healing **at the point of death,** as this verse suggests, or a bringing back to life of one who has already died, as verse 35 suggests. Luke follows Mark closely and retains the same ambiguity, but Matthew resolves the problem by stating clearly at the outset, "My daughter has just died." The point of the story in all three versions is to demonstrate the power of Jesus over life and death.

5:25-34. The healing of this woman is a remarkable example of Jesus' power to heal. Although **faith** must be presupposed to account for her action, and her faith is specifically mentioned at the end of the story as the reason for her cure, nevertheless the actual healing was accomplished by the power of Jesus. It would not be true to the meaning of the story as Mark and Luke tell it, to think of the woman's faith as anything more than that which allowed the power of Jesus to be effective.

5:27. The **garment** of Jesus is not specifically described. Mark does not seem to ascribe any particular significance to it here. Both Matthew and Luke expand the description to "the fringe of his garment" probably out of a closer orientation to Jewish customs (see comment on Luke 8:44).

5:30. Traditions about Jesus were recorded in different ways. A comparison of this verse with Luke 8:45-46 illustrates this very effectively. Note that what is a description by the author in Mark, **Jesus, perceiving in himself that power had gone forth from him,** becomes in Luke a saying of Jesus, "I perceive that power has gone forth from me." Each evangelist apparently felt free to write conversational sayings for Jesus as needed in history.

5:36. Faith—**only believe**—is stressed in this healing, or resurrection, but it differs from the faith of the woman with the flow of blood. Here it is not the faith of the one being healed but that of a third party. The faith of the father is somehow related to the restoration of the daughter.

5:37. The recognition that three disciples, **Peter and James and John,** had a special relationship to Jesus is characteristic of Mark.

5:39. Those who see this story as a healing rather than a resurrection take Jesus' words here literally. Others take them symbolically. **Sleeping** is commonly used in antiquity to describe death.

5:41. Jesus' **taking her by the hand** is a typical healing method in Mark. In 1:31 Jesus heals Simon Peter's mother-in-law in this way.

5:42. Mark's description here is awkward. Matthew leaves out both the walking and the age of the girl. Luke is much more skillful, describing the age of the girl at the beginning of his account.

5:43. The strict charge **that no one should know this** is in harmony with Mark's constant explanation to the reader that Jesus did not seek publicity but preferred to remain the unrecognized Son of God.

J. REJECTION AT NAZARETH (6:1-6a)

The belief of strangers, like Jairus and the woman, is now contrasted sharply with the unbelief of those who supposedly knew Jesus well. Behind this arrangement it is not difficult to see the feeling of the early Gentile church that it really understood Jesus better than the Jewish Christians who had known him personally. Mark's version of his rejection at Nazareth is closely paralleled in Matthew 13:53-58 but is replaced in Luke (4:16-30) by a distinctly different account.

6:2. The astonishment of the people at Nazareth is similar to that which Jesus first aroused in Capernaum (1:22). There, however, he was a stranger. In Nazareth, on the other hand, he was well known already in quite another role. Their rejection is understandable.

6:3. This is the only clue to Jesus' occupation prior to his full-time ministry. It is changed in Matthew 13:55 and Luke 4:22 and by some of the later copyists as well. The thinking of the townspeople seems to have been just the reverse of the early Christians. Whereas the townspeople asked, "How can **the carpenter** be the Lord?" the Christians asked, "How could the Lord have been a common carpenter?"

It is noteworthy that Mark mentions only **Mary** whereas Luke mentions only Joseph. The listing of the names of Jesus' brothers and the mention of his sisters is a very valuable bit of incidental information.

6:4. This saying of Jesus is in the form of a proverb and could be a quotation of a well-known truth, here applied to himself. But since we do not know of other ancient examples of its use, it may have begun with Jesus. We have to assume that Jesus' immediate family did not honor him as a prophet. Matthew 13:57 and Luke 4:24 soften these family implications.

6:5. In place of **he could do no mighty work there** Matthew 13:58 reports simply that "he did not do many mighty works there," and Luke omits any such statement. Mark's version implies that his power to heal was conditioned by the faith of those who desired to be healed.

K. THE MISSION OF THE TWELVE (6:6*b*-13)

The tradition about Jesus' sending the twelve out by twos is preserved in a larger complex of materials. It is a feature of the first three gospels only, and Mark's account seems to be the basic one. The purpose of the mission was apparently to cast out demons and to preach repentance. Matthew 10:7 and Luke 9:2 specifically describe the preaching mission as a proclamation of the kingdom. Some elements of Mark's account are then repeated. Some of Matthew's additional material appears in Luke's account (10:1-16) of the sending out of the seventy, which does not appear in Mark at all. The historical situation behind these accounts is not clear. The return is described in 6:30.

6:6*b*. This short sentence actually seems to stand by itself. It is neither the end of the previous story nor the beginning of the next but simply a link. It literally says that Jesus "went about in a circle."

6:8. The purpose of the **staff** is not clear, and the parallels in Matthew 10:10 and Luke 9:3 forbid taking a staff. The **bag** could be a beggar's sack or possibly a money belt.

6:9. The admonition **to wear sandals** seems to imply a long journey, but they are forbidden in Matthew 10:10. Luke (10:4) forbids them for the seventy. **Two tunics** are forbidden in all accounts.

6:10. This may mean that one should be satisfied with his first invitation and should not seek a better one.

6:11. For one to **shake off the dust** on his **feet** for **a testimony against them** is a traditional Jewish custom, also mentioned in Acts 13:51.

6:13. Healing by anointing **with oil,** a regular practice in ancient times, is mentioned in the gospels only this once. See James 5:14.

L. THE DEATH OF JOHN THE BAPTIST (6:14-29)

The reputation of Jesus leads some to regard him as a reappearance of **John the baptizer.** At this point Mark, realizing that he has not recorded the death of John, attaches a lengthy description of his execution by Herod. Matthew simply follows Mark's rather awkward procedure. Luke has a brief summary of John's imprisonment earlier in his story (3:19-20) and omits the story of his execution.

6:14. The title **King** did not belong to this **Herod;** he was a "tetrarch." Matthew 14:1 and Luke 9:7 make this correction. The reference is to Herod Antipas, one of the sons of King Herod the Great and local ruler of Galilee and Perea.

John . . . has been raised from the dead should probably be understood figuratively to mean that Jesus was similar to John. If literal, it may be a bit of popular superstition, or may reflect some kind of reincarnation belief. The expression **these powers** refers to miracles. Does this not make it necessary to credit John with miracles also?

6:15. The return of **Elijah** was expected just prior to the coming of the Messiah (cf. Malachi 4:5). **A prophet** was a highly regarded person in Jewish piety, second only in esteem to the Messiah himself.

6:17. The reference to **his brother Philip's wife** is probably a mistake. According to Josephus' account of the Herodian family Herodias was not Philip's wife but the wife of another half brother of Antipas who was also named Herod. Some later copyists have tried to bring the two accounts into harmony by reading simply "his brother's wife."

6:20. It is not clear what was intended by **he was much perplexed.** Matthew 14:5 leaves it out, and many manuscripts replace it by "did many things," a phrase which is equally difficult.

6:22. According to Josephus, **Herodias' daughter** was named Salome. It was she who married Herod's half brother Philip.

6:29. John's **disciples** buried him. Christians are likely to regard John simply as the forerunner of Jesus and fail to see him at the center of an important religious movement. He had a group of disciples that continued long after his death, in rivalry to the Christian movement (see above on 2:18-22).

M. SPECIAL GROUP I (6:30–7:37)

6:30-44. *Feeding the Five Thousand.* The story of the feeding of the five thousand (and the four thousand of 8:1-9) is shaped by two completely separate influences. One is the miracle of Elisha in II Kings 4:42-44. The resemblances are too striking to be simple coincidence. The other is the practice of the love feast in primitive Christian worship.

As we have it, the feeding proceeds in the manner of a love feast, giving the sanction of Jesus himself. The miraculous element should not be explained away along rationalistic or naturalistic lines. It was not a great sharing experience, but the demonstration of Jesus as the sustainer of life. John 6:1-14 makes the link with the Elisha miracle closer by specifying "barley loaves" and is much more explicit about the connection between Jesus' miracle and the Lord's Supper.

6:34. The **sheep without a shepherd** image is not used in the accounts of Matthew and Luke. Matthew has already used it earlier in a different setting (9:36). Whereas Mark portrays Jesus as a teacher, Luke (9:11) adds healing activities and Matthew (14:14) mentions only the healing ministry.

6:35-36. The suggestion that the crowd be dispersed to buy food in the nearby villages shows that their needs could have been met without a miracle. Therefore, Mark implies, we should not regard Jesus' miracles as emergency measures when all else failed.

6:37. The question about buying **two hundred denarii worth of bread** is rhetorical and even sarcastic. A denarius was a

Roman silver coin approximately worth about twenty cents, or one day's field labor, according to Matthew 20:2. Obviously the disciples could come up with few such coins, and their specifying this large number pointedly brands Jesus' instruction as absurd. Thus again Mark shows the reader how little the twelve understood their Master. Matthew omits any suggestion of the disciples' buying food, and Luke removes the barb by leaving out the estimated figure.

6:38. The total of **five . . . and two** is seven, the number of loaves in the feeding of the four thousand (see below on 8:1-9). All four gospels have the five-two combination. The elements bread and fish appear in some early Christian portrayals of the Lord's Supper, making the connection between this miracle and the sacrament more explicit.

6:39. The orderly arrangement of the people is reminiscent of Paul's protest that in Corinth the Lord's Supper is disorderly (I Corinthians 11:20-22) and that Christian worship in general "should be done decently and in order" (I Corinthians 14:40).

6:40. The grouping **by hundreds and by fifties** seems to be Mark's personal touch. It is reminiscent of Moses' division of the people in Exodus 18:21. Matthew omits all reference to this. Luke 9:14 has them sitting "in companies, about fifty each."

6:41. It is traditional in Judaism to bless God before breaking bread. Luke 24:30-31 also shows this as a practice of Jesus with his disciples. All twelve disciples act as servers.

6:43. The **twelve baskets** probably are intended to agree with the twelve disciple-servers. These baskets were traditional Jewish food carriers. The expression **broken pieces** appears in an early Christian writing (Didache 9:3-4) as a description of the bread of the Lord's Supper. Matthew, Luke, and John all omit the specific reference to leftover fish.

6:44. Mark's number, **five thousand men,** is repeated in Luke 9:14 exactly and in John 6:10 in a different form. Matthew 14:21 makes it explicit that this does not include the women and children.

6:45-52. *Crossing the Sea.* This story is difficult for modern readers. Though the dominant element is the walking on the water, there are still traces of a stilling of a storm (as in 4:35-41) in the phrases about the **wind.** The chief difficulty is understanding the purpose of the action. Jesus' walking was apparently not to rescue, or even to help, the disciples in their distress. What we have is actually a nature miracle that would leave the reader in no doubt about the status of Jesus as a divine being. Since this is a main concern of Mark, it was probably his reason for including the account in his gospel.

It is possible that he was influenced by Psalm 77:16-19 or that he was writing an allegorical account of Jesus' triumph over death. It is also possible that the story originally belonged to the group of resurrection appearances. It is not likely that we are here dealing with a natural event which has developed legendary proportions.

Matthew has a parallel version (14:22-33) which leaves out the difficult phrase in verse 48, **he meant to pass them by,** but adds an account about Peter walking on the water also. This detracts from Mark's emphasis on the uniqueness of Jesus as the Son of God. Luke omits the whole story. John's version (6:16-21) is similar in spirit to Mark's.

6:48. The **fourth watch** was the last one, from 3 A.M. to 6 A.M. Mark refers to the daytime by hours (twelve, beginning at 6 A.M.) and to the nighttime by watches (four, of three hours each, following Roman custom).

6:49. The explanation that **they thought it was a ghost** suggests the possibility that this experience originally took place after the Crucifixion.

6:50-52. As is customary in Mark, demonstrations of the true nature of Jesus as the Son of God are clear only to the reader; the disciples never seem to see it. Mark concludes that **they were utterly astounded** and then tells the reader that they did not understand the feeding of the five thousand any better, for **their hearts were hardened.** Matthew's version does not give this impression of the disciples at all, but has them recognize him fully (14:33).

6:53-56. On **fringe of his garment** see comment on Luke 8:44.

7:1-23. *Controversy with Pharisees.* This is a composite section dealing with three issues and directed to three different groups. Verses 1-8 treat the problem of unwashed hands, verses 9-13 the Corban vow, and verses 14-23 the problem of kosher food. The first two problems are directed to the Pharisees; the third is expressed first to the people (verses 14-15) and then to the disciples (verses 17-23). Note that since the most ancient manuscripts do not have verse 16, it is omitted from modern versions (see the footnote in the Revised Standard Version).

The general unity of this section implies the early church problem of loyalty to Jewish customs. The solution—namely freedom from them—is here attributed to Jesus himself. It is noteworthy, however, that Paul deals with this problem in I Corinthians 8–10 and Romans 14:1–15:13 as though it were a new one and shows no awareness that Jesus had already solved it in principle. Luke leaves this whole section out, probably because in his judgment the problem was solved by Peter in his experience with Cornelius (Acts 10-11).

7:1-8. Mark's description of Jewish customs certainly implies that his intended readers are Gentile and need this kind of explanation. It also suggests the probability that he too is outside the circle which has firsthand knowledge of these customs, for his explanation is partly inaccurate. He attributes, out of poor information or prejudice, to **all the Jews** what was a custom of the strict Pharisees only.

7:1-5. This seems to be the second official investigation of Jesus (the first being reported in 3:22). The picture of conflict with the authorities is building up. As an actual investigation this is unlikely, for the Jews who did not observe this custom were very numerous and often in high official positions.

7:6-7. The violence of the reply is certainly surprising. It expresses the later hostility between church and synagogue from the Christian point of view.

7:9-13. The criticism of Pharisaism here explains itself. **Corban** was a special gift to God, usually money or property.

Jesus is here condemning abuse of this practice as a pious excuse for neglecting obligations to one's parents.

7:14-23. The question of ritually unclean food (not kosher) is clearly declared solved in this section. The viewpoint is that of the Gentile church. Matthew represents a more conservative aspect of early Christianity. In his reworking of this material (15:1-20) he removes all reference to the non-kosher food which has been made unclean by unwashed hands.

7:15. This is the key verse; the rest is explanation.

7:19. The translation **and so passes on** is a gentle one for a plain statement in the Greek, "and so passes into the privy." It is possible that the explanation **thus he declared all foods clean** is a later addition, but since the statement is harmonious with Mark's Gentile Christian background, it may be original. In any case this conclusion is implied in the whole section.

7:21. The Greek word behind **fornication** means any kind of sexual vice. **Envy** is literally "an evil eye," which may be a reference to the common superstition or may be related to Luke 11:34 (cf. Matthew 6:22-23). **Slander** is literally "blasphemy," a word used of untrue accusations against God and men.

7:24-30. *The Ministry to Gentiles.* Mark now relates a story about Jesus and a Gentile woman, which Luke omits and Matthew alters (15:21-28). It is a symbolic statement of how Jesus went first to the Jews but finally to the Gentiles. Matthew changes this aspect also, having Jesus go "only to the lost sheep of the house of Israel," and makes it simply another healing story.

7:24. That Jesus **entered a house** (of a Gentile) was contrary to the practice of a pious Jew, and thus omitted in Matthew 15:21.

7:26. The identification of the woman as **Greek** is significant. Matthew calls her a "Canaanite" (see comment on Matthew 15:22).

7:27. The **children** are symbolic of Israel, the children of God. **First** is symbolic of the mission of Jesus to his own people. It was only after they rejected him that full attention was paid to the Gentiles. The **dogs** are symbolic of the Gentiles. The overtones of Jewish superiority here are alien to the general spirit of Mark, but the emphasis is related to the general acknowledgment of early Gentile Christianity that "salvation is from the Jews" (John 4:22), or that the actual order of priority is "the Jew first and also the Greek" (Romans 2:10).

7:28. It is highly significant that this Greek woman is the only person in Mark to call Jesus **Lord.** Jesus also refers to himself (or to God?) as "Lord" (5:19; 11:3), and this is certainly the viewpoint of Mark. The recognition of Jesus as Lord in Mark is credited solely to Gentile devotion and insight. This verse is closey related to 15:39. It misses Mark's point here to render "Lord" as "sir," as in several modern translations.

7:29. The woman's daughter is healed **for this saying**—that the **dogs** are entitled to **the children's crumbs.** The real meaning should not be sought in the intentions or personality of Jesus but in the message of Mark to the reader. This message is simply the recognition that Gentiles can claim to share in the salvation of the gospel. The actual historical scene is obscured by these vital issues.

7:30. Note that this is a striking instance of healing from a distance and on the basis of the intercessory faith (implied in the confession "Lord") of a third party.

7:31-37. *Healing the Deaf Mute.* This account gives more about the actual mechanics of healing than is usual in the gospels. Neither Matthew nor Luke repeats the story, perhaps because it resembled too closely a common healing account. It is replaced in Matthew 15:29-31 by a general description of healings.

7:31. The route described here is very unlikely, as Sidon is beyond Tyre to the north and **the Decapolis** (see above on 5:20) is beyond the Sea of Galilee and south. It probably reflects the author's inaccurate knowledge of the geography of Palestine. In his understanding Jesus now works in Gentile territory.

7:37. The astonishment of the people, as is customary in Mark, does not lead to recognition of Jesus as the Son of God. It is the reader of the gospel who is learning this.

N. SPECIAL GROUP II (8:1-26)

This section of Mark is strangely repititious of the previous section. It is not precisely the same, of course, but it has an overall pattern that is not likely to be due simply to coincidence. This may be a reflection of Mark's sources, which in these incidents differed enough so that Mark simply used both of them. It cannot now be determined whether his sources were oral or written; he probably used both kinds.

There also may be some connection between the sequence of events in Isaiah 29:13-19 and these incidents.

8:1-9. *Feeding the Four Thousand.* This story parallels the earlier feeding of the five thousand (see above on 6:30-44). Despite an overall similarity there are some interesting differences. **Seven loaves** replace the earlier "five, and two fish." There are, correspondingly, **seven baskets** of leftovers instead of the "twelve baskets" of the earlier version. This suggests that Jesus was assisted by seven helpers rather than twelve, in striking harmony with the seven deacons of Acts 6:1-6, appointed "to serve tables."

Again the imagery of the love feast of apostolic times appears, this time more in harmony with the organization reported in Acts. Luke, who has an account of the feeding of the five thousand, does not have the feeding of the four thousand at all.

8:4. The failure of the disciples to respond to Jesus' second proposal for feeding the multitudes is simply another instance of Mark's insistence that they never understood. He has already charged that "they did not understand about the loaves" (6:52), and their response to the second situation simply illustrates this theme again.

8:6-7. The blessing of the fish corresponds to the consecration of the elements in the Lord's Supper. This feature is missing from the earlier version. Note that the "two fish" of the earlier version have here become **a few small fish.**

8:8. It is a theme of both versions that more was left over than they had to begin with. This symbolizes the inexhaustible grace of Christ, who is "the bread of life" (John 6:35; all of John 6 is important for understanding the early Christian meaning of the miraculous feeding story).

8:10. *Crossing the Sea.* The crossing of the sea of Galilee to **Dalmanutha** parallels 6:45-52. This version is much simpler, with the walking on the water eliminated, Matthew's version has Jesus cross to "the region of Magadan" (15:39), probably because Dalmanutha is obscure. Since the place is quite unknown, early copyists have made a variety of alterations. It probably illustrates again Mark's unfamiliarity with Palestinian geography.

8:11-13. *Controversy with Pharisees.* This conflict parallels the earlier one in 7:1-23, and it is also an interesting contrast to 6:46-56. In the earlier series the crossing of the sea included an account of Jesus' walking on the water, which was certainly intended as a **sign** of Jesus' divinity. To this was added the general description of his healing ministry, also intended in Mark to be a sign of his divinity. But here these spectacular signs are replaced by a short section against performing signs. This forms the content of the controversy with the Pharisees in this second series. Two different points of view may be preserved here.

8:12. Jesus' refusal to give a sign to the Pharisees is consistent with his constant effort to keep his real identity secret. Mark is saying, not that Jesus did no signs, but that he did not advertise himself in this way. The reader is informed by these mighty acts. The disciples should have been, but were not.

8:14-21. *The Disciples' Failure to Understand.* This paragraph has, at first glance, little relationship to its parallel story in the first series, which was the healing of the Gentile woman's daughter (7:24-30). The more they are studied, however, the more common themes emerge. Both deal with the gospel message symbolically described **bread.** Both deal with the general theme of the failure of the Jews to respond and the necessity of turning to the Gentiles, though the emphasis is different. The theme here is the failure of the twelve, (representing the Jews in general), to understand. The account is full of cryptic, symbolic phrases, left uninterpreted.

8:15. Matthew in an addition of his own (16:12) explains that **leaven** is symbolic of "teaching." This fits the phrase **the leaven of the Pharisees** nicely, but makes **the leaven of Herod** obscure. Matthew changes "Herod" to "the Sadducees," and some later copyists of Mark change it to the equally difficult "the Herodians." Perhaps leaven represents evil influence.

8:17. It is plain that Jesus is dissatisfied with the twelve, presumably for their failure to understand the symbolism of the bread, or his power to supply "bread."

8:18. The expressions in this verse may be read as questions or exclamations. The general treatment of the twelve in Mark would seem to make the exclamatory version more probable. If so, this verse is a high point in Mark's condemnation of the twelve.

8:19-20. The sufficiency of Jesus is not grasped at all. Almost in despair he recounts the signs of the miraculous feedings. The **twelve** and **seven** baskets have made no impression. Pathetically Jesus asks, **Do you not yet understand?** The reader realizes that they do not. One must rely on the Gentile Christian leaders for a true understanding of Jesus.

8:22-26. *Healing the Blind Man.* This story completes the second series of parallel episodes. Its parallel is the healing of the deaf mute in 7:31-37. In both stories the healing is done privately, the process stresses touching, saliva is used, and secrecy is enjoined. These unusual ties are more than coincidence and show the parallel nature of the stories. Both may be a fulfillment of Isaiah 29:18, since this very section of Isaiah has been quoted in 7:6-7. Neither Matthew nor Luke uses either story.

This story is open to the possible objection that Jesus' first attempt is only partially successful. A second action is required to complete the healing. If the blind man is symbolic of Israel, then the story may be an acknowledgment that the conversion of Israel will be in two stages, first the elect and then all Israel as in Romans 10-11.

The story is symbolically related to the description of Peter which follows immediately. Along with the rest of the twelve he has not demonstrated a real grasp of the significance of Jesus. He is blind, so to speak. His "cure" is described as beginning with the confession at Caesarea Philippi. The transfiguration experience is of further help, but even that represents only a partial cure. The story of Peter's full enlightenment is not recorded in Mark.

III. THE MINISTRY BEYOND GALILEE (8:27–9:29)

8:27-30. *Peter's Confession*. Mark here faces squarely the question of the disciples' view of Jesus. In one sense it is a record of their insight, even though it is belated. Peter, as spokesman for the others, affirms his faith in Jesus as the Messiah.

In another sense, however, it is an indictment of the Christology of the twelve, for it reveals a messianic view (see below on verse 29) that falls far short of Mark's Son of God Christology, which was that of early Gentile Christianity in general. Sensitive to this negative aspect of Mark's account, both Matthew (16:13-23) and Luke (9:18-22) make additions to Peter's confession to make it more harmonious with what came to be the "orthodox" view of Jesus.

8:27. The setting near **Caesarea Philippi** is in Gentile territory (see comments on Matthew 16:13*a*).

8:29. The title **Christ** is the Greek translation of the Hebrew "Messiah." Both words mean "anointed one." The concept of the Messiah in Jewish circles implied, not a divine being, but an appointed human.

8:30. As the demons who recognized Jesus' divinity have always been silenced, so now the twelve are forbidden to reveal his messiahship.

8:31-33. *First Prediction of the Passion*. This is the first of three predictions which Jesus makes to his disciples to prepare them for his death and resurrection. But all three are in vain, for Mark's account portrays the disciples as consistently failing to understand.

The point of the threefold attack on the understanding of the twelve is to establish firmly in the mind of the reader the defectiveness of their grasp of the significance of Jesus. To leave no excuse for them, Mark alone of the gospel writers stresses in this first prediction that Jesus was no longer talking in parables and figures but **said this plainly** (Matthew 16:21-23; Luke 9:22).

8:31. On **the Son of man** see above on 2:10. The memory of Jesus' own predictions would almost certainly be affected by the tradition of what actually did happen. The prediction and the fulfillment, therefore, would necessarily be in full agreement as we now have them.

This first prediction interprets the coming resurrection as the victory of Jesus over death in the phrase **rise again.** Jesus is not the passive instrument of God's action. He will not "be raised" from the dead (as in Matthew 16:21 and Luke 9:22), but he himself will rise. This probably anticipates a theology of the atonement which centers in the victory of Jesus over the final demonic enemy, death.

8:32. The reaction of Peter illustrates his lack of understanding and makes it necessary to view his confession of faith in Jesus as the Messiah as less than a full comprehension. Luke leaves out this rebuke altogether, and Matthew softens it by describing the "rebuke" in such a way that it is no longer a rebuke but a protest.

8:33. Jesus, in turn, gives Peter his most serious personal rebuke, calling him **Satan** and accusing him of being **not on the side of God.** The phrase **get behind me** is a Jewish way of saying "begone."

8:34–9:1. *Standards of Discipleship.* This paragraph is a collection of several short sayings of Jesus, arranged here by Mark to give some standards for true discipleship. Three of them existed also in Q, the other collection of traditions about Jesus used by both Matthew and Luke. They are appropriate here because of Peter's failure to grasp the significance of Jesus' coming crucifixion.

8:34. The **multitude** should be understood as including the reader of the gospel. **Take up his cross** is probably a post-crucifixion phrase among the early Christians, here used to express a basic thought of Jesus. It is possible, however, that it was a proverbial expression in the Roman Empire and was used by Jesus without special reference to his own crucifixion. In a cryptic way it expresses the Christian life as the way of the cross, probably as understood in Gentile Christian preaching. Matthew 16:24 repeats the saying exactly, and Luke 9:23 is almost exact, reading "take up his cross daily." Matthew 10:38 and Luke 14:27 use also a Q version of the saying.

8:35. The phrase **and the gospel's** is omitted in Matthew and Luke, probably because their other source, Q, had the same saying without it (Matthew 10:39; Luke 17:33). This is obviously symbolic of the Christian way of the cross. It has overtones of death and persecution in it, on both the historical and the symbolic levels.

8:36. This question calls for a true sense of values. Cf. Luke 12:15-21.

8:38. This certainly reflects the situation a Christian faced under official Roman persecution. To deny Christ is to be saved in this world but to be lost in the next. This saying too is found in Q (Matthew 10:33; Luke 12:9). Matthew does not use the Markan version, but Luke does (9:26). This picture of the end of the present evil age, ushered in by the triumphal **Son of man . . . in the glory of his Father with the holy angels,** is described in chapter 13 much more fully.

9:1. This note of time is important. The apparent meaning is that Jesus expected the end of the age within the current generation (cf. 13:30). This expectation was a feature of the earliest Christian community also.

The failure of this expectation forced theological interpretation such as is found in John 3:18-19; 11:24-25 in one way and in II Peter 3:3-10 in another. It is remarkable that the Christian community preserved a saying of Jesus that was not fulfilled, but it was probably established before it could be so recognized. The absence of an explanation or reinterpretation by Mark probably means that none was needed yet, that some of Jesus' generation were still alive at the time he was writing (but see below on 13:32-37).

The same conditions seem to prevail in the environment of Matthew, who preserves both the sayings without explanation also (16:28; 24:34). Luke preserves them also (9:27; 21:32), but may have understood their fulfillment with the coming of the Holy Spirit at Pentecost. He therefore leaves out Mark's phrase **come with power,** which would tend to make the traditional view necessary. It is interesting that both Mark (13:32) and Matthew (24:36) have one "loophole" explanation, which Luke does not preserve.

9:2-10. *The Transfiguration.* The Tranfiguration represents a special attempt of God to cure the spiritual blindness of the chief disciples, Peter, James, and John. They see Jesus exalted and transfigured; they hear the voice from heaven informing them what it earlier said to Jesus (1:11). But seeing and hearing is not understanding. They do not perceive, or at best they perceive only dimly.

The attempt of some to see this story as the spiritual illumination of Peter, in vision form, runs counter to a main theme in this gospel. To regard it as a misplaced resurrection account, as others do, adds problems, though this is a possibility. Matthew 17:1-8 and Luke 9:28-36 have the story.

9:2. The phrase **after six days** is repeated in Matthew but changed to "about eight days after" in Luke. It is a strange introduction, found nowhere else in Mark, Matthew, or Luke. A similar one occurs once in John, to introduce a resurrection story (20:26), but that is hardly proof that this too must be a resurrection story. The "six days" is probably patterned after Exodus 24:16, so that the heavenly voice comes on the seventh day (the sabbath).

Peter and James and John are later to be pillars of the Jerusalem church, and here they are symbolic of that church's inability to perceive the true nature of Jesus. The high mountain is patterned after the Exodus passage and is not to be located geographically. It is simply a place of revelation. The word behind **transfigured** is exactly the same as the one used by Paul in II Corinthians 3:18 for "being changed" into his likeness. The true nature of Jesus is being revealed to Peter, James, and John—and to the reader, who alone perceives it.

9:3. The fact that the ancient **fuller** (one who bleached cloth) had a low place in society may have led both Matthew and Luke to change the figure of speech to "light" (Matthew 17:2) or "dazzling" (Luke 9:29). The whiteness is symbolic of heavenly things.

9:4. Mark does not explain the presence of **Elijah** and **Moses** with Jesus. Perhaps they were considered the greatest religious figures in Israel's past.

There is in Judaism a traditional connection between the Messiah and Elijah but not between the Messiah and Moses. Among the Samaritans, however, the Messiah was expected to be a reappearance of Moses, and there may be here a blending of Jewish and Samaritan messianic hopes.

Another, more plausible, possibility is that they represent the two official witnesses to the Messiah, mentioned in Revelation 11:3-6. Here verse 6 identifies them figuratively as Elijah (I Kings 17:1) and Moses (Exodus 7:20). These witnesses are reflected also in Luke 16:29-31, where it must be remembered that Elijah symbolized the prophets.

9:5-6. Peter's response is not supposed to be very intelligible, for Mark comments that **he did not know what to say.** His reaction was one of great fright. Jesus is first called "Rabbi" (**Master**) here.

9:7. The **cloud** is a parallel to the cloud of Exodus 24:15-18, and the **voice** is parallel to the voice there. What the voice says is supplied from Psalm 2:7 and represents the Christology of Mark. This is a repetition of the baptismal scene for the benefit of the disciples.

9:8. The disappearance of Moses and Elijah leaving **Jesus only,** suggests that Jesus replaces them in the new order.

9:9. The meaning of this verse includes an acknowledgment that this vision (the word actually used in Matthew's parallel, 17:9) was unknown until after the Resurrection.

9:10. The disciples, as usual, do not understand what **the rising from the dead** means. Matthew and Luke, in harmony with their consistent defense of the disciples, omit this part of Mark.

9:11-13. *The Elijah Prophecy.* This conversation about Elijah may have grown out of the appearance of Elijah in the transfiguration scene. At any rate Mark felt it to be appropriate here. It is based on Malachi 4:5-6.

9:12. The meaning of **to restore all things** is found in the prophecy in Malachi 4:5-6.

9:13. The claim that **Elijah has come** as John the Baptist answered one of the strong Jewish arguments against the early Christians. Jesus could not have been the Messiah, they argued, because Elijah had not come as forerunner. **As it is written of him** is a standard way of referring to scripture, but no such prediction exists in our Old Testament.

It is significant that the early church was by no means in agreement on this identification of Elijah and John. It is flatly repudiated in John 1:21. Matthew 17:13 makes the identification explicit and adds the reassuring, but anti-Markan, detail that "the disciples understood." Luke omits the whole conversation.

9:14-29. *The Demon-possessed Boy.* The healing of the demon-possessed boy (called an epileptic in Matthew 17:15) seems to be a joining of two originally separate stories. It is easier to follow if these are distinguished.

The first is in verses 14-20 and is a simple exorcism of a dumb spirit. The second, verses 21-27, is a more complex account of the exorcism of a deaf and dumb spirit. Verses 28-29 are a poorly adapted conclusion that does not fit either story very well and is left out by Luke and drastically altered by Matthew (17:19-20). The stories probably got confused in tradition because of their striking similarity.

9:14-20. In this first story the disciples' inability to exorcise the demon is explained as due to the faithlessness of the people. Then Jesus seemingly casts it out in spite of the faithlessness, but the ending is replaced by the introduction of the second story. Note that the crowd is present from the beginning.

9:21-27. In this second story the inability of the disciples is not mentioned. The main concern is the faith of the **father.** The **crowd,** always present in the first story, gathers around Jesus in the middle of this second one.

9:28-29. This returns to the theme of the first story and is believed by some to be the original conclusion of it.

IV. PRIVATE INSTRUCTIONS TO THE DISCIPLES
(9:30-50)

9:30-32. *The Second Prediction of the Passion.* In this second prediction of Jesus' death and resurrection (the first was in 8:31-33) Mark leaves no room for doubt as to his intention. He tells the reader that the disciples **did not understand . . . and they were afraid to ask him.**

Verse 31 lays special emphasis on Jesus' teaching his disciples. This is omitted in the parallel accounts (Matthew 17:22-23; Luke 9:43*b*-45), where of course the disciples are defended. Matthew says "they were greatly distressed", and Luke says they were providentially kept from understanding. These are characteristic alterations.

9:33-37. *The Quarrel over Rank.* In the first of two similar episodes (the second is in 10:35-45) the disciples are caught discussing among themselves which of them **was the greatest.** Cf. Matthew 18:1-5 and Luke 9:46-48.

9:33. This is the last mention of **Capernaum** in Mark. **In the house** is Greek idiom for "at home" (see above on 2:1).

9:34. The disciples **were silent** because they were ashamed of their discussion. This unflattering view of the disciples is well drilled into the reader of Mark. Luke 9:46 preserves Mark's account, but Matthew 18:1 alters it drastically in the interest of the disciples.

9:36-37. Mark adds an episode about receiving a child in Jesus' name that does not seem to fit the dispute about rank. Luke has a similar account (9:47-48). Matthew greatly strengthens the episode by inserting two other separate units, (Matthew 18:3 and 18:4) within Mark's.

9:38-41. *The Independent Disciple.* This paragraph consists of a short dialogue between Jesus and John, with two originally separate sayings (verses 40 and 41). The original setting has been affected by the circumstances of the early Christian community. The use of Jesus' name as a formula for casting out demons began after the Resurrection and is here read back into the earlier period.

The problem faced here is the legitimacy of Christian workers who are not in fellowship with the twelve—that is, the leaders of the Gentile Christian church in general. What about those (like Paul) who worked independently? The answer is that they are acceptable to Jesus. It is a dialogue story which Matthew, quite naturally, prefers not to use, and which Luke abridges (9:49-50). Cf. the reverse of verse 40 in Matthew 12:30 and Luke 11:23.

9:41. This saying really has no relationship to the preceding verses. It seems to commend any favorable treatment accorded to Christians in an era of persecution. Cf. Matthew 10:42.

9:42-48. *Sayings on Temptation.* The meanings of the sayings collected here are often obscure. Verse 42 deals with tempting others, verses 43-48 with the problem of one's own temptations.

9:42. The central problem here is the original meaning of **little ones.** The context at first suggests children. Since they are further described as ones **who believe in me,** they seem to be Christian children. But since Jesus sometimes referred to his disciples as children, it seems at least possible that the original reference was to his followers of any age. Cf. Matthew 18:6 and Luke 17:1-2.

9:43-47. Three parallel figures—**hand, foot,** and **eye**—represent the common agents of temptation. They should not be taken literally, of course, because one eye is hardly more to be blamed than the other for visual temptations, nor one foot more than the other for straying from the path.

Behind the word **hell** is the Greek "Gehenna," a transliteration of the Hebrew name of the Hinnom Valley southwest of Jerusalem. At one time this place was used for infant sacrifices to the Ammonite god Molech and later, in contempt, was used as the garbage dump for Jerusalem. Before Christian times the name became symbolic for hell. This is not the same word or concept as the Hebrew "Sheol" or the Greek "Hades."

9:48. This clause is taken from Isaiah 66:24. It is not found in Matthew's version (18:7-9). Most later manuscripts of Mark have added it as verses 44 and 46 also (hence the King James Version), but the early manuscripts have it only at the end (as in the Revised Standard Version). It symbolizes the finality of God's judgment.

9:49-50. *Sayings on Salt.* Three sayings on salt are here grouped together editorially. They are unrelated to each other in meaning.

9:49. This saying is not found in any other gospel. Some manuscripts add "and every sacrifice will be salted with salt." It apparently teaches the acceptance of suffering as a normal experience.

9:50a. Matthew 5:13 and Luke 14:34-35 have a more elaborate version of this saying. Luke recognizes its symbolic difficulty by adding the formula "He who has ears to hear, let him hear." Matthew introduces it with "You are the salt of the earth," making the saying easier to interpret. The original intent is elusive.

9:50b. This is another cryptic saying, found in Mark only, that depends for its meaning on the interpreter. The exhortation to **be at peace with one another** is refreshingly plain and clear.

V. THE JOURNEY TO JERUSALEM (10:1-52)

10:1-12. *On Marriage and Divorce.* This account represents a Gentile Christian adaptation of Jesus' original teaching. The situation presupposed in verses 11-12 is not that of a Palestinian Jewish community (the environment of Jesus) but that of the Greco-Roman world (the environment of the Gentile Christian church). In Jesus' environment adultery was not a crime against the wife but against the other wife's husband. Matthew 19:9 more accurately represents Jesus by omitting the phrase **against her.** Moreover, the wife did not have the opportunity to divorce her husband in Jesus' environment but she did in the customs of the empire. Matthew therefore omits this verse entirely. Luke omits the whole account.

10:1. This verse introduces the journey of Jesus from Galilee to Jerusalem. The geographical route is only vaguely suggested—from there (i.e. Capernaum, 9:33) to **Judea.** It seems intended that the reader understand Jesus as avoiding Samaria by coming down the east side of the **Jordan.** Neither Samaria nor the Samaritans are ever mentioned in Mark. **As his custom was, he taught them.** Matthew's parallel (19:2) stresses healing instead of teaching, and this curiously reverses the main emphasis of both gospels.

10:2-9. The discussion on marriage is related to a widely disputed point in Jesus' time. Followers of the Rabbi Hillel taught and practiced a very lenient interpretation of Deuteronomy 24:1, permitting men to divorce their wives for minor matters. Followers of Rabbi Shammai were much stricter in their interpretation, allowing divorce only on grounds of adultery.

Matthew's version of Jesus' final saying (19:9) adapts it to the views of the stricter party. Mark, however, perhaps not so intimately acquainted with the Jewish discussion, presents a view that is stricter than Shammai's. This view is found also in an earlier Christian writing (I Corinthians 7:10-11).

It is noteworthy that Mark's account here does not proceed in rabbinic fashion, with its citation of scripture against scripture. Rather it is a matter of scripture against the unwritten will of God, after the fashion of Paul, who got his central insights by revelation.

10:4-5. The law of Moses is presented as a concession made necessary by the **hardness of heart** of the people. Actually Deuteronomy 24:1 was a provision of mercy and justice that, in its own time, helped women by requiring divorce rather than mere abandonment. But Jesus probably saw it as an excuse for irresponsible behavior and so adopted a stricter view.

10:6-8. The symbolic meaning apparently intended here is understood as making marriage permanent. The textual basis is Genesis 1:27 and 2:24. The interpretation in verse 8*b* is based on a type of thinking reflected in more detail in I Corinthians 6:15-16.

In this popular ancient view it is not love or the marriage ritual that permanently unites, but the sexual act. This is perpetuated in later, more sophisticated versions of this thinking, such as the Roman Catholic teaching that a valid marriage must include consummation in the sexual act.

This particular explanation may not go back to Jesus himself, since its native environment is non-Palestinian. It reflects a concern with being, or nature, that is non-Semitic and characteristically Greek. Moreover, it implies the monogamous customs of the Gentile world rather than the polygamous customs of the Semitic world. Judaism did not officially abolish polygamy until a thousand years after Jesus.

10:9. The uniting of the two into one is regarded as an act of God, a uniting so mysterious that is cannot be explained in natural terms. The question for us is, How does God unite two people with a genuine unity? The answer is not clear; the sex act is too simple a solution.

10:10-12. That the disciples need a private explanation is characteristic of Mark and naturally omitted in Matthew's parallel.

10:13-16. *Jesus and Children.* The disciples fail here to understand the relation of children to the kingdom. Jesus' indignation at the disciples is omitted in Matthew 19:13-15 and Luke 18:15-17. The brief setting serves only to put the disciples in a poor light and to introduce a very popular saying of Jesus. This saying, like so many of Jesus' sayings, is not clear. Children have all kinds of qualities, some desirable and others not. The interpreter reads in what he feels to be appropriate. The most probable clue, from verse 15, suggests that the kingdom is a gift, not an achievement, like the Gentile Christian doctrine of salvation by grace.

10:17-22. *The Rich Man's Question.* The story of the rich man gives us a fine example of the basic traits of Mark and deserves careful study. There are three other versions of the story, one of which (Luke 18:18-23) follows Mark's very closely, except that the man becomes "a ruler." The changes in Matthew's version (19:16-22) illustrate well the differences between Mark and Matthew. It requires combining versions to get the popular title "The Rich [all] Young [Matthew only] Ruler [Luke only]."

The fourth version is found in the noncanonical Gospel According to the Hebrews, which exists only in fragmentary quotations. In certain respects it has obvious values that lead some to pronounce that it is the best version. This fourth version follows as translated from *Gospel Parallels* (Thomas Nelson & Sons, 1949):

The second of the rich men said to him, "Teacher, what good thing can I do and live?" He said to him, "Sir, fulfill the law and the prophets." He answered, "I have." Jesus said, "Go, sell all you have and distribute to the poor; and come, follow me." But the rich man began to scratch his head, for it did not please him. And the Lord said to him, "How can you say, I have fulfilled the law and the prophets, when it is written in the law: You shall love your neighbor as your self; and lo, many of your brothers, sons of Abraham, are clothed in filth, dying of hunger, and your house is full of many good things, none of which goes out to them?" And he turned and said to Simon, his disciple, who was sitting by him, "Simon, son of Jonah, it is easier for a camel to go through the eye of a needle than for a rich man to enter the kingdom of heaven."

10:17-18. The salutation **good Teacher** is rejected by Jesus, who affirms that goodness belongs to **God alone.** In the sense of absolute goodness, in all its perfection, this would represent the traditional Jewish view. But against the background of Mark's theology and the Gentile Christian community this probably reflects helplessness in the power of sin, as expressed in Romans 7:18.

This does not mean that Mark is portraying Jesus as having a sense of his own sinfulness. Mark is simply using this story to reveal the true answer to the question of salvation. This true answer does not lie in obedience. Even if one could be wholly obedient, one would still lack the essential requirement of salvation, which is complete renunciation of all worldly dependencies and acceptance of salvation as God's gift in trust and faith. From a different theological perspective Matthew changes this opening question and answer, but his version is incompletely changed and clearly a secondary account.

10:19. In Mark's free summary of the Ten Commandments, **do not defraud** is not directly related, and so it is omitted in Matthew 19:18-19 and Luke 18:20. **From my youth** suggests that he is no longer a youth and is therefore omitted in Matthew 19:20, which describes the man as "young."

10:21. The note that Jesus **loved him** is in Mark only. His **lack** should not be understood as his special problem, because in Mark's theology obedience is not the way to salvation. Note that in Matthew's version obedience is the clue to salvation, and the renunciation which is required in Mark is turned into a counsel of perfection, something beyond the actual requirements.

10:23-31. *On Riches and Discipleship.* These sayings appropriately follow the story of the rich man. Matthew and Luke follow Mark's plan here, and Luke actually takes the words of Jesus to his disciples and addresses them to the rich ruler (Luke 18:24).

10:25. This verse repeats in highly exaggerated form the teaching of verse 23. The explanation that there was a Needle's Eye Gate into Jerusalem that a camel could enter only on its knees is a medieval sermon unfounded in fact. The plain meaning is that it is impossible for the rich to enter the kingdom. This is confirmed in verses 26-27.

10:27. The most striking idea in this story is the Gentile Christian conception of salvation as entirely the work of God, his rescue of helpless humanity.

10:28-31. This dialogue between Jesus and Peter is related to verses 17-22 and 23-27 but seems to be a unit in itself. Peter claims, for all the disciples, that they have done what the rich man refused to do, **left everything and followed** Jesus. Jesus replies, in general terms, that renunciation of things in this

151

world will bring everything in return, in both this life and the next.

10:29. The phrase **for the gospel** reflects the situation of the early church and is deleted from the parallel versions (Matthew 19:29 and Luke 18:29).

10:31. This saying is not part of the preceding dialogue, but has been added by Mark, probably to detract from the prestige of the twelve. Luke removes it to an earlier section (13:30). It says that human values are not necessarily God's and, in particular, that the twelve may not be entitled to any special priority finally.

10:32-34. *The Third Prediction of the Passion.* This third prediction, made again privately and personally to the twelve, follows the pattern of the first two (8:31-33; 9:30-32). There is no hint that the disciples now understand, and Luke clearly recognizes this (18:34).

10:32. It may be that we have here a brief glimpse of Jesus moving at the head of a single file of disciples, which would customarily be arranged strictly according to seniority. This was a formalized procedure in first-century Palestine. The amazement and fear of the disciples is a Markan feature omitted from Matthew 20:17 and Luke 18:31.

10:34. On **he will rise** see above on 8:31.

10:35-45. *The Ambition of James and John.* Here James and John are represented as selfishly seeking the chief seats in heaven. This gives Jesus occasion to teach the disciples humility. Since it casts a poor light on the disciples, especially James and John, Luke omits the James-John part entirely. Matthew imperfectly alters the beginning of the story to shift the stigma of selfishness to their mother, transforming it into motherly ambition (Matthew 20:20-28).

10:38. The phrase **drink the cup** is idiomatic for martyrdom. **Baptism** as symbolic for death is found also in Luke 12:50 and Romans 6:3-4.

10:39. This seems to reflect clearly the martyrdoms of James and John. That of James is reported in Acts 12:1-2. The death of John is less certain, with conflicts in tradition. This prediction is itself the best evidence, for had it not been fulfilled it probably would not have been preserved.

10:41. The indignation of **the ten** at James and John makes it difficult to interpret their request in any way that would absolve them from criticism.

10:42-45. The meaning of discipleship is not privilege but service, and Jesus exemplifies this service. His highest service is finally that he gives **his life as a ransom for many.** The ransom phrase is contrary to the thinking of Matthew and Luke. It is omitted in Luke 22:27 in favor of service as good deeds. Matthew 20:28 may be simply a carryover from Mark.

The idea of Jesus' death as a ransom is undeveloped in Mark, but it is certainly related to I Corinthians 6:19-20; 7:23 and Galatians 1:4; 2:20. It is one way that Gentile Christianity expressed its conviction that Christ is God's action to rescue persons helpless in the power of sin. This conviction may be a development of Jesus' own attitude, especially if his own view was shaped by Isaiah 53.

10:46-52. *Healing Bartimaeus.* The healing of Bartimaeus reads like other healings in Mark but introduces the title **Son of David** for Jesus. This title emphasizes the descent of the Messiah from David. Paul acknowledges this in Romans 1:3 but never refers to it elsewhere. The main Gentile Christian view of Jesus as the divine Son of God found the Son of David title more confusing than helpful. It was tolerated only if properly understood. It was eventually easier to describe Christ in other ways, and this even led some to deny his descent from David. Mark's feeling is expressed in 12:35-37, in harmony with John 7:40-43.

10:46. In Aramaic **Bartimaeus** means **the son of Timaeus.** The name is omitted in Matthew 20:29-34 and Luke 18:35-43. Matthew tells the story as a healing of "two blind men."

10:47. On **Jesus of Nazareth** see above on 1:24.

10:52. The healing is by word—as in Luke also. In Matthew Jesus touches "their eyes" and omits Mark's explanation **your faith has made you well.** The words **followed him** imply discipleship, but Bartimaeus is otherwise unknown.

VI. THE MINISTRY IN JERUSALEM (11:1–13:37)

A. THE ENTRY INTO JERUSALEM (11:1-10)

The account of the entry into Jerusalem is a traditional story of the popularity of Jesus. Here it has been theologically adapted to an announcement of Jesus as the Messiah after the manner of the prophecy in Zechariah 9:9. The Fourth Gospel reports that the disciples were not aware of any messianic significance to the entry at the time, but later, reflecting on it, they saw its true significance (John 12:16). Mark's account has been shaped by this later understanding, as is illustrated by the unusual use of **the Lord.**

11:2-3. Mark's intent is probably to illustrate to the reader Jesus' supernatural knowledge. It is possible, however, that Jesus is deliberately fulfilling the prophecy of Zechariah 9:9 and has planned his entry carefully. At this point Matthew 21:4-5 makes explicit the connection between this event and the prophecy of Zechariah. **A colt . . . on which no one has ever sat** is based on the Greek translation of the prophecy, which reads "a new [i.e. unbroken] ass."

B. RADICAL ACTIONS (11:12-25)

11:12-14. *Cursing the Fig Tree.* This story is difficult to understand. As we have it in Mark, the tree is in leaf, but **it was not the season for figs.** Seeking fruit on it nevertheless, and finding none, Jesus lays a curse on it to prevent it from ever bearing fruit again. Then they all go on into Jerusalem, where Jesus drives out the money-changers.

The barren fig tree is probably symbolic of Israel and the coming destruction of Jerusalem. Mark records the episode as an example of the power of Jesus. It is probably a version of an original symbolic teaching, now preserved in Luke 13:6-9. It is significant that Mark and Matthew have this incident but no parable; Luke has a parable but not the incident. Tradition has apparently made the parable into an actual happening. See further below on verses 20-25.

11:15-19. *The Temple Cleansing.* This incident is reported in all the gospels, but at different points in Jesus' life. Matthew, Mark, and Luke put it at the beginning of the last week (Matthew on the first day, Mark on the second, and Luke on an unspecified day). John, however, places it during a Passover two years earlier (2:13-22).

11:15. The persons **who sold** were merchants, profiteering on the pilgrims. The **money-changers** were bankers, exchanging various foreign currencies for money which could be used in the temple. These changers charged a commission, of course. **Those who sold pigeons** (or doves) were selling sacrificial offerings to the pilgrims. The priestly families seem to have had control of this business.

11:16. This prohibition is peculiar to Mark's account, and probably reflects the influence of Jeremiah 17:27. The original prohibition applied only to carrying things on the sabbath, but this was extended eventually to the temple area for all days.

11:17. The scripture quotation is a combination of Isaiah 56:7 and Jeremiah 7:11. Matthew (25:13) and Luke (19:46), out of closer sympathy with a more conservative Jewish Christianity, omit the phrase **for all the nations.**

11:20-25. *The Withered Fig Tree.* The effect of the cursing is discovered the next morning. Naturalistic explanations are beside the point if the incident is simply a variant of the parable of Luke 13:6-9. But since Mark presents it as an incident, further displaying the power of Jesus, he finds some teachings on the power of faith entirely appropriate here. That this was Mark's editorial decision is shown by the appearance of some of these sayings in other settings in Matthew 6:14; 17:20 and Luke 17:6.

11:22-24. It distorts the intention of these verses to take them to mean that a man of faith and prayer can be a powerful magician. God acts through us in accord with his will and not ours. A more carefully phrased expression of the power of faith and prayer is found in I John 5:14.

11:25. This valuable saying on prayer has been placed here by

Mark. Matthew has it much earlier in his gospel (6:14) in an abbreviated form.

C. JESUS IN CONTROVERSY (11:27–12:44)

11:27-33. *The Question About Authority.* The first event of the third day of this last week is a question from the authorities. Since it has already been reported that they are plotting to destroy him (verse 18), it is safer to assume that these questioners are not genuine students but clever hunters. They are seeking to discredit him so that he can be destroyed without reaction from the people. This first question is about Jesus' credentials. His answer is not an answer at all but an evasion. This pattern of evading insincere questions is carried out in the next two questions also.

11:27. The mention that **they came again** is the basis for assuming this to be the third day. That Jesus **was walking in the temple** after having purged it of its mercenaries only the day before shows the strength of his popularity at this time.

11:29. Jesus "answers" their question with one of his own, about John's baptism. This was the occasion of the divine commissioning of Jesus, which was the source of his authority.

11:31-33. Because they cannot answer the question without discrediting themselves, they simply reply, **We do not know.** So Jesus refuses to answer their question. It is a bit too sophisticated here to think that Jesus refused because they would not have understood his answer. He simply dealt cleverly with an insincere question.

12:1-12. *The Parable of the Wicked Tenants.* This parable is so appropriate that both Matthew (21:33-46 and Luke 20:9-19) have left it in this place. It is not really a parable but an allegory on the rejection of the Jews by God, reflecting a later Christian setting. Its theme is "the true Israel."

The rejection of Jesus by the Jews has caused God to **give the vineyard to others,** the Gentiles. This is a major plank in the platform of early Gentile Christianity. The allegory is similar to

Isaiah 5:1-7. The **man** represents God. The **vineyard** is
Palestine. **Let it out to tenants** refers to God's giving of Canaan
(Palestine) to Israel. **To get from them some of the fruit**
symbolizes the obedience God expects. The **servant** and the
others to follow are the prophets, seen by him to exhort
obedience. The **beloved son** is of course Jesus himself.

Verse 8 is symbolic of the crucifixion and rejection of Jesus by
the Jews. Verse 9 is symbolic of the fall of Jerusalem and the rise
of early Gentile Christianity, claiming to be the true Israel. The
Old Testament "prophecy" to support this was found in the very
popular Psalm 118:22-23.

12:13-17. *The Question about Taxes.* The second question **to
entrap him** raised an explosive political issue. What about the
offensive taxes that Rome collected, should they be paid? If
Jesus replied "no," he would be even more popular, but subject
to immediate arrest and execution. If he replied "yes," he would
be in danger of losing his popularity with the people. Jesus,
knowing their hypocrisy, gave an ambiguous answer and let
them interpret it as they wished. **And they were amazed at him.**

12:18-27. *The Question about the Resurrection.* The third
question revolves around a disputed religious question. The
Sadducees did not believe in a resurrection. In ridiculing it they
intended to ridicule Jesus, who shared with the Pharisees a
belief in the resurrection. After one woman has been the **wife** of
seven brothers successively, whose wife will she be in the
resurrection? Jesus' reply is again enigmatic. In effect he says
that the question is inappropriate to life in the resurrection, for
then we will be **like angels.** But how are the angels?

12:19. See Deuteronomy 25:5-6.

12:25. The implication of **they neither marry nor are given in
marriage** is that life in the resurrection will not have these
physical necessities. Angels do not cohabit, for they are
immortal beings. Conception and birth belong only in the age of
mortality. See I Corinthians 15:35-57 for the best commentary
on Jesus' answer.

12:26-27. This argument for the resurrection turns on the
present tense of the verb as God spoke to Moses, saying, **I am**

[not "I was"] **the God of Abraham**]who has long been dead].
Hence Abraham, and the others, must not be dead from God's
perspective. God is a **God . . . of the living,** not the **dead.** But
since it is obvious that Abraham did die, then he must be alive in
some sense other than the ordinary one. He is alive in the
resurrection plans of God; hence the Sadducees **are quite
wrong.**

12:28-34. *The Question about the Greatest Law.* After the
three insincere questions there comes one that seems sincere.
The basic function of this paragraph is to present clearly a central
doctrine of early Gentile Christianity. Righteousness is not to be
understood as strict obedience to a complex code of laws and
customs. The one commandment that is central is the principal
of **love.**

12:29-30. The quotation of Deuteronomy 6:4-5 would be
satisfactory to all Jews. These are the most treasured verses of
Judaism.

12:31. The second quotation, from Leviticus 19:18*b*, uniquely
expressed Christian concern and could hardly be offensive to
anyone. The concluding statement in Mark, that **there is no
other commandment greater than these,** is the affirmation of
early Gentile Christianity. Both Matthew and Luke omit this
affirmation. Matthew 22:40 changes it to make all the other laws
grow out of these two. Luke has rewritten the whole episode
(10:25-28), having the scribe say what Jesus says in Mark.

12:35-37*a*. *The Davidic Ancestry of the Messiah.* This difficult
section seems to be an argument against thinking of the Messiah
(Christ) as a descendant of David. The Messiah was David's
Lord rather than his son, the argument from Psalm 110:1 seems
to say. It would be natural to think that this argument must have
arisen in early Gentile Christianity, which wanted a Lord and
Savior more than a Jewish Messiah, or Son of David.

12:37*b*-40. *Denouncing the Scribes.* This denunciation of
hypocrisy and formalism is greatly expanded in Matthew
23:1-36.

12:41-44. *The Widow's Gift.* Within the temple enclosure,
but outside the building proper, there were 13 offering boxes.

Apparently Jesus sat for a while watching people come up to these boxes and leave their offerings. The **copper coins** are literally "leptons," the smallest denomination of the Greek-Syrian system. Mark explains for his readers that the **two** leptons equal the smallest Roman coin, the "quadrans" (**penny**). Perhaps originally the story was told with only one lepton.

D. THE LAST DAYS (13:1-37)

13:1-4. *The Setting.* This dialogue provides the setting for the longest "speech" of Jesus in Mark. The destruction of the temple is associated with the end of this age and the coming of the kingdom of God. The destruction of the temple actually occurred in A.D. 70 at the hands of the Romans, but without the end of the age.

13:3. The secrets of the end of the age were given, according to Mark, only to the four senior disciples. Neither Matthew (24:3) nor Luke (21:5-7) follows Mark in this. By restricting the revelation to these four Mark indicates that this teaching was not originally a feature of the public teachings of Jesus, nor even of his special instructions to the twelve, but rather something shared only with a very few.

13:5-37. *The Apocalyptic Prophecies.* This complex discourse (the only one in Mark) is often called "The Little Apocalypse" (see comment on Matthew 24:4). In form and content it resembles Daniel 7–12 and the book of Revelation. Technical study of it reveals that it is composite. It is made up of some genuine sayings of Jesus that were expanded and adapted to current community needs in written form before being incorporated into Mark.

This discourse was probably the result of a special interest group, just as today there are groups who find special satisfaction in Daniel and Revelation. Matthew 24-25 and Luke 21 have parallel accounts.

13:5-6. These verses parallel verses 21-23 and may represent two versions of a traditional warning. Cf. I John 2:18.

13:7-8. The expectation of strife and natural disasters at the end is a pattern in apocalyptic thinking. This theme is carried on in verses 24-25. In this understanding salvation comes in the darkest moment. Things get progressively worse until, all at once, they are over. This is fully developed in Revelation. The **birth-pangs** refer to the birth of the new age.

13:9-13. This too is standard theme material. It reflects the problems of persecution and seems to be influenced by the circumstances of Roman persecution of the Christians, but of this we cannot be sure. All apocalyptic literature is "persecution literature," exhorting the faithful to hold on to the end.

13:14-20. The **desolating sacrilege** is apocalyptic code for something. Matthew took it to be the same as referred to in Daniel 9:27 and 12:11, but it is now thought that Daniel refers to an event of 167 B.C. That the term has a hidden meaning is indicated by the parenthetical note **let the reader understand**—quite out of place in a speech.

If it was intended to refer to the desecration of the temple in the war of A.D. 66-70, then that would tell us that Mark was written after that event. Luke 21:20 substitutes for this "sacrilege" a siege of Jerusalem, probably because that is what actually took place.

13:20. The doctrine reflected in **the elect, whom he chose,** although related to the chosen-people idea in the Old Testament, is a distinctively Gentile Christian concept. It is a necessary part of a theological system which understands salvation as God's act to rescue helpless humanity.

13:21-23. See above on verses 5-6.

13:24-25. These wonders are common themes in apocalyptic literature. The view of the universe reflected here is of course prescientific.

13:26-27. The **coming** of the **Son of man** in this fashion was the popular early Christian expectation. It can be seen also in Acts 1:9-11 and I Thessalonians 4:17.

13:28-29. Cf. 4:26-29; James 5:7-8.

13:30-31. These are two originally separate sayings. The phrasing of the second (verse 31) may be influenced by Isaiah

51:6. In it Jesus' words are presented as eternal, a position which they share in Matthew and Luke with "the law and the prophets" (Matthew 5:17; Luke 16:17). Here we can see again the more radical nature of Markan Christianity and the more conservative bent of Matthew and Luke.

13:32-37. The lesson in all this is that, since no one knows the exact schedule for the end of this age and the coming of the kingdom, everyone should be ready at all times. The fact that variations of these watchfulness sayings are found elsewhere in Luke (12:38, 40; 19:12-13) and in Matthew (24:42; 25:13, 14-15), shows clearly that they are editorially arranged here.

13:32. This saying is particularly significant, for it preserves an early admission that Jesus (as the Son) did not have perfect knowledge of all things. Since this seems to conflict with the later beliefs about Jesus, it was a common tendency of the copyists to omit the phrase **nor the Son.** This saying may be connected with later efforts to explain why Jesus' prediction of the end did not in fact happen (see above on 9:1). This explanation would admit candidly that he did not actually know the schedule, for that was reserved for **only the Father.** Note that Luke has reworded the explanation and assigned it to the resurrection period rather than the earthly ministry (Acts 1:6-7).

It is a mistake to regard Mark as intending to emphasize the inferiority of Jesus to the Father; the intention is just the opposite. The Son is not classified among human beings, nor even among angelic beings, but he is superior to both.

VII. The Passion Story (14:1–15:47)

A. Events preparatory to the Crucifixion (14:1-42)

14:1-2. *The Conspiracy.* The emphasis is on urgency and secrecy. This is the best explanation for the actual trial and crucifixion schedule as reported in all the gospels. Jesus was to be disposed of before the Passover; hence there was a hasty trial and execution. Note that Mark's comment on the date (**two days before the Passover**) is reported in Matthew as a saying of Jesus (26:2). Luke simply says that the feast was drawing near (22:1).

14:3-9. *The Anointing of Jesus.* The story of the anointing at Bethany appears, with interesting variants, in all four gospels (Matthew 26:6-13; Luke 7:36-50; John 12:1-8). The purpose in Mark (closely followed in Matthew) is expressed in verse 8—to anoint the **body** of Jesus **beforehand for burying.** The story of the women going to the tomb early in the morning after the sabbath (16:1) expresses the same basic concern.

In the first three gospels the body of Jesus is not properly anointed. This deficiency is met by this account of the Bethany anointing (in some circles) and by the intentions of the women (in other circles). Mark preserves both traditions. Luke, however, uses the story quite differently. John seems to have an independent version that retains Mark's basic purpose, but also reports an official anointing (John 19:39-40).

14:3. Simon the leper becomes in Luke a "Pharisee" named Simon, and in John the incident is reported as happening in the house of Lazarus. The **woman** is not identified in Mark or Matthew. In Luke she is a forgiven sinner, and in John she is Mary, the sister of Lazarus. In Mark and Matthew it is Jesus' **head that is anointed, whereas in Luke and John it is his** "feet."

14:5. The value of the ointment is specified in both Mark and John as **three hundred denarii.** Based on the wages indicated in Matthew 20:2, this sum would approach a laborer's total annual income.

14:7. The meaning is simply that the time for doing something for Jesus was running out. There is no reason to think that Jesus believed poverty to be inevitable. This verse is not a social analysis but simply a statement of present opportunity. Cf. Matthew 26:11; John 12:8.

14:8-9. These verses probably represent the reflection of the community as it pondered the significance of the original event. It is possible that the anointing originally represented a messianic anointing ceremony (cf. I Samuel 9:15-16; 10:1), replaced in Mark's story by the spiritual anointing at the time of the baptism. The anointing-for-burial interpretation has become the official one, however.

14:10-11. *The Defection of Judas.* Judas' betrayal is not completely explained in the gospels. Matthew 26:14-15 and John 12:6 assume a motive of financial greed. John 13:2 and Luke 22:3 seem to make Judas the agent of Satan. But Mark simply reports Judas' betrayal.

Probably Judas failed to understand Jesus and acted in disillusionment. It is possible that he betrayed him in order to force him to reveal his messianic powers and to usher in the kingdom. Mark never reports any repentance from Judas, nor does he tell what happened to him after the Crucifixion.

14:12-16. *Preparation for Passover.* Mark's description of the Last Supper as the Passover meal has been a point of controversy ever since the second century. John states clearly that everything took place before the Passover began (13:1, 29; 18:28; 19:14, 31). In John the Crucifixion occurs at the time of the sacrificing of the paschal lamb, which was on the day before the Passover.

Several things combine to make John's dating preferable to Mark's:

(1) Mark's account itself contains traces of John's view in the expressed plans of the Jewish leaders (see above on verses 1-2; also on 15:46).

(2) A Jewish hearing or trial on the first day of Passover is not very likely.

(3) The earliest Christian literature, the letters of Paul, favors John's view. In Corinthians 5:7-8 the Crucifixion is the Christian Passover sacrifice; in I Corinthians 15:20 the Resurrection corresponds to the "first fruits" of the passover feast. Mark's dating would make both events come a day late for these associations. Matthew and Luke depend on Mark's version and therefore agree with it.

Various efforts have been made to harmonize the two traditions, but Mark states too clearly that the Last Supper was the Passover meal and John just as clearly maintains that the Crucifixion was prior to the beginning of the feast (19:14).

14:12. Mark's Gentile Christian background causes him to be technically inaccurate here. The **passover lamb** was not **sacrificed . . . on the first day of Unleavened Bread** but on the day before. Matthew 26:17 and Luke 22:7 correct this, in different ways. Probably Mark reckoned the days in Gentile fashion, as we do now, from midnight to midnight. The Jewish reckoning is from sunset to sunset. To a Gentile the afternoon sacrifice and the evening meal would all be on the same day. To a Jew, however, the afternoon sacrifice is on the day before.

14:13-16. This unusual account is strikingly similar to 11:1-6. Both accounts seem to have the same significance. They can be regarded as the working out of providential plans, known to Jesus, or they can be regarded as Jesus' own prearrangements.

14:17-21. *Prediction of Betrayal.* In all four gospels Jesus predicts his betrayal. Matthew (26:25) and John (13:26) are more specific than Mark or Luke (22:21-23).

The Christian tradition owes something to Psalm 41:9. Mark's general lack of sympathy with the twelve makes it easy for him to report, matter-of-factly, how one of them betrays him. Matthew involves Judas in remorse, repentance, and suicide. Luke ascribes the betrayal to Satan's influence. Thus both the later evangelists defend the reputation of the twelve.

14:21. The New Testament assumes in many places that the crucifixion of Jesus is according to Old Testament prophecies. If the suffering servant poems of Isaiah 42-53 are regarded as messianic prophecies, then the New Testament assumption is understandable. Since it is known that the early church did associate Jesus with the suffering servant, this is the best explanation for this verse.

14:22-25. *The Last Supper.* Mark reports as the main event of the Last Supper the institution of the Lord's Supper. This is supported by the earlier account in I Corinthians 11:23-25 and may be considered as the "orthodox" version among Gentile Christians of his own day. Paul's account seems to reflect a memorial service. There is little or nothing in the gospel accounts of the supper to justify repeating it ritually. Only in John 6:52-58 is full sacramental significance attached to a very indirect discussion of the custom. In the first three gospels the supper has eschatological significance; it will be repeated only after the kingdom comes.

14:22. The blessing that accompanied the breaking of bread was traditional in Judaism. **This is my body** probably became a ritual phrase before the writing of the gospels. It lends itself well to a variety of interpretations, ranging from the "real presence" interpretation of Roman Catholicism to purely symbolic views like that of the Quakers.

14:24. This expresses well the idea of Jesus' death as a ransom (see above on 10:45), inaugurating a new covenant (cf. Exodus 24:8). The thought of drinking blood was repugnant to Jews and is strictly forbidden in their code of food laws. It is difficult even to imagine an analogy like this arising out of Jewish piety. Luke omits all reference to the wine as blood. Paul claims that his account was received "from the Lord" (I Corinthians 11:23). That probably indicates that the present account arose in Gentile Christianity and is here presented as having occurred earlier.

14:25. The natural meaning here is that the coming of **the kingdom** is expected to take place shortly after the death of Jesus. Matthew's phrasing (26:29, adding "with you") makes this meaning more explicit.

14:26-31. *Predictions of Jesus.* This section contains Jesus' prediction of the desertion of his followers, especially Peter, and of his resurrection appearance to the disciples in **Galilee.** The desertion is understood as a fulfillment of Zechariah 13:7. The resurrection prediction seems to intrude into the desertion discussion. Perhaps its meaning is that after **the sheep** have been **scattered** (by desertion) the risen Lord himself will gather them together again.

Luke omits this prediction on two grounds.

(1) It conflicts with his report that the resurrection appearances were in the Jerusalem area.

(2) In Luke the role of restoring the scattered community is assigned to Peter (22:32).

14:26. The singing of **a hymn** after the supper is most naturally understood as the Hallel (Psalms 113-118 sung in praise to God) of the Passover meal.

14:29-31. Peter's vehement denial of his forthcoming desertion only serves to make it worse when it does happen.

14:32-42. *Jesus in Gethsemane.* This story marks another high point in Mark's denunciation of the twelve. In the hour of Jesus' greatest spiritual anguish they all fall **asleep**, oblivious of the real nature of his struggle. The three leaders are chosen for special companionship at this crucial hour, but they also fall asleep. To drive the point home, it happens three times. Matthew (26:36-46), very surprisingly, makes no effort to soften this picture, but Luke (22:40-46) characteristically explains that they were sleeping "for sorrow" and omits the second and third occurrences.

The historical problem is acute here. If Jesus was accompanied only by sleeping companions, how did anyone later on learn of what went on? The traditional explanation, that Mark himself was the young man of verse 51 and therefore witnessed the whole scene from his hiding place, is mostly an ingenious effort to preserve the literal historicity of the story. This explanation borders on the fancies of the historical novel. See below on verses 51-52.

The Gethsemane story is demonstration in life of the prayer which Jesus taught his disciples, "Thy will be done, on earth as it is in heaven" (Matthew 6:10). Both versions—the teaching and the demonstration—became very popular. Matthew has both, but John has neither, because in it Jesus always does the will of God without struggle. The agony described in the Gethsemane scene of the first three gospels is emphatically denied in John 12:27. It is reflected clearly, however, in Hebrews 5:7-10.

14:34. The admonition to **watch** would be more appropriately translated "keep awake." Thus the disciples' conduct is a direct violation of instructions.

B. THE TRIAL (14:43–15:20)

14:43-52. *Betrayal and Arrest.* The story of the arrest appears in its simplest form in this gospel. The later gospels add both conversation and details and introduce a few changes. Mark's account reports a mob arrest directed by the Jewish leaders. Matthew and Luke follow this, but John reports "a band of soldiers." Judas betrays Jesus with a kiss in Mark and Matthew. Mark's simple story of the attack on the high priest's slave undergoes interesting development in the later gospels.

14:43-46. This is the arrest story proper. It seems to describe Judas' actions as affording positive identification of Jesus for a secret nighttime arrest.

14:47. It is possible that this episode of resistance by a bystander was originally a separate tradition. Matthew identifies this person as a disciple, and John says it was Peter. All the other gospels elaborate the incident and include some form of rebuke by Jesus.

14:48-49. This protest of Jesus is unique in the gospels. Elsewhere he suffers without protest. In Mark he speaks to those who have arrested him. In Matthew 26:55 he is addressing the crowd. In Luke 22:52 he is speaking to "the chief priests and officers of the temple and elders," who are not even present in Mark or Matthew. There is no protest at all in John's account.

The explanation of Jesus' nonresistance is found in scriptural prophecy, retained in Matthew 26:56, but not in Luke. The scripture intended must be a general prophecy of death, such as the Christian interpretation of Isaiah 53, rather than some specific prophecy of the arrest. **Day after day** implies a longer ministry in Jerusalem than Mark reports.

14:50. The desertion of the disciples is reported very directly. It is repeated in Matthew 26:56. Luke omits it, but it is implied in his story. Mark intends to imply simply that they deserted Jesus in fear of being arrested themselves. His sole point is their cowardice.

14:51-52. This **young man** may be an addition to the story that

167

came originally from a Gentile Christian reading of Amos 2:16. If not, it is obscure. It appears in no other gospel and must have been originally a separate tradition from the arrest story.

14:53-65. *The Jewish Trial.* The trial of Jesus before the Jewish authorities is represented in Mark as taking place between midnight and dawn, a most unlikely time. Matthew 26:57-68 follows Mark, but Luke moves the proceedings to the following morning (22:66). The trial itself is based on the accusation of **blasphemy**, but the charge is never justified.

14:53. The **high priest** is correctly identified in Matthew 26:57 as Caiaphas. (The account of John, mentioning both Annas and Caiaphas, needs special study.) The assembly appears to be quite a formal and official session, although in all probability the real hearing was hasty and unofficial. The setting is the home of the high priest.

14:55-59. Jesus was not judged guilty of blasphemy on the testimony of others, for their **false witness . . . did not agree.** It was on his own testimony that he was condemned.

14:61. The silence of Jesus is a Gentile Christian reading of Isaiah 53:7.

14:62. The confession of Jesus is not intended to contradict his silence in the preceding verse. Here it documents from Jesus himself the faith of the evangelist that Jesus truly was a divine being, the Son of God. This confession is for the reader of the gospel. It did not successfully inform the high priest, or anyone else in the story, of his divinity. The great secret is preserved to the end.

14:63-64. The verdict of the high priest is clearly stated but hardly justified. No one among the Jews would have considered a messianic claim to be blasphemous. The condemnation as **deserving death** suggests that this court either could not or did not pass down an actual sentence of death. John states that they could not (18:31), but the evidence on this point is not clear. The establishment of official trial procedures for this period is difficult, uncertain, and finally irrelevant if Jesus' trial was illegal.

14:65. The mocking by the Jews parallels the later mocking by the Romans (15:16-20). The theme of the Jewish mocking is religious whereas the theme of the Roman mocking is political.

14:66-72. *The Denial of Peter.* This is foretold in verse 30. The setting is laid in verse 54. Matthew 26:69-75 follows Mark closely, but Luke 22:54-65 puts the denial before the Jewish trial, rather than after it, bringing together the setting and the denial itself. In Mark **the cock crows twice,** in both the prediction (verse 30) and the fulfillment (verse 72). In all the other gospels there is just one cock-crow. In all four, however, there is a threefold denial (cf. John 18:15-18, 25-27). The four accounts are not agreed on the accusers of Peter. His weeping is augmented in both Matthew and Luke. Mark exposes Peter's weakness; Matthew and Luke emphasize his repentance. Peter's reputation is restored, in very different ways, in Matthew (16:18-19), Luke (22:31-32), and John (21:15-19), but not in Mark.

15:1. *The Jewish Consultation.* The Jewish leaders have a consultation **as soon as it was morning** and deliver Jesus to Pilate. **The whole council** implies an official gathering of the Sanhedrin (see comment on Matthew 26:47-75). This is the occasion which Luke describes as the Jewish trial. Mark has a night trial, a mocking, and a morning consultation. Luke has a night imprisonment and mocking and a morning trial.

15:2-20. *The Roman Trial.* Mark has the simplest account. All the later gospels add details (Matthew 27:11-31; Luke 23:2-25; John 18:28–19:16). All accounts assume a political charge of messiahship in the sense of rebellion against Rome. All accounts declare the innocence of Jesus and the sympathy of Pilate. All include the Barabbas incident, and all leave the reader with the impression that the Crucifixion was caused by hostile Jewish pressure on a weak Roman agent.

It is historically probable that Pilate exercised a stronger role in the trial than the gospels indicate. He is known to have been severe and prompt in putting down possible rebellions (cf. Luke

13:1-2), and indeed was finally recalled to Rome and replaced because of his excessive cruelty to the Jews.

15:2. The charge of kingship was the only point that would concern Pilate. Jesus' reply is ambiguous.

15:5. Mark's report of Jesus' refusal to reply to the charges, as in the Jewish trial, is probably based on Isaiah 53:7.

15:6. This custom is not reported anywhere in ancient literature except in the gospels.

15:7. In Mark **Barabbas** is an insurrectionist. The later gospels tend to transfer him into a common criminal. The name itself means "Son of the Father," and was probably a messianic title.

The scene actually seems to describe the offering to the people of the release of one of two men charged with insurrection plots against Rome. It is even possible that both men were named "Jesus" (in Matthew 27:17 some manuscripts read "Jesus Barabbas or Jesus who is called Christ"). Quite understandably, under these circumstances, the crowd would prefer the experienced revolutionary, Barabbas.

15:15. The scourging was customary in many death sentences. In Luke the scourging is a proposed substitute for crucifixion (23:22). The act itself was a severe lashing, and some men actually died under the lash. This may help explain why Jesus died on the cross sooner than expected.

15:16-20. The mocking by the Roman soldiers emphasizes again the real political element in the charges against Jesus. He was executed as a potential revolutionist.

Matthew follows Mark closely. Luke, in reporting earlier (23:6-12) a trial before Herod that the other gospels do not mention, describes the mocking as done by "Herod with his soldiers."

15:17. The **purple cloak** becomes "a scarlet robe" in Matthew 27:28 and "gorgeous apparel" in Luke 23:11. The clothing of royalty is thus differently described by a generation which knew few actual details. The **crown of thorns** is also mock royalty.

15:18. The **reed** is identified in Matthew 27:29 as the mock king's staff, or scepter.

C. THE EXECUTION (15:21-47)

15:21. *The Journey to Golgotha.* The short journey to the crucifixion place is not described except for this **Simon of Cyrene** incident. It is full of obscurities. Cyrene, on the north coast of Africa opposite Crete, was a Greek city with a large Jewish population. **Coming in from the country** seems to mean no more than that Simon was on his way into the city as the execution squad was going out.

The detail that he was **the father of Alexander and Rufus** suggests that the original readers of Mark would know the sons and that the incident is included because of this personal knowledge. This forms the strongest reason for regarding it as historical, in spite of the denial in John 19:17. Matthew 27:32 and Luke 23:26 preserve Mark's account but reveal lack of acquaintance with Alexander and Rufus by omitting their names. Nothing further is known of Simon, Alexander, or Rufus.

15:22-37. *The Crucifixion.* The details of the crucifixion story are supplied by Old Testament scripture (mostly Psalm 22 and Isaiah 53) more than from firsthand testimony. Nothing is known beyond the simple fact that he was crucified. Neither the location nor the circumstances can be recovered.

15:22. The location of **the place called Golgotha** is unknown. As **the place of a skull** it may have been a place that resembled a skull. "Calvary" is the Latin translation of Golgotha. One tradition explained the name as the site of the burial of Adam's skull. That it was outside the walls of the city is the only certainty.

15:23. This detail may be derived from Psalm 69:21. Matthew 27:34 makes the agreement more exact. It seems to appear again in verse 36.

15:24. The dividing of Jesus' **garments** and the **casting** of **lots** is almost certainly derived from Psalm 22:18.

15:25. The fact that Jesus is crucified at **the third hour** (9 A.M.) emphasizes the hastiness of the trial procedures.

15:26. The inscription is reported, with differences, in all four gospels. It stresses the political nature of the charges against Jesus.

15:27. The **two robbers** crucified with Jesus may be an expression of Isaiah 53:9, 12, explicitly noted in later copies of the gospel.

15:29-31. This detail comes from Psalm 22:7.

15:32. The note that both of the robbers **also reviled him** is modified in Luke 23:39-43.

15:33. The supernatural **darkness** beginning at **the sixth hour** (noon) and lasting for three hours is symbolic. There is no report of it elsewhere in ancient literature. Cf. Amos 8:9.

15:34. Jesus' cry is the opening line of Psalm 22, a psalm which the early Gentile church understood as the words of Jesus (cf. Hebrews 2:10-12) and which supplied many details of the crucifixion story. No other saying from the cross is reported in Mark.

Matthew follows Mark closely, but both Luke and John are independent—from each other as well as from Mark. Of the "seven last words," one is from Mark, three from Luke only, and three from John only. In all cases the evangelists themselves seem to be responsible for them. Mark's original tradition probably contained only a **cry** (as in verse 37), which he then interpreted from Psalm 22:1. Luke (23:46) preferred Psalm 31:5. The quotation, **My God, My God, why hast thou forsaken me?** is given in Aramaic in Mark and in Hebrew in Matthew.

15:35. The confusion with the name **Elijah** would arise more naturally out of the Hebrew form "Eli" used in Matthew 27:46 rather than the Aramaic **Eloi.**

15:36. The offering of **vinegar** to drink may be related to verse 23, and both may be expressions of Psalm 69:21.

15:37. Jesus' death is placed at **the ninth hour** (verse 34), only six hours after the beginning of his crucifixion. This is much shorter than usual and no explanations are offered.

15:38-39. *The Effects.* The effects of the Crucifixion are expressed theologically by Mark. The rending of **the curtain** which protected the Holy of Holies in **the temple** is explained in

Hebrews 9:11-14; 10:19-22 as the high point of the sacrificial offering of Jesus.

The Greek of the centurion's statement could mean either "a son of a god," or "a son of God" or **the Son of God.** Whether the centurion himself was expressing a pagan or a Jewish concept, it is clear that Mark thought of his words as a recognition of Jesus' divinity. This reaction climaxes Mark's conviction, systematically stressed throughout the gospel, that Jesus' Jewish friends never truly perceived his divine nature. It was a Gentile centurion who first recognized it, in sharp contrast to the twelve, who never advanced beyond a vision of Jesus as the Jewish Messiah. It is doubtful that Mark intends to convey the impression that the centurion became a Christian, as later tradition says. The centurion here is representative of Gentile Christianity, which saw the significance of Jesus as the Son of God revealed in the drama of the cross.

15:40-41. *The Witnesses.* The witnesses to the Crucifixion are briefly described as **women . . . who, when he was in Galilee, followed him.** Mark singles out for special mention **Mary Magdalene,** another **Mary, the mother of James the younger and of Joses, and Salome** (cf. Matthew 27:56 and Luke 23:49). Note that they were **looking on from afar** (cf. Psalm 38:11).

15:42-47. *The Burial.* Unless someone specifically requested it, the body of a crucifixion victim was usually left to rot on the cross or simply discarded. Jewish tradition, based on Deuteronomy 21:22-23, requires burial on the same day the death occurs. **Joseph of Arimathea,** a minority leader in the Jewish **council** that condemned Jesus, seems simply to be doing the decent thing for Jesus.

15:46. The purchase of the **shroud** implies that the Passover has not yet begun, for during the feast the shops would all be closed. Tombs **hewn out of the rock** in the Judean hillsides were common at this time. Each tomb was used many times over the centuries.

15:47. The two Marys here are presumably the same as those in verse 40. But it is unnatural in Greek to use the expression "Mary the one of Joses" (literal translation) to designate a mother-son relationship. Without verse 40 it would have to be translated "Mary the wife (or daughter) of Joses."

VIII. THE RESURRECTION (16:1-8, 9-20)

16:1-8. *The Empty Tomb.* The discovery of the empty tomb is made by the women who were the crucifixion witnesses. The two Marys (the second now identified as "Mary the one of James"—see above on 15:47) and Salome go at the first opportunity to anoint the body of Jesus (see above on 14:3-9). The historical center of the story seems to be that there was a tradition that the women visited the tomb and found it empty. The details vary in the other gospels.

16:2. The time is after sunrise (contrast "while it was still dark" in John 20:1).

16:3-4. No further details are known about the size, shape, or position of the stone.

16:5. The **young man** becomes an "angel" in Matthew 28:5, "two men" in Luke 24:4, and "two angels" in John 20:12. Mark's intent was probably to describe an angelic being.

16:6. On **he has risen** see above on 8:31.

16:7. The expression **his disciples and Peter** is strange and remains unexplained. The reference to a promised appearance in **Galilee** is in accord with 14:28, but quite out of harmony with the whole resurrection tradition in Luke-Acts.

16:8. The reaction of the two Marys is one of **trembling and astonishment.** Like all the personal disciples of Jesus in Mark, they do not comprehend his true significance. Their decision to say **nothing to any one,** out of fear, confirms this.

This verse ends very abruptly, apparently before completion of the sentence (the Greek word for **they were afraid** usually means "afraid of . . ."). The earliest manuscripts of Mark end at this point.

The Problem of the Ending. Since the authentic text of Mark breaks off at verse 8, the continuations found in many manuscripts are clearly later additions (see below on verses

9-20). There arises the problem of explaining this abrupt and seemingly incomplete ending. Scholars are divided among four possibilities:

(1) One theory is that nothing has been lost. A minority of scholars find it possible to accept what we have in verse 8 as the original and intended ending. Jesus has risen, and the original disciples are uncomprehending and afraid. The grammatically strange final word **they were afraid** (see above on verse 8) has a parallel or two in ancient literature. But most scholars believe that the existence of two late additions, felt to be necessary by the church, is clear evidence that Mark is incomplete. Logically verse 7 looks forward to a Galilean resurrection appearance that is missing.

(2) A more popular theory is that the author was interrupted at this point and never got to complete his gospel. Whatever the occasion for his stopping work in the midst of a sentence, the assumption would be that it was death which prevented him from ever returning to it.

(3) Another theory is that the original ending was accidentally lost, before Mark was used as a source by Matthew and Luke. Perhaps, depending on the form of the manuscript, the end of the scroll was damaged or the final page was lost. A majority of scholars favor this theory.

(4) A fourth theory, is that Mark's original ending was deliberately destroyed. It has been suggested that the reason for the suppression was this ending's account of Jesus' resurrection appearance to the disciples in Galilee. This would have contradicted the tradition represented in Luke that all the appearances occurred near Jerusalem. Not many scholars have found this a convincing reason, because Matthew's brief ending reports this Galilean appearance, and it survived. Some more drastic cause for dissatisfaction is needed.

A more probable reason for the suppression of Mark's original ending is that it portrayed the disciples as not believing in the Resurrection. Contrary to the usual view, this ending was known to Matthew and Luke. The evidence is found in

Matthew 28:17 and Luke 24:41, each of which preserves a modified version of a tradition that the disciples disbelieved. Each modification is typical of its author's distinctive way of modifying Mark in the interest of the disciples' good reputation. Matthew regularly alters Mark's statement about them, whereas Luke, if he includes it at all, adds an explanation. Thus the presumed Markan original that the disciples disbelieved has been altered in Matthew 28:17 to read "but some doubted." In Luke 24:41 it has been explained that they "disbelieved for joy."

Neither Matthew nor Luke, loyal to the disciples as each was, would have reported doubt or disbelief if it had not been present in their source. On the other hand, Mark's report that the disciples disbelieved the Resurrection is a fitting climax to the characteristic portrayal of them in his gospel, and can be recognized as another aspect of the early Gentile Christian criticism of the leaders of Jewish Christianity.

16:9-20. *Later Additions.* Two attempts to supply a substitute for the missing ending of Mark have come down to us:

(1) The "longer ending" appears in almost all of the later manuscripts and therefore in the King James Version, as well as most other versions. In the Revised Standard Version it is placed in a footnote. Technical study makes clear that it comes from a different author and is based on Luke, John, and some other sources. Since it reports, in typical Markan fashion, the disbelief of the disciples and has the risen Jesus upbraiding them severely **for their unbelief and hardness of heart,** and since it has a typically Markan understanding of the gospel (verses 15-16), there is good reason for thinking that its principal "other source" was the original ending itself. It may therefore be regarded as a revised version of the original.

The best explanation of why the original ending itself was not restored is simply that it was now lost except in the memory of oral tradition. The longer ending, therefore, probably represents a conscientious effort by the church to restore the lost or suppressed ending. The original and primitive elements of the longer ending now appear alongside influences from the resurrection stories of Luke and John.

(2) The "shorter ending" (see the footnote in the Revised Standard Version), found only rarely in the later manuscripts, is obviously a late editorial addition to give the gospel a satisfactory conclusion. It is probably based on Matthew.

THE GOSPEL ACCORDING TO LUKE

William Baird

INTRODUCTION

General Character and Purpose

The Gospel According to Luke is the first half of a two-volume work—Luke-Acts—which constitutes over a fourth of the New Testament. It is the third of the three "Synoptic" gospels. As a part of a historical work Luke resembles the historical writings of its time. Unlike many Greek histories, however, Luke is religious history—it is written with a purpose. As a gospel it follows the pattern of a unique kind of Christian literature. Mark, the earliest gospel, set the pattern for this literature. A gospel is not primarily biography; it is proclamation. Yet as a historical work Luke makes clear that the gospel is preached through history.

In order to accomplish this purpose the author develops an apology for Christianity. He insists that what God has done in history is according to law and order. Thus Pilate, who represents Rome's legal genius, declares repeatedly (23:4, 14, 22) that Jesus is guilty of no crime. The Crucifixion is the responsibility of the leaders of the Jews (23:25). Indeed these priests and rulers have so perverted their heritage as to have abandoned it. Christianity has become the true Judaism, and the coming of its leader heralds the fulfillment of Israel's hope (2:25-38).

The author is also anxious to explain why the end of the world has not come. Mark imagined that the Son of man would return before the first generation of Christians had passed away (Mark 13:30). Now the time has grown late. Why has he not come? To answer this question the author of Luke develops a theology of history—a view of the course of events which is grounded in his faith.

He seems to see history as divided into three eras:
(1) the time of the Jews, which is finished;
(2) the time of Jesus Christ, which is the key to history;
(3) the time of the church, which is now.

This last may be extended into the distant future so that the time of the end remains remote. The time of the church will be the subject of Acts, the second volume, but the first is concerned with Jesus Christ. Luke's presentation of Jesus is marked by some unique features. For example, this gospel has a special interest in the geographical ordering of the story. In 9:51 Jesus sets out on a journey toward Jerusalem—a journey which does not reach its goal until 19:27. Although he immediately enters Samaria, by chapter 10 Jesus is saying things that would make sense only in Galilee.

It may be that Luke's knowledge of Palestinian geography is confused, but more likely he intends to present the whole ministry of Jesus as moving toward the Holy City. The purpose of God in history is to be accomplished in the suffering and death of his Christ.

Jesus is presented as bringing God's salvation to those who need it most—publicans, sinners, Samaritans, and Gentiles. Only in Luke does Jesus dine with Zacchaeus. Only in Luke are we told of the Samaritan whose mercy shames priest and Levites. The Jesus who cares for the poor and the outcasts is portrayed in soft colors. Women play a special role in his ministry, and Jesus is depicted as a man of prayer. Not just the son of Abraham, he belongs to humanity; he is "the son of Adam, the son of God" (3:38).

Authorship

According to tradition this gospel was written by Luke, "the beloved physician" and travel companion of Paul (Colossians 4:14; Philemon 24; II Timothy 4:11). Actually the tradition is not very old. It appears first in the writings of Irenaeus, who was a theologian living in Gaul during the latter part of the second century.

What is the basis for the belief that Luke is the author? It was no doubt early assumed that Luke and Acts were by the same author. This was a valid assumption. Both books reveal similarity of language, style, and thought. Both begin with prefaces which are similar in form and content.

As students began to look at the second volume, they discovered that its author in certain passages referred to the participants as "we." These "we sections" (Acts 16:10-17; 20:5-15; 21:1-18; 27:1–28:16) seemed to identify the author of Luke-Acts as accompanying Paul on these occasions. Since the last of them brings him to Rome, the author must be none other than Luke, who alone remains with Paul in a Roman prison (II Timothy 4:11).

Although these facts could explain the rise of the Lukan tradition, the matter is much more complex. The "we sections" can be explained on other grounds. Inconsistency with Paul's letters raises the question whether Acts could have been written by any companion of his. Actually the traditional identification of the author is of no great importance. In no case can he be recognized as an eyewitness of events in the career of Jesus. His own account is at best secondhand, depending on the works of those who "were eyewitnesses and ministers of the word" (1:2) before him. We can conclude that the author was a competent historian of broad learning and profound faith.

Date and Place of Composition

The exact date and place of the writing of this gospel cannot be known. Since the author uses Mark as a source, and since he seems to have accurate knowledge of the destruction of Jerusalem by the Romans, he evidently wrote after A.D. 70. He must have written before 140, when his gospel was included in the canon of the heretic Marcion. Since the situation of the church reflected in the gospel fits well the political situation of the reign of the Emperor Domitian (81-96), a date from about 85 to 95 is most likely.

According to one tradition Luke wrote his histories in Rome. Another locates his writing in Greece. Since there is another tradition that the evangelist died in one of the Greek provinces, this latter tradition has better support.

Any of these locations assumes the tradition that Luke, companion of Paul, is the author, and presents the same problems. Perhaps all we can say is that the gospel was written from some place where Greek was the primary language and where cultured readers like Theophilus (1:3) would be at home.

Sources and Their Arrangement

As Luke acknowledges in the preface, his gospel is based on a variety of sources. Most basic is Mark. Over half of Mark's subject matter is taken over to constitute about a third of Luke's gospel. Although Luke omits large sections of Mark, and although he inserts into his narrative large blocks of non-Markan material, the basic outline of his first volume is determined by the structure of Mark.

The material which Luke inserts into this outline comes from several sources. For one, he uses the document which scholars have called "Q" (for the German word *Quelle*, which means "source"). This material, which he shares with Matthew, is the basis for about 250 of Luke's total of some 1,100 verses. It consists mainly of teaching material and parables.

Besides this, Luke has a source (or sources) exclusively his own. This material, sometimes called "L," is the ground for around 280 verses. It is the source for Luke's understanding of the birth of Jesus, his special collection of parables, and his dramatic account of the Resurrection. L may be composed of oral tradition as well as written documents. Luke is faithful in following his sources. The way he adapts them to his own narrative is a key to his particular understanding of the gospel.

Language and Style

Luke writes a Greek of high quality. Occasionally he improves on the style of Mark. Foreign words like "rabbi" and "Golgotha," since they might grate on the ear of the Hellenistic reader of the Greco-Roman world, are omitted.

A distinctive feature of Luke's style is his fondness for twofold constructions. He likes double names (e.g. "Martha, Martha," 10:41), repetitious sentences (e.g. 19:31, 34), and parallel illustrations (e.g. Noah and Lot, 17:26-32). This parallelism may reflect the Old Testament conviction that two witnesses are essential to establish evidence (Deuteronomy 19:15). Thus the innocence of Jesus is established not only by the trial before Pontius Pilate but also by a judgment before Herod Antipas. Luke takes the early Christian concept of witness seriously and understands his own work as literary witness (cf. 24:48; Acts 1:8).

I. PREFACE (1:1-4)

1:1-2. In writing a preface to his first volume Luke follows a literary convention of his day. Historians and medical writers often began their work with such an introduction. Luke's preface reveals his dependence on predecessors. **Many have undertaken to compile a narrative,** and he has used their work as sources. Ultimately the gospel tradition is dependent on oral reports which go back to those **who from the beginning were eyewitnesses and ministers of the word.**

1:3-4. Although Luke's reference to previous work is no criticism of his sources, his intention to write a new narrative suggests the superiority of his own endeavor. His proposal to write a better account rests on two claims:

(1) the thorough nature of his research, in that he has **followed all things closely for some time past;**

(2) his intention **to write an orderly account.** The significance of this latter claim is not entirely clear, since the Greek word for "orderly" simply means "one after another," and the order can

be temporal, spatial, or logical. Many have supposed that Luke is proposing a better chronological account or is offering a consecutive narrative. However, in both chronology and sequence Luke offers little which is new; he mainly follows Mark. It may be that the unique feature of Luke's order is geographical—his beginning in Jerusalem, moving from there to Galilee and then back to Jerusalem, ending again in the Holy City.

Who is **Theophilus,** to whom the gospel is addressed? Since the name means "friend of God," some have concluded that it is symbolic—that the book is dedicated to the true Christian. However, since the name has been found in contemporary literary sources, Theophilus is probably a real person. The title applied to him here, **most excellent,** is used in Acts to describe government officials. At least we can conclude that Theophilus is a person of high social rank.

Many have debated his relationship to Christianity. Is Theophilus a pagan whom Luke hopes to convert? Is he a Christian who needs more instruction? These questions seem to ignore the fact that a dedication to a prominent person was a device of Hellenistic literature. Theophilus is probably Luke's patron. The gospel is directed to a wider audience—one which needs to be informed concerning **the things which have been accomplished among us.**

II. PREPARATION FOR THE ACTS OF JESUS (1:5–4:13)

A. THE BEGINNINGS OF JESUS AND JOHN THE BAPTIST (1:5–2:52)

After the complex literary Greek of his preface Luke changes his style to present the birth narrative. This may reflect sources which are Semitic in character, but mainly illustrates Luke's ability to adapt his writing to the narrative. He wants to give his account the religious quality of the Old Testament. Thus he uses poetic and symbolic language.

183

The ultimate source of this material may have been the followers of John the Baptist. They probably believed John to be the long-awaited Messiah and continued their influence as late as the events described in Acts 19:3. Although Matthew has an account of the birth of Jesus, it rests on a tradition independent of the one preserved here.

1:5-25. *The Annunciation of the Birth of John.* Luke sets his story into the context of contemporary history. John is born **in the days of Herod, king of Judea.** The Herod mentioned here is Herod the Great, who ruled from 37-4 B.C. By Judea, Luke means the whole area of Palestine. The parents of John represent Jewish piety at its best. **Zechariah,** the father, is a member of one of the twenty-four divisions of the priesthood. His wife **Elizabeth** is also of priestly descent. Although they are righteous before God, they have not received the blessing of a child.

1:8-10. Zechariah goes to Jerusalem with his division to officiate at the temple. While there Zechariah is chosen **by lot** to offer incense in the holy place. The casting of lots was believed to guarantee divine approval. **Incense** was offered morning and evening. The service was preceded by a call to prayer, and while the priest was in the temple proper, the people remained assembled in the courtyard.

1:11-13. While Zechariah is performing this rare duty, the **angel of the Lord** suddenly appears beside **the altar of incense.** The angel is **Gabriel** (verse 19)—one of the seven archangels of Jewish tradition. Zechariah is shocked, although he might have known that the offering of incense provided the proper setting for supernatural revelation. At any rate the angel brings good news: Elizabeth is to bear a son. His **name** is to be **John,** which means "God is gracious."

1:14-17. Gabriel now bursts into song: The birth of John will bring **joy** to **many** people. The child is to be dedicated to God, and therefore like a Nazirite (cf. Numbers 6:1) **he shall drink no wine nor strong drink.** Since Luke stresses the idea that God's work in history is accomplished through the Holy Spirit, it is noted here that John is to be **filled with the Holy Spirit** from birth.

He also will come **in the spirit and power of Elijah.** The idea that Elijah would come as herald of the end of the world finds its roots in Malachi 4:5. The early Christians interpreted the returning Elijah as the forerunner of the Messiah promised in the Old Testament. Luke, unlike Mark and Matthew, does not explicitly identify John as Elijah. However, the one who comes in the spirit of Elijah has an eschatological mission—a mission concerned with the ending of the age. He is to prepare the people for the coming of the kingdom of God.

1:18-23. When Zechariah hears this he cannot believe. The evidence is all against it: he is **old** and his **wife is advanced in years.** The angel now presents his credentials. He is one who stands **in the presence of God,** so that his predictions are sure. Moreover, Zechariah will be struck dumb because of his unbelief. This traditional experience of dumbness (cf. Daniel 10:15-17) after receiving revelation indicates the overpowering character of the divine word and the miracle of revelation.

Meanwhile **the people** become anxious. According to the ritual they must remain praying until the officiating priest comes out to offer the benediction. When Zechariah belatedly appears, it is evident that some wonder has occurred. The priest can only make **signs;** he cannot speak. After his week of duties is complete, Zechariah goes home to await the work of God.

1:24-25. Elizabeth conceives and praises God for removing her **reproach among men.** Childlessness was blamed on the woman. Elizabeth hides herself **for five months.** Since this was not a customary practice of pregnancy, something symbolic is probably meant. Just as Zechariah's silence awaits the word of God, so Elizabeth's secrecy awaits divine revelation.

1:26-38. *The Annunciation of the Birth of Jesus.* Parallel to the annunciation of the birth of John is the account of the annunciation of the birth of Jesus. The ultimate source of this material may have been the followers of John the Baptist. If so, the annunciation originally would have come to Elizabeth rather than to Mary. This would afford a parallel to the annunciation to

Zechariah as well as explain how Elizabeth knows the name of the child (1:60). Gabriel is again the heavenly actor, while the appearance occurs in **Nazareth,** a town in the hill country of Southern **Galilee.** As usual Luke shows an interest in dates. The event takes place in the **sixth month** of Elizabeth's pregnancy.

1:26-31. The angel comes to **Mary,** a virgin betrothed to a man named **Joseph.** According to the customs of the day, betrothal was an official relationship. It often involved cohabitation culminating in the legal recognition of marriage. Betrothal usually occurred early, so that Mary was probably quite young. Since the child is to receive **the throne of his father David** (verse 32), it is important to note that Joseph is **of the house of David.** Until verse 34 the account seems to assume that Joseph will be the father.

The angel's greeting, that Mary will be especially favored of God, comes as a complete surprise. Some manuscripts add the phrase, "Blessed are you among women" (see the footnote in the Revised Standard Version), and this reading has contributed to the formulation of the "Ave Maria." The real mission of Gabriel is to declare that Mary will **bear a son.** He shall be called **Jesus**—the Greek form of the ancient Semitic name Joshua, which means "the Lord is salvation."

1:32-33. The angel now breaks into song. In form and content this psalm reflects the poetry of the Old Testament. Its main theme is the messianic role of the promised child. He will be **called the Son of the Most High,** like the king addressed in Psalm 2:7. For the Hebrew mind divine sonship did not require a supernatural birth. The child will also inherit the kingdom of David; he will fulfill the Jewish hope of the reestablishment of the Davidic reign. The resulting kingdom will be eternal, as prophesied by Psalm 89:29.

1:34-35. The surprise of Mary comes as a surprise to the reader. Since she is betrothed and about to consummate her marriage, why should the news that she will bear a son come as anything unusual? Originally the surprise may have been, not that she was to bear a child, but that the child would be the Messiah.

Luke has used Mary's question in verse 34 to introduce the doctrine of the virgin birth. On Hellenistic soil, where a supernatural event was the common feature of the births of kings and heroes, a miraculous origin of the Messiah seemed natural. Although she has not had sexual intercourse with a man, which is the literal meaning of verse 34, Mary will bear a child conceived by the power of **the Holy Spirit.** The resulting child will be **the Son of God** in a special sense; he will have a unique nature.

1:36-38. The proof that God can do this is seen in the miracle of Elizabeth. This kinswoman of Mary's has conceived a child in her old age and in spite of her barrenness. With God all things are possible. Since Mary is a relative of Elizabeth, she too may be of priestly descent and thus not of the house of David. In any case she is subservient to the divine election. She accepts the word of God in humble obedience as **the handmaid** (or slave) **of the Lord.**

1:39-56. *Mary's Visit to Elizabeth.* Since Mary has received divine revelation, she demonstrates her faith by immediate action. She goes **with haste** to a town of the **hill country** of Judea. Various efforts to identify this home city of Zechariah and Elizabeth have proved futile. When Elizabeth meets Mary, the child John leaps **in her womb.** This is reminiscent of the struggle in the womb of Rebekah (Genesis 25:22) and signifies that John recognizes the superiority of Jesus before either is born. Elizabeth's exclamation is inspired. She blesses Mary and tells of the action of the fetus within her. Most of all, she calls Mary the **mother of my Lord,** giving to Jesus the title typical of early Christian adoration.

1:46-55. The song which follows is commonly called the "magnificat," from the opening word in Latin. Although it is attributed to Mary, many think it was originally spoken by Elizabeth. Some of the manuscripts actually read "Elizabeth" in verse 46; and its background is surely the song of Hannah (I Samuel 2:1-10)—a hymn which fits Elizabeth better than Mary. For Luke, however, it surely belongs in the mouth of Mary. She is the model of faith who has believed **what was spoken to her**

from the Lord. She is the one who fulfills Jewish expectation.

The poem has two parts. The first expresses Mary's personal thanksgiving. She is the lowly **handmaiden** who will be called **blessed** by all generations. Though she is lowly, God can work through her for the salvation of many. The second half of the song expresses the thanksgiving of the nation. God is the powerful one who has destroyed the enemies, **scattered the proud,** and reduced the rich. The lowly he has **exalted,** and he will remember his promises to **Israel.** Since the poem calls Israel the **servant** of the Lord, it is evident that the servant psalms of the latter part of Isaiah are basic to Luke's understanding of the messianic age.

1:56. After remaining **three months** with Elizabeth, Mary returns to her home. We can assume that, since she came in the sixth month of Elizabeth's pregnancy, Mary stays in Judea until John is born. The **home** to which she returns is probably that which she shares with Joseph in Nazareth.

1:57-80. *The Birth of John.* Elizabeth delivers her child and there is great rejoicing. The promise of the angel is fulfilled. The idea that **neighbors and kinsfolk** should join in the naming of the child is traditional. That the ceremony of circumcision and the giving of the name coincide may represent a later practice.

At any rate the account is characterized by two miracles. The first has to do with the naming of the child. As was often the custom the guests assume that the boy should be named **after his father.** Elizabeth insists that his name should be John, even though none of his family is known by that name. **Signs** are made to Zechariah, who now appears to be deaf as well as dumb. Taking up the father's prerogative to name his son, he scratches "John" on the **writing tablet** of wax on wood. The agreement between father and mother seems divinely inspired. Besides, another wonder occurs at once: Zechariah, who was struck dumb, is able to talk. The news spreads throughout the neighborhood and an expectant question is raised: **What then will this child be?**

1:67-75. Zechariah, who has received the miraculous gift of speech, prophesies under the guidance of the Spirit. Traditionally his song is called the "Benedictus" from the first word in Latin. In content it appears to be a typical Jewish messianic hymn.

In this first part the prophecy stresses the fulfillment of Jewish eschatological hopes. God has visited his people with salvation and redemption. The **horn of salvation** is a symbolic way to refer to the power of God. All the predictions of the **prophets** shall be fulfilled, and the **covenant** with **Abraham** will be remembered. The **enemies** who are being overthrown would be identified as the Romans by the Jewish interpreter, but for Luke they are the foes of Christ, or the persecutors of the church. Throughout this section of the poem the child John is seen to fulfill the typical expectation of a nationalistic Jewish Messiah.

1:76-79. In this second part John is presented under the Christian interpretation as the forerunner of the Messiah, **the prophet** of the end time who will **prepare** the way of the Lord. Here the Elijah motif of Malachi 4:5 is taken up, and **the Lord** in verse 76 is no doubt to be identified as Jesus. The main feature of this preparation is to make way for God's saving and redemptive action. Verse 78 is difficult to translate, but the meaning is clear: with the prophetic activity of John the messianic age has dawned. The idea of God's revelation symbolized by **light** is typical, while the concept of the rising of the sun of righteousness is found in Malachi 4:2.

1:80. John's growth is reminiscent of the development of Samuel (I Samuel 2:26) and of Samson, who like John was dedicated to God as a Nazirite—one separated from others by a special vow. That John becomes **strong in spirit** points to the inner development of his life. Some have taken the statement that he was **in the wilderness** from his youth to indicate that John was raised by the sectarians of Qumran, the community which preserved the Dead Sea Scrolls. If this is true, he certainly broke with them before he embarked on his mission. Their message was to a select few while his was to all Israel. The time of John's **manifestation to Israel** is the time of expectation; his appearance heralds the preaching of the kingdom.

2:1-20. *The Birth of Jesus.* Jesus is born in **Bethlehem.**

According to Luke this event occurred in the Judean city because of an imperial census. **Augustus,** Roman emperor from 27 B.C. to A.D. 14, decreed that the entire empire **should be enrolled.** Whether or not this census actually occurred has been debated. There is no other record of a universal census at this time, and an imperial enrollment within the realm of Herod the Great seems unlikely. There actually was a Palestinian census in A.D. 6, which was precisely the time **when Quirinius was governor of Syria,** but this is over ten years too late.

On the other hand, some recent research into Roman practices has indicated that a census may have involved two steps: (a) the enrollment in which the data were collected, and (2) the assessment in which the actual taxation was declared. The enrollment did require that a man appear for census in the area where he owned land, and on some occasions his wife came along. It may be that Caesar controlled the taxation within Herod's kingdom. Evidence has been found that P. Sulpicius Quirinius, though not yet governor of Syria, was a viceroy in this area after 12 B.C. Thus, although Luke's picture is not entirely accurate, an enrollment could have been held in Palestine during the reign of Herod the Great, perhaps around 6 B.C.

2:4-7. Actually Luke's purpose here is more theological than historical. He, like Matthew, wants to show that Jesus was born in the city of David. Since he is the Son of David and the Messiah, he must be born in a messianic city, in Bethlehem, from whom "shall come forth for me one who is ruler in Israel" (Micah 5:2).

Here Mary gives **birth to her first-born son,** wraps him **in swaddling cloths,** and lays **him in a manger.** The information that **there was no place for them in the inn** is misleading. The word translated "inn" is better rendered by "guestroom." The intention is to contrast a place of human lodging with an area for feeding animals. The **manger** is a feeding trough for stock. It could be located under the house or out in the open. In all of this the birth of Jesus is presented in simplicity and humility.

2:8-12. Whereas Matthew brings wise men from the East,

Luke relates the coming of Judean **shepherds.** These humble pastoral folk are **out in the field** at night with their **flock.** This feature of the story would argue against the birth's occurring on December 25 since the weather would not have permitted it. Suddenly **an angel of the Lord** appears to them accompanied by the radiance of heavenly **glory.**

Since light is the typical symbol of divine revelation, the angel's message can be accepted as word from God. This message announces **good news . . . to all the people;** the birth of Jesus has universal significance. The one who is born is **Savior,** and he is to be confessed as the Messiah and Lord of all men. The **sign** that all this is true can be seen in the simple surroundings of the birth (cf. Isaiah 7:14-15).

2:13. The angel is suddenly accompanied by the **host** of heaven, who join in praises **to God in the highest.** The second part of their hymn is not entirely clear. Some Greek manuscripts read "on earth, peace, good will among men," and the Latin versions have "peace to men of good will." The Revised Standard Version is to be preferred here. Not only is it based on the best text, but the notion that divine peace depends on human attitude is totally against the theology of Luke. For him the new situation on earth is due to the grace of God in the gift of Jesus Christ.

2:15-20. The shepherds act immediately on the revelation which they have received. At Bethlehem they see Mary, Joseph, and the child Jesus. This lowly birth is only a sign of the great things which the angel has promised. The shepherds relate their heavenly vision, to the wonder of all. We are given the impression that a large crowd of witnesses is present. Mary, who is again rapt in awe and wonder, treasures all these things **in her heart.** The shepherds return **glorifying and praising God** much as the angels did. They set the pattern for the Christian mission, witnessing to all what they have **heard and seen.**

Luke's picture of the birth of Jesus is presented in the quiet tones of pastoral life. The shepherds are depicted, as often in Hellenistic literature, with an aura of beauty and purity. They remind us of the peaceful flocks of the shepherd king whose successor has been **born this day** in Bethlehem.

2:21-40. *The Destiny of Jesus.* Jesus is taken to Jerusalem for the fulfillment of religious duties and the prediction of his destiny. First he is circumcised on the eighth day, according to the ancient custom, and given the name announced by the angel Gabriel. Then he is taken to the temple in Jerusalem. In recounting the events there Luke seems to have combined two Old Testament rituals.

The ceremony of **purification** is described in Leviticus 12. According to this text the mother is considered unclean after the birth of her son for seven days, and on the eighth he is circumcised. Counting from that day, the mother is to remain separate thirty-three days longer. At the end of that time, or forty days from the birth, she is to offer a sacrifice. For a poor woman who could not afford a lamb this sacrifice could consist of **a pair of turtledoves, or two young pigeons.**

The second ceremony which Luke assumes is the redemption of the firstborn. According to Exodus 13:2, 12-13, which is quoted here, a firstborn child is considered **holy,** or belonging to the Lord. He must be redeemed with an offering of five shekels. Luke gives the impression that the purification sacrifice suffices for the redemption offering. Actually the former was performed by the mother while the latter was the duty of the father. Neither had to be offered at the temple. Luke is anxious to have parents and child together in Jerusalem since it is the place of Jesus' destiny.

2:25-32. That destiny is announced by **Simeon,** the aged prophet who has been awaiting **the consolation of Israel**—that is, he has been looking for the messianic age. The Holy Spirit has informed him that he will not die before the Messiah comes. The Spirit inspires him to go to the temple at just the moment when the parents of Jesus are performing their duties. It is clear to him that in Jesus his hopes are fulfilled.

Taking the child in his arms he pronounces a prophetic hymn which in traditional liturgy is called the "Nunc Dimittis," from the opening words in Latin. The main point of the poem is that

salvation has now come and that this salvation is for all people. Not only will there be **glory to . . . Israel,** but there will be **a light for revelation to the Gentiles.** Since he has seen this salvation, Simeon can **depart,** meaning that he is prepared to die.

2:33-35. Mary and Joseph (who is called **his father**) marvel at what has been said. Then Simeon offers a special blessing to the **mother.** This blessing seems to reflect two Old Testament symbols: **fall and rising** (cf. the stone of stumbling of Isaiah 8:14) and the **sword** (cf. Ezekiel 14:17). In context these figures make two important points: that the coming of the Messiah means first decision and judgment, and second, suffering. The suffering pierces the **soul** of the mother of Jesus—a prediction of his passion.

2:36-38. As a parallel witness to Simeon the ancient **prophetess, Anna,** appears. Jewish tradition recognized the validity of seven prophetesses, among them Hannah of I Samuel 2. Anna's **great age** is emphasized. **Till she was eighty-four** is literally "till eighty-four years," which could refer to the period of her widowhood and make her age over a hundred. She is continually in the temple enclosure praying and **fasting.** Her presence, along with that of Mary, indicates that the events described in verses 27-38 took place in one of the outer courtyards where women were allowed. Anna, like Simeon, arrives **at that very hour** when Jesus is dedicated. She gives thanks to God and also indicates that the hope of **redemption** is fulfilled in the child.

2:39-40. The parents and child return to **Nazareth,** their home in **Galilee.** Jesus, much like John (1:80), grows in strength and **wisdom.** It is important to note that **everything according to the law of the Lord** has been performed. Jesus is presented as "born of woman, born under the law" (Galatians 4:4).

2:41-52. *The Boyhood of Jesus.* The **temple** is again the seat of activity for the young Jesus. This is possible because his parents are pious Jews who annually attend the feast of the **Passover.** The law required every faithful Jewish male to go to Jerusalem three times a year. On this occasion Jesus is **twelve years old.**

He has just become a "son of the Law," and therefore accepts his duty to attend the feast.

The Passover festival, joined with the feast of Unleavened Bread, lasts seven days. When the festival is finished, the parents return toward Nazareth, assuming that Jesus is with relatives or friends. A search at the end of the day's journey, however, indicates that the lad is lost. **After three days** Mary and Joseph find him in the temple **among the teachers.** The "three days" would include the journey from Jerusalem, the return, and one day of searching within the city.

Jesus is primarily presented as a learner who listens and asks questions—in contrast to the paintings which portray him in the attitude of a preacher—but **his answers** indicate a precociousness which amazes his audience.

2:48-50. Mary's reaction contains a mild rebuke: **Son, why have you treated us so?** Joseph is again described as **your father.** Jesus' answer is utterly baffling to his parents—a fact which indicates that this material comes from a tradition other than that which has described the miraculous birth. Jesus expresses surprise that they have been seeking him, but his reason is not entirely clear. The Greek reads literally, "Did you not know that I must be (in, among) my Father's?" This idiom allows the translation ". . . about my Father's business" (King James Version), but the more likely meaning is **in my Father's house.** The important thing for Luke is that Jesus is in the temple.

2:51. Mary again keeps all **these things in her heart.** Parents and child return to the Galilean home, and he is **obedient to them.** This situation is seen to be only temporary, however, for they do not adequately understand the role he is to play, while he—even in his youth—seems to anticipate what his destiny must be.

2:52. Jesus' growth **in wisdom and in stature, and in favor with God and man** reminds us of the development of the prophet Samuel (cf. I Samuel 2:26). In any event Jesus is reared in a home of true Jewish piety; he obeys his parents, he follows the law. Like Moses and the other heroes of his time Jesus is a precocious child. Most important of all, he calls God "Father" and recognizes a unique relationship with the Almighty which will determine his whole life.

B. THE WORDS AND DEEDS OF JOHN THE BAPTIST
(3:1-22)

3:1-6. *The Prophet in Historical Perspective.* Considerable time has elapsed since the previous narrative. Again Luke is anxious to set his account in the context of contemporary events. It is **the fifteenth year** of the Emperor **Tiberius;** this would be A.D. 28-29. The rulers of Palestine are listed. Over **Judea** is **Pontius Pilate,** a procurator appointed by Rome. He ruled from A.D. 26 to 36, and his presence in Palestine is confirmed by an inscription found recently at Caesarea, his capital city. Ruler of **Galilee** is **Herod**—a son of Herod the Great known as Herod Antipas, whose realm also included Perea, east of the Jordan. The title **tetrarch** originally referred to the ruler of a fourth of a region, but in Hellenistic times it could be used for any ruler of a petty kingdom. Since Luke lists four Palestinian rulers here, he may intend the title to carry its original meaning. Over **Ituraea and Trachonitis** rules **Philip.** He too was a son of Herod the Great and half brother of Antipas; his area was to the north and east of the Sea of Galilee. **Lysanias** is tetrarch of **Abilene**—a region still farther to the north. It is known that a certain Lysanias ruled this region in the first century B.C., but the man mentioned here is perhaps Lysanias II.

3:2a. Luke also gives the religious setting of his story. It takes place during **the high-priesthood of Annas and Caiaphas.** This statement is confusing, since there could be only one high priest at a time. According to Jewish custom a man was appointed to the office for life. The Romans, however, prevented this practice and appointed high priests by their own authority. Thus Annas held the office from A.D. 6 to 15, while Caiaphas (his son-in-law) was recognized as high priest from A.D. 18 to 36. Perhaps the Jews still considered Annas to hold the position, or it may have been that Annas was the real power behind the high-priesthood of the younger man.

3:2b-3. The important event of this time is the coming of **the word of God** to John the Baptist. This clearly puts John within the tradition of Israel's prophets upon whom, like Jeremiah, "the word of the Lord came" (Jeremiah 1:2). In contrast to Mark 1:45 and Matthew 3:1, 5, John is presented here as going out into **all the region about the Jordan** to preach.

His message has two main features: a call to repentance and the demand of baptism. The idea that he preached **a baptism of repentance for the forgiveness of sins** is dependent on Mark 1:4. For Luke repentance has become practically synonymous with conversion, while baptism is the action which symbolizes the acceptance of the new faith.

3:4-6. Mark is also Luke's source for the quotation from Isaiah. Luke modifies his source at two points:

(1) He omits the first part of the quotation which Mark erroneously attributes to Isaiah (actually from Malachi 3:1).

(2) He lengthens Mark's quotation of Isaiah 40:3 to include verses 4-5. The result of this second change is to stress the universality of the coming salvation: **all flesh shall see the salvation of God.** Luke's understanding of John is similar to the rest of early Christian tradition. He is **the voice . . . crying in the wilderness** to **prepare the way of the Lord.** The **Lord** here is Jesus; John is the forerunner of the Christ.

3:7-20. *The Message of John.* Luke omits the description of John found in Mark 1:6. The presentation of John's message of doom is based on Q. Verses 7-9 are practically identical with Matthew 3:7-10. Whereas Matthew presents these words as spoken to the Pharisees and Sadducees, Luke reports that they are directed **to the multitudes.** In content this Q material declares the wrath, or judgment, of God. Before it sheer dependence on descent from **Abraham** is of no avail. Judgment is imminent; **the axe** is already at **the root of the trees.**

3:10-14. John's message of judgment has demanded **fruits that befit repentance.** In a passage which has no parallel Luke describes what this means. The multitudes ask, **What then shall**

we do? John answers that those who have abundance should **share** with the needy; this is true for both food and clothing.

Representatives of various groups now come to inquire what the fruit of their repentance should be. The tax collectors, or publicans, were notorious on two counts. First, they had sold out to the Romans who had farmed the collection of taxes out to them. Second, they were constantly tempted to charge a rate as high as the traffic would bear. John's advice is directed to this latter sin: **Collect no more than is appointed you.**

Next **soldiers also** came. Since Jews were exempt from service in the Roman legions, these may have been troops of Herod Antipas. The Baptist demands that they refrain from the typical evils of soldiery—**violence,** extortion, and discontent. That these social commands are not entirely in harmony with John's eschatology seems evident. Perhaps Luke is attempting to define repentance in terms meaningful to an ethical Greek. Some of Jesus' teachings from the Sermon on the Plain (6:17-49) are thereby anticipated.

3:15-18. Luke's presentation of the messianic preaching of John is based on Mark and Q. Only Luke, however, records the question of the people **concerning John, whether perhaps he were the Christ.** Luke therefore makes John's denial of his own messiahship and confession of one **who is mightier** than himself more explicit than the other evangelists. The figure of the slave who is not even **worthy to untie** his master's **sandals** is taken from Mark 1:7, while the symbol of the terrible thresher is based on Q (cf. Matthew 3:12).

The linking of **Holy Spirit** and **fire,** found also in Matthew, has special significance for Luke. It anticipates the events of Pentecost (Acts 2:3-4), when "tongues as of fire" will be distributed upon those who receive the Spirit. Luke adds the editorial note that **with many other exhortations, he preached good news.** John's note of doom has little to commend it as "good news," but by Luke's time the words had become a technical term for preaching in the mission of the church.

3:19-20, Luke adds a final note about the end of John's career.

This account reflects John's criticism of Herod's marital relations, but the story of John's death as recorded in Mark 6:17-29 is lacking in Luke. It may be that this historian is intentionally correcting Mark's mistaken notion that Antipas' wife had been married to Philip. In any event Luke is anxious to complete his story of John so that he can go on to Jesus. The Baptist will appear again in chapter 7, but from now on his significance is solely in relationship to the Christ.

3:21-22. *The Baptism of Jesus.* Among those who come for baptism is Jesus. Luke's account of this event is based on Mark 1:9-11, though some traces of Q can be seen. The resulting narrative has three unique features:

(1) Luke makes baptism subordinate to the coming of the Spirit. In fact the actual baptizing of Jesus is not described, but is only a part of a dependent clause which points to the important event: **the Holy Spirit descended upon him.**

(2) Luke tells us that the coming of the Spirit is preceded by a period of private prayer. Luke, more than any other of the gospel writers, depicts the prayer life of Jesus. The connection between praying and the coming of the Spirit is found also in Acts 8:15.

(3) Luke says that the Spirit descended on him **in bodily form, as a dove.** The rabbis described the brooding of the Spirit in the creation and Luke surely understands his account in a symbolic fashion. The point is to show that the event of the Spirit's coming is not subjective but an actual act of God. This real possession of the Holy Spirit is basic to Luke's whole understanding of the ministry of Jesus. He is the one who has the Spirit; he is the one through whom God acts.

3:22*b.* Revelation by a **voice . . . from heaven** was a traditional feature of rabbinic debate. Perhaps the text should read: "Thou art my Son; today I have begotten thee" (cf. the footnote in the Revised Standard Version). It is clear that Luke understands Jesus to stand in a special relationship to God—a relationship that defies ordinary definition and demands a whole set of symbols which point to the divine.

C. THE GENEALOGY OF THE SON OF GOD
(3:23-38)

Luke's account presents two problems: the relation of this genealogy to that of Matthew 1:1-16; and the tension between the genealogies and the virgin birth. Since the genealogies of Luke and Matthew differ, they probably rest on different traditions. Both depend to some degree on the Old Testament. Luke's list makes use of passages like Genesis 5:3-32. The main differences between Matthew and Luke are:

(1) Matthew begins with Abraham and traces the descendants down to Jesus, while Luke starts with Jesus and lists the ancestry back through **Abraham** to **Adam** and finally to God.

(2) Matthew's genealogy includes forty-two generations, while Luke's total is seventy-seven. Even within the same period, from Jesus to Abraham, Luke has fifty-six names while Matthew has only forty-two.

(3) The names of the two lists, though agreeing at many points, differ especially between Joseph and Zerubbabel. Luke lists the father of Joseph as **Heli** while Matthew has Jacob.

Luke is aware of the tension between genealogy and virgin birth. He says that Jesus was **the son (as was supposed) of Joseph.** The fact that he lists Joseph indicates that Luke intends to trace the ancestry of Jesus through his earthly father. The notion of some interpreters that Luke is proposing a genealogy through Mary is without support.

It is possible, of course, that Luke wishes to establish the Davidic descent of Jesus by listing the legal father of Jesus. At any rate he is alert to the fact that a genealogy which traces the divine sonship through human ancestors is not entirely consistent with the belief that Jesus is conceived by the Spirit. Most likely Luke is true to the various traditions he has received. Though not entirely harmonious, they point to a confession which transcends biological beliefs. Jesus is both son of David and Son of God.

That symbolic ideas are involved is clear from Luke's total of seventy-seven generations. Apparently the figure is the result of two important Hebrew numbers: seven is the normal holy digit, while twelve is the true number of God's people. Jesus initiates the twelfth, or perfect, generation; seven times eleven equals seventy-seven, or the number of generations before Christ.

The use of Adam involves another typical Lukan idea—the universal significance of Jesus. He is not simply the Jewish Messiah, son of Abraham and son of David. He is the **son of Adam,** the son of the father of the whole human race.

D. The Temptation of Jesus (4:1-13)

Jesus has received the Spirit at baptism. Now **full of the Holy Spirit,** he is **led by the Spirit** into the **wilderness** to be **tempted by the devil.** The source of this account is Q (cf. Matthew 4:1-11).

4:2b-4. In introducing the first temptation Luke makes the fasting of Jesus more explicit—**he ate nothing in those days.**

4:5-8. Luke presents the temptations as occurring in a different order from that reported in Matthew. The second temptation is described as the vision of **all the kingdoms of the world in a moment of time.** It may be that Luke envisages the temptations moving west from the wilderness of the Jordan to the mountains and finally into Jerusalem. In any case he does not say that this temptation occurred on a mountain. Instead **the devil took him up,** as if Jesus is taken up into the air. For Luke the mountain is a place of prayer and revelation, not a place for temptation.

4:9-12. The third temptation is practically the same as Matthew's second. For Luke it is climactic, since important events occur in the Holy City; it is the place of Jesus' destiny.

4:13. Luke's account of the ending of the temptation narrative differs from that of Matthew, who speaks of ministering angels not mentioned by Luke. For him the important thing is that the **devil departed from Jesus until an opportune time.** Since the devil does not again appear in this gospel until he comes to enter Judas (22:3), the period of Jesus' life is a time when Satan has been expelled. It is the time when God's purposes are being fulfilled in history.

To be sure, Luke understands the temptation in terms consistent with the tradition. After his baptism Jesus must wrestle with the meaning of his divine sonship. He rejects all temptations to be a popular or miracle-working messiah. He interprets his role by means of the Old Testament. That he is the Son of God is confirmed by his defeat of Satan.

III. THE ACTS OF JESUS IN GALILEE
(4:14–9:50)

A. PREACHING AND REJECTION IN NAZARETH (4:14-31)

4:14-15. *A Summary.* The source of this summary of Jesus' work in Galilee is Mark 1:14-15. Luke makes some interesting changes. For one thing he does not say that Jesus' work began after the arrest of John, but points out that **Jesus returned in the power of the Spirit.** The Holy Spirit which he received at baptism becomes the ruling force in his whole ministry. Luke also fails to say that Jesus was preaching the imminent coming of the kingdom of God. As often, he avoids details which would focus upon the futuristic features of eschatology.

4:16-30. *Jesus' Reading from Isaiah.* In presenting Jesus' mission as beginning in **Nazareth,** Luke departs from the order of Mark. Although his account has a few points of contact with Mark's later report of a ministry in Nazareth (Mark 6:1-6), the source of this narrative is basically Luke's special material, L. However, Luke is aware of the fact that Jesus did not really begin his ministry in his home town. In verse 23 he makes it evident that previous work had been done at Capernaum. Luke's order therefore must have been shaped by some purpose other than the historical. It attempts to present a kind of prefiguring of the whole mission of Jesus. Although accepted by others, Jesus is rejected by his own.

Luke's story is a comment on Mark 6:5—a passage omitted by

201

Luke—which says that Jesus "could do no mighty work" in Nazareth. Luke points out that Jesus has done mighty works elsewhere after his own people have rejected him and because this mission to others was of the very purpose of God.

4:16-17. The actual mission to Nazareth took place in **the synagogue.** Since it was his custom to be there on the sabbath, Jesus is presented as a faithful Jew. His behavior in the synagogue is according to regular practice. Any layman could participate, and the posture for reading was to stand, while one sat to expound. The text which Jesus reads was a familiar one—Isaiah 61:1-2. It would be found in a scroll from the treasured collection of the synagogue.

4:18-21. The surprising thing is Jesus' interpretation. **Today this scripture has been fulfilled in your hearing** means that Jesus understands his own mission as fulfilling the ancient prophecy. He is the one **anointed . . . to preach good news to the poor;** his baptism was the event of his anointing with the Spirit. Jesus is the one who will **proclaim release to the captives and recovering of sight to the blind.** The latter anticipates Jesus' ministry of physical healing, whereas the former, along with the declaration that he will **set at liberty those who are oppressed,** refers to Jesus' ability to cast out the demons who hold persons in bondage. In a deeper sense the entire ministry of Jesus provides a salvation from the forces which oppress all humans.

Most important, Jesus announces **the acceptable year of the Lord.** It might be better to translate this "the year of the Lord's favor," as in Isaiah 61:2, for it means that now is the time of God's fulfillment. Now is the acceptable time; all of the prophetic expectations reach their accomplishment in Jesus Christ.

4:22-24. The reaction to this sermon seems to be double. While **all spoke well of him,** there are some who doubt. **Is not this Joseph's son?** The evidence is against his being the Messiah.

To make this division even sharper, Jesus tells two proverbs. The first gives voice to his critics: **Physician, heal yourself.** This means that Jesus is being challenged to begin his work at home. Instead Jesus has been performing acts of power in rival **Capernaum.**

The second proverb says, **No prophet is acceptable in his own country.** This is Jesus' reply to the first. The reason a prophet cannot perform his works at home is that no one there is ready to accept him.

4:25-27. Jesus goes on to alienate his countrymen further. This time he takes up two biblical illustrations. In the first **Elijah** provides never-failing meal and oil for a **widow** (I Kings 17:8-24). The point is that she comes from **Zarephath in the land of Sidon.** Though there were many widows in Israel, God sent his prophet to a woman of the Gentiles. Similarly **there were many lepers in Israel at the time of . . . Elisha** (II Kings 5:1-27), but God's healing came to none of them. Instead his power cleansed a Gentile—**Naaman** of Syria. Thus what Jesus is doing is according to the purpose of God: to abandon his own who have rejected him and turn to those who are ready to receive.

4:28-30. The angry crowd puts Jesus out of the synagogue, **out of the city,** and tries to destroy him. This account of an attempt to push Jesus over a cliff is recorded nowhere else in the New Testament. The traditional place can be viewed by modern visitors to Nazareth—a high bluff overlooking the plain of Esdraelon. Jesus escapes, and his ability to pass **through the midst of them** seems miraculous. This effort to execute Jesus is prophetic; it looks forward to his death in Jerusalem. Just as Jesus is rejected in his home town, so he will be destroyed by the rulers of Israel. His escape, however, makes possible a mission elsewhere, just as his resurrection will make possible a mission to the world.

B. Activity in the Vicinity of Capernaum
(4:31–5:16)

4:31-37. *An Exorcism in the Synagogue.* After describing the ministry in Nazareth, Luke presents Jesus as going **down to Capernaum.** The journey did involve descent. Nazareth is in the hill country, while Capernaum is on the edge of the lake, over six hundred feet below sea level. A synagogue on the northern shore of Galilee has been excavated which, though dating from about A.D. 200, probably rests on the site of the Capernaum synagogue of Jesus' day.

The account here is taken from Mark 1:21-28. Luke informs the non-Palestinian readers that Capernaum is **a city of Galilee** and omits Mark's notice that Jesus' authority was acknowledged as superior to that of the scribes.

4:33-37. Luke preserves the main content of Mark's story. The preaching of Jesus evokes a protest from a demoniac. Luke makes it clear that the man is possessed by **the spirit of an unclean demon.** Since Luke's readers believe the world is populated by hosts of demons, good and bad, it is important to point out that this spirit is evil. The demon, as in Mark's version of the story, recognizes the true nature of Jesus—he is **the Holy One of God,** the Messiah.

In describing the exorcism Luke heightens the miracle by saying that the man was **thrown . . . down in the midst** of the synagogue, yet without **harm.** The crowd is amazed at the power of Jesus and asks, **What is this word?** Here Luke employs the Greek *logos,* which had become in his time a technical term for the "word" of Christian preaching. That Jesus had the power to cast out demons is attested by the historical evidence, although demon possession and exorcism reflect a world view foreign to our own.

4:38-44. *Healings at Simon's House.* Luke has omitted Mark's account of the call of the first disciples (Mark 1:16-20). Instead he presents the story of a group of healing miracles at the house of Simon (see comment on Mark 1:29-39). He has shortened Mark's account. For example, in his story of the healing of **Simon's mother-in-law** he omits the names of Andrew, James, and John. However, Luke does give a fuller description of both the disease and the healing. Only he tells us that the mother-in-law **was ill with a high fever.**

Although this has been interpreted as illustrating Luke's clinical interest, his description of the manner of healing shows no evidence that the author was a physician. He says that Jesus **rebuked the fever.** Surely the Hellenistic doctors knew that fever was a symptom rather than a cause of disease, while the method of cure reflects the ancient notion that evil spirits were responsible for human malady.

4:40-41. Since it is the sabbath, large crowds cannot come for healing until the holy day has ended at sunset. Again Luke heightens the miraculous by noting that Jesus healed **every one** that came. Mark merely says he cured "many." The mode of healing is again described, for Jesus is shown as laying **hands** on his patients. As in the synagogue the **demons** recognize Jesus to be **the Son of God.** This is further clarified by the note that Jesus **would not allow them to speak, because they knew that he was the Christ.** The demons recognize what ordinary people do not see: Jesus is the Messiah, whose power threatens their very existence.

4:42-44. Since he is in danger of being understood as a miracle worker, Jesus departs to **a lonely place.** Though Luke usually emphasizes Jesus' prayer life, he does not say here that Jesus was praying. Instead of being pursued by the disciples, Jesus is followed by **the people,** who are anxious to retain this powerful practitioner. Jesus insists that he must go on to other cities. His purpose is to announce **the kingdom of God.**

This is the first time this phrase has been introduced into Luke's narrative. For him it means that God's rule has come into history in Jesus himself. His power over the demons is proof of this. Moreover Jesus follows the divine intention; he **was sent** from God **for this** very **purpose.** Luke concludes that Jesus **was preaching in the synagogues of Judea,** which does not mean a mission to the south. **Judea** to Luke usually means Palestine.

5:1-11. *The Call of Disciples.* As a substitute for Mark's call of the first disciples Luke records the account of the miraculous catch of fish. This story has no parallel in the other gospels. The fact that Jesus sometimes **taught the people from** a **boat** is mentioned in Mark 4:1, but most of Luke's narrative is taken from his special tradition, L.

Some think the original was a post-resurrection story, because a kind of parallel is found in John 21 and because the confession of Simon would make better sense after his denial. At any rate Luke presents this event as occurring by the lakeside as Jesus is teaching. Typically Luke calls the sea **Gennesaret** and refers to it as a **lake;** the word "sea" would be understood by his readers as describing the Mediterranean. The message of Jesus is again called **the word of God** (see above on 4:33-37).

5:4-9. Jesus gives the command for Simon to **put out into the deep.** That symbolic ideas are involved is seen in the fact that catching fish is a sign of the Christian mission. The deep is the abyss (cf. 8:31) from which all persons must be saved. When Jesus commands that he should **let down your nets** Simon responds with a title of respect, **"Master."** But his doubts are evident: **We toiled all night and took nothing!** Nevertheless, he is obedient. The resulting catch is so great that nets are breaking and two boats begin to sink.

At this point Simon falls down before Jesus and cries, **Depart from me, for I am a sinful man, O Lord.** He recognizes Jesus to be more than master; he is the exalted Lord of all. Simon's confession of sin indicates that he has doubted Jesus. He has not believed that Jesus is the Christ, and he has not realized that the power of God is at work in him.

5:9-11. As well as Simon, **James and John** are astonished. These together make up the inner circle; Andrew is not mentioned. The three are called to participate in Jesus' divine mission. **Henceforth** they **will be catching men.** The phrase translated **henceforth** means "from the now," "from now on." "Now" is a favorite word of Luke's. It means that God's eschatological purposes are at this time being fulfilled in history. The disciples respond, leaving **everything** to follow their Lord. Thus the call of the disciples is given a dramatic setting. The mission of God is grounded in the miracle of divine action.

5:12-16. *Healing a Leper.* Jesus' power to rescue is seen in this story, which is based on Mark 1:40-45. Although he shortens the account and adds his own introduction, Luke reproduces Mark's narrative faithfully. He tells us that the man was **full of leprosy** so that the seriousness of the disease is certain. The leper addresses Jesus as **Lord,** thus offering a kind of confession. The belief that Jesus healed him out of compassion is missing from

Luke's narrative, and the warning **to tell no one** is less severe.

Luke also adds his own ending to the story: Jesus **withdrew to the wilderness and prayed,** which reveals Luke's interest in Jesus as a man of prayer. This ending also serves to correct Mark's notion that "Jesus could no longer openly enter a town" (Mark 1:45). In this text Jesus is again presented as faithful to Jewish ritual requirements (Leviticus 14:2-32), but the man who goes **to the priest** gains his main importance as a witness to the people of what God has done.

C. CONTROVERSIES WITH THE PHARISEES (5:17–6:11)

5:17-26. *Healing a Paralytic.* Luke begins a series of stories which illustrate the growing conflict between Jesus and his opponents. The healing of the paralyzed man is recorded in Mark 2:1-12. Luke's account is shorter and less vivid. For example, he leaves out the detail that the paralytic is carried by four men. Luke's narrative also includes references of special interest to his readers. He explains that scribes are **teachers of the law** and assumes a non-Palestinian architecture in noting that the sick man was let down **through the tiles.**

He displays his typical interest in the Christian mission— Jesus' hearers come from **every village of Galilee and Judea and from Jerusalem.** Although the source for this information could be Mark 3:7 it is unlikely that Jesus had such an extensive following at this stage of his career. Similarly Luke's notice that the man who had been healed **went home, glorifying God** stresses the importance of Christian witness. Throughout the story Jesus is presented as the exalted Christ, the **Son of man,** who has the power and **authority** to forgive sins—a prerogative which the Jews assigned to God only.

5:27-32. *The Call and Feast of Levi.* The source for this account is Mark 2:13-17. Luke shortens the introduction by omitting the information that the event occurred beside the lake. The commitment of Levi is heightened; Luke tells us that **he left everything.** This seems out of harmony with the rest of the story, for if Levi left everything how could he make a **great feast in his house?**

Luke has the opponents criticize the disciples instead of Jesus. It is the church, rather than its Lord, which is being attacked. The mission must go to those who need it most. Jesus came, not **to call the righteous, but sinners.** Only Luke adds that the call is **to repentance,** thus indicating that people are required to respond to the work of God.

5:33-39. *Fasting and Rejoicing.* At the feast of Levi the question is raised as to why the disciples do not fast. The answer shows that Jesus has little interest in religious customs and that his message, in contrast to that of John the Baptist, is one of joy.

Two illustrations, the patch on a **garment** and **new wine** in **old wineskins,** show that the faith embodied in Jesus is radically new. The source is Mark 2:18-22, and Luke offers only minor changes. For one thing he makes the parable of the patch ludicrous. No one tears a **new garment** to patch an **old;** the result would be the ruin of both. Luke also adds a unique conclusion to the episode. Since **the old is good** no one wants to drink new wine. This saying, which is lacking in some manuscripts, may represent the irony or humor of Jesus. More likely it originates in the later life of the church. At a time when Christians are being challenged with a mission to the world some hold to the outmoded ways of Judaism.

6:1-11. *Concerning the Sabbath.* Two incidents illustrate the controversy over keeping the holy day. The story about "harvesting" grain on the sabbath is based on Mark 2:23-28. The sin of the disciples is not that they ate grain which did not belong to them but that they "worked" on the sabbath day. Luke makes this clear in his description of the disciples as plucking **ears of grain** and **rubbing** them **in their hands.**

6:3-5. In defending this action Jesus cites an incident from the career of David (I Samuel 21:1-6). Luke omits Mark's mistaken reference to Abiathar as high priest at that time. After verse 4 some manuscripts add the following saying: "On the same day he saw a man breaking the sabbath by working and said to him, 'If you are doing this deliberately, you are blessed: but if you are acting out of ignorance, you are transgressing the law and are accursed.'" It is unlikely that these words are authentic, but they indicate the early Christian belief that the sabbath should be intentionally broken.

Luke omits Mark's word that "the sabbath was made for man, not man for the sabbath"—a statement indicating that Jesus originally said that *man* (the meaning of the Aramaic idiom "son of man") is **lord of the sabbath.** For Luke the meaning is that Jesus Christ, the exalted Lord, is ruler of the sabbath. He has abrogated ritual laws and his followers need not obey Jewish regulations about holy days.

6:6-11. The second incident concerns a man with a serious malady. Luke notes that it is his **right hand** which is **withered** and specifies the **scribes and the Pharisees** as Jesus' opponents on this occasion. With typical supernatural power Jesus knows the **thoughts** of his accusers. He does not, as in Mark, look at them with anger. Instead it is the foes of Jesus who are **filled with fury.** Luke does not list the Herodians among them, since these would have been unknown to his non-Palestinian readers. The healing of the man illustrates Jesus' belief that the sabbath is a time **to do good.** Of course no rabbi imagined that the sabbath was a day **to do harm,** yet for Jesus not to do good was an evil in itself.

D. THE CALL OF THE TWELVE (6:12-16)

To aid in the mission Jesus enlists twelve disciples. This list of names, with minor variations, is found in Mark 3:13-19; Matthew 10:1-4; and Acts 1:13. Some scholars do not believe the selection goes back to Jesus himself, since the lists are not entirely consistent. Luke names **Judas the son of James** where Mark and Matthew have Thaddaeus. In his unique introduction to the account Luke says that Jesus **continued all night in prayer;** thus the choice of the twelve is by divine guidance.

Luke has Jesus confer on them the title "apostle." For Luke the important thing about the **apostles** is their official position in the early church. Perhaps this explains his omission of their more charismatic functions, "to preach" and "to cast out demons" (Mark 3:14-15). It may be this more refined view of ecclesiastical office which has led Luke to avoid the description of James and John as "sons of thunder" (Mark 3:17).

E. THE SERMON ON THE PLAIN (6:17-49)

6:17-26. *Setting, Blessings, and Woes.* In order to declare the demands of discipleship Jesus presents a sermon. Most of its contents can be found in Matthew's Sermon on the Mount. But since Matthew includes much material which is found in other contexts, we can conclude that Luke probably follows Q more faithfully. Luke prefers to preserve the mountain as a place of prayer and vision; he has Jesus come down to **a level place** to deliver the sermon. The account of its setting is based on Mark 3:7-11. Again the mission of Jesus is presented as casting an influence over a wide area. The crowd which comes from distant places is anxious **to touch** Jesus, for a sort of supernatural force emanates from his person.

6:20-23. Luke is usually credited with presenting the Beatitudes in their more original form (see comment on Matthew 5:3-12). He lists only four and presents four "woes" in parallel. In contrast to Matthew the form of Luke's account is briefer and less interpretative. He has Jesus bless the poor and the hungry without offering any spiritual interpretation.

As well as showing Luke's interest in the lower classes this formula sounds an eschatological note. The poor symbolize the pious of Israel who await the coming of the Lord. The vivid character of Luke's blessings can be seen in the third beatitude—the contrast between weeping **now** and laughing in the time to come. Throughout this section of the sermon Jesus is presented as speaking directly to his listeners: **Blessed are you.**

6:24-26. The woes, together with the blessings, show the reversal of values in the time of fulfillment and also reflect the prophetic condemnation of the oppressors (cf. Isaiah 65:13). The woes have no parallel in Matthew.

6:27-45. *The Demands of Love.* This section of the sermon is also drawn from Q (cf. Matthew 5:38-48). First Jesus is presented as requiring love and rejecting retaliation. Luke's reporting here is fuller than Matthew's. The love which discipleship demands, like the love of God, extends to those who do not deserve it: to **your enemies,** to **those who hate you,** to **those who curse you,** and to **those who abuse you.** Luke then gives concrete examples of this love which are found also in Matthew.

6:32-36. Luke's presentation of a love which reaches out to those who do not love you is more explicit than Matthew's. Verse 34 has no parallel; it declares that the disciple must **lend** without expecting to be repaid. That no bank could operate on such principles is obvious, but the demand of love conforms to no ordinary standards. Instead one must **be merciful, even as your Father is merciful.** This form of the command is more original and more demanding than Matthew's. To be perfect in the Old Testament is a human attainment; to be merciful is an attribute of God.

6:37-38. Luke's word forbidding judging is similar to Matthew 7:1-5, but his description of giving is fuller. The one who forgives and gives receives in return **good measure, pressed down, shaken together, running over.** This figure of speech is borrowed from the grain trade; it represents filling a container to full and overflowing. The word translated **lap** refers to a fold of cloth gathered over the girdle—a sort of big pocket which could hold a large quantity of one's personal possessions.

6:39-45. Into the discussion of judging Luke inserts the parable of the **blind** leading the **blind** (cf. Matthew 15:14) and the saying that **a disciple is not above his teacher** (cf. Matthew 10:24-25). These words seem out of context here. The connection appears to be with what follows. The saying about the **speck** and **log** in one's **eye** indicates that the leader must have good vision. A blind man is not a good guide for the blind.

211

But if one judges his brother, this shows that he does not have good sight; he cannot be a leader or teacher.

All of this describes the kind of leadership needed in the church of Luke's day. The word about the **good tree** and the **good fruit** makes the same point (cf. Matthew 7:16-20). There must be a unity between the inner and the outer person. Only the truly **good man out of the good treasure of his heart** can produce **good.** Disciples are those who do not judge, whose vision is clear, whose heart is right.

6:46-49. The Parable of the Builders. Luke, like Matthew, concludes the sermon with a parable taken from Q (cf. Matthew 7:24-27). Essentially the same, the parables make clear that Jesus expects his words to be obeyed. Luke's version seems to imagine a non-Palestinian urban setting. Instead of choosing a place to build, his builder **dug deep, and laid the foundation upon rock.** Rather than the torrential rains of Palestine, Luke depicts the swelling of some important river. In any event the house falls if it is not properly constructed. Likewise one falls if one does not do the word of the Lord. Perhaps Luke is describing the testing which comes upon the church.

F. ACTS OF HEALING (7:1-50)

7:1-10. The Centurion's Slave. Although the source is Q, Luke's account is longer than Matthew's (cf. Matthew 8:5-13). The story recounts the cure of a Gentile's servant and approves this centurion's faith as greater than any Jesus has encountered in Israel.

The unique feature of Luke's narrative is its failure to relate any direct contact between the centurion and Jesus. Instead two delegations are sent as intermediaries. The first, composed of the leaders of the Jewish congregation, points out that the foreigner is deserving of help; **he loves our nation, and he built our** place of worship. Thus the centurion is a "God-fearer"—a Gentile sympathetic to the Jewish religion.

7:6-10. The second delegation brings the message that the

centurion is **not worthy to have** Jesus **come under my roof.**
Luke's form of the story heightens the officer's humility, since it
also implies that the centurion is unworthy to come into Jesus'
presence. At any rate the Gentile is a man who knows both how
to exercise and how to accept authority. His submission to the
authority of Jesus is a sign of his faith.

Luke does not include Matthew's word that "many will come
from east and west," since he uses it elsewhere (13:28-30). Yet
its message echoes a Lukan theme: the mission to the ends of the
earth is begun by Jesus himself, even though the work is to be
accomplished through intermediaries.

7:11-17. *The Widow's Son.* The story of the raising of the
widow's son comes from Luke's special material, L. It is without
parallel in the gospel tradition. The background of the account is
found in I Kings 17:17-24, where Elijah gives life to a widow's
son, and in II Kings 4:32-37, where Elisha performs a similar
miracle. When Luke concludes his narrative by noting that the
people exclaim, **A great prophet has arisen among us,** it is
evident that a major purpose of the story is to present Jesus in
parallel to the powerful prophets of old.

7:11-12. A town some six miles southeast of Nazareth has been
identifed as the ancient site of **Nain.** Outside the east gate a
cemetery is located. According to Jewish custom a person was
buried late in the afternoon of the day of death. Since honoring
the dead was considered a meritorious work, the large funeral
procession is to be expected.

7:13-17. In introducing Jesus to the story Luke calls him
Lord. Jesus is the Lord of life with power over death. The
motivation for his action is **compassion;** nothing is said of faith.
Jesus touches the corpse, contaminating himself with ceremonial uncleanness of death. The Jews carried their dead
enshrouded upon a stretcher; the term **bier,** or casket, reflects
Luke's familiarity with the customs of the Greek world. At Jesus'
command the young man rises from the dead. Jesus is the one
who calls the living forth from the dead. Not only is this miracle
a sign that Jesus is a **prophet;** it also indicates that **God has**

visited his people. This means that God is present in the act of Jesus. Little wonder that **fear seized them all.**

Although Luke understands it as a miraculous event, the primary significance of this resurrection is its meaning for faith. It expresses the Christian's conviction that life comes through encounter with Jesus Christ. The story also prepares for the witness to John the Baptist: "the dead are raised up" (verse 22).

7:18-35. *The Significance of John.* The stage is now set for introducing the messianic question of John the Baptist. Luke's source for the account is Q (cf. Matthew 11:2-19). First John sends representatives to inquire about Jesus' messiahship. They are told **to tell John** that they have seen the messianic prophecies fulfilled in the acts of Jesus. Luke, with his usual fondness for a double witness, suggests that **two of** John's **disciples** are sent. He also gives the messianic question more emphasis through repeating it a second time. In his account the acts of fulfillment are accomplished immediately before the eyes of John's emissaries; **in that hour** Jesus **cured many of diseases and plagues and evil spirits** (cf. Isaiah 29:18-19; 35:5-6; 61:1). Luke's normal stress on eschatological fulfillment in the present moment of Jesus' mission is evident.

7:24-30. Now that John's question about Jesus has been answered the narrative proceeds to relate Jesus' view of John. In essence John is recognized as a **prophet** who plays the role of forerunner of the Messiah. Although **among those born of women none is greater than John** he still belongs to the old age. **He who is least in the kingdom of God is greater than** John, and the new age has started to come in Jesus.

Luke inserts a parenthetical sentence which further evaluates John's work. He notes that those who submitted to John's baptism, the ordinary **people** and the sinful **tax collectors, justified God;** that is, they acknowledged that God's way was just. On the other hand, those who refused the baptism of John, **the Pharisees and the lawyers, rejected the purpose of God.** All of this indicates that Luke accepts John's mission as determined by the plan and purpose of God.

7:31-35. The parable of the fickle **children** illustrates the reaction of the hearers of both John and Jesus. John has come as an ascetic and the people suppose him possessed. Jesus has come **eating and drinking** and they charge him with excesses. The final saying of Jesus is perhaps proverbial. It suggests that true **wisdom** is approved **by all her children.** In contrast to the foolish children of the parable these children of wisdom are those who have accepted John and Jesus. In them the wisdom of God—his purposes in history—are manifest.

7:36-50. *The Forgiveness of Sins.* Luke has a fondness for banquet scenes. Here he uses one as the setting for Jesus' forgiveness of a gross sinner. Although there is some relationship to Mark 14:3-9, the source of this narrative is L. The previous story has concluded with a description of Jesus as a friend of sinners. Now that description is illustrated with an actual event.

Jesus, who is still on relatively good terms with his opposition, is invited to the **house** of **Simon,** a **Pharisee,** for dinner. As the meal proceeds, a sinful **woman** washes Jesus' **feet** with her **tears,** wipes them with her **hair,** kisses his feet, and anoints them with ointment from **an alabaster flask.** Since the position for eating is to recline with feet away from the table, the woman approaches Jesus from **behind.** However, **if** he **were a prophet,** as his actions seem to indicate, he would know **what sort of woman this is.** To be touched by her is to be contaminated with her sin. Just what kind of sinner she is has not been made clear, but it is implied that her sin is of the lowest sort, perhaps prostitution.

7:40-43. To counter Simon's criticism Jesus tells a parable. His ability to perceive the thoughts of his host, of course, proves him to be truly a prophet. The parable tells of a **creditor** who **had two debtors.** One owed him **five hundred denarii,** while the other's debt was **fifty.** Since one denarius was a day's wage for common labor, it is evident that the first debtor owed a large amount. The creditor forgave them both. **Which,** asks Jesus, **will love him more?** Simon answers, with Jesus' approval, **The one . . . to whom he forgave more.**

7:44-46. Next Jesus applies the parable to the situation at hand. Simon has failed to offer Jesus the ordinary courtesies of a guest. He has not provided for the washing of Jesus' feet; he has not presented Jesus with the **kiss** of greeting; he has not honored Jesus by anointing his **head with oil.** The woman, by way of contrast, has offered all these duties with utmost humility. Simon's failure to accept the responsibilities of a host gives the story a certain sense of unreality, although it is possible that Simon treats Jesus without respect as an inferior guest.

7:47-48. Jesus concludes his application by saying, **Her sins, which are many, are forgiven, for she loved much.** Actually this conclusion is not supported by the parable, in which we were told that one who was forgiven much loved much. The same point is made in the latter part of verse 47 when Jesus goes on to say that **he who is forgiven little, loves little.**

Luke's reversal could indicate that the woman was previously forgiven by Jesus and now is expressing the love which results. Most likely Luke is not aware of any tension. The love and forgiveness of God is always present before its appropriation by persons.

7:49-50. It is clear that Luke has combined more than one tradition here. The final words of the passage introduce the debate about the right to forgive sins, which is out of context. Moreover, the expression that the woman's **faith has saved** her introduces ideas which are foreign to the narrative.

G. TEACHINGS OF THE KINGDOM OF GOD (8:1-56)

8:1-18. *The Purpose of Parables.* Luke begins this section with a description of the ministering women. Although reference to their activity is found in Mark 15:40-41, this passage is without exact parallel. It indicates that Jesus' Galilean ministry was supported by a group of well-to-do women who had benefited from his power to cast out **evil spirits** and cure infirmities. Specifically, **seven demons** had been exorcised from **Mary . . . Magdalene,** who is not necessarily to be identified with the sinful woman of the preceding passage. To be sure, the

town of Magdala had a reputation for prostitution. **Joanna,** the
wife of Herod's steward, is mentioned again in 24:10. **Chuza,**
the name of her husband, has been found in inscriptions from
Nabatea, but about the man and his office nothing is known.
Susanna is mentioned nowhere else in the biblical record. Luke
says that there were **many others.**

Although Luke had a special interest in women's place in the
kingdom's ministry, his story is probably based on good
historical data. The manuscripts which read that the women
provided for **them** are to be preferred to those which say "him";
the ministry was to Jesus and the twelve, not simply to Jesus
alone.

8:4-8. During this preaching mission Jesus delivers the
parable of the sower. Here Luke returns to Mark (4:1-25) for the
first time since 6:17. In an abbreviated form Luke reproduces
the story of the sower who **went out to sow** and whose seed fell
on a variety of soils. Luke adds that the seed which **fell along the
path . . . was trodden under foot.** Instead of "rocky ground" he
says that some fell on **the rock** and **withered away, because it
had no moisture.** Apparently Luke is thinking of a thin layer of
soil over a shelf of rock. Luke adopts only Mark's high estimate
of the harvest from the good ground; it **yielded a hundredfold.**
On verse 8*b* see comment on Matthew 13:9.

8:9-10. Luke's account of the reason for speaking in parables is
much milder than Mark's. For one thing Luke applies this
purpose only to the parable under discussion, not to all parables.
He also omits Mark's word that this explanation is spoken to the
twelve "alone" and refrains from describing those who do not
understand the parables as "those outside."

Most important, Luke drops Mark's idea that the parables are
spoken "lest they should turn again, and be forgiven." Mark was
attempting to explain how some could hear the parables of Jesus
and not understand. He believed that the answer must be found
in the very intention of God (cf. Isaiah 6:9-10, which Matthew
quotes here). Luke recognizes that the **secrets,** or mysteries, of
the kingdom remain hidden, but he avoids the conclusion that

matters are destined to remain so. His very purpose is to make the message of Jesus clear.

8:11-15. In interpreting the parable of the sower Luke follows Mark. The parable had been turned into an allegory (see comment on Matthew 13:10-17) in an earlier stage of the tradition. This allegory reflects the missionary situation of the early church. At some points Luke's application is clearer than Mark's. He interprets the seed as the **word of God,** thus employing the technical term for the Christian gospel (see above on 4:33-37). He also describes those who **believe** and are **saved,** presenting a system of salvation which is supported by the early chapters of Acts. The allegory is not entirely clear. While the seed is said to be the word, it is soon identified with the variety of hearers.

8:16-18. These concluding sayings are more in harmony with the original purpose of the parables. **A lamp** is put **on a stand** so that **those who enter may see.** That which is hidden shall **be made manifest.** Those who hear will be able to understand increasingly. Jesus intended his parables to reveal the purposes of God.

8:19-21. *Jesus and His Relatives.* Whereas Mark located this story just prior to the parable of the sower, Luke puts it immediately after. Luke shortens Mark's account and presents the clash between Jesus and his family in much milder form. This is partly because Luke does not present the story in the context of the charge that Jesus is beside himself. Since this setting is lacking, what meaning can the account have in the context of Luke? The answer seems to be found in the climax of the story: the true relatives of Jesus are **those who hear the word of God and do it.** Thus this narrative carries on the activity just announced in the parable; the mission of God creates a new order of relationships.

8:22-25. *Commanding the Winds.* Luke begins a series of powerful miracle stories based on Mark. The stilling of the storm is drawn from Mark 4:35-41. In essence the story tells how Jesus was able to quiet a raging storm. Luke again calls Galilee **the lake.** He does not say that it is evening, although that could be inferred from the fact that Jesus **fell asleep.** The title **Master** is used for Jesus; he is recognized as the one of authority. His rebuke of the disciples is slightly softer than in Mark.

Whereas the nature miracles appear to us to involve triumph over natural law, Luke understands them in the setting of a world controlled by supernatural forces. A sudden storm is caused by a demon, and Jesus' rebuke of wind and waves confirms this world view. The point of the story is to reveal to the disciples one of the mysteries of the kingdom—the power of Jesus. Indeed he does the very things which God can do (cf. Psalm 107:25). The disciples raise the expectant question, **Who then is this?**

8:26-39. *Casting Out Demons.* Still following Mark's account of astounding miracles (Mark 5:1-20), Luke records the healing of the Gerasene demoniac. Essentially the story describes the cure of a man possessed of a number of demons. After recognizing Jesus as the Messiah this **Legion** of evil spirits invades a herd of swine, causing them to rush to their destruction at the bottom of the lake. Luke seems to assume that the **country of the Gerasenes** is non-Jewish territory, since it is **opposite Galilee** (on the geographical and textual problems in this see comment on Mark 5:1-20). His concern is to show that the power of God is effective even outside Palestine.

8:31-39. Only Luke tells us that the demons begged not to be sent **into the abyss.** The abyss, here symbolized by the depths of **the lake,** represents hell or the place where evil powers are kept captive for final judgment.

8:34-39. When Luke points out that the man **who had been possessed with demons was healed,** he uses the Greek term which also means to be saved. According to Luke **the people in the surrounding country . . . were seized with great fear.** This probably should not be taken to mean that they are worried about their economic losses but that they stand in awe of the mighty acts of God. Just as demons have been driven into perdition, so a man has received salvation.

8:40-56. *Healing a Woman and Raising a Girl.* Luke's third great miracle story in this section of his gospel is the raising of Jairus' daughter. Into this story is woven the healing of the woman with the hemorrhage. The source is Mark 5:21-43. In relating this restoration of life Luke presents the second witness of Jesus' power to raise the dead (cf. 7:11-17). The cure of the woman illustrates Luke's word from 6:19: "All the crowd sought to touch him, for power came forth from him." According to Luke, Jairus' **daughter**, like the son of the widow of Nain, is an **only** child. The two miracles are already joined in Mark's account, but Luke seems to find some connection in the fact that the daughter is **about twelve years of age** and the woman has been ill **for twelve years.**

8:42b-48. Luke abbreviates Mark's account. For one thing he fails to say that the woman had "spent all that she had" on "many physicians" and that she "was no better but rather grew worse." Instead of indicating sympathy with the medical profession this omission probably reflects an effort to remove irrelevant detail. Luke, like Matthew (9:20), says that the woman **touched the fringe of his garment.** This refers to the tassel on the corner of Jesus' garment which was thrown over his left shoulder—a reminder of Israel's obligation to the law (cf. Deuteronomy 22:12).

8:49-56. Luke adds a promise that the young girl will **be well,** using again the Greek word meaning both "healed" and "saved" (see above on verses 34-39). Luke does not give the Aramaic words of Mark 5:41—a typical omission.

Luke makes it clear that the mourners know **that she was dead.** The understanding of death and resurrection, however, betrays Greek ideas. In saying that **her spirit returned** Luke illustrates the Hellenistic belief that death involved the departure of the spirit from the body. As in the case of the widow's son the miracle has its meaning for faith. This is seen in the fact that only **Peter and John and James** are taken along to witness the raising; the private character of the miracle is even clearer in Mark. The meaning for faith is obvious. Jesus is the one who gives salvation to the dead now.

H. INSTRUCTIONS TO THE DISCIPLES (9:1-50)

9:1-6. *The Mission of the Twelve.* Luke continues to follow the order of Mark. Mark's account of the rejection at Nazareth has been omitted, but Luke has used this material previously (4:16-30). The report of the sending out of the twelve is based on Mark 6:6*b*-13; there are minor agreements with Matthew 10:1-14. In essence the fact that Jesus called the disciples to share in his mission is recorded. The form of the mission reflects practices of the earliest community rather than those of the time of Jesus or of the time of Luke.

Luke's account suggests that the twelve were given **power** as well as **authority over all demons.** The task is not only **to heal** but **to preach the kingdom of God.** Surprisingly Luke, in spite of his fondness for double witness, omits Mark's detail that they went out "two by two"; he will employ this description of the mission in his account of the sending out of the seventy (10:1-16). The radical dependence on God is seen in the fact that **no staff** is to be allowed. The story shows that the church's mission had its origin in the career of Jesus, that the mighty deeds of Jesus are repeated by the leaders of the church.

9:7-9. *The Reaction of Herod.* The mission has its effect on the highest authority. In describing the reaction of Herod Antipas to Jesus, Luke follows Mark 6:14-16. The word here that Herod **beheaded** John is Luke's only reference to the Baptist's death; he has not recorded the story of John's execution (Mark 6:17-29). In general the account reports the popular opinion about Jesus—an opinion confirmed by the record of Peter's confession (verses 18-22). Luke more accurately refers to Antipas as **the tetrarch** (see above on 3:1). In contrast to Mark's report that Herod identified Jesus with the risen John, Luke insists that the tetrarch raises the expectant question: **Who is this?** Luke also adds the note that Herod **sought to see** Jesus. This desire will be fulfilled at the trial of Jesus (23:8).

9:10-17. *Feeding the Crowd.* When the twelve return from their mission Jesus performs the miracle of the feeding of the five thousand. The source is Mark 6:30-44. Luke has shortened the story. Basically the tradition reports that Jesus fed a multitude of people by miraculous means. To the early church this act symbolized the Eucharist; the blessing and breaking of bread prefigured the Lord's Supper. Only Luke notices that the event took place in the vicinity of **Bethsaida**—a name which means "house of the fisher."

Luke also points out that the activity of Jesus on this occasion is twofold: preaching **the kingdom of God** and curing **those who had need of healing.** In Luke's account the concern is not only with **provisions** but also with a place **to lodge.** The church which offers teaching and salvation, provides through its central act of worship the basis for all of life.

9:18-27. *The Confession of Peter.* This account is based on Mark 8:27–9:1 and follows Luke's "great omission"—that is, the material of Mark 6:45–8:26 which is missing in Luke. Luke may have intentionally abandoned Mark here, or he may have used an edition of Mark which did not include this material.

Luke's account of the confession follows Mark closely though with variations. For example, Luke does not locate the event in the Gentile city of Caesarea Philippi but leaves the reader to suppose it occurred on Jewish soil. In noting that Jesus **was praying alone** when he raised the question about his popular identity Luke gives a divine setting. The answer confirms the report about Jesus which Herod received (verses 7-8). The actual confession differs slightly in all three Synoptic gospels. Luke's version—**the Christ of God**—is early in form and reflects simple recognition of Jesus' messiahship.

9:23-26. Peter's effort to dissuade Jesus from his suffering role and the subsequent rebuke from Jesus (Mark 8:32-33) are omitted by Luke. Perhaps he prefers to preserve the reputation of the apostolic leader, but more likely Luke wants nothing to detract from the necessity of the Christ's journey to Jerusalem. Discipleship demands following Jesus on this way of suffering.

The call to **take up** the **cross daily** may reflect, as many have claimed, a post-resurrection effort to spiritualize the demand of martyrdom and express in terms of Jesus' own crucifixion the realization that suffering is of the essence of the Christian life.

On the other hand it is possible that Jesus depicted discipleship under the demand of martyrdom and used as a symbol the cross, which was the common instrument of execution under the Romans. On verse 24 see comments on Matthew 10:39 and Mark 8:35.

9:27. Luke does not suggest that **some standing here** will see the kingdom come "with power" (Mark 9:1). Yet some who have witnessed the confession will see the **kingdom of God** manifest immediately in the transfiguration of Jesus.

9:28-36. *The Transfiguration.* Jesus' suffering has been predicted; now his glory is revealed. Luke's source is Mark 9:2-8. His account is slightly longer.

9:28-32. Luke says that this event occurred **eight days after** the confession rather than Mark's "six." Using the Roman method of reckoning time, he seems to assume a date one week later. Again Jesus is presented at prayer. To the story Luke adds that **Moses and Elijah . . . spoke of his departure.** That is, they are discussing the ultimate result of Jesus' trip to **Jerusalem**— his death, resurrection, and ascension. Only Luke points out that **Peter and John and James . . . were heavy with sleep.** This suggests that the transfiguration occurred at night—a setting which would magnify the radiance of the **raiment** which **became dazzling white.**

9:33-36. Luke makes it clear that Peter did not know **what he said** and that the fear of the disciples arose with the coming of the **cloud.** They are afraid of losing their master and in danger of failing to listen to the **Chosen** one of God. This event, which reflects the post-resurrection faith, is presented as happening **in those days;** that is, in the history of Jesus the glory of the risen Christ is revealed.

9:37-50. *The Weakness of the Disciples.* When Jesus comes down from the mountain **on the next day,** he is met by a man whose son is possessed by a demonic spirit. The account of their encounter is based on Mark 9:14-29. Luke abbreviates the story by omitting such details as an argument between the disciples and the scribes and a lengthy description of the history of the disease. He adds that this son is an **only child.** After rebuking **the**

unclean spirit Jesus gives the boy **back to his father** much as he did the widow's son (7:15)—an expression reminiscent of I Kings 17:23. Stress is put on the fact that the miracle is accomplished by the power and **majesty of God**—a power which Jesus possesses and which eludes the disciples.

9:43b-45. Unlike Mark 9:30-32, Luke connects the following account directly to this incident. Jesus gives another prediction of his passion. More emphatically than Mark, Luke indicates that the disciples do **not understand** and that the meaning of the **saying** is **concealed from them** by their lack of faith. The Passion is taken seriously by Luke, since no prediction of the Resurrection is included here. The point of the story is to indicate that Jesus is to be removed from the disciples. Doing the work of God will depend on them and the power of their faith.

9:46-48. Proof of their lack of understanding is seen in the disciples' argument about greatness, which Luke, in contrast to Mark, attaches immediately to these sayings. Jesus' answer to their debate indicates that true greatness is to be found in lowliness. The power of God works through the lowliness of faith.

9:49-50. That power can operate even in those who do not belong to the official group (see comment on Mark 9:38-41). At any rate the ministry in Galilee is now finished. God's acts of power have been performed. Jesus has been recognized as the Messiah. The disciples do not fully understand, yet the destiny of Jesus is determined. He must go to Jerusalem.

IV. THE JOURNEY TO JERUSALEM (9:51–19:27)

Throughout these chapters Jesus is presented as a wandering teacher. The source for this section of Luke is mainly Q and L. Actually very little of the material demands the setting of a journey. Although the trip is mentioned on occasion (9:51; 13:22; 17:11), the purpose is not historical but theological. The divine intention of Jesus' mission is to go toward suffering; the demand of discipleship is to follow.

A. The Cost of Discipleship (9:51-62)

9:51-56. The story of Jesus' rejection by a Samaritan village is from Luke's special material, L. Again the evangelist makes it clear that Jesus goes to Jerusalem **to be received up,** that is, to be crucified, raised, and ascended. Hostility between Samaritans and Galileans is traditional, but the reason for the rejection of Jesus is his purpose to go beyond them; **his face was set toward Jerusalem.** Seeing this rejection, **James and John** suggest that he call **fire down from heaven** much as Elijah did (II Kings 1:9-10). Some manuscripts say that Jesus rebukes them because "you do not know what manner of spirit you are of." His mission is not like Elijah's; his intent is to undergo suffering, not cause it. Just as he was rejected at the beginning of his Galilean ministry by Nazarenes, so he is rejected at the beginning of his journey to Jerusalem by Samaritans.

9:57-62. These verses based largely on Q (cf. Matthew 8:18-22). Luke presents the person who hopes to follow Jesus simply as a **man** rather than a "scribe," as in Matthew. He adds the word about saying **farewell to those at . . . home** and putting the **hand to the plow.** This simply indicates that the demand of the kingdom is absolute. No other duty can detract from following Jesus.

B. The Mission of the Seventy (10:1-24)

10:1-12. *The Sending of the Seventy.* Only Luke relates the mission of the seventy (or seventy-two, as some manuscripts read) disciples. The source of the account, however, is Q's account of the mission of the twelve (cf. Matthew 9:37–10:15). Apparently Luke has created this narrative to symbolize the later mission of the church to the Gentiles. Traditionally the

Jews conceived of seventy or seventy-two non-Jewish nations.

Luke describes the participants as going out **two by two**—a practice illustrated in his description of the Gentile mission in Acts. He adds the advice that the disciples should **salute no one on the road.** The mission is urgent and allows no time for the complexities of oriental greetings. This urgency is also seen in Luke's emphasis on the belief that **the kingdom of God has come near.** The Gentile mission prepares for the accomplishment of the rule of God. The journey toward Jerusalem makes possible universal salvation.

10:13-16. Woes on Palestinian Cities. Although he is theoretically on a journey through Samaria, Jesus is presented as hurling woes on cities of Galilee. This probably betrays Luke's hand in the construction of the travel narrative more than it indicates an ignorance of Palestinian geography. In any case, the account is from Q (cf. Matthew 11:20-24). The importance of the sayings is their connection with the mission of the seventy. They make the point that the preaching of the Gentile mission involves the word and authority of Jesus; **he who hears you hears me.**

10:17-24. The Return of the Seventy. Only Luke tells of the sending of the seventy and the result of their mission. The disciples return confessing Jesus as **Lord** and declaring how the **demons are subject to us in your name.** The seventy have the power to perform the same sort of exorcisms as Jesus. They exercise this power, however, through their relation to him; the very announcement of the name of Jesus drives the demonic forces into defeat.

Next Jesus tells of his vision of **Satan** falling **from heaven.** When this vision was seen is not certain, but it seems to have been during the mission of the seventy. The fall of Satan indicates that the prince of demons has been overcome. The mission to the Gentiles defeats the reign of evil.

10:19-22. Jesus says that he has given the disciples **authority to tread upon serpents and scorpions.** This power was predicted by the Old Testament (Psalm 91:13). Since the rabbis used scorpions and serpents to symbolize demonic forces, the expression suggests that the **spirits are subject** to the disciples. Yet something is more important than power over the demons—having **your names written in heaven.** This is an Old Testament allusion (cf. Exodus 32:32-33) which indicates that those whose names are inscribed in the heavenly book are those who share in the kingdom of God.

10:21-24. To these sayings Luke attaches some material from Q (cf. Matthew 11:25-27; 13:16-17). Jesus has just said that the names of the faithful are written in heaven. Now he offers a prayer, thanking God that revelation has been granted to **babes,** that is, to the humble ones who participate in his mission. Then he turns to the disciples and offers them a blessing. They have seen what **prophets and kings** longed to see—the revelation of **the Father** through **the Son.**

C. THE QUESTIONS OF PEOPLE (10:25–11:13)

10:25-37. *Eternal Life and the Neighbor.* Since Jesus has spoken of revelation, an expert in the law tries to **put him to the test.** Luke's source is Mark 12:28-31. Whereas Mark has the question raised by a scribe, Luke mentions **a lawyer.** The question for Luke concerns **eternal life** rather than the most important commandment. These changes would make the material relevant to Hellenistic readers, who knew little about scribes and cared less about the Jewish law. That keeping the law was essential to eternal life was an Old Testament concept. Luke has the lawyer, instead of Jesus, answer the question about **what is written in the law.**

10:29-32. In order **to justify himself,** or to find some way to escape the demands of the law, the lawyer raises a question, **Who is my neighbor?** Jesus tells the parable of the good Samaritan in answer.

This parable is without parallel in the other gospels. The meaning of the story is clear. A man went down the dangerous road **from Jerusalem to Jericho.** Attacked and beaten by thieves, he was left beside the road to die. First a **priest** and then a **Levite** came along and **passed by on the other side.** These two represented the religious leaders of the Jews, and Jericho was a residential center for priestly families. Perhaps they had completed their service in the temple and were anxious to get home. Just why they passed by the needy man is not stated. Possibly they feared contamination from the dead or were reluctant to associate with the lowly "people of the land."

10:33-35. The introduction of the **Samaritan** into the story was shocking. In contrast to priest and Levite the listeners might have expected a layman. But the man from Samaria represented both racial impurity and religious heresy. Without fear of contamination or exposure to the robbers, this stranger treated the **wounds,** brought the unfortunate to the nearby **inn,** and left enough money to care for him. **Oil and wine** were believed to have curative and antiseptic value. **Two denarii** represented about two days' wages.

10:36-37. When Jesus asks the question, **Which of these . . . proved neighbor to the man who fell among the robbers?** some scholars see evidence that the story is out of context. The question of the lawyer was, Who is my neighbor? The question of the parable is, Who acted like a neighbor? Perhaps Jesus changed the question. One must not escape the demand of the law by asking Who, but respond to the divine demand by seeking How. In any case the commandment is clear: show love to those who need it.

10:38-42. *The True Service.* Having illustrated the command to love one's neighbor Luke describes the meaning of the commandment to love God. The story is taken from L. In contrast to the Samaritans, who have rejected Jesus, **Martha** receives him as guest in **her house.** This home, according to John 11:1, is located in Bethany, but Luke does not imagine Jesus to be so near Jerusalem at this time. While Martha is **distracted with much serving,** her sister **Mary** sits **at the Lord's feet** and listens **to his teachings.** She acknowledges him as her Lord.

10:40-41. The amount of distraction may indicate that Martha has a crowd of guests to serve, and according to custom serving honored guests is an important duty. Little wonder that she complains to Jesus about Mary's inefficiency. His response is a mild rebuke; Martha is **anxious and troubled about many things.**

10:42. The rest of Jesus' answer varies in the different manuscripts. Some read **one thing is needful,** while others say "few things are needful, or only one." It is also not clear whether the one which is needed refers simply to the number of dishes of the meal or has some spiritual significance. Probably both are true. The dishes of food represent devotion to the Lord. Not many things are needed, but only one dish. **Mary has chosen the good portion,** for her "dish" is to hear and obey the word of God.

11:1-13. *Prayer.* One may sit at the Lord's feet through prayer. Luke's account of the Lord's Prayer is based on Q (cf. Matthew 6:9-13). Since Matthew's version is longer and contains liturgical additions, Luke's form of the prayer is probably closer to the original.

11:1. Matthew puts the prayer in the context of the Sermon on the Mount, while Luke presents it in the setting of Jesus' own **praying.** That John's **disciples** pray is confirmed by 5:33.

11:2-4. The simple appellation **Father** no doubt stands for the Aramaic *Abba*—the term of direct address which a child used for his own father. The force of the eschatological note **thy kingdom come** is not reduced, as in Matthew's version, by reference to doing the will of God on earth. However, Matthew's "debts" and "debtors" are probably more primitive than Luke's effort to explain debts as **sins.**

11:5-8. The parable of the **friend . . . at midnight** is found only in Luke. It tells the story of a man who receives a late guest. Since there is no opportunity to buy food he goes to a friend's house and asks to borrow **three loaves**—the amount of bread needed for a meal. The friend replies that he does not want to be bothered. The door, barred with a beam through a ring, is difficult to open, and the whole family is in bed on a mat on the floor. Nevertheless he will get up and give the provision, not out of friendship, but because of the **importunity,** or persistence of the request.

The point of the parable is not that God is like a man who does not want to be bothered and answers prayers only because he is tired of listening. Rather it is the typical rabbinic argument from the lesser to the greater. If even this reluctant man responds to requests, **how much more** will God, who is anxious to meet our needs.

11:9-13. To the parable Luke attaches other sayings from Q (cf. Matthew 7:7-11) which also indicate the surety of answer to prayer. Here the illustration is from fatherhood rather than friendship. If earthly fathers **know how to give good gifts . . . , how much more will the heavenly Father.** Luke omits Matthew's word about loaf and stone and adds the illustration that a father will not give a **scorpion** for an **egg.** He also suggests that God's gifts are of a higher category. He will **give the Holy Spirit to those who ask him.**

D. Controversies and Conflicts (11:14-54)

11:14-28. *Concerning Exorcisms.* The activity of the Spirit of God is contrasted with the activity of the evil spirits. The source of this account is Q (cf. Matthew 12:22-30), although some relationship to Mark 3:22-27 is evident. After Jesus has cast a **demon** out of a **dumb man** (Matthew says that he is blind as well), the charge is made that he exorcises demons by **Beelzebul** (or Beelzebub), **the prince of demons.**

Jesus' argument is twofold:

(1) If he were casting out demons by the prince of demons, then **Satan** would be fighting **against himself.**

(2) If he casts out demons by Beelzebul, the accusers' own exorcists deserve the same charge.

11:20. Whereas Matthew says that Jesus' exorcisms are "by the Spirit of God," Luke reads, **it is by the finger of God that I cast out demons.** This form is probably more original. It is a vivid way to point out that the works of Jesus are ultimately the acts of God.

11:23. This saying is not in harmony with 9:50, but here the intention is to enlist persons in the battle on the side of God.

11:24-26. The word about the unclean spirit who returns to his former dwelling with **seven other spirits more evil than himself** is taken from Q and is almost identical with Matthew 12:43-45. The saying indicates that in the battle people are constantly threatened with the power of Satan.

11:27-28. The brief word about the woman who cries, **Blessed is the womb that bore you,** is found exclusively in Luke. It means, "How happy the mother of such a son must be!" and is a sort of messianic confession. Jesus' response indicates that in the struggle against evil the important thing is not to give lip service to himself or his mother but to **hear the word of God and keep it.**

11:29-36. *Concerning Signs.* The source for this material is Q (cf. Matthew 12:38-42). Luke has noted how a woman has missed the point of Jesus' mission. Now he indicates that the crowd has done the same. Taking up the request for a sign (verse 16) Jesus replies that **no sign shall be given . . . except the sign of Jonah.**

Luke's understanding of the sign is probably more original. Whereas Matthew sees the three days and three nights of Jonah in the belly of the whale as a symbol of the resurrection of Jesus, Luke presents the sign simply as Jonah's preaching of repentance. The meaning is that someone **greater than Solomon** and Jonah **is here.** People should not ask for a sign but listen to his message.

11:33-36. The sayings about **light** are based on Q (cf. Matthew 5:15; 6:22-23). In context they indicate that the message of Jesus is clear and is seen **when your eye is sound.** This figure describes the person of integrity and singleness of purpose. If one responds to the light of God's word with one's total being, then the **whole body** (or whole person) **is full of light.**

11:37-54. *Woes to Pharisees and Lawyers.* Luke puts these sayings into the setting of a Pharisee's meal. The source is Q (cf. Matthew 23:1-36). The woes to the Pharisees are provoked by

231

the notice that Jesus fails to practice ceremonial hand washing **before dinner**. Within the passage Luke presents six woes—three spoken to the Pharisees and three answering the question of a lawyer.

11:39-41. In the saying concerning the **inside** and **outside of the cup** Luke speaks of giving **alms of those things which are within.** This could represent a mistranslation of the Aramaic original, which may have said "purify the things within." Or it might suggest that true almsgiving has to do with the inner person.

11:44. Luke's form of this saying is different from the parallel in Matthew 23:27-28. He envisages **graves** beneath the ground upon which people unwittingly **walk** and are defiled. The evil of the Pharisees is concealed, but it contaminates Israel.

11:47-51. Luke adds that **apostles** as well as **prophets** are sent by God and killed by men. He thinks of the later leaders of the church and the persecutions which they endure. When he adds that **blood . . . may be required of this generation** Luke perhaps thinks of the destruction of Jerusalem.

11:53-54. Luke ends his account with an editorial note concerning the attempt of **the scribes and the Pharisees** to find evidence of Jesus' error.

E. The Demands of Discipleship (12:1–13:9)

12:1-12. *The Necessity of Confession.* Surrounded by a huge **multitude** Jesus cautions his disciples to **beware of the leaven of the Pharisees.** This expression is found in Mark 8:15 without explanation. Luke has Jesus interpret this leaven as Pharisaic **hypocrisy**—a hypocrisy seen in the inner, hidden corruption of the Pharisees.

12:2-9. These verses are based on Q (cf. Matthew 10:26-33) and describe how hypocrisy can be avoided. Basically one must **fear** only him who controls one's eternal destiny. One must trust God, who cares even for the **sparrows.**

Matthew's version omits reference to the **Son of man.** Here

Jesus seems to distinguish himself from that figure. Yet Jesus is the representative of the coming Son of man—the exalted Messiah of the end time—since those who confess Jesus will be acknowledged by the Son of man in the future.

12:10-12. Since Jesus is only a veiled emissary of the Son of man on earth, blasphemies against him can be forgiven (cf. Matthew 12:32). Blasphemy **against the Holy Spirit will not be forgiven,** since it would involve rejection of the very action of God which forgives. Luke seems to understand the unpardonable sin as a failure to listen to the Holy Spirit in the hour of trial (cf. Matthew 10:19). It is in the mission of the church that the power of the Spirit to save or to condemn is operative.

12:13-21. *The Threat of Covetousness.* The parable of the rich fool, found exclusively in Luke, is told in the setting of a discussion about inheritances. According to Jewish custom the older son in a family of two received two thirds of the father's possessions. The man who asks the question is probably the younger brother, and it is implied that the older son has not divided the inheritance with him. Jesus refuses to judge between them, noting that covetousness is a threat to both.

12:16-21. To illustrate his point he tells a parable. A certain man had an abundance of crops. To take care of the excess he built larger **barns.** Then he said to his soul (his inner self), **You have ample goods for many years.** While he is enjoying his abundance the rich man is interrupted by the word of God: **Your soul is required of you.** That is, the man is required to die; his possessions are of no avail. Luke adds the note that **he who lays up treasure for himself . . . is not rich toward God.** The true way to lay up treasures will be explained later (verse 33). The parable illustrates the fate of the man who loves neither God nor neighbor.

12:22-34. *The Futility of Anxiety.* Although the disciple is not to lay up treasure for himself, he need **not be anxious** about the basic needs of life. Luke's source here is Q—material which Matthew includes in his Sermon on the Mount (Matthew 6:19-33). Basically the text tells the faithful to put their trust in

God. As he cares for **ravens** and **lilies,** so he will provide for the needs of his people.

When Luke adds that they should avoid anxiety because they **are not able to do as small a thing as that,** he may mean that they cannot add a **cubit** (about eighteen inches) to their "stature" (one possible meaning of the Greek word). Adding to one's **span of life** (another possible meaning of the same word) is hardly a small thing.

12:32-34. Luke's reference to the **little flock** is unique. Taking up a common Old Testament figure he describes the disciples as the sheep of God. This suggests that they are the humble people who are ready to accept the divine rule. In contrast to Matthew, Luke suggests that these faithful ought to play an ascetic role: **Sell your possessions, and give alms.**

12:35-47. *Exhortation to Watchful Waiting.* Rather than concern for possessions the disciples should show readiness for the coming of **their master.** Verses 35-38, although similar to Matthew 25:1-13, are from Luke's special material, L. Like faithful servants the disciples must be ready for their returning Lord.

The admonition that their **loins be girded** refers to binding up the loose Palestinian robe, ready for action, ready for service. That their **lamps** should be **burning** indicates that the crisis comes at night. Since Jewish night was divided into three watches, readiness at the **second** or **third** denotes wakefulness at the time of one's greatest temptation to sleep. When spoken by Jesus, these words stressed the need to be prepared for the coming kingdom. In the time of Luke they urge readiness for the return of the Christ—a coming which has been delayed.

12:39-46. The same point is made in the following verses. Here the source is Q (cf. Matthew 24:43-51). If a **householder** knew the **hour** that a **thief** would arrive, he would be prepared; so the faithful must be ready for the unexpected **coming** of the **Son of man.** Peter asks if this parable is for the disciples or **for all.** Although no answer is given, it is clear that this Lukan question implies instruction to the leaders of the church. The **wise steward** of the Lord's work will be found active when **the**

master comes. The servant who presumes on the master's delay will be severely punished.

12:47-58. Responsibility of leaders is also the theme of Luke's unique conclusion. The view that conscious sins are more severely punished than unwitting errors is common to Jewish theology. Continuing his illustration from the servant-master relationship, Luke suggests that intentional disobedience deserves **a severe beating,** while disobedience out of ignorance results in **a light beating.** The leader of the church, who has been granted special knowledge of the divine will, is required to fulfill a higher standard of responsibility.

12:49-59. *The Certainty of Judgment.* To be sure, the disciples will face judgment. Verses 49-56 are from L, although minor parallels are found in Matthew 10:34-36; 16:2-3, and Mark 10:38.

12:49-50. The judgment is presented under two figures. The idea of casting **fire upon the earth** could suggest either punishment or purification. The second figure, **baptism,** may support the latter. In any case the baptism Jesus is **to be baptized** with refers to his martyr's death. This death releases the Spirit, which both judges and purifies the **earth.**

12:51-53. The coming of Jesus brings division within the household. The **five** who are **divided** are probably the **father,** the **son,** the **mother** of the son's bride, her **daughter** (the bride), and the son's mother as the **mother-in-law** of the bride, who is thus **daughter-in-law** as well as daughter. **Three against two and two against three** may indicate a conflict between the older generation (father, mother, and mother-in-law) and the younger (son and his bride). In the context these verses mean that the encounter with Christ brings a crisis. The response of faith creates a division within the people.

12:54-56. The words about the weather carry on the theme of judgment. Jesus turns to the crowd. When they **see a cloud rising in the west** they know that **a shower is coming.** The sea is to the west and rain storms come from that direction. When they **see the south wind blowing** they know that **there will be**

scorching heat. The desert is to the south and torrid winds originate in that area. The point is that the **multitudes** know how to read the signs of the weather, but they do not know how **to interpret** the signs of **the present time.** The sign of the present is the appearance of Jesus; his preaching heralds the coming of the kingdom of God.

12:57-59. The discussion is carried further in these verses. The source is Q (cf. Matthew 5:25-26). The meaning is clear: just as a prudent man agrees with his **accuser** while they are on the way to the **magistrate,** so a wise man should be reconciled to God before the judgment comes. The way is short and the judgment severe. One does not escape until he pays **the very last copper.** The coin which Luke has in mind, the lepton, was scarcely worth anything; it is the widow's "mite" mentioned in 21:2.

13:1-9. *The Need of Repentance.* In view of the coming judgment Israel must repent. This passage is closely connected with the previous one, since Luke speaks of **some** who were **present at that very time.** No parallel is to be found in Mark or Matthew.

Those present remind Jesus of **the Galileans whose blood Pilate had mingled with their sacrifices.** The historian Josephus reports an occasion when the Roman governor massacred some riotous Jews in Jerusalem and another, evidently after Jesus' crucifixion, when he destroyed some Samaritan worshipers on Mt. Gerizim. Luke's incident seems different from either of these. It must have occurred near the temple in Jerusalem, where Galilean Jews would come to sacrifice. Similarly there is no other account of the fall of the **tower in Siloam** which was fatal to **eighteen** citizens of Jerusalem.

In both cases Jesus draws the conclusion that those who perished were not **worse offenders** than those who escaped. He refutes, therefore, the Jewish doctrine of retribution—the doctrine that those who receive special punishment must be guilty of some great sin. Instead Jesus finds everyone guilty before God, **all** in need of repentance.

13:6-9. The parable of the **fig tree** indicates that there is still time to repent. It may be Luke's substitute for Mark's account of the cursing of the fig tree (Mark 11:12-14, 20-21). The use of a **vineyard** as symbol of the people of God is a typical Old Testament figure. Although the fig tree has not produced fruit for **three years,** the **vinedresser** requests a **year** for cultivating and fertilizing. If it does not bear fruit then, it will be **cut down.** So also Jesus comes with a call for repentance; Israel is granted a final chance.

F. HEALING AND TEACHING (13:10-35)

13:10-17. *A Crippled Woman.* This narrative is taken from Luke's special tradition, L. The setting is a synagogue where Jesus has been teaching. He encounters a woman who has been ill **for eighteen years**—a fact which indicates the seriousness of her malady. Apparently she is afflicted with a sort of paralysis, since she is **bent over** and cannot **fully straighten herself.** When it is said that she has a **spirit of infirmity** and that **Satan** has **bound** her, it is clear that her contemporaries considered her disease the result of demon possession.

The fact that Jesus calls to a woman would seem strange to them. It shows that the call of repentance is given to all, even the lowly and the helpless. Jesus, like the healers of his time, **laid his hands upon her;** he has the power to save. The power, of course, comes from God whose praise the patient proclaims.

13:14-17. Since it is **the sabbath** the **ruler of the synagogue** is **indignant.** His word is an adaptation of Deuteronomy 5:14; man is not to work—or to heal—on the sabbath. Jesus replies that since the law allows one to **lead** his animal **to water** on the holy day it ought to make possible the release of a person from demonic power. He describes the woman as a **daughter of Abraham**—a rare expression which identifies her as one of the faithful people of God.

Jesus does not note that care for one's animals was allowed

237

only if certain conditions, such as the distance to the watering place, were met. The ruler of the synagogue might have replied that livestock need water every day; a woman who has been paralyzed for eighteen years could wait till tomorrow. Jesus, however, announces another doctrine of the sabbath. It is the time when the work of God should be done, the message of repentance declared, and God's salvation offered.

13:18-21. *Parables of the Kingdom.* Although Luke presents Jesus as still speaking in the synagogue, both of these parables are drawn from Q (cf. Matthew 13:31-33). The **mustard seed** parable is also found in Mark 4:30-32. Luke's version of the mustard seed parable is abbreviated. He does not say that the mustard is the "smallest of all seeds" or that its **tree** is the "greatest of shrubs." In essence both parables contrast small beginnings and big endings. Although Jesus' announcement of the kingdom of God awakens only a meager response, the kingdom will come with a power which challenges all Israel and includes people of all the world.

13:22-30. *The Narrow Door.* Those who are included in the kingdom are now described. Although parallels are found in Matthew, this passage is based on L. The setting is the journey **toward Jerusalem.** The discussion is provoked by a question put to Jesus: **Will those who are saved be few?** The answer by implication is "Yes," since **many . . . will seek to enter and will not be able.**

13:24-29. Whereas Matthew 7:13-14 conceives of a "hard way" and a "narrow gate," Luke imagines the **door** of a house. This door is also **narrow** and thus difficult to enter. However, the possibility of entering is now open, so that Jesus can urge his listeners to **strive to enter.** One strives presumably by hearing the words of Jesus and doing them (cf. 6:47). When the door is closed, the time to enter has passed. Those who **stand outside** knocking will claim acquaintance with the **Lord.** Did he not pass through their village, eating with them and teaching in their **streets?** Jesus, who is now presented as host in the house, will not recognize them; their works are evil. But while the door is ajar those who **weep** and **gnash** their **teeth** catch a glimpse of the messianic banquet. Who is seated there with the patriarchs and **prophets?** Indeed, those who come from the four corners of the world (cf. Isaiah 49:12). Israel has been rejected, but Gentiles are participants in the **kingdom of God.**

13:30. The saying about the **last** and the **first** finds a parallel in Matthew 19:30; 20:16. The first represent the Jews to whom Jesus has come. The last are the Gentiles with whom the church's mission is effective.

13:31-35. *Jerusalem and the Prophets.* In contrast to Jesus' prediction of Israel's rejection, Luke records a prophecy of Jerusalem's rejection of Jesus. Verses 31-33 are without parallel in the other gospels. Since Jesus is presented as being on good terms with the Pharisees, and since the encounter with Herod Antipas might better fit the Galilean ministry, it may be that this event originally occurred earlier in the career of Jesus. At any rate the view of Herod seems to have become more negative than that described in 9:9. Then he wanted to see Jesus; now he wants to **kill** him.

13:32-33. In calling Antipas **that fox** Jesus could be adopting either Old Testament or Greek usage. For the Old Testament the fox was an animal of destruction; for the Greeks he symbolized craftiness. Jesus' cryptic words about **today and tomorrow, and the third day** indicate that his time of ministry is short. The third day also alludes to his resurrection, when he will **finish my course.** Above all Jesus must do his work. He will be killed, to be sure, but Herod cannot interrupt his destiny. **It cannot be that a prophet should perish away from Jerusalem.** The death of Jesus is according to the plan of God.

13:34-35. These verses are based on Q (cf. Matthew 23:37-39). In the context of Luke they make it evident that the fate of Jesus and the fate of Jerusalem are related. Jesus will be rejected just as the ancient prophets have been stoned and killed. This rejection will seal the doom of the city; its **house is forsaken.** Only as Israel recognizes the messiahship of Jesus will it be redeemed.

G. AT A PHARISEE'S TABLE (14:1-24)

Into the narrative of the journey to Jerusalem Luke inserts a pause. Jesus dines at the house of a Pharisee. The wanderer, as at the house of Martha (10:38-42), is received as guest. The banquet was a typical setting for the utterances of Hellenistic teachers, and Luke employs the meal as the site of a collection of Jesus' sayings.

14:1-6. *Healing on the Sabbath.* This passage is found exclusively in Luke. In a sense it is parallel to 13:10-17. The **ruler,** who belongs **to the Pharisees,** could be either a leader of the synagogue or a member of the sanhedrin, the Jewish ruling council. Apparently other Pharisees are present to watch Jesus; they hope to trap him. A man appears who is afflicted with **dropsy.** This malady involves an excess of liquid in the tissues of the body. It is a symptom, not a disease. According to the rabbis the condition resulted from sins of unchastity.

14:3-6. Jesus asks the **lawyers and Pharisees**—the experts in the law—whether it is proper **to heal on the sabbath.** When they remain **silent** he takes hold of the man and cures him; the power to heal operates through Jesus. At once he puts another question to the critics: **If a son or an ox** tumbles into a well, who will not work to save it on the sabbath? Some manuscripts suggest that it is an ass, not a son, who has fallen into danger. Again the sabbath is interpreted as a time to do God's work, but more seriously than in the story of the crippled woman. There the stress was on caring for the normal needs of livestock; here it is a question of life or death.

14:7-17. *Place of Honor.* The situation of the meal makes possible a parable, again from L. When invited to a **wedding feast,** or to any important festival, one should not select the **place of honor.** Palestinian feasts involved an arrangement whereby guests reclined on couches in groups of three. The center grouping was considered a place of esteem and was awarded on the basis of office, wealth, or power. If **a more eminent man** comes late—a practice not infrequent among the prominent—the man who has chosen the high place may be asked to step down.

Instead one should take **the lowest place,** so that he may be requested to **go up higher**—a request which evokes the honor of all. The advice reflects simple social prudence and is reminiscent of ancient Jewish wisdom (cf. Proverbs 25:6-7). That this parable is directed to the Pharisees is perhaps hinted by their love of the "best seat" (11:43).

14:11. This verse has parallels elsewhere in the gospels (18:14; Matthew 18:4; 23:12). It summarizes the meaning of the parable: the **one who exalts himself will be humbled** and vice versa. At the end of time values will be reversed (cf. 1:46-55).

14:12-14. The host is told how guests should be invited. One ought not ask those who can return the invitation, but rather **the poor, the maimed, the lame, the blind.** It may be that Jesus originally stressed only the poor. They would fit the context better; the others may prepare for verse 21. If they do belong in the original, their inclusion marks a sharp contrast to contemporary religious practice. The lame and the blind were forbidden entrance to the temple. The invitation of God, however, includes the lowly.

In dealings with their fellows people should display the same sort of mercy. No reward for such action can be expected in this age, but in the time to come—**at the resurrection of the just**—God will bless the merciful. It is not necessary to conclude that Jesus is adopting the notion that only the righteous will be raised. He is simply saying that those who obey God will share the blessings of the righteous in the end time.

14:15-24. *Invitations to the Banquet.* The mention of the resurrection suggests a discussion of the future. The remark of one of the guests provides a transition from the earthly meal to the messianic banquet. Although a parallel is found in Matthew 22:1-10, Luke's account represents an independent version of the same tradition. A guest declares that **he who shall eat bread in the kingdom** is **blessed.** This offers the opportunity for Jesus to announce a parable which describes the invitations to the messianic feast. The parable rests on Jewish invitation customs.

Actually the host sent two. The first was the primary invitation; the second announced the moment when the banquet was ready. Failure to respond to the second after accepting the first was considered gross discourtesy.

14:16-22. In Jesus' story a man invites many to a great feast and **at the time for the banquet** sends **his servant.** The response is a variety of excuses—purchase of **a field,** acquiring **five yoke of oxen,** marriage—all considered more important than attendance. These refusals suggest that all sorts of worldly involvements are considered more important than the invitation to enter the kingdom.

Perhaps Jesus too envisages two invitations: one at the time of his preaching, the other at the moment when the kingdom comes. In any case another invitation is offered. **The poor and maimed and blind and lame** are asked to attend. That is, those whom the Jews consider unworthy—tax collectors and sinners—are invited as replacements for the Pharisees.

14:23-24. There is still room for more. The master sends his servant out into the **highways and hedges,** or into the country. Since Israel has rejected the invitation Gentiles will be brought in. The order to **compel** them could better be translated "urge." Perhaps Luke has in mind the oriental custom whereby the stranger was taken by the arm and drawn into the house.

The application is clear. Those who do not accept the invitation of Jesus shall not taste the messianic meal; they shall not share the blessings of the end time. That these words are spoken to the listeners of Jesus and not just the servant of the parable is seen in the fact that the **you** of verse 24 is plural.

H. RENUNCIATION AND DISCIPLESHIP (14:25-35)

14:25-27. *Demands of the Kingdom.* The announcement that the kingdom is open to all leads to the assembling of **great multitudes.** Now it is seen that sharp demands are laid on those who are invited. The source is basically L. First the kingdom demands renunciation of the family. This saying has a parallel in

Matthew 10:37-38. To Matthew's list of "son or daughter" Luke adds **wife . . . , brothers and sisters, yes, and even his own life.** This last demand is illustrated by the word about bearing one's **cross,** which comes from Q (cf. Matthew 10:38) and duplicates a similar word previously taken from Mark (see above on 9:23-26). The cross, a symbol of execution, indicates that a man must renounce all to follow Jesus.

14:28-33. *Parables.* The two parables about building a **tower** and preparing for **war** have no parallel in the other gospels. The two suggest a contrast: the tower is a simple farm building or vineyard watchtower of the ordinary farmer; the battle is the concern of a **king.** In both cases the parables illustrate the cost of the kingdom. One who seeks to enter must be aware of its demands.

Actually these two parables do not clearly illustrate the idea of renunciation which is stated in verse 33. Instead they give the idea of careful calculation. Yet Jesus may hope to suggest that calculation will have only one conclusion. The demand of the kingdom is absolute; **all** must be renounced.

14:34. *Preservation of Character.* The word about **salt** is common to the Synoptics (cf. Matthew 5:13 and Mark 9:50). Palestinians knew that salt extracted from the Dead Sea or the Mediterranean had to be pure. So the disciple must preserve his true character—absolute obedience to the rule of God.

I. JESUS AND SINNERS (15:1-32)

15:1-10. *The Lost Sheep and the Lost Coin.* Jesus' invitation to the lowly has evoked a response from **tax collectors and sinners.** For this he is rebuked by **the Pharisees and the scribes** and in response declares these parables. Although the story of the lost sheep may be found in Q (cf. Matthew 18:12-14) Luke's special material seems to have the two parables already joined.

15:3-7. The lost sheep parable has its background in such Old Testament passages as Ezekiel 34:12. The shepherd who has a **hundred sheep** seeks diligently for **one which is lost.** When he finds it **he lays it on his shoulders.** This was a typical way to carry sheep, revealing care and concern. The shepherd rejoices and calls his friends to share his joy. In application Jesus insists that there will be a similar celebration **in heaven** (one way of saying "God") over one repentant sinner.

15:8-10. The parable of the lost coin is without parallel in the other gospels. It tells of a **woman** who has **ten silver coins**—literally "drachmas." These were Greek-Syrian coins of approximately the same silver content as the denarius but officially discounted by the Roman administration. For the average Palestinian woman ten drachmas would represent the savings of many months. When the woman of the parable loses one, perhaps hearing it drop on the stone floor, she lights **a lamp** and sweeps **the house** until she finds it. She too celebrates her joy with **friends and neighbors.**

The application is similar: the repentance of the individual sinner results in **joy before the angels of God** (that is, in the court of heaven, meaning that God himself rejoices). Both parables show that God's love persistently seeks the lost and rejoices at their redemption.

15:11-32. *The Two Sons.* To the parables of the lost sheep and lost coin Luke joins the story of the lost son, traditionally called the parable of the prodigal son. Its omission from the other gospels is striking. But the genius of the story, together with its Semitic terminology, establishes its authenticity.

15:11-12. According to the story the **younger** of two sons asks to receive his inheritance, which by Jewish custom, amounted to a third of his father's possessions. According to normal practice the division of a father's property was determined during his lifetime, but his sons did not actually receive their inheritances until his death. Some heirs, like this younger son, tried to get their portions earlier. A son granted such a privilege had to renounce all further claim on the estate. The father in the parable, since he has servants, is a well-to-do landowner. Apparently the sons are unmarried—a fact which could establish their ages as under twenty.

15:13-16. After the request is granted the young son sets off to a far country. By implication he goes to the Jewish communities overseas. He spends his wealth **in loose living,** which could mean either extravagance or immorality. After a **famine** strikes the youth is reduced to poverty. He takes employment as a swineherd.

To the Jews the pig was an unclean animal and caring for it was the lowliest of occupations. A rabbinic saying declares, "Cursed is the man who rears swine, and cursed is the man who teaches his son Greek philosophy." Symbolically it is suggested that the young man has rejected the law. In this lowly condition he eats the **pods that the swine ate.** These are the foot-long pods of the carob tree, used in Palestine for animal fodder and sometimes eaten by the poor. The rabbis considered eating them to be an act of penance.

15:17-24. The depth of his situation leads the young man to come **to himself.** He thinks of his father's abundance and resolves to return, confessing his sin and offering himself as servant. Sin **against heaven** means sin against God. While the son is still a distance away the father runs out to meet him and embraces and kisses him. The motive of the father's action is **compassion.** It is evident that he has been looking for his son's return all along. When the son repeats his confession, the father makes him, not a servant, but an honored son. Not work clothes, but **the best robe,** is put upon him; not the yoke of slavery, but the **ring** of sonship; not the barefoot service of slaves, but the sandals of a son. A great feast is held with the young man as honored guest.

15:25-30. The **elder son** is in the field working. The sound of **music and dancing** comes from the house; he has not heard this since his brother left. Inquiring of a household slave, he learns of his brother's return and is angry. The father goes out to the elder son, just as he had to the younger. He is met with reproach from the angry youth: **These many years I have served you** and for this received no reward. Not even a **kid** from the many in the father's flock has been provided for his celebrations. Yet for his younger brother, whom he accuses of infidelity and immorality, there is killed **the fatted** (literally "grain-fed") **calf.**

The father's reply is true to the parable, but not to the actual economy of men: **All that is mine is yours.** In fact the feasting of the younger son has depreciated the possessions of the elder. But it is not so with God. His grace abounds to self-righteous as well as sinner. The final statement of the father repeats the early basis for rejoicing, **Your brother was dead, and is alive; he was lost, and is found.**

Although it is commonly agreed that a parable makes only one point, this story has a double moral: (1) God loves the sinner and forgives him on the basis of his repentance. (2) The Pharisees ought to respond at the salvation of sinners just as God does. The younger son stands for the sinners and tax collectors; the elder son represents Pharisaic self-righteousness. Perhaps the two points are basically the same: God's saving love goes out to sinner and self-righteous alike.

J. The Threat of Riches (16:1-31)

16:1-13. *The Crafty Steward.* Jesus has just spoken to the Pharisees. Now he directs a parable to the disciples. The source is L. A certain **rich man** has received the report that **his goods** are being wasted by his **steward.** The steward is told that he must give an **account of your stewardship**—he must close the books—and give up his position.

16:3-7. The steward seeks a way to provide for his needs after he is **put out** of his stewardship. He is **not strong enough to dig, and . . . ashamed to beg**—a saying which was proverbial. He decides to help the master's creditors reduce their debts, so that they will offer hospitality in his time of need. He tells a man who owes **a hundred measures of oil** to **write fifty** and one who is in debt for **a hundred measures of wheat** to **write eight.** He is suggesting that each falsify his promissory note. The debts are large in both cases, since 100 measures of oil totals about 550 gallons, and 100 measures of wheat is equal to something over 500 bushels.

16:8-9. The conclusion of the parable can probably be taken as words of Jesus. The term translated **master** really means "Lord" and is one of Luke's typical titles for Jesus. If so, he commends **the dishonest steward for his prudence,** noting that the **sons of this world** (literally "age") **are wiser . . . than the sons of light.** When Jesus says that the former are wiser **in their own generation** he implies that the wisdom of the righteous is concerned with **their** generation—the age to come.

Interpretation of this parable has led to considerable debate. For example, it is suggested that Jesus is only commending prudence. Just as the unrighteous are prudent in the affairs of this world, so the righteous must be prudent in regard to the matters of the kingdom. Others see a typical argument from the lesser to the greater. If even an unrighteous steward knows how to deal with the matters of the world, how much more the sons of light ought to know how to respond to God. Perhaps the parable is best interpreted in context: just as the steward faces a crisis, so does the disciple. In time of crisis radical decision must be made.

16:10-13. The additional sayings indicate how this decision is to be made. The first contrasts true riches with **the unrighteous mammon.** The disciples must seek the former and reject the latter. Faithfulness in spiritual things begins in the common questions of honesty. The saying about **two masters,** paralleled in Matthew 6:24, attempts to avoid a misunderstanding of the parable. In no way does it suggest that disciples are to follow the steward in their use of money. Indeed their prudence has to do with true riches. They **cannot serve . . . mammon,** which means possessions or wealth acquired by evil means.

16:14-18. *The Demands of the Kingdom.* Luke inserts here a collection of sayings about money and Pharisees which are taken from L and Q. The Pharisees, who have overheard Jesus' rejection of mammon, scoff at him. Luke's charge that they are **lovers of money** may be confirmed by the fact that the Pharisees were urban businessmen who were gaining economic prominence. Their effort to **justify** themselves **before men** probably refers to their effort to attain righteousness by giving alms. According to Jesus, God is not impressed by external righteousness but knows the **hearts** of men. In God's economy values are reversed.

16:16-18. In these verses taken from Q (cf. Matthew 11:12-13; also 5:18, 32) Luke draws the distinction between the old era and the new sharply. **John** is the dividing line. In this context those who enter the kingdom **violently** are probably the Pharisees who strive for righteousness by their own effort. Nevertheless God's demands remain secure; not **one dot of the law** will **become void.** The will of God is even more demanding than the Old Testament acknowledges, as the prohibition of divorce shows (cf. Mark 10:11-12).

16:19-31. *The Rich Man and Lazarus.* Still speaking to Pharisees, Jesus relates a parable found exclusively in Luke. It points out that the law, which has just been under discussion, is understood better by the religiously disenfranchised than by the Pharisees.

The parable contrasts two men. The **rich man** is **clothed in purple** (the expensive robe of royalty) **and fine linen** (a luxurious undergarment). He **feasted sumptuously every day**; his whole life is a constant feast. The **poor man named Lazarus,** on the other hand, would be happy to eat the crumbs from under the **table.** Since he lies at the **gate,** he may be lame. **Full of sores,** he is tormented by odious **dogs.**

At death the poor man is carried **to Abraham's bosom,** while the rich man finds himself in **Hades.** It is not clear whether these situations are an intermediate or a permanent state. Being in Abraham's bosom probably symbolizes companionship with the patriarch at the messianic banquet. **Hades** is a place of **flame** and **torment.** The rich man asks aid from Lazarus and is reminded that the situation after death is exactly reversed. Abraham points out that **a great chasm has been fixed,** so that communication between the two realms of the dead is impossible. Judgment has been final, and the situation beyond the grave cannot be modified.

16:27-31. The rich man then requests that Lazarus be sent to his **brothers,** for **if some one goes to them from the dead, they will repent.** Abraham insists that if they ignore **Moses and the**

prophets, even a resurrection will not convince them. This means that the law itself is the word of God which men should obey. Texts like Isaiah 58:7 demand food and hospitality for the poor. In the context of Luke the resurrection of Christ is implied. Even when the risen Lord comes to men many will not have faith.

K. FORGIVENESS AND FAITH ON THE GROUND OF GRACE (17:1-19)

17:1-10. *Sin, Forgiveness, and Faith.* Luke now includes a collection of sayings spoken to the disciples. He presents Jesus' description of the fate of one who causes an offense to **one of these little ones** and applies this teaching to the life of the church. That the later situation is reflected is seen in the probability that the disciples of Jesus had no servants.

Although there are parallels in Matthew, and even Mark, Luke may be using here his special source, L. The word translated **temptations to sin** is sometimes given as "stumbling blocks" but literally refers to the trigger of a trap or snare. The point of the saying is that he who causes one of God's faithful to be ensnared by evil deserves severe judgment.

17:3-4. However, if one of these little ones sins, he should be forgiven. Jesus suggests that the disciple should first **rebuke him** (warn him or address him earnestly). Luke's form of the forgiveness teaching is different from that in Matthew 18:21-22. There one is to forgive "seventy times seven," while here the disciple is to forgive **seven times in the day.**

17:5-6. Just as they must forgive, so also the disciples must have faith. Luke portrays them as asking for an **increase** of **faith;** they say, "Bestow on us more faith." That an increase would be fitting is seen from a comparison of their faith with **a grain of mustard seed.** If faith were even that tiny size it could do the impossible—not, as in Matthew 17:20, move a mountain, but uproot a **sycamine tree** and plant it **in the sea.** The sycamine is apparently the common black mulberry or perhaps the sycamine fig.

17:7-10. The parable of the unworthy **servant** is found only in Luke. It describes a servant or slave of a farmer who works all day in the fields and then is required to serve his master in the evening. His eventual right to **eat and drink** is not understood as a reward for extra services; he has done only what was his **duty.** Thus the disciple can make no claim on God; he simply obeys the Lord's will. What he receives is by the grace of God. He is one of the little ones who has learned the meaning of faith.

17:11-19. *The Thankful Leper.* One who receives the divine grace ought to be thankful. To illustrate this point Luke records the healing of **ten lepers**—a narrative not found elsewhere in the gospels.

Jesus is again described as **on the way to Jerusalem.** The remark that **he was passing along between Samaria and Galilee** has been interpreted to mean that Jesus is moving from west to east, but it is possible that Luke conceives of the border between Galilee and Samaria as running north and south. Although lepers were not allowed in Jerusalem, they could abide in a **village** if they **stood** their **distance.** Apparently they have had some previous encounter with Jesus, since they call him by name and use the title **Master,** which his disciples sometimes employed. Instead of crying "Unclean" they ask for **mercy.**

Jesus sends them **to the priests.** Only the officials in the Jerusalem temple could establish their health and assure their restoration to the religious community. The sending is a kind of test; Jesus has spoken no word of healing. On noting his cure **one** of the lepers, **a Samaritan,** returns to give **thanks.** He praises **God,** who is the ultimate source of his salvation, and falls prostrate before Jesus, who has performed it. The Master, who notes that the thankful man is a **foreigner,** makes him an example for Israel.

As well as showing the need of gratitude to God the story illustrates the nature of **faith,** about which the disciples have asked in verse 5. It is the sort of thankful response to God's grace which makes a person well; it is the faith which saves.

L. The Coming of the Kingdom (17:20–18:34)

17:20-37. *The Days of the Son of Man.* Apparently the healing of the leper is taken as an eschatological sign. The Pharisees ask when the kingdom is coming. Luke replies with material drawn from his own sources, though with some parallels in Q. The result is an adaptation of Jesus' words to the eschatology of the author.

First it is stated that the **kingdom** does not come with dramatic **signs** which can be **observed**. Instead the reign of God is "within you" (the more common meaning of the Greek preposition) or **in the midst of you** (a meaning favored by scholars as more consistent with other references to the kingdom in the gospels). Thus on the lips of Jesus this remark could mean that the kingdom is an inward reality, or that it has started to come into history with his own mission. For Luke it could mean that the kingdom is present in the church through the gift of the Spirit.

17:22-37. The **days of the Son of man,** on the other hand, will come in the distant future. One should not be misled by advice which cries, **Lo, there!** . . . **Lo, here!** since the Son of man will come like a flash of **lightning.** Though there has been some delay, Luke assures his readers that the end of time will come and the triumphant Messiah will be visible to all. Yet before this happens **he must suffer many things and be rejected;** Jesus is identified as the Son of man, and the route to triumph leads through Jerusalem.

Because of this hiddenness of the Messiah his triumphant coming will be as a surprise. **As . . . in the days of Noah** and of **Lot** men were going about their ordinary business, so in the days of the Son of man judgment will come unexpectedly. When this happens no one should be distracted by the concerns of this world. Salvation can be lost in the last moment, as it was for **Lot's**

wife. The judgment will come as a crisis which divides: of **two men** sleeping side by side or **two women** turning a millstone together only one will be **taken.**

Again the question of **where** is raised. The answer is symbolic and likely proverbial: **Where . . . the eagles** (or "vultures") are **gathered.** Wherever men refuse to be alert and ready for the Son of man in faith, there will be the judgment.

18:1-8. *The Vindication of the Elect.* In spite of the delay of the Son of man, Christians should continue to **pray** and not despair. To illustrate the need of persistent prayer Luke introduces a parable which has no parallel in the other gospels. It is similar to the parable of the friend at midnight (11:5-8).

The **judge** is corrupt. The **widow** is one of the typical needy of the Bible. Since her case is brought before an individual, it probably concerns money, perhaps an inheritance. She **kept coming** asking vindication, so that finally the judge answers. The root meaning of **wear me out** is "beat me under the eye," but Jesus probably intends the figurative idea.

18:6-8. In the application **the Lord** uses the typical argument from the lesser to the greater. If an **unrighteous judge** hears the pleas of a woman because of her persistence, how much more will God respond to the continual prayers of his people.

The translation of verse 7b is uncertain. According to the usual meaning of the verb it reads literally, "and he is [or "is he"] long suffering over them." This might be taken to mean that God will show patience in hearing the cries of his elect. In this context, however, the emphasis seems rather on the speedy vindication of God's chosen—**Will he delay long over them?** Luke no doubt sees this applied to the church in time of trial. The important thing is that **faith** will be found on earth—that this kind of prayerful hope will persist—when the Son of man finally comes.

18:9-14. *The Pharisee and the Tax Collector.* Instead of having faith in God, some trust **in themselves.** The point is illustrated by another parable found only in Luke. It contrasts **two men** who go to the Jerusalem **temple to pray.** Since they go at the same time, it is probably one of the prescribed hours of prayer—9 A.M. or 3 P.M. **The Pharisee** takes the stance of pride and thanks God that he is not guilty of the sins of many men—that tax collector, for example. He does more than the law requires. The Pharisaic fondness for Monday and Thursday fasting was not required of all Jews, and tithing was enforced only for agricultural products, not of **all** that one received.

18:13-14. The **tax collector** takes the stance of penitence. He simply casts himself on the mercy of God and confesses his sinfulness. In commenting on the story Jesus insists that the tax collector is pronounced righteous and the Pharisee not. The worst sort of sin is self-righteousness. One is **justified** by trust in God, not in one's own efforts. The final verse, which has frequent parallels in the gospels (14:11; Matthew 18:4; 23:12), refers to the reversal of situations in the end time.

18:15-17. *Children and the Kingdom.* Another example of faith is seen in the coming of children. Here Luke returns to his Markan source (Mark 10:13-16), which he abandoned at 9:50. His mention of **infants** shows that the children are small. Luke omits Jesus' indignation with **the disciples** and his blessing of the children. He stresses the idea that Jesus **called** the children. To **enter** the kingdom one must have a childlike trust.

18:18-30. *The Rich Man and the Kingdom.* Again the question of entering the kingdom is raised. Luke answers with a narrative drawn from Mark 10:17-31. His account omits some of Mark's vivid detail. There is no mention of the man's running to Jesus or of the fact that Jesus "loved him." However, Luke does reproduce the statement that **no one is good but God alone** (cf. Matthew 19:17). For Luke the man is **a ruler,** perhaps a member of the sanhedrin or a leader of the synagogue.

Luke also adds that renouncing one's family is **for the sake of the kingdom of God.** The story makes the point that entering the kingdom demands more than obedience to the law. It requires surrendering possessions and home. The one who makes this decision receives **in this time** spiritual blessings and **in the age to come eternal life.**

18:31-34. *The Fate of the Son of Man.* The decision about the kingdom involves an understanding of the fate of Jesus.

Following Mark 10:32-34 Luke presents his sixth prediction of the passion (9:22, 44; 12:50; 13:33; 17:25). He apparently considers Mark's introduction unimportant but finds the mention of **Jerusalem** important to his theme. The long journey is about to reach its goal.

Luke omits Mark's reference to the verdict of the chief priests and scribes because it is not entirely in harmony with his own passion narrative. Instead he stresses that the rejection of the Son of man is fulfillment of prophetic prediction. This prepares for 21:27 but, more important, indicates that the destiny of Jesus is according to the purposes of God. The failure of the disciples to understand is emphasized by repeating the remark three different ways. Their lack of understanding is not due to a lack of clarity in Jesus' words, but to the inadequacy of their own faith.

M. Events in Jericho (18:35–19:27)

18:35-43. *Sight to the Blind.* In order to understand, the disciples' eyes must be opened. Luke illustrates this with a miracle story based on Mark 10:46-52. He omits the request of the sons of Zebedee in Mark 10:35-40. Whereas Mark reports that Jesus healed a blind beggar named Bartimaeus as he was leaving Jericho, Luke speaks merely of **a blind man** and locates the cure **as he drew near to Jericho**—perhaps to provide a setting for the Zacchaeus narrative. At any rate, since the incident occurred in the vicinity of Jericho, he is describing Jesus as drawing closer to Jerusalem.

The main theme of the passage is the recognition of Jesus as the Jewish Messiah—he opens the eyes of the blind (cf. Isaiah 35:5). Jesus is called **Son of David** in preparation for his triumphal entry into Jerusalem. There the disciples will see and believe.

19:1-10. *Salvation to Zacchaeus.* This narrative is found only in Luke. The blind man and Zacchaeus present a double witness to Jesus as the bringer of salvation. Zacchaeus is described as a

rich man who has made his wealth through the despicable practice of collecting taxes.

The word translated **chief tax collector** has been found nowhere else in Greek literature, but it no doubt describes one who supervised tax collecting. Jericho, situated on an important commercial route, was a center of taxation.

Since he is **small of stature** Zacchaeus climbs a tree in order to see Jesus. This **sycamore tree** has no relation to the American sycamore. It is a variety of fig which resembles a mulberry tree.

19:5-8. Jesus, displaying prophetic power, addresses Zacchaeus by name. The tax collector receives the Lord into his house as guest. Again the typical murmuring of the crowd occurs, for Jesus enters the home of **a sinner.**

Verse 8 has perhaps been inserted, since Jesus' remark in the following verse is directed to the objections of the crowd, not to the tax collector's promise of restitution. The pledge that he would **restore . . . fourfold** is reminiscent of the Old Testament requirement to return four sheep for one which was stolen (Exodus 22:1).

19:9-10. The important thing is that **today salvation has come to this house.** The moment of encounter with Jesus is the time of redemption. The salvation of the household anticipates a typical theme of the Acts narrative, for example, Acts 10:2 and 11:14. The tax collector, though viewed as an outcast, is restored to the people of God; **he also is a son of Abraham.** It is to just such sinners that the Messiah is sent (cf. 15:4, 8).

19:11-27. *The Demand of Faithfulness.* Since the Messiah is approaching Jerusalem his followers imagine that the **kingdom** is **to appear immediately.** Luke answers that mistaken notion with a parable of Jesus. Although there is some relation to Matthew 25:14-30, Luke has his own version of this illustration. Apparently Luke has changed an original parable into an allegory that shows his own historical and eschatological interest. The background of the story is seen in Palestinian history where Herodian princes went to Rome to confirm their **kingly power** and Jewish embassies asked Caesar to deny it.

19:12-19. According to the parable a **nobleman went into a far country to receive a kingdom.** Luke sees this as a sign that Jesus will receive his kingly power, not in Jerusalem, but in some distant time. Before the kingdom comes with power there will be delay.

Before leaving, the nobleman gives an equal sum of money to **ten of his servants.** The amount is a **pound**—literally "mina," the term in the Greek-Syrian monetary system for one hundred drachmas (see above on 15:8-10). Though the talent of Matthew's version was sixty times as much, a mina had enough purchasing power to start a businessman in **trade.** When he returns as king the nobleman asks the servants to give an account of their stewardship. That only three of the ten report indicates a parallel with Matthew and shows that ten is a round number. The first servant has increased the one pound ten times, while the second returns five. These faithful servants are granted **ten** and **five cities,** respectively—illustrating a huge return from a small investment.

19:20-25. The third servant has hidden his pound **in a napkin**—a neck scarf worn for protection from the sun—and has made no profit at all. At least the **money** could have earned **interest** in the **bank.** This return without increase leads to serious judgment. The one pound is taken away and given to the servant who earned ten. Objections, omitted in some manuscripts, are raised by the observers in verse 25.

19:26-27. The conclusion makes two points: (1) **To every one who has will more be given; but from him who has not, even what he has will be taken away.** This expression is found elsewhere in the gospels (Mark 4:25; see comment on parallels). It declares that the rule of God calls for fearless venture. He who does not produce the fruits of repentance and faith is not worthy of the kingdom at all.

(2) The **enemies** of the king will be slain. Those who oppose the kingly power of Jesus will be destroyed. These are the Jerusalem leaders whose rejection of the Messiah seals the fate of their city.

V. The Acts of Jesus in Jerusalem
(19:28–24:53)

A. Entry into Jerusalem (19:28-46)

19:28-40. *The King Who Comes in the Name of the Lord.*
Although the latter part of Luke's passion narrative is unique
(sometimes showing parallels with John), the early sections
follow Mark. The major difference is that Luke includes the
lament over Jerusalem and the cleansing of the temple as part of
the entry itself. The account of the entry is based on Mark
11:1-10.

19:28-34. In preparation two disciples enter a village and **find
a colt.** Luke stresses the idea that the **Lord has need of it**—a
phrase repeated a second time. Only Luke notes that the
owners inquire about the **untying** of the colt, so that they give a
tacit approval to Jesus' triumph. In no sense should this be
interpreted as prearranged. Jesus knows of the colt by prophetic
power.

19:37-40. Only in Luke do we read of **the descent of the
Mount of Olives.** This makes possible a view of the whole city
from the east and prepares for the lament which follows. Luke
also refers to **the whole multitude of the disciples,** perhaps to
suggest a large crowd which has followed all the way from
Galilee.

The hymn of praise does not mention Jesus as the Son of
David (cf. Mark 11:10); that has already been confessed in 18:39.
Emphasis instead is placed on his present kingship, and the
words of praise are reminiscent of the heavenly choir of 2:14.
The Pharisees' attempt to get Jesus to **rebuke your disciples**
(found only in Luke) illustrates the activity of the enemies who
oppose his kingship (cf. verse 27). But if the disciples should be
silent, cosmic forces would speak; **the very stones would cry
out.**

19:41-44. *The Fate of Jerusalem.* At the sight of the city Jesus
weeps. The account is based on L. Jesus expresses the wish that
the city **knew the things that make for peace.** These things

would be those which lead to right relationship with God, including repentance and recognition of Jesus as Lord **today.** But Jerusalem does not know; these things **are hid from** her **eyes.** The multitude has sung of **peace in heaven** (verse 38), yet in Jerusalem there shall be destruction. Eschatological judgment is to be fulfilled in history.

Although Jesus may have predicted the fall of the city, Luke's description reflects knowledge of the events of A.D. 70. In particular the **bank** which the **enemies will cast up** suggests the wall which the Romans constructed around Jerusalem during their siege.

19:45-46. *The Cleansing of the Temple.* This record is based on Mark 11:15-19, but Luke shortens the account drastically. In linking the cleansing to the entry narrative he destroys Mark's chronology, which presented particular events as occurring on certain days of the passion week. The cleansing prepares the temple for Jesus' Jerusalem ministry—a ministry which seems to have lasted several days (cf. verse 47). Most important, the structure of Luke's narrative makes the cleansing of the temple the goal of the entry. Indeed the temple is the goal of the trip to Jerusalem. There the old religion is encountered; there the new teaching is given; there the mission of the church is begun (cf. 24:53).

B. Opposition to Jesus (19:47–21:4)

19:47–20:8. *The Question of Authority.* Luke's general statement about the Jerusalem ministry is based on Mark 11:18-19. His major purpose is to present a sharp contrast between the leaders and the people. As well as **chief priests** and **scribes** Luke lists **principal men** among the Jerusalem officials. These were probably lay members of the sanhedrin. **The people,** on the other hand, are not called "the multitude" or the "crowd" (Mark 11:18). They are potentially the people of God. Luke has no account of the cursing of the fig tree (Mark 11:12-14).

20:2-8. The debate about authority is drawn from Mark 11:27-33, which Luke follows faithfully. He does add that Jesus is **preaching the gospel** as well as **teaching.** The question for Luke concerns the authority of the church's message. He also notes that the leaders are afraid **the people** will **stone** them if they fail to acknowledge **John** as **prophet.** Possibly Jesus is to be seen as cleverly evading the question, but more likely the theme is positive: "John's authority is from God; so is mine."

20:9-19. *The Parable of the Evil Tenants.* The one who has been questioned puts his opponents in question. Jesus does this by a parable; the leaders of the Jews perceive that it is spoken **against them.** The source is Mark 12:1-12.

20:9-15. Luke makes some interesting changes. For one, he says that the man who went to **another country** was gone **for a long while.** Until the time of John the prophetic word had not been heard for generations. Luke also increases the climax of the story: the only one killed is the **son.**

Post-crucifixion motifs are involved here. This is seen by the fact that Luke reverses Mark's order so that the son is **cast out of the vineyard** and then **killed,** reflecting the tradition that Jesus was executed outside the city.

20:16-19. When the listeners imagine what judgment might befall these tenants, they cry, **God forbid!** That is, they fear that such condemnation might come upon themselves. To the quotation of Psalm 118:22-23 Luke adds an allusion to Isaiah 8:14-15. The cornerstone has become a stone of stumbling. Rejection of Jesus means judgment upon Jerusalem.

20:20-26. *The Question of Tribute.* What relation does the authority of Jesus have to the authority of Rome? This question is answered on the basis of Mark 12:13-17. Luke's use of the narrative has one main purpose: to make the political innocence of Jesus absolutely clear.

Luke accomplishes this by editorial work at the beginning and end of the account. In the introduction he points out that **spies** are sent to watch Jesus so that evidence may be found **to deliver him up to the authority and jurisdiction of the governor.** At the end of the story Luke shows that no incriminating evidence has been found; **they were not able . . . to catch him by what he said.** On the lips of Jesus the word about rendering **to Caesar . . . and to God** may suggest that the realm of Rome is unimportant in face of the kingdom of God. To Rome belongs the unrighteous mammon symbolized in the coin. Luke is implying that obedience to the will of God brings one into no conflict with Caesar.

20:27-40. *The Problem of the Resurrection.* Luke proceeds to give a fuller description of the realm of God. His source is Mark 12:18-27. He presents Jesus as more tolerant of the opposition, omitting Mark's two statements that the Sadducees are "wrong." Luke stresses the idea that the life of the resurrection is totally different from the realm of Caesar. Similarly those who share it have a new nature. They become **sons of God through being sons of the resurrection.**

Perhaps Luke thinks of this new nature as present in the life of faith. Not only do the faithful worship a living God but they also **all live to him** through their response to Jesus. Luke ends the story with an editorial note which again shows that no one **dared to ask him any question.** Jesus has answered both Pharisees and Sadducees.

20:41-44. *The Christ and the Son of David.* To make it perfectly clear that Jesus is not a political ruler Luke introduced Mark's argument that the Christ is not **David's son** (Mark 12:35-37). Luke of course does not intend to deny that Jesus is the Davidic Messiah; he has previously argued that Jesus is the son of David (1:32; 3:31). However, he does insist that Jesus is not the nationalistic leader that the Jews expect. Above all the title "son of David" is not fully descriptive of him; he must be called **Lord.**

20:45–21:4. *The Scribes and the Widow.* Jesus now attacks his opponents directly. The source is Mark 12:38-44, which is followed carefully, though abbreviated. Luke does add that these words are spoken **to his disciples . . . in the hearing of all people;** those attacked are foes of the church. Jesus warns of the pride and pretense of the **scribes** and contrasts their imaginary piety with the genuine offering of a **widow.** She is a type of the poor who accept the demands of the kingdom, who know that one's whole life is dependent on God.

C. A Discourse on the End of History (21:5-37)

21:5-7. *The Fate of the Temple.* Luke's apocalyptic section (see comment on Matthew 24:4) is based on Mark 13. Its major feature is the separation of the destruction of Jerusalem from the eschatological events of the future. This feature reflects Luke's doctrine of the end, which is shaped in part by the delay of the Lord's return in triumph.

The prediction about the temple has a slightly different setting from that described in Mark 13:1-4. Here the word is apparently spoken in the temple and to a larger group than just the disciples. Although Jews marvel at the **noble stones** of the temple, this center of worship shall be destroyed. The "prophecy," as Luke well knows, is to be fulfilled in A.D. 70 by the siege and destruction of Jerusalem by the Romans.

21:8-11. *Signs of the End.* This part of the discourse is based on Mark 13:5-8. Luke makes some important modifications. For him the threat is not simply that imposters come in the Messiah's name but that these false Christs say, **The time is at hand.** The real heresy is the belief that the end is coming soon. In truth **the end will not be at once.** This is why Luke omits Mark's word that historical and cosmic **signs** are "the beginning of the sufferings." He wants to avoid the impression that omens on earth and in heaven provide evidence that the messianic age has already started.

21:12-19. *Persecution of the Faithful.* Again Luke changes his Markan source. He points out that persecution will take place **before all this**—that is, before the end comes. In describing the persecutions he mentions those who are put in **prisons;** he probably thinks of the imprisonments which he will describe in Acts (e.g. 4:3 and 5:18). The prophecy that the faithful will be **brought before kings and governors** is fulfilled in the life of Paul.

Luke omits the saying which implies that the end will come after the gospel is "preached to all nations" (Mark 13:10). For him the Gentile mission is a historical reality, but the triumphant Lord has not yet returned. The promise that the disciples will be given **a mouth** is a way of saying that they will be told what to say. In Hebrew anthropology the organ stands for the function which it performs.

21:16-19. Verses 16 and 18 seem to be in contradiction. In verse 16 **some** will be **put to death,** but in verse 18 the faithful are promised that **not a hair of your head will perish.** Luke may be contrasting two different groups. Or he may be suggesting that though the Christians are persecuted, or even executed, they cannot be ultimately destroyed; their salvation is sure.

21:20-24. *The Destruction of Jerusalem.* This crucial section of Luke's eschatological discourse is based on Mark 13:14-20, but the intention of Mark's passage has been changed. Mark was concerned with happenings of the end of history. Luke is describing an event which has occurred in history—the destruction of the Holy City. In place of Mark's "desolating sacrilege"—an apocalyptic symbol borrowed from Daniel 12:11—Luke has a reference to **Jerusalem surrounded by armies.** Similarly Luke directs the warnings to **those who are inside the city.** Though what happens in the **days of vengeance** is historical, it fulfills **all that is written.**

21:24. Luke's word that **Jerusalem will be trodden down by the Gentiles** refers to the capture and razing of the city by the Romans. By **the times of the Gentiles** he may mean the era of the Gentile mission. The rejection of Jesus means the destruction of the city, but it is from Jerusalem that the Gentile mission is launched. The time of the Gentiles is the time of the church; it continues until the coming of the Son of man.

Although the fate of Jerusalem is sealed already by its rejection of Jesus, Luke does not agree that the days have been "shortened" (Mark 13:20). The coming of the Lord is an event distinct from the destruction of Jerusalem.

21:25-33. *The Coming of the Son of Man.* Luke now turns to the future—the cataclysmic return of the Son of man. His source is Mark 13:24-32, but he makes interesting changes. To the description of the cosmic signs he adds **the roaring of the sea,** probably from Old Testament passages like Psalm 65:7. It seems strange that after showing such an interest in heavenly messengers in the birth stories, he omits any reference to the sending of angels here. Probably he wants nothing to detract from **the Son of man coming in a cloud.**

Only Luke has the word that **when these things begin to take place** the faithful will know their **redemption is drawing near.** The concept is rare in the Synoptic gospels. Luke's idea that redemption is granted, not through the death of Christ, but through his return, is striking.

21:29-31. Luke follows Mark's version of the parable of the fig tree closely. Its point is that as one can observe the signs of nature and know **summer** is at hand, so one can see these cosmic signs and know the end **is near.** Here the understanding of signs contradicts Jesus' word that the "kingdom of God is not coming with signs to be observed" (17:20). But this simply shows that this whole passage represents the eschatological tradition of the church more than the teachings of Jesus.

21:32-33. In discussing the time of the end Luke omits the idea that the Son does not know the day or hour (Mark 13:32). Luke's Christology is too high to allow a limitation of the Lord's knowledge. **This generation will not pass away till all has taken place** is open to two interpretations. If it refers to Jesus' generation, it means that all things began to be accomplished in the destruction of Jerusalem; if to Luke's generation, it means that the events of the end are not too distant.

21:34-37. *Exhortation to Watchful Waiting.* Luke omits Mark's parable of the man who went on a journey and adds his own ending to the discourse. It stresses the need for watchful waiting, since the **day** of the Lord will come **like a snare**—that is, as a surprise. The effect of this eschatological event will be universal—**upon all who dwell upon . . . the whole earth.** Luke's own generation is reflected here. It is a time when **hearts** can **be weighed down** with **cares** of this life—that is, when the vital expectation of the end is dying away.

21:37-38. This is Luke's summary of the Jerusalem ministry. **The temple** has been the seat of Jesus' teaching, which apparently has been carried on for several days. At night he has **lodged on the mount called Olivet**—information not necessarily inconsistent with the mention of Bethany in Mark 11:11, since this village is just beyond the crest of the hill. However, Luke probably thinks of the place of lodging as identical with the place of prayer (22:40). He emphasizes the fact that the people assemble **early** to hear Jesus. This indicates the eagerness of their response in contrast to the villainy of the leaders.

D. The Last Supper (22:1-38)

22:1-6. *The Conspiracy Against Jesus.* Luke's account is based on Mark 14:1-11, although the narrative of the anointing at Bethany is omitted. Luke makes the mistake of identifying **the feast of Unleavened Bread** with **the Passover.** They are actually two different festivals, the former following immediately after the latter and lasting seven days.

Luke's saying that the feast **drew near,** in contrast to Mark's "two days," is another indication that he thinks of a longer ministry in Jerusalem. He follows Mark's dating but omits the report that Jewish leaders sought to avoid killing Jesus during the feast. Probably Luke has noted its inconsistency with Mark's account of the arrest on the evening when the Passover was eaten and the execution during the feast of Unleavened Bread.

22:3-6. The distinctive feature of Luke's narrative is the statement that **Satan entered into Judas.** The last appearance of Satan was in 4:13, where the devil "departed from him until an opportune time." Apparently he has been absent during the whole ministry of Jesus. The opportune time is now—the time of the Crucifixion. Satan has entered Judas, so that this **member of the twelve** and the leaders of the Jews who follow him have become instruments of Satan's power.

22:7-13. *Preparation for the Passover.* Although he abbreviates the account, Luke follows Mark 14:12-16 faithfully. By omitting Mark's question by the disciples, however, he implies that Jesus took the initiative for the supper. He also identifies the two sent to make the preparations as **Peter and John**—heroes of early episodes in Acts. The story of locating the **upper room,** like that of finding the colt (19:30-34), suggests, not prearrangement, but prophetic power. Like Mark and Matthew, and in disagreement with John, Luke identifies the supper as a Passover meal (see comments on Matthew 26:17-29; Mark 14:12-16; John 13:1).

22:14-23. *Eating in Anticipation.* Since the ceremony of the Passover includes more than one cup, possibly only the second cup (verse 20) is involved in the institution of the Lord's Supper.

22:14-19. The supper is primarily an anticipation of the messianic banquet. When Jesus is reported as saying that he has **earnestly desired to eat this passover** it is not clear whether he actually partakes of the supper or not. In some manuscripts his pledge is that he will **not eat it** "again" until the supper **is fulfilled in the kingdom of God.** Yet whether he eats or not, one thing is clear: the elements of the supper look forward to the coming of the kingdom. The joyous feast of the future cannot take place, however, until Jesus' purpose is accomplished. That will happen at his death—an event dramatically anticipated in the breaking of the bread. To share in this supper will make **the apostles** participants in the fate of Jesus as well as guarantee their presence at the messianic meal.

22:21-23. Still at the **table,** Jesus predicts his betrayal. The account is based on Mark 14:18-21. In contrast to Mark, Luke locates this prophecy immediately after the words which institute the Lord's Supper. The effect of this change is to make it clear that even those who share in the supper are in danger of falling away. The passage also shows that, even though Jesus' death is accomplished by Satan through the betrayer, the destiny of Jesus is **determined** by God. The guilty, however, is not absolved but becomes the object of the divine **woe.**

22:24-38. *The Misunderstanding of the Disciples.* Here Luke presents Jesus as offering a discourse at the table—a theme more fully developed in John. The question about the identity of the betrayer leads to a discussion of greatness. Jesus replies that in the kingdom it is not measured by the standards of the world. There **kings . . . exercise lordship** and **authority** and are called **benefactors**—a title actually applied to Hellenistic rulers. In the kingdom the **greatest** is the **youngest, and the leader** is **one who serves.** The youngest may reflect the "young men" who perform duties in the early church (cf. Acts. 5:6, 10). The example of service is seen in Jesus himself. He is not **one who sits at table** but **one who serves.**

22:28-30. Those who share this table will participate not only in his **trials** but also in the messianic banquet. The promise that they will **sit on thrones judging the twelve tribes of Israel** (cf. Matthew 19:28) is simply another symbolic way to say that they will share the blessings of the end time.

22:31-34. According to Luke the prediction of Peter's denial is a part of this discourse rather than a saying spoken on the road (Mark 14:29-31). Luke basically uses his own material. The idea that **Satan demanded to have you** (plural in the Greek) is reminiscent of Job. Just as he has engineered the betrayal, so the devil puts the disciples to the testing which leads to denial.

Although Luke does not say that all the disciples support Peter's pledge of fidelity (cf. Mark 14:31), he does imply that all are involved by his use of the plural of **you** in verse 31. The figure of sifting **like wheat** is borrowed from Amos 9:9, where it symbolizes judgment of Israel. Peter's promise of faithfulness includes the idea that he is ready to undergo imprisonment; after the Resurrection this pledge will be kept. Indeed the central feature of the saying is the allusion to Peter's experience of the risen Christ. Though he will deny Jesus, the resurrection faith will lead Peter to turn **again** and **strengthen** the other disciples.

22:35-38. These verses are without parallel in the other gospels. In view of the imminent testing the disciples must be prepared. Jesus refers back to the mission of the twelve (9:1-6), when they were sent out without **purse or bag or sandals**—equipment more clearly forbidden for the mission of the seventy (10:4). He then asks, **Did you lack anything?** At their denial he declares that the present time of trial is utterly different. **Now they need everything they can get their hands on, even a sword.**

The testing is serious—a matter of death for Jesus and persecution for the church. Jesus' death has been predicted by the Old Testament (Isaiah 53:12), which indicates that he will be executed like a common criminal. For Jesus, of course, the testing is a matter of the spirit, and the sword is a symbol of conflict and death. The disciples misunderstand completely: **Look, Lord, here are two swords.** Resigning himself to their blindness, Jesus ironically cries out in despair, **It is enough.**

E. THE ARREST (22:39-62)

22:39-46. *Prayer on the Mount.* After the discourse Jesus and the disciples go to the Mount of Olives. Luke's account of Jesus' prayer there is parallel to Mark 14:32-42, although it may reflect his special tradition. He abbreviates the story by reporting that Jesus prayed and returned to the disciples only once instead of three times.

22:39. That it was Jesus' **custom** to go **to the Mount of Olives** confirms the previous information (21:37) that this hill east of Jerusalem was the place of lodging during the ministry to the city. This customary action may hint too that the wrestling described in the prayer has gone on for some time.

22:40. Luke refers simply to the **place** of prayer, omitting as usual Mark's Aramaic—the name "Gethsemane." He emphasizes the meaning of the event more for the faith of the church than for the experience of Jesus. **Pray that you may not enter into temptation** in Mark's version is a rebuke to the disciples for their failure to watch. In Luke's account it is the instruction to them as they come to the place and is repeated when they are aroused from sleep. The stress is on the church's need for preparation to face the testing of persecution.

22:41-42. Luke omits Mark's separation of Peter, James, and John from the rest of the disciples. He adds that Jesus **withdrew . . . about a stone's throw**—a Greek and biblical expression

267

which describes a short distance—and says that he **knelt down** instead of "fell on the ground." Jesus' prayer is not precisely the same in any two of the Synoptic gospels. Luke omits the Aramaic "Abba" of Mark, although his term **Father** means the same. All three accounts agree that Jesus prays that God's **will**, not his own, **be done.**

22:43-44. These verses (see the footnote in the Revised Standard Version) have no parallel in the other gospels. Though not found in some ancient manuscripts, they seem to represent Lukan style. The **angel** who comes to help in time of trouble is a typical feature of Jewish martyr stories. Misunderstanding of verse 44*b* has given rise to the common expression "sweat blood," but the meaning is rather that **his sweat** rolled down **like great drops of blood** from a wound, suggesting the anxiety involved in the experience.

22:45-46. Luke excuses the disciples' lack of watchfulness by explaining that they were **sleeping for sorrow,** and Jesus' rebuke is very mild (see above on verse 40).

22:47-53. *Betrayal and Capture.* This narrative is apparently based on both Mark 14:43-52 and L. Luke observes that **Judas** leads the **crowd**—information which indicates that Satan's purposes are being accomplished through **one of the twelve** (cf. verse 3). The impression is given here that Judas approaches, but does not actually **kiss,** the **Son of man.** Jesus' consciousness of the betrayer's intention is a sign of prophetic power. The question about **the sword** is reminiscent of verses 35-38. Use of the sword results in the wounding of **the slave of the high priest.** Luke and John 18:10 agree that it is his **right ear** that is **cut off.**

It is not clear in the Greek whether Jesus' response is directed to the use of the sword or to the act of capture. It may be translated either **No more of this,** meaning no more use of the sword, or "Let them have their way" (New English Bible), forbidding further interference with the arrest.

22:52-53. Jesus' words rebuking his captors are directed, not as in Mark to those who are sent out by the Jerusalem leaders, but **to the chief priests and officers of the temple and elders**

themselves. The mention of the officers is exclusive with Luke and refers to officers of the temple police.

Jesus' rebuke gets its force from the setting. Although he is **day after day** teaching **in the temple,** his enemies come to capture him at night. This setting makes possible a symbolic remark: **This is your hour**—that is, the hour of their triumph. But the character of the hour is signified by the night as evil. It is **the power of darkness.**

22:54-62. *The Denial of Peter.* From this section of the passion narrative Luke has omitted the flight of the disciples (Mark 14:50), the escape of the young man (Mark 14:51-52), and the trial before the sanhedrin at night (Mark 14:57-61). The result of the last omission is to place the denial of Peter prior to the hearing before the sanhedrin in the morning. Luke has thus put Jesus and Peter together in the courtyard of the high priest's house as a setting for the denial. The source is probably Luke's special material L, plus Mark 14:66-72.

22:54-60. The account of the three denials is slightly different from Mark's. For example, the second charge is made by **some one else,** whereas Mark attributes it to the **maid** again. Luke presents only the second charge to Peter, while Mark has this form of accusation in the first and third encounters. To add to the climactic character of the narrative Luke allows **an hour** to elapse between the second and third denials.

He also improves the character of Peter by omitting Mark's report that this future leader of the church invoked a curse upon himself and swore. Perhaps Luke conceives of a progression of denial: in the first Peter denies his association with Jesus; in the second he denies his association with the disciples; in the third he makes an absolute denial, for he does not know what they are talking about.

22:61-62. Mark's idea that the **cock** would crow twice is lacking in Luke. Only one crowing is necessary to give the disciple the sense of guilt. The words that Peter **went out and wept bitterly** are not found in some manuscripts and may be assimilated from Matthew 26:75. Only Luke includes the most dramatic note of the entire narrative: **The Lord turned and looked at Peter.**

F. THE TRIALS (22:63–23:25)

22:63-71. *Before the Council.* Although Luke does not include the trial before the sanhedrin at night, he records a hearing before that council in the morning. The source of the account is probably L edited by use of Mark 14:53-65. Here the mockery takes place before the hearing rather than after it as in Mark. The content of the two accounts is similar. Jesus is **blindfolded . . . , struck,** and asked **who** hit him; a prophet should have the power to identify his assailant. Luke omits Mark's information that the mockers, probably to be identified as the temple police, spit on Jesus.

22:66-68. Luke's version of the hearing conforms more closely to Jewish legal practice. It is not held illegally at night as Mark's describes. Much of Luke's narrative follows Mark's nocturnal trial. The report that false witnesses were brought in and the charge that Jesus intended to destroy the temple are omitted.

Luke's trial is more theological than historical. The questioning is unrealistic, since it is done, not by the high priest, but by the whole assembly in chorus. First they ask if Jesus is **the Christ.** To this he responds that they would **not believe** if he told them. They do not know the nature of the Messiah.

22:69-71. In contrast to Mark's reference to seeing the Son of man in power, Luke has Jesus announce that **the Son of man shall be seated at the right hand of the power of God.** For Luke the moment of Jesus' rejection is the time of his triumph. This occurs **now** at the moment of decision about Jesus.

The statement about the Son of man leads to the question, **Are you the Son of God?** Thus Luke interprets the title "Son of man" at its highest level—the level of the divine nature of the Christ. Jesus' reply, **You say that I am,** can be taken as either affirmation or denial. Luke's intention is to place the responsibility of decision on the Jewish leadership. They assume his response to be an affirmation and therefore blasphemy **from his own lips** which seals his condemnation. In a deeper sense these words declare a theological truth: Jesus' own words send him to his death. No official verdict is pronounced; Jesus is sent to another authority.

23:1-5. *Before Pilate.* Although verse 3 has a parallel in Mark 15:2, Luke's narrative here is based primarily on his special tradition, L. His purpose is to present Jesus as innocent, to confirm the guilt of the Jewish leaders, and to absolve the Romans of any injustice. This is accomplished by Pilate's threefold declaration that he finds **no crime** in Jesus (verses 4, 15, 22). The guilt of the Jews is supported by the information that **the whole company** of the council **brought** Jesus to Pilate and made false charges against him.

In essence the charge is that Jesus is a revolutionary. He forbids the people **to give tribute to Caesar**—an accusation which Luke's readers know to be erroneous (20:25)—and he says that **he himself is . . . a king.** Since kingship becomes the dominant motif of Luke's account, it bears a certain similarity to John 18:29–19:22.

23:3-5. Jesus' response to the question is similar to his answer before the council: **You have said so.** Pilate understands this to be a denial. If Jesus were claiming to be king, evidence of insurrection would be sure. When Pilate declares Jesus' innocence, the accusers give further evidence of his sedition. Their charge that he has been **teaching throughout all Judea, from Galilee even to this place** not only provides the ground for sending Jesus to Herod, the ruler of Galilee, but summarizes the whole mission of Jesus.

23:6-12. *Before Herod.* Discovering that Jesus is **a Galilean,** Pilate sends him to **Herod** Antipas, who is **in Jerusalem,** perhaps to attend the feast. As we were told in 9:9, Herod has been hoping **to see** Jesus. Now we discover that his purpose has been to behold some act of power. Although **questioned . . . at some length** Jesus makes **no answer,** and presumably performs no miracle. His silence adds an aura of mystery to the proceedings, as well as fulfills prophecy (cf. Isaiah 53:7).

271

23:11-12. Herod is no doubt exasperated. He **with his soldiers** treats Jesus **with contempt.** This mockery takes the place of the mocking by the troops of Pilate in Mark 15:16-20; Luke prefers to present a "Jewish" ruler in the role of persecutor rather than Rome.

When he says that the soldiers put **gorgeous apparel** on Jesus, he uses the same term which Josephus employs to describe the royal robe of Solomon. With sarcasm Jesus is being treated as king. After the mockery Herod sends Jesus back to Pilate. It is clear from verse 15 that his verdict is "not guilty." **Herod and Pilate became friends** apparently because each recognized the other's authority. Since this hearing is not found elsewhere in the gospels, some doubt its historicity. It seems unlikely that a Roman governor would recognize the rights of a petty tetrarch outside his own jurisdiction. In any case the purpose of the narrative is perhaps revealed in Acts 4:25-28. There Herod and Pilate are explicitly mentioned as fulfilling the prophecy of Psalm 2:2, that "kings . . . set themselves, and the rulers take counsel . . . against the LORD and his anointed." For this prophecy to be fulfilled there must be a king as well as a governor involved in the trial of Jesus. Moreover, Luke's interest in two witnesses is again visible. Not only Pilate but also Herod finds Jesus innocent.

23:13-25. *Before the Crowd.* After Jesus is returned Pilate assembles **the chief priests and the rulers and the people.** He repeats the charge, reaffirms his own verdict, and announces Herod's agreement. Since Jesus has done **nothing deserving death** the governor proposes a comparatively mild punishment and **release.** These verses are found exclusively in Luke.

23:18-23. The crowd cries for **release** of **Barabbas**—a man imprisoned **for an insurrection . . . and for murder.** Here Luke turns to Mark 15:6-15. Luke states clearly that Pilate wants **to release Jesus.** The mob, swayed by the demonic power of the leaders, demands crucifixion, even though Pilate affirms his belief in innocence for **a third time** and repeats his proposal to **chastise** and **release** Jesus. But the crowd is urgent and ultimately prevails.

23:24-25. Luke's presentation of the outcome is ironical. Barabbas, who is apparently guilty of insurrection and murder, is released. Jesus, who is innocent of insurrection and has come to save Jerusalem, is condemned. Luke makes it clear, however, that the leaders of the Jews are really guilty. He says that Pilate **delivered** Jesus, not "to be crucified," as Mark expresses it, but **up to their will.**

G. THE CRUCIFIXION (23:26-56)

23:26-31. *The Way to the Cross.* Luke, more than Matthew and Mark, stresses the procession to the Crucifixion. Although verse 26 finds a parallel in Mark 15:21 the narrative is drawn from Luke's unique tradition. **Simon of Cyrene** symbolizes the true disciple; he takes up the cross and follows Jesus. The background of the wailing **women** is found in Zechariah 12:10. Jesus applies the idea to the present situation; they should not **weep** for him but for themselves. **Jerusalem,** not Jesus, is in serious danger. When its destruction comes—a fate sealed by the rejection of Jesus—the childless will be most fortunate. The call **to the mountains** is a quotation from Hosea 10:8, while the word about **green** and **dry** wood is proverbial. The two figures stress the seriousness of the city's future. One will do anything to hide from its horrors. If Jerusalem can commit a crime like the Crucifixion, how great will be her punishment in the crisis of judgment.

23:32-43. *The Place of the Skull.* Luke's account of the crucifying appears to be based on both L and Mark 15:22-32. It does not include the Aramaic word "Golgotha," but only its translation, **The Skull.** The saying **Father, forgive them; for they know not what they do** is found exclusively in Luke. It is not, however, in some important manuscripts. But it is probably original since it is consistent with Luke's general portrait of Jesus and finds a parallel in Acts 7:60.

A major feature of this narrative is the idea that sinners are given another chance, especially those who have acted in ignorance. Another emphasis of the account is the sharp distinction drawn in verse 35 between the **people,** who simply **stood by, watching,** and the **rulers,** who **scoffed** at Jesus. The scoffing ridicules the acknowledgment of Jesus as God's **Chosen One**—a title which presents the Messiah as the Elect of God (cf. 9:35). The **inscription** on the cross is not precisely the same in any two of the gospels. Luke places the words **This is the King of the Jews** at the end of his description of the mockery as a climax.

23:39-43. The penitent thief is described only in Luke. In contrast to the other criminal this man confesses his guilt and expresses faith. Although he is without hope, the penitent asks that Jesus **remember** him when he comes in his **kingdom.**

Jesus' statement, which has led to considerable debate, is perhaps not intended to stress the time of the thief's entrance into Paradise. As often in Luke, **today** or "now" may refer to the time of salvation which is the time of encounter with Jesus. However, Luke may wish to stress the conviction that Jesus at death comes into his power as king—an event which occurs "today." **Paradise,** which basically means "garden," is used by Jewish authors of this period for the abode of the righteous dead, referring to either the intermediate or the final state. When stripped of its symbolism, the narrative simply suggests that the repentant sinner can receive salvation now through faith in Jesus Christ.

23:44-49. *The Death of Jesus.* Here Luke has combined his special material with Mark 15:33-41. His explanation of the **darkness**—that **the sun's light failed**—led some early readers to assume an eclipse, and alter the text accordingly. But at Passover time, when the moon is full, an eclipse of the sun is impossible. This fact forced others to change the text to read "the sun was darkened." They correctly interpreted Luke as stressing supernatural events, as his inclusion of the rending of the temple **curtain** shows.

This curtain separated the holy place from the Holy of Holies. The tearing of the curtain allows two possible interpretations:

(1) The entry to God's dwelling is open; the death of Jesus provides access to God.

(2) God has left the temple, splitting the curtain in two; the death of Jesus means judgment on Israel.

23:46. The word "My God, my God, why hast thou forsaken me?" and the discussion about Elijah reported by Mark and Matthew are missing in Luke. Instead he includes the saying **Father, into thy hands I commit my spirit.** It seems unnatural for Jesus to cry **with a loud voice,** but some have noted that this occurred at the time of the trumpet call to evening prayer. The prayer of Jesus comes from Psalm 31:5 and suggests that at his death his spirit returns to God, from whence it came.

23:47-49. The **centurion** comes from Mark's narrative. Luke has him merely confirm Pilate's verdict that Jesus is **innocent.** This Roman officer presents a kind of parallel with the penitent thief, indicating that the chance for repentance is still open.

Two other groups observe the cross. **The multitudes,** who have watched silently, return **home** in a mood of penitence. The **acquaintances** probably include the disciples, since Luke has not reported their flight. The **women** are the ministering women of 8:1-3. Together these are witnesses of the death of Jesus so that they may become witnesses of his resurrection (cf. Acts 1:22).

23:50-56. *The Burial.* Luke's account modifies Mark 15:42-47, perhaps on the basis of his own tradition. **Joseph . . . of Arimathea,** somewhat in parallel with Simeon (2:25), is presented as **a good and righteous man.** Luke says that he **had not consented to** the **purpose and deed** of the sanhedrin even though he was a **member.** Mark's information that Pilate inquired about the death of Jesus is lacking. Luke also omits Mark's explanation that **the day of Preparation** means "the day before the sabbath" (cf. John 19:14). **Was beginning** is literally "was dawning"—perhaps a reference to the appearance of the evening star, since the sabbath began at sundown. The fact that the women **saw the tomb** makes it possible for them to find it on Easter morning. In contrast to Mark, Luke suggests that these women **prepared spices and ointments** before the sabbath.

275

H. The Resurrection (24:1-53)

Although he uses Mark, Luke's account of the Resurrection is unique. For one thing he groups all the events into a single day and presents them under the motif of the early church's celebration of Easter. He also depicts all the appearances of the risen Christ as happening in the neighborhood of Jerusalem.

24:1-12. *The Empty Tomb.* The story of the women coming to the tomb is similar to Mark 16:1-8. The women are named in verse 10, but the list is different from Mark's.

24:4-5. At the tomb the women meet, not one, but **two men** dressed in **dazzling apparel.** Luke's fondness for two witnesses is again apparent. Faced with these heavenly messengers the women are afraid and look **to the ground.** The men offer a mild rebuke, **Why do you seek the living among the dead?** A majority of manuscripts add, "He is not here but has risen," but it is usually supposed that this has been taken over from Mark.

24:6-7. The important difference from Mark is the word about **Galilee.** In Mark's account it is announced that the risen Christ "is going before you to Galilee," but Luke says, **Remember how he told you, while he was still in Galilee.** This refers to prediction of the Resurrection **on the third day** presented in Galilee (9:22), but Luke's real intention in this modification is to keep all resurrection narratives in the vicinity of Jerusalem.

24:8-12. The women do not flee, as in Mark's account, but return **to the eleven** and bear witness. The latter are the leaders of the church—**apostles.** In spite of the witness they do **not believe.** This report of the empty tomb is not adequate for faith. Most ancient texts add verse 12 (see the footnote in the Revised Standard Version), in which Peter runs to confirm the women's story. Although this may have been added to Luke under the influence of John 20:3-10, it could be original. Sometime before verse 34 Simon Peter has an experience of the Resurrection.

24:13-35. *The Pilgrims of Emmaus.* This is the most dramatic resurrection narrative in the New Testament. It is found only in Luke. He makes it clear that the event took place **on that very**

day, on Easter. The site of **Emmaus** has never been positively identified; four modern villages have been considered as possibilities. According to the story **two** disciples are walking **from Jerusalem** to this town. One of them is called **Cleopas,** who is sometimes identified with Clopas, the father of Simeon, who succeeded James as leader of the Jerusalem church. Luke's intention is to give the story a quality of history; the name of one of the two is known.

24:15-18. As they walk along **discussing** the recent happenings in Jerusalem, they are joined by the risen Jesus, who is not recognized. We are told that their **eyes were kept from recognizing him.** This probably does not mean that some miracle of blinding has occurred, but that a special opening of the eyes is necessary for seeing the risen Christ. Proof of the inward character of this blindness can be seen in the fact that even when they stand **still** they do not know the identity of the other pilgrim. When Jesus expresses ignorance of the recent events Cleopas is surprised. His response is open to slightly different translations, but its meaning is clear: the event of the Crucifixion is widely known.

24:19-24. To answer Jesus' question the two disciples tell the basic elements of the message of Jesus. They have accepted him as a **prophet.** The **chief priests and rulers** of Jerusalem are guilty of his **death.** The disciples hoped he was the Messiah, but now their hopes have been dashed. The reference to the **third day** hints knowledge of Jesus' prediction of his resurrection. To be sure **women** have found no body and claimed a **vision,** while others have tested their report. Yet for all the evidence of an empty tomb no one has seen the risen Lord.

24:25-27. Jesus criticizes their lack of faith, using the whole Old Testament to prove that **the Christ should suffer . . . and enter into his glory.** Specific texts which make these points are not easy to find, but Luke believes the total witness of **Moses and all the prophets** is that the Messiah's role involves a suffering which leads to triumph.

24:28-31. Arriving at the home of the travelers, Jesus is invited to share their hospitality. Suddenly the stranger assumes the role of host. Taking **bread,** he blesses and breaks it, and the disciples' **eyes were opened.** The breaking of bread is reminiscent of the feeding of the five thousand (9:16) and the Last Supper (22:19). This indicates that the miracle of seeing the risen Christ occurs in the celebration of the Lord's Supper. This is not to suggest that his reality is to be found only there, or that the fellowship of the church somehow creates the resurrection faith. It is simply observed that in this event of the church's worship the risen Christ is made **known** (verse 35).

24:32. When the two disciples exclaim, **Did not our hearts burn within us while he talked to us on the road?** they confess that the experience of the Resurrection illuminates their whole past. The **scriptures,** once so opaque, now are **opened** through the risen Christ.

24:33-35. When the pilgrims return **to Jerusalem** they find that **the eleven** have already heard the good news. The report that **the Lord . . . has appeared to Simon** confirms Paul's account of the Resurrection (I Corinthians 15:5; see above on verses 8-12).

The Christ who at first is invisible, who then appears at places removed in distance, who appears again and vanishes, is hardly an ordinary person. Although the following verses will partially blur this image, it is evident here that Luke, like Paul (I Corinthians 15:44, 50), supports belief in a spiritual resurrection.

24:36-49. *The Appearance in Jerusalem.* This narrative is without parallel in the other gospels. It seems to rest on a different tradition from the Emmaus story, since the disciples are **startled and frightened.** If they had already heard the reports of Peter and the two from Emmaus about the risen Christ, his appearance would not have been so shocking.

As a matter of fact, the purpose of this account is to refute the beliefs of docetism—a heresy which asserted that Jesus only seemed to have a physical body. In announcing that the risen Christ has **flesh and bones** Luke apparently wants to avoid the notion that the risen Lord has no concrete reality. The word rendered **spirit** here would better be translated "ghost." Christ is no vaporous specter. He can eat **a piece of broiled fish.**

24:44-49. Again it is stressed that the death and resurrection of Christ are according to scripture. Christ is not only the fulfillment of the Old Testament but also its interpreter. Most important, his interpretation must be announced to the world. The message of **repentance and forgiveness of sins** granted through Christ must be preached **in his name to all nations.**

The punctuation of the passage is not clear, so that it is not certain whether the preaching or the witnessing is to begin **from Jerusalem** (see the Revised Standard Version footnote), but the two are essentially the same. Witnessing is not to occur at once, for the disciples must **stay in the city** until they receive **power from on high.** This will take place on Pentecost (Acts 2:1-4). Now it is clear why the events of Jesus' death and resurrection occur near the city. Jerusalem is the traditional messianic center; there the prophets have been executed; there the Christ is raised; there the risen Lord establishes his mission to the world; there the church will begin.

24:50-53. *Departure from Bethany.* This account has no parallel in the other gospels, but its relation to Acts 1:9-11 has created a problem. Both texts describe the ascension of Christ. The words **and was carried up into heaven,** in most manuscripts, make this clear. But while the Acts narrative presents the Ascension as occurring forty days after the Resurrection, this account includes the departure of Jesus as an event of Easter day.

Perhaps Luke, concerned less with chronology than with theology, presents both accounts to make different points. An ascension soon after the death of Jesus seems historically probable, as the promise to the penitent thief implies (23:43). Of course the Ascension cannot occur until the resurrection appearances of Easter have occurred. The Acts account wishes to stress the importance of the risen Christ for the founding of the church. Thus Christ is the end of the gospel and the beginning of the mission.

24:52-53. After Jesus has departed the disciples return **to Jerusalem with great joy.** They praise God, who has accomplished all these things. Luke's gospel ends as it began—**in the temple.**

THE GOSPEL
ACCORDING TO JOHN

Massey H. Shepherd, Jr.

INTRODUCTION

The gospel of John was published in the Roman province which then was the Western part of Asia Minor. It dates from not later than the early years of the second century. Its sources and circumstances of origin remain veiled in mystery. Yet no document has influenced so powerfully the hearts and minds of Christians. Nor has any book of the New Testament received so many diverse interpretations of its meaning and judgments of its historical value.

The enormous amount of critical and devotional commentary which the gospel has evoked is perhaps its strongest claim to an authentic inspiration. The testimony *of* Jesus and *about* Jesus in this gospel meets all sorts of people with manifold insights of revelation.

The gospel itself encourages an ever-deepening search for meaning. Throughout the work there are explicit notices that Jesus' contemporaries did not understand the true purpose of his sayings and actions. His mother and brothers, his disciples and friends, the Jewish rabbis and priests, the Samaritan woman, Pontius Pilate—all of them miss the point of his sayings and are dumbfounded by his behavior. Everything in the gospel is a "sign" that points to a fulfillment. Each fulfillment is not only in the historic "hour [which] is coming, and now is" when Jesus accomplishes his mission from God, but in a judgment that separates those who believe and those who do not believe in him both now and in the "last day."

Purpose

The author is explicit about his purpose. The work is a gospel—an account "written that you may believe that Jesus is the Christ, the Son of God, and that believing you may have life in his name" (20:31). Did he know other written gospels? If so, was his aim to correct, supplement, or displace them? These questions have received diverse answers, in both ancient and modern times. The similarities of basic structure and content with the other gospels are matched by noticeable differences— in chronology, style, and method of presentation. These characteristics of the work have been evaluated by reference to the variant traditions about the author and the circumstances of his writing.

From the early third century a tradition was established that John the apostle dictated the gospel in old age. John had knowledge of the other gospels but he wrote from his own reminiscences, supplementing them with accounts of Jesus' ministry before the imprisonment of John the Baptist. Many modern interpreters are also persuaded that John depended on his own independent traditions, not on any previous written gospel. Others, however, believe that he used Mark, and a few find literary relationship with Luke.

Clement of Alexandria, writing around 190, said that John "last of all, perceiving that external facts had been shown in the gospels [i.e. the Synoptics], and urged by his disciples and inspired by the Spirit, composed a spiritual gospel." That is, the Synoptic gospels give us history; John gives us theological interpretation. This view has been popular until recent times. But the distinction is overly simplified. Each of the gospels has a theological evaluation of the history it records. This is what makes it gospel and not mere biography.

Like all other gospels this book was designed for use by Christians—for witness and preaching to potential converts, for teaching and worship within the church community and for meditation of those who "dwell" and "abide" in Christ and his life-giving words and sayings. The gospel is universal in scope—for "the world"—not only for those who have seen and heard Jesus with their own eyes and ears but for those whose belief is responsive to the testimony of eyewitnesses.

Date, Place, and Situation

The time and place of publication of the gospel can be approximately determined. Apart from considerations of authorship and its use of other gospels, internal evidence suggests a date after the destruction of the Jewish temple in Jerusalem in 70. It was also probably after the expulsion of Jewish Christian believers from the synagogues, which was effective around 85-90.

The earliest known references to the gospel are disputed. Some scholars believe that it was known to the martyr-bishop of Antioch, Ignatius, whose letters to churches in Asia around 115 show several phrases of possible allusion. The letter of Bishop Polycarp of Smyrna, whom tradition considered a disciple of the author, does not cite the gospel. But it does contain a quotation from I John, which is generally considered later than the gospel. The eminent Gnostic theologian Valentinus certainly knew and used the gospel in his meditation The Gospel of Truth, written around 140. Circulation of the gospel in Egypt by the second quarter of the second century is attested by a papyrus fragment of the text of 18:31-33, 37-38.

All this evidence agrees with the testimony of Irenaeus, bishop of Lyons (around 177-200), who was a native of Smyrna and in his youth a hearer of Polycarp. Irenaeus says that "John" delivered his gospel to the elders in Asia, remaining among them until the time of the Emperor Trajan (98-117).

There is no good reason to doubt the unanimous tradition of

Irenaeus and his contemporaries that the gospel was published in Ephesus—despite the theories of some modern critics that its origin was possibly Antioch or Alexandria. Christians, with their ideas and writings, shared the ease of travel and communication of the Roman Empire. A book produced in any urban center would soon find its way to other cities. It would not take several years or a decade for a book published in Asia to circulate in Syria or Egypt or in Rome and the West.

All early Christian writings were written to meet specific needs and situations. This gospel is no exception. Even the casual reader will note throughout a confrontation, explicit or implicit, with the "Jews"—so much so that Jesus himself often appears as one separate from and opposite to the Jews. Yet there is no denial of his Jewish identity, whether in contrast to a Samaritan (4:9, 22) or to a Gentile (18:35).

The author's concern with Judaism is not that of the apostolic age, which was the mission to the Gentiles and their acceptance in full fellowship with Jewish Christians who continue to keep the Old Testament law. His problem is a more subtle one: a Judaizing form of Christianity. This form open to Jew and Gentile alike, adhered to Jewish practices and legal demands but interpreted them in general, universal terms drawn from Hellenistic cosmology and philosophy. In such a scheme the scandal of God the Word-made-flesh in Jesus of Nazareth and his decisive once-for-all act in suffering and dying for the sin of the world are incredible, if not blasphemous. They did not deny the coming of a heavenly "Christ," but their interpretation of scripture did not persuade them that he could be a man from Galilee (see below on 7:40-52).

This Jewish-Hellenistic construction—combining outward observance with spiritualized interpretation—had its roots in the apostolic age. Paul combated it constantly. It was especially virulent in Asia in the latter first and early second centuries. The seer of Patmos identified them as those "who say that they are Jews and are not" (Rev. 3:9). Ignatius' letters to the Asian churches are a persistent attack on the problem of those who preach Christ but continue to observe Judaism.

The same controversy is reflected, though with more speculative opponents, in I John and in the Pastoral letters, which also date from this period and were addressed to leaders of the church in Asia and the Aegean islands. The author of the gospel sees the crux in a right interpretation of the Old Testament, as fulfilled and perfected in the incarnate Son of God, who is none other than the historical Jesus:

The law was given through Moses; grace and truth came through Jesus Christ. (1:17).

It is Moses who accuses you, on whom you set your hope. If you believed Moses, you would believe me, for he wrote of me. But if you do not believe his writings, how will you believe my words? (5:45-47).

You are his disciple, but we are disciples of Moses. We know that God has spoken to Moses, but as for this man, we do not know where he comes from. (9:28-29).

Author

The acceptance of the gospel in the New Testament canon in the late second-early third century was a seal of acceptance of its authorship by John son of Zebedee, one of the twelve apostles of Jesus. Though contested at that time, this official view held the day without serious challenge until recent times. It is still stoutly defended by many able scholars, Catholic and Protestant. Its strongest support is the testimony of Irenaeus, who claimed to have received the tradition firsthand, when a youth, from Polycarp.

The tradition would perhaps be stronger if it did not claim too much, for in addition to the gospel it claims John as author of the three letters and Revelation. Distinguished theologians of the ancient church, were doubtful that the same hand produced both the gospel and Revelation. They were keen enough to note the differences in these writings both of literary style and of doctrinal vewpoint. They resorted therefore to a two-John hypothesis: (1) the apostle, who wrote the gospel and letters, and (2) a "disciple of the Lord," who composed Revelation.

Support for this thesis was found in a book of Oracles of the Lord by Bishop Papias of Hierapolis (around 60-130), a contemporary of Ignatius and Polycarp, who distinguished two Johns: an apostle, one of the twelve, and a disciple, who lived to his own times. But it is not clear from the surviving fragments of his work to what John he ascribed the books under that name. Many modern scholars ascribe Revelation to the apostle—as did Justin Martyr, around 150—and the gospel and letters to the "disciple."

The gospel itself has an appendix (chapter 21), which includes a colophon (verses 24-25) ascribing the "witness" of the gospel to the unnamed "beloved disciple" who lay close to Jesus' breast at the Last Supper (cf. 21 20-24). The church in Asia identified the "beloved disciple" as John, as is clear not only from the testimony of Irenaeus but more especially from a letter of Bishop Polycrates of Ephesus (around 190) preserved by Eusebius. In listing the "great luminaries" who have "fallen asleep" in Asia, Polycrates mentions John, "who leaned on the Lord's breast, who was a priest, wearing the sacerdotal breastplate, both martyr and teacher." It is notable that he does not call John an apostle.

The colophon distinguishes two stages in the composition of the book: the "disciple" who bears witness, and "we" who attest to the truth of his testimony. This suggests a posthumous publication by disciples, or an editor, of the eyewitness disciple.

Indications of editorial revision have often been noted—for example, 2:21-22 and 4:2, not to speak of the appendix itself. There are abrupt transitions both of geography and of discourse. Chapter 6 would seem to make more sense if it preceded chapter 5. The dangling summons of 14:31, "Rise, let us go hence," intrudes in the middle of a long discourse; and the logic of argument and exposition in chapters 7, 8, and 10 is curious. There is no manuscript evidence to support any transpositions of the text; nor is there evidence that the gospel ever circulated without the appendix. Nonetheless editorial work seems plausible.

There is a growing consensus that the author—whether "disciple" or "witness"—had access to good historical traditions stemming from Palestine. His facts, as well as his interpretations, must be taken seriously. He knew the geography of Palestine and the customs of the Jews better than Mark, and he may have had Judean associations more immediate than those of the Synoptic gospel writers.

He was undoubtedly a Jew, one whose native tongue was the Aramaic spoken by Jesus. He thinks and writes in a Semitic idiom. The sayings of Jesus he records, however different in style from those of the Synoptics, betray the same Semitic parallelism of structure. Yet he writes a clear and grammatical Greek. Efforts of some scholars to prove that the gospel was translated from Aramaic have not won general acceptance. His Hellenistic culture has perhaps been exaggerated, but it was not negligible. He was more than a match for his theological opponents.

Structure

The gospel shows apparent dislocations of content, together with a "spiral" method of exposition—that is, words and phrases once introduced are later taken up and developed in new combinations. This makes it difficult to outline the gospel in any definitive way. The gospel lacks the continuous flow of narrative in which teachings are inserted, as in Luke, or the topical divisions of narrative plus teaching that characterize the five-fold arrangement of Matthew. Commentators have generally analyzed it as follows:

(1) Chapter 1, which introduces all the titles and interpretations of Jesus used throughout the gospel.

(2) Chapters 2–11, consisting of narratives of a series of "signs," each pointing to the death-resurrection theme of the following chapters, interspersed with discourses and controversies about the true nature of Jesus' revelation.

(3) Chapters 12–20, which contain the passion and resurrection narrative, including a long discourse to the disciples and final prayer at the Last Supper.

(4) Chapter 21, the appendix.

In addition to this conventional analysis there is another illuminating one that views the gospel as presenting the manifestation of the Christ to the world (chapters 1–4), to the Jews (chapters 5–12), and to the disciples (chapters 13–21).

I. INTRODUCTION OF THE MESSIAH (1:1-51)

1:1-18. *The Prologue.* The gospel opens with a hymn that celebrates God's revelation of himself to the world. From all eternity God has existed with his **Word,** who is his mind and purpose and the agent of his self-disclosure. By his Word he created the world, and imparted to it **life** for fellowship with him and **light** for knowledge of him. But his gifts of life and light, ever present and ever active, have been resisted or ignored by his creation. They have even been rejected among those especially chosen as **his own people,** the Jews. Finally the Word revealed God's **glory** by becoming himself a man of **flesh** like other men. In the person of Jesus Christ the character of the eternal and invisible God, in all the fullness of his love and truth, has been made known.

The prologue hymn thus summarizes the themes developed in the gospel:

Jesus the Christ is the agent of a new creation (chapters 1–2).

He is the life of the world (chapters 3–6).

He is the light of the world (chapters 7–9).

He is rejected by his own people (chapters 10–12).

But he is acknowledged by all who believe in him (chapters 13–20).

The author has inserted in the hymn several prose comments—in modern works they would be footnotes—that anticipate the "witness" to God's Word of revelation which he will unfold in his gospel:

(1) The testimony of John the Baptist (verses 6-8, 15), the final prophetic voice to announce the appearance of the Word among men.

(2) The belief of the new people of God (verses 12-13), who are his **children,** not by reason of natural birth or race, but by their faith in his Word.

(3) Jesus the Word himself (verse 17), in whose incarnate life God surpassed even the glory of **grace and truth** which he revealed to Moses when he gave the law on Mt. Sinai.

Much learned discussion has been devoted to the sources of this prologue hymn. Its cue is undoubtedly Genesis 1, the Old Testament creation song "in the beginning"—and possibly also Mark 1:1, the "beginning" of the gospel. Note the imitation of it in I John 1:1-4. Basic is the Old Testament concept of the word of God. God spoke and it was done—in the act of creation, in the gift of the law, in the mouth of the prophets.

The Word is also the wisdom of God that is reflected in the reason and moral sense of upright men and women and in the order and beauty of creation. Non-Jewish readers of the gospel would recognize this concept of the Word, in Greek *Logos*. The term came into Greek philosophy with Heraclitus of Ephesus, and both Stoics and Platonists made much of the *Logos* as the "mind of God" reflected or immanent in the intelligibility, rationality, order, and harmony of the universe.

The Jewish philosopher Philo of Alexandria, a contemporary of Jesus, attempted a synthesis of the Jewish and Greek concepts of the *Logos* as the image of God's mind in creation, in the law, and in human reason. But none of the philosophers, as Augustine testified, approximated the originality of the gospel in an affirmation that the **Word became flesh.**

1:19-34. *John the Baptist.* The gospel presupposes that its readers already knew John the Baptist as a prophet of the coming Messiah. It assumes the early tradition of Christian believers that John's preaching and baptism were the introduction to the public ministry and work of Jesus. It knows that John left behind him many admiring disciples, who continued his work, often in conscious rivalry with the disciples of Jesus. To many Jews John was the preeminent **prophet**—like Moses or **Elijah,** who were the expected precursors of the Messiah. Many may have considered John the very Messiah (**Christ**) himself.

1:19-28. In this gospel John the Baptist denies categorically all claim to any special status or authority in Judaism. He states this before the **priests and Levites** sent by the temple officials, the Sadducees, and **from the Pharisees,** the teachers of the law in the synagogues. Yet he is no less, in all humility, a **voice** of God—**sent from God** (verse 6)—not merely as a forerunner to the true Messiah, but as the first witness to and believer in him. He is indeed a "burning and shining lamp" (5:35), a light that testifies to the true Light now appearing **after** him in time but existing **before** him in all eternity. "He must increase," John says, "but I must decrease" (3:30).

1:29. The title of Christ as **Lamb of God** is peculiar to this gospel and to Revelation, in which, however, a different Greek word for "lamb" is used. There has been much discussion about the proper interpretation of this title. It is one example of an amazing subtlety in the Johannine writings of using terms and expressions that combine many themes and evoke many images and symbols.

One thinks at once of the Passover lamb, for the gospel is explicit in dating the death of Jesus on the afternoon of the "Preparation" day, when the paschal animals were slaughtered (18:28; 19:14). The chronology of the gospel is built around the three Passover seasons when Jesus performed impressive "signs": the cleansing of the temple (2:13), the gift of the bread of life (6:4), and the raising of Lazarus from the dead (11:55). The gospel shares with Paul an interpretation of Christ as "our Passover" who is sacrificed for us (cf. I Corinthians 5:7-8).

Yet the Passover sacrifice, though a commemoration of deliverance from bondage, was not in any sense an observance "that takes away sin." Hence others see here a reference to Isaiah's suffering servant—the lamb slaughtered for the sin of many (Isaiah 53:7-12). This would be a fulfillment of the most poignant prophecy of the Old Testament regarding God's ultimate redemption of mankind in and through his chosen people.

Another view relates the symbol of the Lamb to the ram figure of Jewish messianic expectation—the militant, victorious ruler and leader of God's flock, who will finally make an end of sin in the world. It is this figure that dominates Revelation. It is the Lamb who stands in heaven as one that was slain, the Lamb who stands on Mt. Sinai with the hosts of his saints, the Lamb who overcomes the armies of the evil beasts, the Lamb who summons the redeemed to the marriage supper with his bride—the King of kings and Lord of lords.

1:30-34. John's baptism **with water** is in the Synoptic gospels an instrument of "repentance for the forgiveness of sins" (Mark 1:4; cf. Matthew 3:11; Luke 3:3; Acts 13:24). In this gospel it is never so described. It only points to him who alone can take away sin, and who **baptizes with the Holy Spirit.** Hence the author avoids any mention of Jesus' baptism by John, for this would imply that Jesus was himself a sinner needing forgiveness. Instead John witnesses to the descent of the Spirit on Jesus, revealing him as the **Son of God** (cf. Mark 1:10-11). Thus "John did no sign, but everything that John said about this man was true" (10:41).

1:35-51. *Call of the Disciples.* The gospel author has his own traditions and interpretations about the gathering of the disciples that are not altogether in accord with the narratives of the Synoptic gospels (cf. Mark 1:16-20; Mathew 4:18-22; Luke 5:1-11). John the Baptist, not Jesus, takes the initiative in the calling of the disciples. It takes place in Judea, not in Galilee. The first four disciples are Andrew and Peter, Philip and Nathanael, not Peter and Andrew, James and John.

1:35-40. The unnamed disciple of these verses has often been taken to be the gospel author himself—John son of Zebedee. But the context suggests that he is Philip (cf. verse 43). The sons of Zebedee, James and John, are mentioned only in the appendix (21:2). In fact the author never gives us a list of the names of the twelve disciples, as do the Synoptic writers (Mark 3:16-19; Matthew 10:2-4; Luke 6:14-16; Acts 1:13), though he refers to them (6:70-71). The names which he introduces from time to time in his narratives are the same as those of the Synoptics except for Nathanael.

1:41-45. Andrew and Philip are prominent in the gospel as disciples who lead others to Jesus (cf. 6:5-9; 12:20-22). Both of them bear Greek names. They are said to come from **Bethsaida,** a large city on the northeastern bank of the Jordan River's entrance into the Sea of Galilee, where Jews and Gentiles met in daily exchange. The city is a fitting symbol of the universal outreach of the gospel. Andrew and Philip, themselves convinced that Jesus is the **Messiah** promised in scripture, become the first missionaries: Andrew finds Simon, Philip finds Nathanael.

The gospel does not overlook, however, the eminence of Simon Peter in the early tradition. He receives from Jesus, at the time of his calling, the special nickname **Cephas,** meaning "Rock." At a critical moment in Jesus' ministry Peter leads the other disciples in loyalty and confession of faith (6:68-69; cf. Matthew 16:16-19). And Peter will assume his prominent role, as in the Synoptic gospels, in the passion and resurrection narratives (chapters 13; 18-21).

1:46-51. The figure of **Nathanael** is enigmatic. He is mentioned only here and in the appendix (21:2), where he is said to come from Cana, a Galilean village about nine miles north of Nazareth. Verse 46 suggests a certain rivalry between the two Galilean towns. Efforts have been made, without success, to identify him with one of the twelve—with Bartholomew, Matthew, or Simon the Cananean, none of whom are mentioned in this gospel. Others believe him to be the elusive "beloved disciple" of the gospel.

Were it not for 21:2 the most likely alternate name for him would be Thomas—a nickname that means "Twin." Thomas has a significant role in the gospel (cf. 11:16; 14:5; 20:24-29). And in the ancient tradition of the church in Asia, preserved by Bishop Papias of Hierapolis, the names of the disciples occur in this order: Andrew, Peter, Philip, Thomas, James, John, Matthew.

Nathanael is certainly portrayed as a very real person—devout, cautious, a bit stubborn, but also curious. Yet the author has subtly made him an ideal disciple, to whom Jesus gives the promise of witness to the final glory of revelation at the end of the ages. His name means "God has given," and so Jesus will describe his disciples in his prayer to the Father. His hometown Cana, not mentioned in the Synoptic gospels, is to be the scene of the two first "signs" of Jesus' glory in Galilee (cf. 2:1-11 and 4:46-54).

Jesus indicates that Nathanael is a true **Israelite** without **guile**—unlike the dissimulating Jacob, after whom the Jews adopted the name Israel (Genesis 32:28; 35:10). Unlike the "Jews" also, who are the antagonists of Jesus in this gospel, Nathanael's abode is **under the fig tree,** an Old Testament symbol of the shelter of the true Israelites in the age to come (cf. Micah 4:4; Zechariah 3:10), dwelling in peace and safety (cf. I Kings 4:25). But the vision of this coming age, which Jesus promises the disciples is portrayed in an imagery that recalls at once Jacob's dream of a ladder to **heaven** and the traditional figure of the **Son of man** coming on the clouds with the **angels.**

II. THE SIGNS OF THE MESSIAH (2:1–11:57)

Like a symphonic overture chapter 1 has unfolded a theme. Out of the hiddenness of eternity and the obscurity of time there emerges a historical figure bearing titles both heavenly and earthly—the Word, the Son of God, the Lamb, the Teacher, the Messiah-King of Israel, the Son of man. Geographically he moves within a territory bounded by the wilderness of Judea and the nothern limits of Galilee, with his home village Nazareth. Chronologically he is placed by reference to the prophet who precedes him and the disciples who follow him. His human name is Jesus. He brings the life and light, the grace and truth of God; he baptizes with the Holy Spirit; he opens the way to the kingdom of God.

This extraordinary appearance is measured within the compass of a week, which is itself symbolic. A new creation replaces the week of the old creation (Genesis 1). More important, it looks to the final week of this revelation on earth, the Passover week when Jesus is slain, when what is foreshadowed will be "finished." The clue to this chronological symbolism is the phrase that links the introduction to the "book of signs" that follows it without break: **on the third day** (2:1). For the third day is the day after this week, the day of Resurrection, the day that is the sign to which all preceding signs point.

The term "sign" has a peculiar nuance in this gospel. Ordinarily the word refers to a miracle ("signs and wonders") that may or may not lead to belief in the miracle worker. In this gospel Jesus himself generally refers to such deeds as his "works." He refuses, as in the Synoptic gospels to work "signs" on demand of the unbelieving (2:18; 6:30; cf. Mark 8:11-12). That he did many signs not recorded in the gospel is stated several times by the author (2:23; 12:37; 20:30). Certain ones, however, have been selected as significant in revealing the true nature of Jesus' person. More especially, they are pointers to the meaning of his death and resurrection. It is around these "major" signs that the gospel narratives and discourses are unfolded, from the miracle at Cana to the raising of Lazarus. Most of them, though not all, are miracles.

A. Manifestation to the World (2:1–4:54)

2:1-12. *The Miracle at Cana.* Each of the gospels begins the story of Jesus' ministry in Galilee with incidents and sayings appropriate to its thematic emphasis. John selects the first of Jesus' **signs** which **manifested his glory,** and as a result of which **his disciples** not only followed him but **believed in him.** The scene is laid in **Cana**—possibly as a link with the preceding call of the "true Israelite," Nathanael. It begins a cycle of stories and discourses which will return for a second sign in Cana (4:46-54), and which will introduce the manifestation of Christ to the world of Jews, Samaritans, and Gentiles.

The incident is an excellent example of the author's ability to tell an interesting story. The details are inherently plausible but at the same time full of symbolic meaning. He is a consummate allegorist (see comment on Matthew 13:10-17). It will be noted that in this gospel Jesus never imparts his teaching by parables, though he often uses allegories.

The miracle takes place **on the third day,** an unmistakable pointer to the resurrection and exaltation of Jesus. The village wedding feast is a foretaste—with the **good wine** supplied by Jesus—of the "marriage supper of the Lamb" (Revelation 19:7-9; cf. Matthew 22:2-14; Luke 12:36-37). The water jugs of Jewish purification ceremonies have become empty (cf. Mark 7:1-4). They are now to be filled with the new wine of the last times (cf. Amos 9:13-14)—and wine in abundance. In this miracle Jesus produces some 120 gallons, an excessive amount indeed if intended merely as wine needed for the local feast. Numerous early Christian paintings and sculptures associate the Cana miracle and the feeding of the multitude (chapter 6) with the feasting of the redeemed in the age to come.

Wine is also the symbol of blood. The first miracle and sign of Moses leading to the deliverance of the people of God from bondage in Egypt was the turning of water into blood (cf. Exodus 7:14-24). The gospel author stresses the life-giving water and blood that Jesus will give his disciples to drink (cf. 4:13-15; 6:53-56). The final sign of this new life in the Spirit is attested in the streams of water and blood that flow from his pierced side when his death is accomplished (cf. 19:34-35; I John 5:6-8). Many interpreters, both ancient and modern, see in this symbolism specific reference to the cleansing and empowerng gifts of Christ in the sacraments of baptism and the Lord's Supper.

2:3-4. The conversation of Jesus with his mother suggests hidden meaning—at least to the Christian reader. Mary appears only here and at the foot of the cross (19:25-27), where she is committed to the care of the beloved disciple. In both places Jesus addresses her in an unusually formal manner, as **woman.** She is gently rebuked for her trustful attempt to induce Jesus to perform a sign before his proper **hour**—that is, the time chosen by his Father for his death and glorification. This cannot be anticipated by any kind of human intervention. Nonetheless

Jesus does perform a sign—a sign that points to the final accomplishment of his "hour."

As "woman" Mary symbolizes the believing church (cf. Revelation 12:1-6). But the church cannot bring to pass the "works" of Jesus until he has fulfilled his ministry and mission and returned to his Father.

2:12. This verse is somewhat awkward. It may perhaps be an editorial insertion. It summarizes Jesus' early Galilean ministry, centered in **Capernaum,** which is treated more fully in the Synoptics (cf. Matthew 4:13; Mark 1:14; Luke 4:31). It differs from the Synoptic tradition in dating this ministry before the arrest of John the Baptist and in associating Jesus' family with his disciples during this period (cf. Mark 3:31-34) though the author notes later (7:5) that Jesus' brothers did not believe in him.

2:13-25. *The Cleansing of the Temple.* The miracle at Cana has suggested that Jesus' revelation fulfills and supersedes the ordinary daily ceremonies of the Jewish cultic system. The cleansing of the temple illustrates the theme with reference to the very heart and center of Jewish sacrificial worship.

In the Synoptic gospels (Mark 11:15-18; Matthew 21:12-16; Luke 19:45-48) this bold act of Jesus is placed within the last week of his life. There it is portrayed in terms of prophetic protest against the profanation of the temple by fraudulent practices in its precincts. It recalls the condemnation of Jeremiah 7:11. It is a purification of the holy place, making it fit as a "house of prayer for all the nations" in the coming messianic age. Its effect is to solidify the opposition of the Jewish religious leaders to Jesus and to engage them in a concerted effort to "destroy" him.

The incident as recorded in this gospel bears all these meanings and more. It is placed near the beginning of Jesus' ministry, at Passover time. Though it is not a miracle, it is no less a **sign** of what will be fulfilled in his death and resurrection. Significantly Jesus drives out not only the wicked **money-changers** but also the innocent animals. Thus he points to a more drastic "purification" of worship: the end of the old cult of animal sacrifice and the inauguration of a worship "in spirit and truth."

2:19-22. The **temple,** begun in 20/19 B.C., was not finished till A.D. 64 and then was destroyed by the Romans in 70. Its destruction was probably predicted by Jesus (cf. Mark 13:2; Luke 19:43-44). The prophecy was used against him at his trial before the sanhedrin (cf. Mark 14:57-59; 15:29).

Possibly the original form of Jesus' prediction is preserved in verse 19, with reflection on its true meaning and purport. He is the true "Lamb of God, who takes away the sin of the world" (1:29). His sacrificed **body** is the new **temple** in and through whom the disciples and believers will offer a spiritual sacrifice acceptable to God, in a living building not made with hands. The theme is a basic one throughout the New Testament.

2:23-25. To summarize the preceding narratives the author introduces briefly the question of **signs.** The sign of the cleansing of the temple, not being a miracle, is not immediately obvious even to Jesus' disciples, much less to the populace. Those who believe in him by this time are still overly impressed by the miraculous as such. Jesus consistently rejects this basis for belief. It is too shallow. Jesus himself knows how people are easily swayed by the merely marvelous—"signs and wonders." He does not **trust himself** to human **witness.** Insight into his true signs comes only by revelation from God (cf. 3:31-36; 5:19-24).

3:1-21. *Discourse with Nicodemus.* The author now turns from Jesus' encounter with the Jewish cultic system to an encounter with its legal system. This is represented by a distinguished Pharisee, who as a **ruler of the Jews** sits on the supreme council of the sanhedrin. Nicodemus is known only from this gospel. He was undoubtedly one of the more liberal Pharisees, open to new teachings and interpretations. Though he was attracted by Jesus' signs, there is no clear evidence in the gospel that Nicodemus was a "secret believer" in Jesus. But later he defends Jesus from unjust accusations (7:50-51) and joins with Joseph of Arimathea in providing for him a decent burial (19:39).

Nicodemus' fairness and adherence to strict rules of judicial procedure remind one of another great Pharisee, Gamaliel, who protects the rights of the early disciples (Acts 5:34-39).

297

The interview of Nicodemus with Jesus is marked by mutual courtesy, respect, and concern for issues of utmost importance. Its secrecy, **by night,** is simply a matter of caution on the part of Nicodemus, in view of the hostility of the Jewish leaders toward Jesus. Despite the marked difference in worldly status of the two men, each respectfully addresses the other by the title of **Rabbi** or **teacher.** But the conversation leads to no agreement, for Nicodemus really does not comprehend what Jesus is talking about. In fact Nicodemus fades out of the picture after verse 9 as Jesus' discourse appears to address a wider audience—a stylistic device characteristic of this gospel.

3:3-13. One would expect the conversation to revolve about the problem of whether salvation is possible through keeping the law. The rabbis taught that when all Israel kept the law, the kingdom of God would come. Jesus, however, immediately moves the discussion to a different level. Salvation in the **kingdom of God** requires a new birth. This, by an ambiguity of the Greek word, is also a birth "from above," from heaven itself—a birth not merely in a baptism of **water,** such as John the Baptist offered, but a birth through the operation of the **Spirit.** Such a birth is possible only by belief in the Son of man and Son of God, namely Jesus himself.

3:14-15. To illustrate this teaching, so incredible to Nicodemus, Jesus uses a sign—not one of his own, but one of **Moses** the lawgiver. When the people of God sinned **in the wilderness** through disbelief, they were afflicted with serpents, and many of them died. But through Moses' intercession God gave them a sign—the standard of the bronze **serpent**—that whoever looked on it and believed would live (Numbers 21:4-9). So it shall be with the Son of man, when he is **lifted up** on the standard of the cross, a cursed thing like the serpent itself. Whoever believes in him will have **eternal life.**

3:16-21. Thus the discourse with Nicodemus becomes a pointer to the final sign of Jesus' death and resurrection. At the same time it recapitulates the broad themes of the gospel prologue. **Light** and **life** have come into the world in the person of God's only Son. Those who receive him and believe in his name are reborn, not by fleshly means, but by God. Hence the distinction between those who believe and those who do not is evidence of the arrival of the final **judgment.** God himself does not make this judgment. Rather he ratifies a judgment which persons make for themselves by their own decisions.

3:22-36. *Discourse with John's Disciples.* The discussion with Nicodemus about baptism in **water and the Spirit** leads the author to a return to the question of the relation of Jesus and John the Baptist and of their respective disciples. In the only passage in all the gospel tradition that intimates that Jesus himself ever **baptized** he locates Jesus in **Judea** while John carries on similar activity in northeast Samaria at **Aenon.**

In contrast to the priestly and rabbinic traditions John the Baptist represented the last and greatest figure of the prophetic strain in Judaism with his insistence on spiritual repentance and renewal. Of all Jews he was closest to Jesus, both in the relationship of master and pupil and in teaching about the coming kingdom of God.

As we have seen (1:19-34), John the Baptist is portrayed in this gospel not only as a forerunner but as a first witness to Jesus. In this passage John's testimony is reaffirmed and underscored. He makes no claim for himself. He is from the **earth;** Jesus is from **heaven.** His fullest joy is to be accounted the **friend of the bridegroom** (cf. Mark 2:19-20). On Jesus, more than on any other prophet, God has poured out his Spirit beyond measure. Jesus utters the true **words of God.** Belief in him and obedience to him are decisive as to whether one comes to life or to wrath in the coming age.

It is indeed a remarkable testimony. Some scholars believe, however, that verses 31-36 are words of Jesus, not of John the Baptist, since the style is very similar to Jesus' words to Nicodemus. It is suggested that they be transposed, probably to follow verse 21—or else that verses 22-30 should follow 2:12.

The setting of John's witness is the rivalry of John's and Jesus' disciples for adherents to their respective leaders. More especially it concerns the question, raised by an unidentified **Jew,** about the meaning of their baptisms.

In the Synoptic gospels the tension between the two groups of disciples is not over baptism but concerns customs of fasting and prayer (cf. Mark 2:18-22 and Luke 11:1). Many scholars see here a reflection of early Christian polemic against a sect of Baptist disciples. But the attempt to locate such a group in Ephesus, where this gospel was probably written, on the basis of Acts 18:24–19:7 is very problematic.

Several Christian writings of the second century refer to Jewish baptist sects in Samaria and Transjordan that may owe something to John the Baptist's teaching and practice. One source, the Clementine Recognitions (1:60), records a controversy with Christians by a disciple of John who claimed for the Baptist the title of messiah "inasmuch as Jesus himself declared that John was greater than all men and all prophets" (cf. Matthew 11:7-11). In Iraq today there is a small baptist sect known as the Mandeans who claim a direct descent from John the Baptist's ministry and teaching.

The gospel author, more by implicit suggestion than by explicit statement, considers John's baptism as a **purifying** rite comparable to similar Jewish ceremonies. He certainly does not account it a sacramental "new birth" in the Spirit, conveying the forgiveness of sins, like Christian baptism. In this view of John's baptism he is in agreement with the first-century Jewish historian Josephus, the only source outside the New Testament we have for the career of John:

[He] was a good man and commanded the Jews to practice virtue, by exercising justice towards one another and piety towards God, and to come together to baptism. For the baptism would be acceptable to God if they used it, not for the putting away of certain sins, but for the purification of the body, the soul having previously been cleansed by righteousness. (Antiquities 18:116-19, trans. C. K. Barrett.)

4:1-42. *Discourse with a Samaritan Woman.* The location of John's baptizing in Samaria (3:23) provides the link that leads to Jesus' mission to the Samaritans. The editorial transition in verses 1-3, however, is awkward, and verse 2 contradicts 3:22.

The schism between the Jews and Samaritans was quite as bitter as described in verse 9. This is reflected also in the Synoptic gospels (cf. Matthew 10:5; Luke 9:51-56). The origin of their separation and hatred is generally traced to the time of Nehemiah, in the fifth century B.C. But there is no clear evidence of a formal religious schism until the Samaritans built a temple of their own on Mt. Gerizim near **Sychar,** which was ancient Shechem. This was done probably after their revolt against Alexander the Great in 331 B.C., when Alexander rebuilt the city of Samaria as a Hellenistic colony.

The faithful remnant of Samaritans then retired to the site of Shechem, hallowed by traditions of the patriarchs **Jacob** and **Joseph** and the establishment of the nothern kingdom of Israel. In 128 B.C. the Jewish Maccabean ruler John Hyrcanus destroyed the Samaritan temple and attempted to suppress the separate Samaritan cult. When the Romans took over control of Palestine in 64-63 B.C., however, the Samaritans were free to restore their independent religious customs.

On the surface the mission of Jesus to the Samaritans appears to have happened accidentally through a chance conversation. Yet it is undoubtedly a providential development that anticipates the spread of the gospel, first in Jerusalem and Judea, then in Samaria, then to the end of the earth.

In the Synoptic gospels only Luke exhibits any special appreciation by Jesus of the despised Samaritans (Luke 10:30-37, 17:11-19). In this gospel the Jewish feeling of superiority to and aloofness from the Samaritans is expressed by Jesus in verse 22, but this only heightens the dramatic contrast. His willingness to enter into communication with them, and specifically with a Samaritan woman of disrepute, is a circumstance as startling to the woman herself as it is to Jesus' disciples. It is the author's peculiar way of indicating that the **Savior of the world** came indeed to "seek and to save the lost" (Luke 19:10).

4:7-15. Jesus' discourse with the woman, like that with Nicodemus (3:1-15), develops on two levels of meaning. The woman thinks of **water** in earthly terms of necessity for man and beast, whether it comes from wells or cisterns, fountains or streams. This was a natural concern in Palestine, where water supply is not always sufficient, much less abundant. Jesus, however, speaks of **living**—that is, flowing water as a sign of **eternal life,** whose source is God, whose depths are in his wisdom, and whose abundance is assured in the new Jerusalem, the city of God of the coming age.

Jesus is himself, of course, this gift of life-giving water. He will later make this more explicit (7:37-39) and identify the living water with the Holy Spirit, who will be given after his glorification. Hence many interpreters see here also a cryptic reference to baptism, such as the reference to water and Spirit in the discourse with Nicodemus.

4:16-26. The woman only begins to comprehend that a prophetic statement is being made after Jesus unexpectedly reveals his insight into her personal life. She immediately becomes defensive and shifts the conversation to argument about differences of Jews and Samaritans. Jesus picks this up with the reminder of their common hope in the messianic age, when estrangement will be transcended in worship **in spirit and truth.** The discussion closes with Jesus' dramatic revelation: **I . . . am he**—an anticipation of his remarkable "I am" sayings in later incidents of the gospel.

4:27-42. The universal mission of the Christ is then implied in two ways:

(1) The disciples are forewarned by Jesus of the imminent **harvest** (cf. Matthew 9:37 and Luke 10:2).

(2) The disreputable woman herself becomes the agent of evangelism among her fellow Samaritans.

Salvation has broken through the rigid confines of orthodox Judaism, though the disciples are slow to comprehend this extraordinary fact. **One sows and another reaps.** John the Baptist, Jesus himself, the Samaritan woman, and the Hellenist Philip (Acts 8:4-13) sowed the seed in Samaria. The Jewish-Christian church would have misgivings (cf. Matthew 10:5), but the apostles found there a rich harvest (cf. Acts 8:14-25).

4:43-45. A Transition. This transitional passage is even more

difficult and contradictory than that in verses 1-3. Jesus' remark
about his rejection in Galilee recalls Mark 6:4, yet this stands in
immediate connection with the author's statement of Galilean
welcome. But it may be that their welcome is based on a
misunderstanding of his signs (cf. verse 48; 2:23-25). They judge
him as a wonder worker yet do not believe in him for his true
significance.

4:46-54. *Healing of a Nobleman's Son.* This story brings us
again to **Cana** (see comment on 2:1-12) and a **second sign** in
Galilee. The miracle is a variant of the healing of the centurion's
servant in the Synoptics (Matthew 8:5-13; Luke 7:1-10). The
official is undoubtedly a Gentile. In all four gospels Jesus
performs his acts of mercy for Gentiles at a distance and solely in
response to their insistent faith. His mission is primarily to
Israel. But the incidents of his concern for Gentiles in distress
indicate his universal mission to all who come to him in trustful
belief.

The time of the cure is noted as the **seventh hour,** or at 1 P.M.
This may be merely a detail of the story without significance.
But the author rarely gives details without hidden significance.
It is about the seventh hour that Jesus is crucified (cf. 19:14) and
fulfills all signs.

B. CONTROVERSY WITH THE "JEWS" (5:1–10:42)

Chapter 5 continues without break the cycle of Jesus' signs
that point to his death and resurrection. But a new emphasis is
seen. In chapters 2–4 his signs have suggested the uniqueness of
his person in an all-encompassing circle, beginning with his
family, disciples, and friends. It then reaches out to his people,
the Jews—priests, Pharisees, disciples of John the Baptist—and
then with increasing reserve to Samaritans and Gentiles. The
arrangement rests on historical tradition, yet is symbolic: the
Christ is the Savior of the world.

With chapter 5, however, and continuing through chapter 12,
the attention of the gospel is concentrated on the "Jews." These

are not only Jesus' historical antagonists but also symbolic of Judaizing Christians of the author's own day who thwart the universal mission of Christianty (see Introduction). The narratives and discourses are all related to specific Jewish festivals—sabbath (5:9*b*-10), Passover (6:4), Tabernacles (7:2), Dedication (10:22). At the close there is another Passover (11:55), that of his death and glorification.

In this midsection of the gospel Jesus speaks more openly of himself and his relation to God the Father. The discourses become increasingly controversial and embittered. Tension mounts. The "hour" approaches.

5:1-9. *Healing of a Paralytic.* The first incident of this new section occurs in Jerusalem on a **feast of the Jews,** which is identified as the **sabbath.** The story has parallels in Mark 2:1-12 and 3:1-6—the healings in Capernaum of a paralytic and of a man with a withered hand. The latter also occurs on the sabbath and is the occasion of a similar controversy with the Pharisees. There is a suggestion also, though less prominent here than in the Synoptic gospels, that the healing of the body is accompanied by the forgiveness of sin.

The locale of the incident has been confirmed by modern excavation of a **pool**—whether of **Bethzatha** or Bethesda or Bethsaida—north of the temple area, to which the **Sheep Gate** no doubt gave entrance.

The story has several "Johannine" characteristics. Jesus performs his sign on his own initiative and his peculiar knowledge of men (verse 6). He chooses one of many possible subjects for his saving action—in this case a sick man of little initiative himself and of scant gratitude. The sick man is a personification of the impotence of Judaism. The charge against him of breaking the sabbath by carrying his **pallet** is but a foil for the weightier charge against Jesus for **working** on the sabbath. The narrative sets the stage for the discourse.

5:10-47. *Discourse on the Sabbath.* In the Synoptic gospels Jesus' controversy with the Jews over the proper observance of the sabbath revolves about the question of priorities: the need of men versus religious restrictions. The argument in this gospel goes deeper. Jesus defends his work on the sabbath by appeal to God the Father's work on the sabbath. God's rest on the sabbath does not mean—as even the rabbis admitted—that God does not continue his providential care of the world during the sabbath. On the sabbath he brings men and women to birth, and also to death and to judgment. Thus Jesus works on the sabbath, as his Father works still—raising persons from spiritual death to eternal life. Indeed the **hour** is at hand, the decisive hour of death and **resurrection** and **judgment**—for the **Son of man** has come.

The issue between Jesus and the Jews is thus shifted from sabbath observance to decision about the person of Jesus, who identifies himself with the **Father** (cf. Mark 2:28: "the Son of Man is lord even of the sabbath"). What then is the authority to support Jesus' exalted claim? The testimonies are threefold:

(1) The **witness** of John the Baptist, in whose **light** the Jews rejoiced **for a while.**

(2) The **works** of Jesus himself, who claims only that he does God's will.

(3) The **scriptures,** indeed **Moses** himself, on whose writings the Jews set all their confidence and hope. Moses, like Jesus, did not seek his own glory but only the salvation of God's people (Exodus 32–34). He predicted the coming of a "prophet" like himself who would speak God's words (Deuteronomy 18:15-22, and he foresaw Israel's breaking of the covenant (Deuteronomy 31:16-29). These themes are to be continued and developed in later controversies.

6:1-15. *Feeding of the Multitude.* The scene is abruptly shifted to Galilee. Many interpreters would transpose the order of chapters 5 and 6. But transitions are always abrupt in this gospel, and there is no certain clue as to editorial rearrangements.

The miracle of the feeding of the multitude is the only incident of Jesus' ministry in Galilee which this gospel shares with the Synoptics (Mark 6:32-44; Matthew 14:13-21; Luke 9:11-17. It also shares the sequel: the miracle of Jesus' walking on the water; a discourse on bread, here much developed, however (cf. Mark 8:14-21); and, most significant of all, a decisive separation from Jesus of his popular following in contrast to the continuing loyalty of the twelve disciples. Note the prominence in this account of Philip and Andrew (see above on 1:41-45) and the emphasis on Jesus' controlling initiative—**he himself knew what he would do.** The moral of the story is that the disciples do not yet believe that Jesus can satisfy the need of so great a multitude from so small an offering. But the unnamed youth who gives his lunch represents all who give what they have, without reservation, into Jesus' hands, that he may make it serve many. More is left over, even so, than what was offered— **twelve baskets,** one for each of the twelve disciples!

The feeding miracle in all the gospels is a decisive conclusion to Jesus' Galilean ministry. It is a final **sign** of the awaited **prophet**—like Moses' feeding the people of God in the wilderness with manna (Exodus 16) or like Elisha's multiplying barley loaves for hungry men (II Kings 4:42-44). The people recognize the sign, but they misinterpret the nature of Jesus' messiahship. They wish to make him a **king,** a temporal ruler to restore the independence of Israel and give them material goods (cf. verse 26). But Jesus' "kingship is not of this world" (18:36).

In refusing this role Jesus loses his popular following, including **many of his disciples** (cf. Mark 8:11-21). His enemies among the Jewish leaders are to use this occasion, for the later charges that he is a revolutionary leader against Roman authority (18:33-37; 19:12-16).

As with all the signs in this gospel, the feeding of the multitude points to the climactic ending in Jesus' death and resurrection. The incident is dated at **Passover.** Jesus' giving **thanks** over the food is expressed by the verbal form of *eucharistia* ("thanksgiving" or "Eucharist"), which by the time the gospel was written had probably already become a common term for the commemoration of Jesus' Last Supper.

The miraculous crossing of the sea, the discourse on the **living bread . . . from heaven,** the subtle reference to Jesus' ascension and gift of the Spirit, and many other allusions suggest the new redemptive Exodus that Jesus will accomplish. Peter's confession (cf. Mark 8:27-30) anticipates the confession of the church, as of all true believers, in the **Holy One of God.**

6:16-24. *The Walking on the Sea.* Jesus' withdrawal from the people and the discples leads to a somewhat complicated and elaborate account of movements to change the scene to a synagogue in Capernaum. There may be some editorial rearrangement here. In any case, the gospel follows the tradition recorded in the Synoptics (cf. Mark 6:45-54) of Jesus' miraculous walking on the sea to meet his disciples and calm their fears during a sudden squall.

Some interpreters see in this narrative one of the major signs of Jesus, but the evangelist does not develop the story in his customary manner of expounding signs. The discourse which follows refers exclusively to the miracle of the feeding rather than to the walking on the water. The exodus theme, noted above, is doubtless veiled here. The stormy waters are symbol of passage from bondage and death to freedom and life. The appearance of Jesus suddenly and unexpectedly, with his reassurance **do not be afraid,** reminds one of the situation in which his resurrection appearance takes place (cf. 20:19-23; Matthew 28:10; Luke 24:36-39). His emphatic **It is I**—literally "I am [he]"—is a second revelation of his person (cf. 4:26) that will be picked up and developed in the discourses and controversies to follow.

6:25-71. *Discourse on Bread of Heaven.* The theme of this discourse, **I am the bread of life,** elaborates the true meaning of the feeding miracle, which the people have misunderstood. The style and manner of its development are already familiar from previous discourses in the gospel. Question and answer, even argument, between Jesus and his audience reveal that Jesus is speaking from a deeper level of spiritual insight than that of his hearers. Dialogue shifts into proclamation, and this in turn produces controversy and division. The spiritually discerning hold on to belief. The materially minded reject Jesus' claims. Yet even the former follow more in faith and hope than in full understanding.

6:27-40. The dialogue has close parallels with the conversation with the Samaritan woman (chapter 4), the symbol of **bread** here being comparable to the symbol of water there. The bread given in the miracle of feeding, as well as the **manna** given to God's people in the wilderness, is perishable, sufficing only for the day. It cannot give **life to the world** much less **eternal life.**

Jewish writers and teachers had all used the manna as a type of life in the world to come. Now this true bread, this word of God, this heavenly food, this life raised up **at the last day** is revealed. And faith in him is fulfillment in doing the **will** and the **work** of God. Note that in this gospel such matters as faith and truth are not abstract; they are positive commitment, action, obedience.

6:41-51. The opposition to Jesus now shifts from the **people** (verse 24) to the **Jews,** those who oppose the revelation of God in the Word-made-flesh (see Introduction). Such extraordinary claims come from the **son of Joseph, whose father and mother we know.** They **murmur** against him who is sent from God as did the fathers who **died** in the wilderness. No sign, no miracle, no testimony of truth convinces them (cf. Luke 16:31). Verse 45 quotes Isaiah 54:13.

6:52-59. But Jesus presses further. He, the living bread from heaven for the life of the world, is given as **flesh** to eat and **blood** to drink. This is no doubt a reference to the Eucharist. It comes unexpectedly, since as yet the holy supper of bread and wine has not been instituted. For this reason many scholars consider verses 52-56 a later editorial insertion.

But the evangelist speaks to many levels among his readers. It is not strange that he should in this way anticipate what one would expect him to relate in chapter 13. He is not interested in mere historical sequence. These verses are his way of pointing to an "institution" of "This is my body; this is my blood." The Christian reader gets the message, as in the veiled allusions of the miracle at Cana or the cleansing of the temple.

6:60-65. Obviously the **disciples** find these words a **hard saying.** Similarly they do not understand his words and actions at the Last Supper until after his revelation of resurrection in the breaking of the bread (see below on 21:1-14). To eat flesh and to drink blood was naturally offensive to a Jew. The crisis of belief is now upon the disciples. They "murmur" and **take offense.** The scandal of Jesus confronts them also with decision. Can they understand that Jesus speaks of final things—of the Spirit that gives life?

6:66-71. Simon Peter makes the leap of faith and speaks for all the twelve except one. From this point on only Jesus' intimate band, and a few others, keep following. And indeed stronger tests of their faith are yet to come.

This is the only passage where the evangelist specifically speaks of the **twelve,** almost casually assuming that his readers know the tradition. Here also he first mentions the betrayer **Judas.** But the evangelist does not give us any more of a clue than do the Synoptic gospel writers for the motives of Judas' treachery. From this point on in the gospel we continually meet the impending shadow of Jesus' death.

7:1-52. *Discourse at a Feast of Tabernacles.* This long interlude of controversy and growing bitterness of the **Jews** toward Jesus is peculiar to this gospel. Transitions are abrupt; themes are involved and follow no logical sequence; a general impression is given of confusion, with controversies unresolved, actions frustrated, language increasingly abusive. The overriding theme, if any, is that the **Jews sought to kill him.** The interlude is continued in 8:12-59.

7:2. The background is the celebration of the **feast of Tabernacles** (Booths), one of the major festivals of Judaism, held at the beginning of autumn. It was a pivotal time. The feastings of the gathered harvest were combined with hope for renewed prosperity in the coming year. Its focus was in the temple. Brilliant illuminations of the temple precincts were characteristic, as were special water libations rooted in ancient rainmaking ceremonies to insure good crops. The people lived in temporary shelters or "booths" reminiscent of harvest and vintage conditions, but reminders, more seriously, of their pilgrimage condition in this world as dependents on God's gracious providence. In this setting Jesus' words about **thirst** (7:37) and **light** (8:12) have their peculiar reference.

7:3-9. The section opens with the taunting challenge of Jesus'

brothers, whose disbelief in him is matched by their interest, if sincere, in his signs. The contrast with the faith of his disciples (6:68-69) is striking, the more so because of his brothers' sarcasm. The Synoptic gospels are more ambiguous about Jesus' brothers (cf. Mark 3:31-35). Luke places them among the believers after the Resurrection (cf. Acts 1:14). As usual Jesus does not rise to the bait of this challenge (cf. 2:23-25) but keeps his own counsel and control of his actions.

7:10-31. The evangelist shows realism in setting a scene. This is clearly seen in the gossip and argument about Jesus at the festival, followed by the dramatic public appearance of Jesus **about the middle of the feast.**

An argument is going on about his authority as a teacher, since he has not **studied** in the manner of rabbinical training. So Jesus breaks in and takes up the question—exactly where he left off at the last festival he attended in Jerusalem (chapter 5). He is to be judged, not by **appearances** or conventional credentials, but by what he says and does. Least of all is he to be judged by his family background or the place of his upbringing.

7:32-39. Another misunderstanding in this controversy arises from Jesus' reference to his going away—a theme to be developed again in his farewell discourse to his disciples (chapter 14). He points of course to the consummation of his mission, his return in glory to his Father, and the pouring out as **rivers of living water** of the Spirit. His opponents see his promise as a plan to carry his message beyond Judea and the people of God—not only to the **Dispersion,** who were Jews living outside Palestine, but to the Gentiles, as though he were some sectarian teacher seeking a following wherever he might gather it. They cannot see his coming as a fulfillment of God's purpose for his people Israel, that through them God may fulfill their destiny to bring salvation to the whole world. Their pride and exclusiveness blind them to the true mission of Jesus, and hence of themselves in God's plan of salvation.

7:40-52. The question of where Jesus comes from (cf. verse 27) is now taken up again. The evangelist of course knows of Jesus' true origin—**descended from David, and comes from Bethle-**

hem. But even Matthew and Luke, which narrate in detail Jesus' birth in Bethlehem and his human descent from David, represent him in his public ministry as "Jesus of Nazareth," a Galilean. Jesus himself challenges the claim that the Messiah is to be descended from David, so embedded in Jewish expectations (cf. Mark 12:35-37).

The truth about the Christ rests on divine not human credentials and authority (cf. Mark 11:27-33). It is no matter if he does come from **Galilee,** or that they cannot find in their **scripture** a clear indication that the **prophet** like Moses would **rise from Galilee.**

7:52-8:11. *Jesus and the Adulteress.* This passage is omitted or set off in many modern editions of the gospel since it does not appear in the oldest and best manuscripts. In some manuscripts it occurs after Luke 21:38. Though probably not an original part of this gospel, it need not be taken as an unauthentic tradition about Jesus. It conforms to all we know of him as one who came to seek and to save the lost, to offer God's forgiveness and acceptance. Its inclusion here in later texts was probably suggested by 8:15, 46. The story certainly does not mean that Jesus either condoned sin or did not acknowledge the justice of the law. His compassion indicates his concern for the motives of the woman's accusers, with regard both to her and to himself (cf. 2:24).

8:12-59. *Continuation of the Tabernacle Discourse.* The discussion of where Jesus comes from and where he is going continues. His opponents, who judge only **according to the flesh**—that is, think in earthly frames of reference—misunderstand him at every point. Some think his reference to going away indicates suicide—perhaps their own deathwish for him in view of the constant frustration of their schemes to kill him. Jesus picks up this suggestion to probe more deeply into the issues of death and life, falsehood and truth, bondage and freedom. But the controversy continues at cross-purposes and ends in insults and name-calling.

8:31-47. The argument comes back again to earthly descent and pride of race and blood. The Jews insist on their status and destiny as **descendants of Abraham.** This is their guarantee of ultimate freedom and of life in the age. Jesus rejects this claim categorically. Salvation comes only to those who believe the word of God in Jesus, the **truth** that alone delivers women and men from sin and makes them **free.** The "Jews" father is not Abraham, who believed God, but the **devil,** the **father of lies,** who from the beginning led men into sin and death.

8:48-59. The ultimate blasphemy of Jesus' opponents is reached when they accuse him of demon possession (cf. Mark 3:22-30). His answer is the most absolute and categorical claim of his true person made in this gospel: **Before Abraham was, I am.** In the Old Testament "I am" is the name of God (cf. Exodus 3:14). So they pick up **stones** to slay the blasphemer. The issue is now decisively drawn, but the proper "hour" is not yet. The judgment of who is the true blasphemer in this confrontation is suspended.

9:1-41. *Healing of a Blind Man.* The incurable spiritual blindness of the "Jews" is now dramatically illustrated in the great sign of healing a man physically **born blind.** The details of the miracle story recall examples in the Synoptic gospels of Jesus' healing the blind (Mark 8:22-26; 10:46-52). This was the expected fulfillment of the Messiah's coming role (cf. Isaiah 29:18; 35:5; 42:7; Matthew 11:5; Luke 7:21-22).

The parallel with the Synoptics is further indicated by the **sabbath** setting of the miracle (cf. Mark 3:1-6; Luke 13:10-17; see above on 5:10-47). There is no necessity of performing this work on the sabbath; the blind man could easily be healed on another day. But to Jesus the sabbath is a sign of the new age of God's work of re-creation. It is not merely a day of rest, closed by the **night . . . , when no one can work.**

Another interesting detail, which indicates how the evangelist uses allusive symbolism, is the reference to the **pool of Siloam,** where the healing takes place. This pool, at the southeastern extremity of Jerusalem was the source of water used at the Tabernacles ceremonies (cf. 7:37). Isaiah noted how Israel refused these waters and hence would be overwhelmed by waters of another river (Isaiah 8:5-8).

Not only the symbolism of water but more especially that of light is taken up in the story: **I am the light of the world.** Jesus is the "true light that enlightens every man . . . coming into the world" (1:9), both physically and spiritually. Yet sin causes one to love darkness rather than light (cf. 3:19). People have struggled in darkness since the sin of Adam, preferring evil to good, blind to their own condition, until the light comes to open their eyes to God.

Thus the revelation of the true light unfolds to the man whose eyes Jesus opens. At first he sees Jesus simply as a **man** who helps and heals. Such a man, however, cannot be a **sinner** if he does such a work—**he is a prophet.** With greater confidence the healed man argues with those who deny the fact that such a prophet must come **from God.** Now he is forced to decision: remain secure in the **synagogue,** or reach out to faith yet dim—though now he can see—in the **Son of man.**

Thus the story of an earthly healing of a man's sight is a parable of a spiritual pilgrimage to unshakable faith. It is indeed a **marvel.** The blind man comes through to Jesus against every natural obstacle—his own puzzlement, his parents' cowardly fear of getting involved, his religious leaders' unfair advantage in argument from authority, and the threat of excommunication. The moral is clear: only those are blind who will not see.

Many see in this narrative a sacramental reference, comparable to the eucharistic allusions of chapter 6. They point to many parallels in the ancient church's liturgy of baptism—anointing, washing, confession of faith—and in the interpretation of baptism as release from the guilt of original sin and enlightenment by faith in Christ.

10:1-42. *Discourse at a Feast of Dedication.* The parable and allegory of verses 1-18 are a new discourse of Jesus. They have been abruptly inserted to bridge the controversies with the Jews at the festivals of Tabernacles and Dedication (Hanukkah) respectively.

Actually verses 19-21 appear to pick up the end of chapter 9. Verses 22-30 seem to develop the new theme of chapter 10. Verses 31-39 seem to elaborate chapter 8. This apparently illogical sequence has provoked many theories of editorial, or accidental, changes from the evangelist's original order. But no one rearrangement is generally agreed to.

The Hanukkah feast was instituted in 164 B.C. by Judas Maccabeus. It celebrated the rededication of the temple three years after its defilement under Antiochus Epiphanes by sacrifices to Zeus on its altar. The festival took place in mid-December, and its ceremonies were modeled on those of Tabernacles, especially the kindling of lights—hence its popular name "Feast of Lights." In Jesus' time the priestly families who controlled the temple were a wealthy, aristocratic group, the Sadducees, conservative in religion though liberal in manners of living, politically subservient to the Romans, and generally unpopular with the people. They were hardly exemplary pastors of the Lord's flock according to the Old Testament ideal figure of the shepherd.

Jesus' parable of the good shepherd is thus an apt prelude to a feast celebrating the purifying of the temple. It is based on Ezekiel 34, one of the lessons assigned in the synagogues during the feast. The parable has a sharper edge to it than the tender parable of the lost sheep in the Synoptics (Matthew 18:12-13; Luke 15:3-7). It is closer to the saying recorded in Matthew 9:36 (cf. Mark 6:34).

Verses 1-5 comprise the only parable in this gospel. They are followed by an allegorical interpretation, verses 7-18, similar to the development of the parable of the sower in the Synoptics (Mark 4:13-20). But the **thieves and robbers** should not be exclusively applied to the priests. They include all messianic pretenders and revolutionaries who destroy the flock by their worldly ambitions.

Some would see the allegory as a more immediate reference to the situation of the church in the evangelist's own time—the **hireling** representing false teachers and the **wolf** representing the Roman persecutors. Whatever the allegorical interpretation, the evangelist emphasizes the love of the true **shepherd,** Jesus, who is willing to **lay down my life for the sheep.** The death-resurrection theme is accented in verses 17-18.

C. THE RAISING OF LAZARUS (11:1-57)

11:1-44. *The Miracle.* The last and climactic sign of death-resurrection in the gospel is the raising of Lazarus. It is more stupendous than the messianic signs of raising the dead recorded in the Synoptic gospels (Mark 5:21-24, 35-43; Luke 7:11-17). Here the miracle is deliberately heightened, by the delay until Lazarus has been dead **four days.** It was a popular belief that soul and body were finally separated after three days—with no hope of resuscitation. Lazarus' resurrection thus points to Jesus' resurrection. The event forces decision on belief or disbelief in Jesus (verses 45-53); his enemies understand that the die is cast. It is this decisiveness for faith, in a miracle that surpasses any possibility of rational explanation, that gives the incident its primary dramatic tension.

For, one must ask, what is the motive for this sign? It is not compassion, despite the obvious sympathy of Jesus for his close friends, or his own personal grief; otherwise Jesus would come speedily to heal him before death. It is hardly a compassionate act to bring a man back from the peace of death to the trials and sufferings of this life. Nor are we given any hint that Lazarus, once restored to life on earth, has any special mission to fulfill.

The true motive is baldly stated by Jesus: **it is for the glory of God, so that the Son of God may be glorified by means of it.** Thus the theme of glorification of God in the death and resurrection of Jesus is announced, and will be elaborated further in the coming passion narrative. It has already been hinted in 1:14; 2:11; 7:18.

The raising of Lazarus is also a test, not only of Jesus' disciples and friends, and of the "Jews," but of Jesus himself. Jesus takes a great risk. It is not a risk of proving unable to raise Lazarus, of having his prayer to God unanswered. Jesus never doubts that God will hear him in this crisis. It is rather the risk of disbelief in him, despite the great sign, that will bring about his final rejection.

The disciples have intimations of this: **Let us also go, that we may die with him.** The sisters, Mary and Martha, believe in him but can project their faith and hope only **at the last day.** Jesus summons to faith and decision *now:* **I am the resurrection and the life; . . . whoever lives and believes in me shall never die."**

Who then is Lazarus? Why should he be singled out by personal name from among all the recipients of Jesus' signs in this gospel? This question cannot be answered definitively. His was a common name among the Jews—Eleazar ("God helps"). Some scholars believe that the evangelist selected it from the parable of the rich man and Lazarus (Luke 16:19-31), a story of life after death, but this seems unlikely. Luke does tell us of Jesus' friendship with Mary and Martha (Luke 10:38-42), yet it does not mention a brother or the location of their home at **Bethany** (on verse 2 see below on 12:1-11).

Jesus' **love** of Lazarus is emphasized. This indication of love for disciples begins here to be intensified and is especially directed to a particular disciple "whom Jesus loved" throughout the passion and resurrection narratives. Tradition has of course identified this "beloved disciple" with the evangelist, and more specifically with John the son of Zebedee. But many scholars today believe that Lazarus is the beloved disciple—though there is no reason to suppose that he was included among the twelve.

We have here an example of the evangelist's subtlety in weaving together historical persons with symbolic types—as he did with Nathanael, or the Samaritan woman. Lazarus represents every believer who loves Jesus and is loved by him—whom the Lord will raise up at the last day. So also Jesus' words **Take away the stone** and **Unbind him, and let him go** speak not only to the historical event of Lazarus' resurrection but more deeply to every believer's condition: "Release from the stony heart of sin; let go to life in God."

11:45-57. *The Reaction of the "Jews."* On hearing of the raising of Lazarus the council of **chief priests** and **Pharisees** meets to decide what must be done. **It is expedient for you that one man should die for the people, and that the whole nation should not perish.** This counsel of the high priest **Caiaphas** is crucial. It is a decision made in hatred, fear, and expediency. By sacrificing an innocent man, the council reckons that it can save its own position and prestige—indeed can save the whole country from war and destruction. The people, or at least all too many of them **believe** this man Jesus to be the Messiah. This means war with the **Romans**—no matter that Jesus has rejected all temporal, revolutionary claims, no matter what he has really said and done. The high priest prophesies without knowing it.

So God confounds the evil counsels of men to bring about his own purposes of salvation. The death of Jesus is not for one people alone, much less for their political security. It will be the agency by which God brings into one reconciliation all his children **scattered abroad.**

Caiaphas' supposedly humane policy of course came to nothing, even in the course of historical events. Within a generation the Jewish revolt against Rome, in which no Christian disciples took part, ended in the destruction of Jerusalem and of the temple—the latter never to be rebuilt. To the evangelist and his first readers the irony of the high priest's statement had become evident.

11:54-57. The geographical framework of the Lazarus miracle is not without hidden meaning. Jesus has come forth from the wilderness **across the Jordan** (10:40) where his earthly ministry began with the preaching of John the Baptist (cf. "Bethany beyond the Jordan," 1:28). He now retires to a place near the edge of the **wilderness** before his final return to Passover for the fulfillment of his destiny. Yet so obtuse are many that they engage in the same gossip about Jesus at this climactic time as they did before the feast of Tabernacles.

III. The Passion and Resurrection (12:1–20:31)

A. The Preparation (12:1-50)

The incidents and sayings in this chapter are transitional. Verses 1-19 relate to the coming passion, the anointing of Jesus for burial and the entry into Jerusalem. Verses 36*b*-50 summarize the proclamation of Jesus in his earthly ministry. The bridge between them is verses 20-36*a*, in which is again set forth the death-resurrection theme and the glorification of Jesus that brings judgment and light to the whole world.

The final week of Jesus' earthly life fulfills the promise of the first week of his ministry. As the first week opened with his baptism and consecration to his mission, this last week opens with his anointing and consecration for his fulfilled mission in death. The first week ended in the joyous wedding feast that manifested his glory to the disciples. The last week ends in another Galilean feast that reveals his resurrection glory and seals his disciples' faith and obedience.

12:1-11. *The Anointing.* This scene is comparable to the account in Mark 14:3-9, with details that recall also the incident in Luke 7:36-50. It differs from the Synoptic story in being placed before the triumphal entry. It depicts, as it were, an anointing not only for burial, but for his kingship, now to be acclaimed and then rejected in its earthly dimension, though revealed to faith in its eternal glory. It differs further in being located in the home of Lazarus rather than of one Simon the leper, thus being linked to the preceding story. It differs in highlighting Judas the betrayer as the one who objects to the costly waste.

The variations are undoubtedly due to differences that arise from stories transmitted by oral tradition. Hence the attempts of later interpreters to associate Mary of Bethany with the sinful woman of Luke 7:36-50 and the sinful woman with Mary Magdalene (Luke 8:2) are farfetched.

12:4-7. The portrayal of **Judas Iscariot** as a **thief** is more pronounced than in the Synoptic gospels (cf. Mark 14:11). This may be intended to suggest the reason for Judas' treachery (cf. 13:29). But the real motives of Judas are difficult to ascertain, and the author is possibly nearer the truth in his indication that the devil took possession of him (6:70; 13:2, 27).

12:8. This saying is a reminder that costly gifts of devotion to Jesus neither preclude nor exclude the obligation of concern for the poor.

12:12-19. *The Triumphal Entry.* Jesus' entry into Jerusalem is narrated also in much the same way as in the Synoptics (cf. Mark 11:1-10; Matthew 21:1-11; Luke 19:29-40). But John uses the story as a link between the sign of Lazarus' raising from the dead and the glorification of Jesus and his true kingship as revealed in the impending death and resurrection. The **crowd** who acclaims him represents the **world** which **has gone after him**—but a world very different from those who desire a temporal kingship, though his enemies do not know this.

12:20-36a. *Jesus' Hour.* The decisive **hour has come** (cf. 2:4). Not only the Judean **crowd** look to the revelation of the **King of Israel** (verses 12-13). The **Greeks** from the wider world now appear seeking Jesus. They have been brought by that peculiar pair of Johannine disciples, **Philip** and **Andrew,** from the city of Bethsaida, where Jew and Gentile intermingled. These Greeks are representatives of the Hellenistic world—whether Greek-speaking Jews of the Dispersion or Gentiles. For Jesus the Messiah-King, the Son of man, is now to be **lifted up** on the cross that he may **draw all men** to himself (cf. 3:14-15).

12:27-36a. It is a moment of portent. While the Jews and Greeks watch, Jesus in agony makes his final decision of obedience unto death, in servanthood and sonship. Such obedience is indeed the glorification of God. And God answers: He has **glorified** his **name;** he will **glorify it again.** It is **judgment;** it is the overthrow of Satan; it is salvation. Who comprehends it? Is it merely the sound of thunder or is it the voice of an **angel?** Both material and spiritual perception of revelation are mixed, depending on whether one is in the **light** or in **darkness.**

In no other passage has the evangelist displayed more remarkably his powers of suggestive symbolism than in these verses. The reverberation contains the whole symphony of sounds associated with the voice of God, from the ancient creation Psalm (Ps. 29:1-4) to the final song of the saints in the age to come (Revelation 14:1-2).

12:36b-50. *The End of Public Discourse.* This epilogue concludes Jesus' public ministry—his manifestation to the world and to the Jews. From this point on his teaching is confined entirely to the inner circle of his disciples. These are words of judgment—not that he judges but that people judge themselves by virtue of their response to him. They are also a reflection of Christian judgment on the varying responses to the gospel. The citation from Isaiah 53:1 is paralleled, with similar interpretation, by Paul (Romans 10:16) and that from Isaiah 6:10 is quoted also in Matthew 13:14-15 and Acts 28:25-27.

In characteristic Johannine fashion the theme of the **commandment** of God with which the section closes picks up an earlier suggestion in 10:18. This will be unfolded in more detail in coming discourses in chapters 13–16. Its basis is Deuteronomy, the prophetic book of the law.

B. The Last Supper (13:1–17:26)

The most obvious characteristic of this account of the supper is the lack of any formal institution of the Eucharist with the elements of bread and wine (cf. Mark 14:22-24; 26:26-28; Luke 22:17-19). Many theories have tried to explain this omission—for example:

(1) The author's chronology, according to which this was not a Passover meal (see below on 13:1).

(2) At the time of writing the Eucharist was a "secret" not to be revealed to an unbaptized reader.

(3) The evangelist was not interested in sacraments themselves.

(4) He presupposes his readers know both the Synoptic gospels and the rites of the church.

The fact is, the evangelist chooses his own way to use, or allude to, tradition. In no place does he give any hint of an institution of baptism. Yet baptismal and eucharistic themes constantly recur throughout the gospel. The Eucharist is specifically referred to in 6:51-56.

13:1. *The Johannine Chronology.* The evangelist dates the supper **before the feast of the Passover** instead of equating it with the Passover meal as do the Synoptics (cf. Mark 14:12; Matthew 26:17; Luke 22:7-8). He places the Crucifixion on the eve of Passover, when the lambs were sacrificed (cf. 18:28; 19:31). The Crucifixion is the slaughter of the true paschal lamb. By implication the true paschal feast is the meal of the risen Lord with his disciples on the day of the Resurrection. This discrepancy in chronology has been occasion for endless debate.

All four gospels agree that the Last Supper was held on Thursday evening and that the Crucifixion took place on Friday. But John is explicit that Friday was not the Passover feast day but the day of Preparation (19:31), and that in this year Passover and the sabbath coincided.

There is no way to resolve this conflict of dating by astronomical calculation, since we do not know the exact year of Jesus' death. It was sometime between 29 and 33. In his time the new moon of the month Nisan, in which Passover was celebrated at the full moon, was determined by observation, so that weather conditions might cause a twenty-four-hour delay in proclamation of the beginning of the month. Outside Palestine, in the Jewish Dispersion, the date of the feast was calculated by fixed tables of the moon months. Hence it is possible that the Synoptic gospels represent a memory of the fateful year of Jesus' death based on a fixed calendar, whereas this gospel goes back to Palestinian tradition and a memory that in the year of Jesus' crucifixion the Passover fell a day later than the reckoning of fixed calendars.

13:2-20. *The Foot Washing.* This has been subject to diverse interpretations. Many see it simply as a final acted parable of humility and love that opens the discourse on the theme of Jesus' relationship to his disciples and theirs in turn to one another. Others see in it a veiled sacrament of the "baptism" or consecration of the apostles. Some Christian groups in the course of history have taken it literally as a special ceremony instituted by Jesus. Another problem concerns the textual tradition of verse 10. Many ancient manuscripts of good authority omit the words **except for his feet.**

Jesus' act is certainly an example of the humble, selfless

service, even to the most menial deeds of kindness, that characterizes the true disciple-servant who shares with him his master-servant role in his kingdom. This is explicit in Jesus' own interpretation of his act (verses 12-17). The story is exactly comparable to the words of Jesus at the supper recorded in Luke 22:24-30. His kingdom is not a realm where some are great in authority and privilege and others are slavish in lowly service. In his kingdom the greatest is the least—the servant of all (cf. Mark 10:42-45). This is his final lesson to his disciples. And the Eucharist is, if nothing else, his instrument through which he serves us with his whole life and we serve one another in sharing servanthood of all that we are and possess. The foot washing is a profound exposition of the Eucharist, of that most intimate relationship of Jesus with the members of his body the church.

In this sense Jesus' washing of the disciples' feet is indeed their baptism into his death, their consecration into his priesthood and kingship. As Mary anointed him for his unique fulfillment of his destiny (12:3) with costly ointment poured out on his feet, so he now "anoints" his disciples' feet with the lowly cleansing water, that they may have full **part** in him. They have **bathed** (in the baptism of John?), but they need this final anointing and purification from himself.

The revelation of Jesus is now completed for his disciples (cf. **I am he,** verse 19) and their mission is established. In humility and love the Father sent the Son. Now the Son in humility and love sends the disciples. Whoever **receives** them receives Christ, just as whoever receives Christ receives the Father. The last discourse will develop the theme.

13:21-30. *Identification of the Traitor.* This incident has many similarities to the account in Mark 14:17-21, but the evangelist uses it as to introduce the "beloved disciple" (but see above on 11:3). The Christian reader would assume that the disciple **whom Jesus loved** is one of the twelve, though this gospel does not limit the number of disciples at the supper to the twelve (cf. Mark 14:17; Matthew 26:20). And though the tradition has identified this disciple with John son of Zebedee, nothing in the gospel itself would lead one to that conclusion. It is certainly possible that the beloved disciple is John. But his role here and in the narrative of the Crucifixion and Resurrection (cf. 19:26; 20:2; 21:20) suggests a person whom the evangelist employs as a "type" of the true disciple—a merging of historical and typological witness so characteristic of his method of presentation (for example, Nathanael, the Samaritan woman, the man born blind, and Lazarus).

The beloved disciple lies close to the **breast** of Jesus. This recalls the Prologue, where it is said that Jesus is "in the bosom of the Father" (1:18). It is another indication by the evangelist that the intimate union of Jesus with his disciples is image of his intimate union with the Father.

Neither this gospel nor the Synoptics make clear why the disciples do not react more positively to the identification of the traitor. But they are obviously unaware of its implication.

13:31–16:33. *The Farewell Discourse.* This lengthy discourse is found only in this gospel. Yet it corresponds in many ways to the "apocalyptic" discourse of Jesus before his passion recorded in Mark 13, Matthew 24, and Luke 21. For it deals, in a very different style and manner, with the imminent departure of Jesus and the consequent fate of his disciples, and with his return to them in deliverance.

In fact there are two discourses here. They are separated by the strange summons of 14:31, **Rise, let us go hence,** and the allegory of the vine (15:1-9). They conclude with a final question, **Do you now believe?** (16:31). Both discourses deal with the same themes—the impending death, bodily departure, and continued presence of Jesus, and the consequences of these events for the life and mission of the disciples.

The parallelism of the two discourses is evident. The first (13:31–14:31) speak of the immediate fate of Jesus and his disciples in the impending crisis of his death. The second (15:10–16:33) projects this experience into the future life of his disciples—that is, the church—and their respective followers in the world. The distinction, however, is not absolute. The evangelist always anticipates themes for further comment.

This interweaving of present and future gives the discourse a dramatic tension. In the immediate situation the disciples will falter; Peter will indeed deny him; they do not understand what he is saying, do not know who he truly is; they will be scattered and leave him alone to his fate. Yet they will not really fall away. Only one, Judas, has irrevocably gone out into the **night** of the world which has rejected him. They will be valiant in witness even unto death, and in tribulation they will find joy. Though denial and desertion lie immediately ahead, they will **follow—** and **lay down** their lives for him as he is now going to lay down his life for them. The suffering of Jesus will be their suffering. His triumph will be theirs also.

A little while, and you will see me no more; again a little while, and you will see me (16:16; cf. 13:33 and 14:19). This prediction is the basis of Jesus' discourse. The "little while" is of course the impending time of his death and departure. But the evangelist uses two Greek words for "see" which cannot easily be distinguished in English translation. In the first clause they are no longer to see him present physically. But in the second they will see him in his glorified, exalted life, in a vision that includes but surpasses mere physical sight. This second verb is used of the resurrection appearances in 20:18, 25, 29. It is a seeing that is also knowing; for though "no one has ever seen God" (1:18), **he who has seen me has seen the Father** (14:9).

In order that this seeing may take place, Jesus must **go to the Father** (14:28)—ascend into heaven—to his **Father's house** (14:2), heaven being commonly viewed as God's temple. This departure is not an occasion of **sorrow** but a cause of **joy** (16:20). Only thus can Jesus open the **way** to eternal life (14:6). There he is to **prepare a place** (14:2) for those who will **follow** him (13:36). And only by his return to the Father can he send **another,** his **Spirit,** who will be with the disciples at all times and in all places (14:16-17). So long as he is bound within his fleshly body he is limited by time and space. His ascension assures his presence to his own people wherever they may be, forever. It is promise also of **greater works** than even he could do in his earthly life, for then **whatever you ask in my name, I will do it** (14:12-14).

Who is this "other" whom Jesus will send? The evangelist

calls him by a title peculiar to the Johannine writings, *parakletos,* literally "one called alongside," to help. The term is variously translated as "advocate" (I John 2:1, where it is applied to Jesus himself), **Counselor,** "Comforter" (King James Version), but is better simply transliterated "Paraclete." The discourse makes plain that the Paraclete is the **Spirit of truth,** the **Holy Spirit.** He comes from the Father in Jesus' name and **dwells** with the disciples. He is in fact the presence of God in Christ continuing with his faithful servants after the ascension of Jesus, fulfilling and perfecting his work. Only the disciples will know him, for the **world cannot receive** him (14:17).

The work of the Paraclete is two-fold. Within the fellowship of Jesus' disciples he is the guide and teacher of truth, to **bring to . . . remembrance** what Jesus said (14:26) and reveal those **things that are to come** by virtue of what Jesus accomplished (16:13). Thus he is to **declare** all that is of Jesus and about Jesus and so **glorify** him as Jesus has glorified the Father (16:14).

The Paraclete is also to **witness,** through the testimony of the disciples, to the world ouside, convicting it **of sin and of righteousness and of judgment** (15:26-27; 16:8-11). He directs the disciples both in their preaching of the gospel and in their steadfast testimony in persecution. The love, the prayer, the obedience of the Christian disciple are the gift of grace of the Paraclete. This Spirit Jesus breathes on his disciples in the Resurrection (20:21-22; cf. 14:27).

This conception of the Paraclete is rooted in the Old Testament witness to the Spirit of God who comes upon the prophets to inspire them to speak God's words. But in the New Testament the Holy Spirit is poured forth not only on specific chosen witnesses but on all the faithful believers in Christ (cf. Acts 2:33; I Corinthians 12:7-13). The Farewell Discourse has been a primary source for the development of the ancient church's doctrine of the Trinity.

The allegory of the vine (15:1-9), which binds together the two parts of the discourse, also has its roots in the Old Testament idea of Israel as God's vine. A crucial parable of Jesus recorded in the Synoptics (Mark 12:1-12; Matthew 21:33-46; Luke

325

20:9-19) makes the same comparison. Here the use of the figure includes all the Old Testament associations of God's care for and judgment on the vine. At the same time it goes beyond them by its identification of Jesus as the **true vine.** Thus Jesus is the true Israel, in whose stem are incorporated the **branches** of the people of God, who find their fulfillment and life in him. The allegory is comparable to his discourses on the bread of life in chapter 6 and the good shepherd in chapter 10. It is another revelation of "I am." It is also a Johannine commentary on the "fruit of the vine" (Mark 14:25), the cup of the Eucharist.

17:1-26. *The High Priestly Prayer.* The few prayers of Jesus recorded in the Synoptic gospels are invariably short and addressed with intimate immediacy to his "Father." The two examples already given in this gospel—11:41-42 (cf. Matthew 11:25-27) and 12:27 (cf. Mark 14:36)—share these characteristics, and each of them is a "cry" of Jesus at a moment of great tension.

The extended prayer of this chapter is more serene and meditative, gathering up the themes of the preceding discourse. It is both a final resolution of Jesus' obedience to the death which will be his glorification and an intercession for the fruits of his work after his ascension. The literary form no doubt is due to the constructive skill of the evangelist—for example, verse 3 is hardly the way one would expect Jesus to address his Father. It is in a sense another discourse.

The popular title of this chapter is "The High Priestly Prayer" of Jesus; it is his consecration of himself as the mediator of salvation. It expresses exactly what the author of Hebrews wrote of his eternal intercession: "He is able for all time to save those who draw near to God through him, since he always lives to make intercession for them" (Hebrews 7:25). It sums up the Johannine concept of the work of Christ.

The prayer has four focuses of concern:

(1) Jesus' offering of himself for his Father's purposes (verses 1-5);

(2) his concern for the destiny of his disciples after his ascension (verses 6-19);

(3) the outreach of intercession to all future believers until the end of time (verses 20-23);

(4) the expectation of final consummation in the age to come (verses 24-26).

The **glory** of Jesus—**before the world was made,** the fulfillment of his **hour . . . on earth,** and his return eternally to God's **own presence**—all this will be manifested to the world in the unity in **truth** and **love** of all his disciples and believers. Such unity will suffer many strains, including temptations and persecutions. Here the evangelist no doubt thinks of the schisms and trials of his own generation, which will be repeated in coming generations.

But the last and the eternally continuing prayer of Jesus is that the unity of love and purpose he has with his Father will be reflected in the unity of the church in himself, and that the mission he received and fulfilled from his Father will be the same mission of all who find **joy fulfilled** in his discipleship throughout all ages.

This consummate prayer of Jesus must be the prayer of all who follow him. Many commentators have seen in it an exposition of the succinct Lord's Prayer of the Synoptic gospels. In both cases there is a curious lack of reference to the Spirit.

C. The Crucifixion (18:1–19:42)

Both in the order of the narrative and in many details the Johannine passion story is closer to the Synoptic tradition than any other extended portion of the gospel. Yet the differences, both in omissions and in additions (on the difference in chronology see above on 13:1), give it a tone and interpretation that is quite distinctive. In general it magnifies the "kingship" of Jesus. He goes to his death, not in weakness and humiliation, but as a hero fulfilling his destiny in triumph.

The physical frailty and anguish of Jesus are not emphasized. They are certainly not omitted —for example, the cruel and sardonic mockery of the soldiers and the final agony of thirst.

But there is no wrestling in agony of spirit in Gethsemane; he is able to bear his own cross; and he does not suffer the taunting mockery of those who watched him die.

Here Jesus is in full control of what happens. His arrest is not possible without his voluntary submission. He does not remain silent, for the most part, either at his trial before the chief priests or in the presence of Pilate. He defends himself and his teaching with dignity and forthrightness. He reminds Pilate in no uncertain terms that he is powerless either to crucify or to release him without divine permission. Indeed the trial before Pilate becomes a judgment on the governor himself. And in death's last throes Jesus utters, not a cry of despair, but a word of accomplishment: **It is finished** (cf. Mark 15:34-37, though note the more peaceful ending in Luke 23:46).

18:12–19:22. The Trial. The political overtones are prominent in this account, in ways both paradoxical and ironic. The preliminary hearing before the Jewish high priest is more in the nature of an investigation than a trial. No specific charge, whether of blasphemy or of messianic claim, is formulated. The Jewish authorities simply turn him over to Pilate as an **evildoer.** Yet as the trial before Pilate proceeds, the issue becomes clear: Jesus' kingship challenges the kingship of Caesar.

Neither the Jews nor Pilate really believes that Jesus is the **King of the Jews,** and Jesus positively rejects any claim to be a temporal ruler. The hyprocrisy of the Jews is evident to Pilate; so he mocks them when they object to the **title,** the inscription stating the charge, which he has ordered placed on the cross. It is evident also to Pilate that Jesus is innocent. But he yields to the fear of his own political position when they say, **If you release this man, you are not Caesar's friend.** Were it not for Jesus' dignity the whole proceeding would be a farce.

There is no doubt that the evangelist himself places the major blame for the tragedy on the "Jews" and attempts, albeit unsuccessfully, to exonerate Pilate by portraying him as yielding to pressure. This slant—evident also in Matthew and Luke—has unfortunately been a source of unwarranted anti-Semitic attitudes among later generations of Christians. But it reflects a situation of the evangelist's own times. On one hand was the increasing hostility between church and synagogue, and on the other hand the desire of Christians in the face of persecution to attest their loyalty to the Roman government and to minimize the threat posed by their messianic hopes.

19:25-27. *At the Cross.* A unique scene in this account is the appearance of Jesus' **mother** and the **disciple whom he loved** at the foot of the cross. In the Synoptic gospels the women watch from a distance; the disciples have all fled into hiding. It is of course possible that the evangelist preserves here a true factual memory. Many commentators believe it reflects a later tradition from Ephesus, where they assume the mother of Jesus lived in the area of John the son of Zebedee. But the scene has symbolic meaning. Mary represents the church (see above on 2:1-12), the believing community. The disciple represents every individual believer (see above on 13:21-30). Thus in his final act on earth Jesus entrusts to those who love him and believe in him the care of his church.

19:28-37. *The Death of Jesus.* The cruel punishment of crucifixion, which the Romans took over from the Carthaginians and Persians, was inflicted only on slaves and "foreigners," usually for robbery or sedition. It might last for several days before death at last occurred from hunger and thirst, exhaustion, or bleeding from wounds—including the wounds of scourging, which usually preceded it. Breaking the **legs** of the crucified added to the agony, though it hastened the end—and was possibly a precaution against escape. Jesus' death within three hours was unusual (cf. Mark 15:44-45), but he had already suffered much abuse. The Jewish law required that the body of an executed criminal displayed as a public example should be buried by nightfall. It is doubtful, however, that the Romans respected this law, even when the following day was a special Jewish holy day.

The author's interest in the circumstance that Jesus' legs were not broken has possibly two allusions:

(1) the Passover lamb that is sacrificed should not have a broken bone (Exodus 12:46; Numbers 9:12);

(2) the psalmist noted that the Lord keeps all the bones of the righteous so that "not one of them is broken" (Psalm 34:20). In all the gospels much of the passion narrative is considered as fulfillment of Old Testament passages viewed as prophetic of the Christ.

That Jesus' **side** was **pierced** after his death—a fulfillment of Zechariah 12:10—is another of the peculiar features of this account, one of great importance to the Johannine authors (cf. 20:25, 27; Revelation 1:7). The motive behind the soldier's spear thrust is not clear.

More mysterious is the issue of **blood and water.** There is no adequate medical explanation for such a phenomenon. Yet the author solemnly affirms this "miracle," for it undoubtedly served as a final and consummate sign of the meaning of Jesus' death and triumph. That there is a deep symbolic significance to the blood and water is evident. But interpreters, both ancient and modern, have not agreed about its exact meaning. Most obvious perhaps is the sense that in the self-offering of Jesus all the old legal rites of purification and sacrifice are fulfilled and brought to an end. Others, however, see in the sign a hidden reference to the church's sacraments. The life of Jesus, now closed on earth, continues to flow into the life of his followers in his Spirit-empowered gifts of baptism and the Eucharist—or what the ancient church significantly called the "paschal mystery."

19:38-42. *The Burial.* The burial of Jesus is similarly related in all four gospels. It was important testimony to the real fact of his death, in contrast to later theories, found in some of the apocryphal gospels, that Jesus, not being a real human being, departed to his Father before his actual death on the cross. The ancient orthodox creeds also emphasize the fact that Jesus was "buried." Without such a fact the tradition of the empty tomb is meaningless.

19:38-40. As one might expect, this account has its own peculiar details. **Joseph of Arimathea,** whom the Synoptics identify as a member of the Jewish "council," is here described as a secret believer. He is associated with **Nicodemus** (cf. 3:1-10;

7:50-51), who is presumably a similar believer. In contrast to the mean manner of Jesus' death these men provide him with a sumptuous burial, including **linen cloths** wound about the body and a lavish supply of **spices,** according to Jewish **custom.** Nicodemus provides these spices at the time of burial. There is no mention of the loving women who in the Synoptics watch to see where the body is laid. Chapter 20, however, assumes that at least one of them knows where it is.

19:41-42. The tomb is a new one, so far unused and thus an honorable place for Jesus. This gospel alone locates it in a **garden** near the place of crucifixion.

This close association of place of death and place of burial has been attested at least since the fourth century. It was then that the Church of the Holy Sepulchre in Jerusalem was first erected by the Emperor Constantine on the holy sites. Recent investigations underneath the present church confirm that this could have been the site of the crucifixion and burial, but do not—and possibly cannot—confirm a garden setting of the tomb.

Symbolism is always allusive in this gospel. The fact that Jesus was betrayed in a garden and buried in a garden may be the evangelist's way of emphasizing that what was lost in the Garden of Eden by sin and disobedience is now recovered in a garden by obedience unto death. So Paradise is regained.

D. The Resurrection (20:1-31)

The account of the empty tomb and the appearance of the risen Christ to his disciples has many similarities to the tradition recounted in Luke. But there are Johannine emphases and details that are distinctive.

20:1-18. *The Empty Tomb.* In each of the Synoptic gospels several women come to the tomb for the purpose of completing preparation of the body for burial. In this account, however, only one woman is mentioned, **Mary Magdalene.** Her reason for visiting the tomb perhaps should be assumed to be devotion to her buried Lord.

20:2-10. These verses seem to be an expression—or correction—of the tradition in Luke 24:11 about the disciples' reaction to the report of the empty tomb. Peter and the beloved disciple hasten to verify the testimony. Though they do not see Jesus, they are convinced. In this narrative the evangelist in his subtle way refers to the primary experience by Peter of the Resurrection (cf. Luke 24:34; I Corinthians 15:5). The beloved disciple, who actually arrives first at the tomb, becomes a representative of all believers, both among the disciples and among all those who accept the disciples' witness, beginning with Peter. It is interesting to note that Peter is the first to see. The beloved disciple is the first to see and believe.

20:11-18. Verse 11 takes us back to Mary Magdalene at the tomb, as though verses 2-10 were an interruption. She now sees the **two angels** (cf. Luke 24:4; only one in Mark 16:5; Matthew 28:2-3), but before they deliver any message Jesus himself appears. The vision is real, but she cannot grasp him, for the truth of his resurrection is not yet fully revealed. She can only report that she has seen him and he has spoken to her.

20:19-23. *First Appearance to the Disciples.* The scene now shifts to the closed room, presumably in Jerusalem (cf. Luke 24:33-49), where the frightened disciples are hiding. Jesus identifies himself by showing the marks of his passion. He bestows on them the full grace of his risen and glorified life: **peace,** the true peace that restores them to inner security and fearlessness; mission, the command to take up his work; and power, the gift of the **Holy Spirit,** which is his life, for it is his gift alone by which the disciples can declare the forgiveness of sins. The Resurrection thus brings into being the church—its unity, its commission, its endowment. All that Jesus has won is now given to his disciples.

20:24-31. *The Response of Thomas.* In Matthew 28:17 we are told that at the resurrection appearance "some doubted." In view of the stupendous nature of the event this is understandable. Is it only a vision, or possibily a hallucination? Here the doubt is made concrete in the person of Thomas. Jesus must not only be seen; he must be handled—the whole person must be grasped. And Thomas' doubt—representing that of all who come after him—is turned to certainty. Those who have never seen the Christ can believe in him, for they can touch his very body from which his blood outpoured. It is not fanciful to see here a reference to the Eucharist. We can also see a reference to the very material love of Christian believers one for another and for the whole world.

The resurrection narrative thus builds up into a dramatic climax. First there is the evidence of the empty tomb, then the vision of what this empty tomb signifies. Jesus is risen and alive. The vision becomes concrete in the experience and acceptance of grace and of empowerment for redemptive mission, and finally by incorporation through faith in his glorification through suffering.

The final response, **My Lord and my God!** is the believer's answer to the initial proclamation: "The Word was God. . . .No one has ever seen God; the only Son . . . has made him known" (1:1, 18).

IV. APPENDIX: ATTESTATION OF WITNESS (21:1-25)

The obvious ending of the gospel in 20:30-31 is followed by two narratives and colophon, which all commentators denote as an "appendix" (see Introduction). The fact that verse 24 distinguishes the **disciple who is bearing witness** and the **we** who vouch for his witness suggests an editorial compilation. Evidences of this have been noted here and there in the gospel text itself. Thus many believe that this chapter is a later addition—though careful studies of its vocabulary and style are inconclusive, and there is no evidence that the gospel ever circulated without it.

Both subject matter and style recall especially chapter 6—a miraculous feeding and a confession by Peter. It is possible that editorial rearrangement—whether by the author or others—

tranferred to this place incidents that in the original plan of the gospel were included in the Galilean ministry. Thus the **third** manifestation of Jesus to his disciples may have been the third miracle of his revelation in Galilee (cf. 2:11; 4:54). The testing and call of Peter might logically have followed his confession in 6:69.

21:1-14. *The Miraculous Catch of Fish.* This episode, with its setting at the **Sea of Tiberias** (cf. 6:1), has similarities to the story in Luke 5:2-11. These are seen in the initiative of Peter, followed by his call to discipleship; the mention of the sons of Zebedee, the only time in this gospel; and the heavy weight of fish. The story may well be a completion of the unfinished and unfulfilled promise of Mark 14:28; 16:7 of an appearance to the disciples in Galilee.

But the author has given the tradition a Eucharistic allusion, comparable to that in the feeding of the multitude in chapter 6—the risen Lord is made known in the breaking of bread (cf. Luke 24:35; Acts 10:41). Note that Jesus has already prepared the breakfast of bread and fish before the fish are brought in by the disciples. Note too that it is the beloved disciple who is first to recognize the Lord, as it was he who was first to believe in the Resurrection. The number of fish, **a hundred and fifty-three,** has inspired many attempts at symbolic interpretation. Jerome, for example, declared it the total of species of fish, and Augustine discovered it is the sum of the numbers 1 to 17, which in turn is the sum of the symbolic numbers 10 and 7.

21:15-19. *The Dialogue with Peter.* This scene is also allusive in the Johannine manner. The three-fold question and answer correspond—by way of restoration—to the three-fold denial of Peter before the Crucifixion (13:38; 18:17-18, 25-27). It is also a reaffirmation of Peter's call, with that of other disciples, to **follow** Jesus, and the Johannine recognition of Peter's leadersip in the apostolic band of disciples. He receives his commission, as representative of all the apostles, to shepherd the Lord's flock. He also receives the promise that he too, like his Lord the Good Shepherd, will lay down his life for the sheep. Verse 18 has generally been taken as a reference to the tradition that

Peter suffered martyrdom, probably by crucifixion in the persecution of Nero, A.D. 64.

21:20-25. *The Future of the Beloved Disciple.* Peter's love is now equated with that of the beloved disciple. His question about the fate of this companion is both a natural curiosity about the destiny of the man himself and a deeper allusion to those whom the beloved disciple represents figuratively. The colophon (verse 24) makes clear that the beloved disciple—whoever he was—had died by the time the gospel was published. But in a sense the beloved disciple does not die; he remains until Jesus comes again (verse 22). In every generation, from the time of Jesus' resurrection until the end of the world, disciples whom Jesus loves and who love Jesus in return shall remain with us. Whether soon or late, the summons of Jesus comes to every disciple, to **follow** him to bear **witness** to him.

FOR FURTHER STUDY

MATTHEW

A. H. McNeile, *The Gospel According to St. Matthew*, 1915; older work, but still the best technical commentary in English. G. D. Kilpatrick, *The Origins of . . . Matthew*, 1946; illuminating study of the background. T. W. Manson, *The Sayings of Jesus*, 1949; exposition of the sayings in Q and the special sources of Matthew and Luke, with a discerning treatment of all the discourse material in Matthew. K. Stendahl, *The School of St. Matthew*, 1954; technical analysis of the Old Testament quotations in Matthew, with special attention to the interpretive method found in the Dead Sea Scrolls. F. V. Filson, *Commentary on . . . Matthew*, 1960; a helpful recent commentary. G. Bornkamm and others, *Tradition and Interpretation in Matthew*, 1963; penetrating study of the distinctive characteristics of the gospel tradition as edited in Matthew, with emphasis on the miracles, the church, and the law.

MARK

Benjamin Bacon, *The Beginnings of the Gospel Story*, 1909; somewhat out-of-date, but still very helpful. B. H. Branscomb, *The Gospel of Mark*, 1937; a useful commentary on the Moffatt translation. F. C. Grant, *The Earliest Gospel*, 1943; very helpful on the background of Mark. F. C. Grant in *Interpreter's Bible*, 1951. Vincent Taylor, *The Gospel According to St. Mark*, 1952; best modern technical commentary. Sherman Johnson, *The Gospel According to St. Mark*, 1960; best modern nontechnical commentary, with an original translation. C. E. B. Cranfield in *Interpreter's Dictionary of the Bible*, 1962; and N. Perrin in *Interpreter's Dictionary of the Bible Supplement*, 1976.

LUKE

John Martin Creed, *The Gospel According to St. Luke*, 1930. William Manson, *The Gospel of Luke*, 1930. S. MacLean Gilmour in *Interpreter's Bible*, 1952. Henry J. Cadbury. *The Making of Luke-Acts*, 2nd ed., 1958. A. R. C. Leaney, *The Gospel According to St. Luke*, 1958. Hans Conzelmann, *The Theology of St. Luke*, 1960. C. K. Barrett,

Luke the Historian in Recent Study. 1961. Vincent Taylor in *Interpreter's Dictionary of the Bible,* 1962; W. C. Robinson, Jr. in *Interpreter's Dictionary of the Bible Supplement,* 1976.

JOHN

Beginning students would do well to orient themselves by reference to a dictionary article such as the classic one of Baron Friedrich von Hügel in *Encyclopaedia Britannica,* reprinted since 11th ed., 1911, or of J. N. Sanders in *Interpreter's Dictionary of the Bible,* 1962, and D. M. Smith in *Interpreter's Dictionary of the Bible, Supplement,* 1976, and to critical and thematic surveys such as those of W. F. Howard, *Christianity According to St. John,* 1946, and *the 4th Gospel in Recent Criticism and Interpretation,* 4th ed., 1955. The great commentaries in English are those of J. H. Bernard, 2 vols., 1929; E. C. Hoskyns and F. N. Davey, 1940; C. K. Barrett, 1955; R. H. Lightfoot, posthumous, 1956; and R. E. Brown, S.S., 2 vols., 1966-68. Less extensive commentaries are by W. F. Howard in *Interpreter's Bible,* 1952; Alan Richardson, 1960; and A. M. Hunter, 1965. The magisterial commentary in German of Rudolf Bultmann is available in English translation (1971), and one may gain insight into its positions from D. M. Smith, Jr., *The Composition and Order of the 4th Gospel,* 1965. The vols. of C. H. Dodd are fundamental: *The Interpretation of the 4th Gospel,* 1953, and *Historical Tradition in the 4th Gospel,* 1963.

Special studies of influence are: B. W. Bacon, *The Gospel of the Hellenists,* 1933; Percival Gardner-Smith, *St. John and the Synoptic Gospels,* 1938; J. N. Sanders, *The 4th Gospel in the Early Church,* 1943; Oscar Cullmann, *Early Christian Worship,* 1953, Part II; Aileen Guilding, *The 4th Gospel and Jewish Worship,* 1960; J. A. T. Robinson, *12 New Testament Studies,* 1962, pp. 94-138; André Feuillet, *Johannine Studies,* 1965; R. E. Brown, S.S., *New Testament Essays,* 1965, pp. 51-213.

ABBREVIATIONS AND EXPLANATIONS

ABBREVIATIONS

D — Deuteronomic; Deuteronomist source

E — Elohist source
Ecclus. — Ecclesiasticus
ed. — edited by, edition, editor
e.g. — *exempli gratia* (for example)
ERV — English Revised Version
esp. — especially

H — Holiness Code

J — Yahwist source
JPSV — Jewish Publication Society Version

L — Lukan source
LXX — Septuagint, the earliest Greek translation of the Old Testament and Apocrypha (250 B.C. and after)

M — Matthean source
Macc. — Maccabees
MS — manuscript

N — north, northern
NEB — New English Bible

P — Priestly source
p. — page
Pet — Peter
Phil. — Philippian, Philippians
Philem. — Philemon
Prov. — Proverbs
Pss. Sol. — Psalms of Solomon
pt. — part (of a literary work

Q — "Sayings" source

rev. — revised
RSV — Revised Standard Version

S — south, southern

trans. — translated by, translation, translator

viz. — *videlicet* (namely)
Vulg. — Vulgate, the accepted Latin version, mostly translated A.D. 383-405 by Jerome

W — west, western
Wisd. Sol. — Wisdom of Solomon

QUOTATIONS AND REFERENCES

In the direct commentary words and phrases quoted from the RSV of the passage under discussion are printed in boldface type, without quotation marks, to facilitate linking the comments to the exact points of the biblical text. If a quotation from the passage under discussion is not in boldface type, it is to be recognized as an alternate translation, either that of another version if so designated (see abbreviations of versions above) or the commentator's own rendering. On the other hand, quotations from other parts of the Bible in direct commentary, as well as all biblical quotations in the introductions, are to be understood as from the RSV unless otherwise identified.

A passage of the biblical text is identified by book, chapter number, and verse number or numbers, the chapter and verse numbers being separated by a colon (c.f. Genesis 1:1). Clauses within a verse may be designated by the letters *a, b, c,* etc. following the verse number (e.g. Genesis 1:2*b*). In poetical text each line as printed in the RSV—not counting runovers necessitated by narrow columns—is accorded a letter. If the book is not named, the book under discussion is to be understood; similarly the chapter number appearing in the boldface reference at the beginning of the paragraph, or in a preceding centered head, is to be understood if no chapter is specified.

A suggestion to note another part of the biblical text is usually introduced by the abbreviation "cf." and specifies the exact verses. To be distinguished from this is a suggestion to consult a comment in this volume, which is introduced by "see above on," "see below on," or "see comment on," and which identifies the boldface reference at the head of the paragraph where the comment is to be found or, in the absence of a boldface reference, the reference in a preceding centered head. The suggestion "see Introduction" refers to the introduction of the book under discussion unless another book is named.

Palestine under the Herods

- – – Boundary of Herod's kingdom at its greatest extent

Divisions, A.D. 6-17
I Under Roman Procurators
II Tetrarchy of Herod Antipas
III Tetrarchy of Philip
★ Fortresses

0   10   20 Miles
0   10   20 Kilometres

Grid lines mark 50 kilometre squares

MARE INTERNUM (Mediterranean Sea)

PROVINCE OF SYRIA

ITURAEA   ABILENE

TRACHONITIS

BATANAEA

GAULANITIS

AURANITIS

GALILEE

DECAPOLIS

KINGDOM OF HEROD

SAMARIA

JUDEA

PEREA

IDUMEA

Wilderness of Judea

Lake Asphaltitis (Dead Sea)

NABATAEAN KINGDOM

Damascus (A City of Decapolis)
Sidon
Zarephath (Sarepta)
Tyre
Paneas (Caesarea Philippi)
Raphana (A City of Decapolis)
Ptolemais
Mt. Carmel
Chorazin
Capernaum
Bethsaida-Julias
Gennesaret
Tarichea
Magdala
Sea of Galilee
Camala
Dium
Sepphoris
Nazareth
Abila
Dora
The Great Plain
Scythopolis
Pella
Caesarea (Strato's Tower)
Plain of Sharon
Sebaste (Samaria)
Pella
Gerasa
Apollonia Sozusa
Neapolis
Mt. Ebal
Mt. Gerizim
Alexandrium
Amathus
R. Jabbok
Antipatris
Joppa
Phasaelis
Lydda
Thamna
Gophna
Archelais
Jericho
Gadara
Philadelphia (Rabbah)
Jamnia
Gazara
Emmaus (Nicopolis)
Cyprus
Betharamphtha
Azotus
Jerusalem
Bethany
Hyrcania
Ascalon (Free City)
Bethlehem
Herodium
Kh. Qumran
Settlement of Medeba (Dead Sea Sect)
Agrippias (Anthedon)
Betogabri
Adora
Hebron
Callirhoe
Gaza
Machaerus
Raphia
Idumea
Masada
Beersheba (Beer-sheba)

MAPS ADAPTED FROM OXFORD UNIVERSITY PRESS BIBLE MAPS

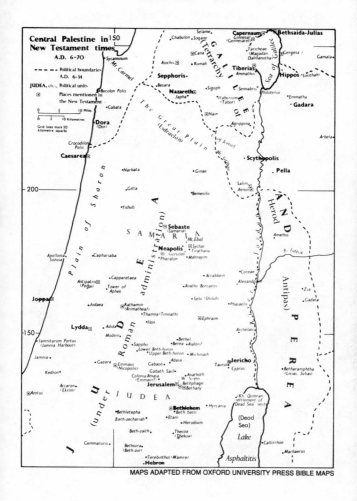

Central Palestine in
New Testament times
A.D. 6–70

- - - - Political boundaries
A.D. 6–34

JUDEA, etc., Political units
⊡ Places mentioned in
the New Testament

0   5   10 Miles
0   5   10 Kilometres

Grid lines mark 50
kilometre squares

150

Sycaminum
Mt. Carmel

Selame
Chabulon
Asochis ⊡
Rumah

Capernaum ⊡
Ginnesar
(Gennesaret)
Tarichaea
Magadan
Dalmanutha?

Bethsaida-Julias

Gergesa·

Gamala·

Sepphoris ⊡

Besara
Nazareth ⊡
Japha·

Cana ⊡

Sigoph

Sennabris ⊡

Tiberias ⊡
Ammathus

GALILEE OF (Tetrarchy of)

Hippos ⊡
·Sinithah?

·Emmatha

·Gadara

Dora
(Dor)

Gabata

·Itaburium
(Tabor)

⊡ Nain

Philoteria·

Crocodilon
Polis

The Great Plain
(Esdraelon)

Mt. Gilboa

Agrippina·

·Arbela

Caesarea ⊡

·Narbata

·Ginae

·Scythopolis

Pella ·

GILEAD (Herod Philip?)

·Gitta

·Bemeselis

Salim ⊡
Aenon?

·Amathus

·Yishub

S A M A R I A

·Sebaste
(Samaria)

Mt. Ebal
·Sychar
Tirathana

B. Jabbok

Apollonia
Sozusa·

·Capharsaba

Neapolis ⊡
Mt. Gerizim
·Pharaton

·Mahnaym

·Coreae

(Antipas)

·Zia

·Gadara

Antipatris ⊡
(Pegai)
Tower of
Aphek

·Capparetaea

·Acrabbein
·Anathi Borcaeus

·Alexandreion

Joppa ⊡

·Judaea

Rathamin
(Arimathea?)

·Selo (Shiloh)

·Phasaelis

·Thamna (Timnath)

⊡ Ephraim

·Archelais

Lydda ⊡

·Adida ⊡

·Ilon

Roman administration)

Iamnitarum Portus
(Jamnia Harbour)

·Modein

·Sappho
·Lower Beth-horon
·Upper Beth-horon

·Bethel
·Berea ·Aialon?

·Michmash

·Jericho ⊡

·Cyprus

·Betharamphtha
(Livias, Julias)

Jamnia·

·Gazara

Emmaus ⊡
(Nicopolis)

Gabaon·

Colonia Amasa
(Emmaus?)

Gabath Saul·

·Taurus

·Anathoth
Bethphage
⊡ Bethany

Kedron·

Accaron
(Ekron)

⊡Azotus

J U D E A
(under

Jerusalem ⊡

·Hyrcania

Kh. Qumran:
settlement of
Dead Sea sect

JUDEA)

·Bethletepha

·Beth bassi

·Beth zechariah
·Etam

·Herodium

(Dead
Sea)

Lake
Asphaltitis

·Beth-zaith

·Thecoa
(Tekoa)

Gemmaruris·

Bethsura
(Beth-zur)

·Terebinthus (Mamre)

·Hebron

·Callirrhoe

·Machaerus

200

150

MAPS ADAPTED FROM OXFORD UNIVERSITY PRESS BIBLE MAPS